THE LIBRARY OF HISTORY AND DOCTRINE

TRADITION IN THE EARLY CHURCH

TRADITION IN THE EARLY CHURCH

R. P. C. HANSON
*Lightfoot Professor of Divinity
in the University of Durham
and Canon of Durham*

Philadelphia
The Westminster Press

This book is dedicated to
The Revd. Canon Alan Richardson, D.D.
Professor of Christian Theology in the University of Nottingham
with admiration, gratitude and affection

© SCM Press Ltd 1962

Library of Congress Catalog Card No. 63-7925

PRINTED IN GREAT BRITAIN

CONTENTS

1 Oral Tradition   7
  1 The meanings of 'tradition'   7
  2 Method of transmission   9
  3 Laws of tradition   17
  4 Secret tradition   22
  5 Examples of oral tradition   35
  6 Conclusions   50

2 The Creed   52
  1 Early formal teaching   52
  2 The early baptismal creed   59
  3 The baptismal creed and the rule of faith   64
  4 Other forms of creed   68

3 The Rule of Faith   75
  1 References in the fathers to the rule of faith   75
  2 The contents of the rule of faith   85
  3 The rule of faith as tradition   94
  4 The relation of the rule of faith to Scripture   102
  5 The formation of doctrine   117
  6 Conclusions   124

4 Custom and Rite   130
  1 Traditional custom   130
  2 The tradition of the See of Rome   144
  3 Apostolic succession   157
  4 Traditional rites   168
  5 Two examples from the fourth century   176

5 The Canon of the New Testament   187
  1 The beginnings of the Canon   187
  2 The development from evidence to oracle   201
  3 Norms of canonicity   213
  4 Uncanonical tradition   224
  5 Conclusions   234

6 Tradition as Interpretation   237
   1 Tradition as a source of evidence   237
   2 The nature of the Canon of Scripture   245
   3 Tradition as the scope of Scripture   252

Appendices
   A. Cyprian's *Testimonia*   261
   B. Irenaeus, *Adversus Haereses* 3.3.1   265
   C. Heretical tendencies in *The Gospel according to the*
     Hebrews   266
Bibliography   268
Index of Names   276
Index of References   279

ABBREVIATIONS

CSEL   Corpus Scriptorum Ecclesiasticorum Latinorum.
ET   English translation.
GCS   Die griechischen christlichen Schriftsteller der ersten drei
       Jahrhunderte.
HE   Eusebius, *Historia Ecclesiastica.*
JTS   *Journal of Theological Studies.*
LCL   Loeb Classical Library.
NS   New series.
PA   Origen, *Concerning First Principles (Peri Archon).*
PE   Origen, *Concerning Prayer (Peri Euches).*
PG   Migne, Patrologia Graeca.
PL   Migne, Patrologia Latina.
SC   Sources chrétiennes.
TWNT   *Theologisches Wörterbuch zum Neuen Testament,* ed. G. Kittel,
       Stuttgart, 1933 ff.

ACKNOWLEDGEMENTS

I would like to express my gratitude to Miss Jean Cunningham of the staff of the SCM Press for her help in preparing this book for the press and to my former colleague, Miss Molly Whittaker, M.A., M.Litt., B.D., for the expert supervision which she has kindly given.

I

Oral Tradition

1. The Meanings of 'Tradition'

THE WORD *tradition*, even in its purely theological or ecclesiastical usage, is employed today in a wide variety of meanings. It can be used to mean a piece of historical information independent of scriptural sources handed down from an early period in the Church, as one might say that Eusebius records a tradition that Abgar, King of Edessa, wrote a letter to Christ and received one in reply from him. It can be used to mean a separate and recognizable source of Christian information and doctrine presumed to have existed from the very beginning of Christianity and to derive from Christ and his apostles, and to supplement the New Testament authoritatively, as when it is claimed that this dogma or that one is founded on tradition in addition to or instead of Scripture. It can mean the doctrine of the Church as it has been taught and developed from the earliest times, the Church's interpretation of the Gospel though not the Gospel itself, as when one speaks of the tradition of Christological teaching of the early Church fathers. It can be used for the whole teaching of the Church, things taught and manner of teaching, and development of the teaching, and also for everything that is handed down from the beginning in Christianity, Gospel, doctrine, ethics, order, practice and custom. It can be applied to the Bible alone, which is in one sense the Christian tradition *par excellence*. And within the Bible, both Old and New Testaments, various traditions, pieces or bodies or series of information handed on, can be detected.

It will be the aim of this book to distinguish the nature and function of different sorts of tradition within the historic Christian faith. The main task which the book will set itself will be to examine as fairly and as fully as possible the likelihood of the survival of original, authentic tradition within the Christian Church outside the Bible, to see whether there are solid grounds for concluding that independently of the New Testament any considerable or significant amount of original and trustworthy information about Jesus (to put the matter in the simplest and barest terms) could have survived, and whether it actually has survived. It must be obvious to anyone who has thought about the subject at all that all Christian tradition must have been originally oral. Our Lord left no written records behind him after his earthly ministry. The earliest history of the Church, the Book of Acts, does not suggest that anybody thought of writing down an account of the works and words of Jesus for several years after the Resurrection. The conviction held apparently by everybody in the earliest period of the Church's existence that the world was about to end with the Advent of Christ would make it unlikely that anybody should take the trouble to put the tradition into written form. If society, civilization and the fabric of the universe are about to collapse, the writing of history is at a discount. This oral tradition must have been passed on from teacher to pupil or from preacher to audience in an increasingly wide circle for some time before any of the oral tradition was put into writing. Scholars have recently concentrated closely upon this oral period in their examination of the origins of Christianity, and nobody who is occupied with the history of early Christianity can afford to ignore it. After some time, however, some of this purely oral tradition began to be written down. How soon this happened is a matter of dispute and conjecture. Some have held that the Passion Narrative of St Mark's Gospel may have achieved written form as early as AD 40 or a little later. Others might put forward St Paul's account of the Gospel and list of the Resurrection appearances of Christ (I Cor. 15.1–7) as deriving in this form from a period earlier even than St Paul's conversion, perhaps as early as AD 35. The earliest gospel is almost universally admitted to be that of Mark, though this does not preclude the possibility that some of the sources of the other gospels, and perhaps even some of the sources of Mark's Gospel, if they can be identified, were written down earlier than 65. The earliest epistle is probably I Thessalonians, though some would maintain that Galatians was written even earlier, before St Paul had set foot on the soil of Europe. In course of time, more and more documents conveying or commenting upon or witnessing to this early oral tradition appeared, until by the end of the first Christian century almost all the books of the New Testament as we know it today had been written and were circulating more or less widely in the Church.

We must not, however, assume that once the New Testament was written all oral tradition which had not in the New Testament found its way to written form immediately disappeared. Texts can be cited from the New Testament itself, such as John 21.25 and II Thess. 2.15, to suggest that this did not happen. Further we have evidence that there were other traditions in existence at that period as well as those enshrined in the New Testament. Some of them have survived in apocryphal gospels or acts or epistles or apocalypses.

Again, recent archaeological research has brought to light a number of documents dating from the second century AD which contain sayings, and sometimes accounts of actions, attributed to Jesus which are not found in the New Testament; these documents are often called *agrapha*. Their contents may well have been known in the first century, and we must not rule out the possibility that some of them may be original and authentic. But even if we lay aside for the present written tradition outside the New Testament, we must reckon with the possibility, indeed the probability, that oral tradition about Jesus continued to be handed on in the Church even after the first century. After all, the Church had from the very beginning been teaching its converts and edifying its faithful with traditional material, which it called the Gospel or the *kerygma* (preaching), and it continued to do so right through the first and second centuries. At no moment did the Muse of History, nor a Committee of Evangelists, nor an Ecumenical Council of first-century bishops, nor any other body, official or unofficial, formally announce that the Christian Church was deriving the material for its teaching henceforward from written rather than oral tradition. Gradually the documents of the New Testament achieve a position of authority within the Church. Gradually they are singled out from all other possible sources of information or funds of tradition as the written tradition *par excellence*. By about the year 170 the New Testament, substantially in the form in which we now know it, is recognized widely in the Church as authoritative Scripture, comparable to the Scripture of the Old Testament. Up till then oral and written tradition have been existing side by side in the Church, with the possibility still open that either may be as authoritative and reliable as the other, though we have to assume that as the period goes on the possibility of oral tradition being reliable must be at least to some extent restricted by the increasing authority given to the New Testament.

2. Method of Transmission

We must retain in our minds the impression of the process just described if we are to make a proper inquiry into the subject of oral tradition. It would next be useful to ask what can be said about the methods whereby these two forms of tradition, oral and written, were handed on.

It is much easier to answer the question in respect of written tradition than of oral. The written tradition was transmitted by the normal process of copying manuscripts in force in antiquity, a process which has been carefully examined by experts in textual criticism. By the nature of the case, we cannot so carefully examine the process whereby oral tradition was handed on. It may be instructive, though it is not directly relevant to the subject of this chapter, to investigate briefly the manner in which the tradition which was finally included in a written form in the New Testament was handed on during the period while it was still orally delivered.

The normal word for tradition in the New Testament, *paradosis*, occurs thirteen times in the New Testament, nine of them referring to the *halakah* or Rabbinic elaboration of the Law,[1] and three of them denoting Christian tradition or traditions,[2] with one uncertain.[3] The word in the New Testament always means that which is handed on and never the deliverer or process of delivery of it. But there are other passages in the New Testament where Christian tradition is referred to without the actual word *paradosis* being used.[4] The contents of this tradition are not often precisely stated, but presumably they included at least some of the words and works of Jesus, and also probably some short sterotyped formulae, such as the account of Jesus' actions at the Last Supper, a brief Christological statement and a list of Resurrection appearances.[5] The occurrence both of a common pattern of *kerygma* in early speeches in Acts, in several passages of St Paul, and in Mark's summary of Jesus' preaching in Galilee[6] suggests that a summary of the main points of the Gospel may have formed part of these Christian traditions. The early Christians knew, of course, of the existence of Jewish tradition, but a difficulty arises when we try to illuminate the process of handing on Christian tradition by analogies from Jewish practice. Jesus himself clearly repudiated (or at least radically criticized) the *halakah*,[7] and from a very early period the Church followed its Master in this rejection, at least as regards the *halakah* as a total system or way of life, though many Christians for the first few centuries may have observed individual customs prescribed in the *halakah*.

---

[1] Matt. 15.2, 3, 6; Mark 7.3, 5, 8, 9, 13; Gal. 1.14.
[2] I Cor. 11.2 and II Thess. 2.15 and 3.6.
[3] Col. 2.8; but this passage could not refer to Christian tradition.
[4] Luke 1.2; Rom. 6.17; I Cor. 11.23 ff.; 15.1 ff.; II Peter 2.21; Jude 3.
[5] So at least Rom. 6.17; I Cor. 11.2, 23 ff. and I Cor. 15.1 ff. would suggest. See Büchsel's article on παραδίδωμι and παράδοσις in *TWNT*, II.
[6] See C. H. Dodd, *The Apostolic Preaching and its Developments*.
[7] See all the references to *paradosis* in Matthew and Mark; cf. Acts 6.14 and Gal. 1.14.

O. Cullmann, however, in his investigation of this subject,[1] has suggested that in one sense an analogy can be discerned between the *halakah* and the earliest Christian tradition. He sets out to show that when St Paul refers to *paradosis* from the Lord he really means 'Church tradition which has a parallel in the Jewish *paradosis*'.[2] Jesus had rejected the 'tradition of the elders' (Mark 7.3; Matt. 15.2), and had attacked those who wanted to 'hold fast to the tradition'.[3] But St Paul uses this very term to describe the tradition which he has received from the Lord, even saying, 'Hold fast to the traditions.'[4] His other references to Christian traditions are in the same vein.[5] The words of I Cor. 11.2, 3 are particularly illuminating. Here St Paul says 'which I also received from the Lord'; this 'also' occurs again in I Cor. 15.1 and 3, and implies a formula of passing on something received. When therefore St Paul says that he received something 'from the Lord', he means that he received it by mediation through the Church.[6] The content of this tradition is evidently moral rules which concern the life of the faithful,[7] and a summary of the Christian message expressed as a formula of faith and combining the facts of the life of Jesus and their theological interpretation,[8] and finally single narratives from the life of Jesus.[9] Cullmann believes that the tradition of the words of Jesus must have been 'already very advanced' in Paul's day: 'They must have played a more important role than the relatively small number of words of Jesus quoted by Paul (I Thess. 4.15; I Cor. 7.10; 9.14) would lead us to suppose.' No doubt St Paul received his tradition of these words from the other apostles.[10] Cullmann then advances his theory that Paul took Jesus, or rather the Lord (*Kyrios*), as himself constituting a substitute for the Jewish 'tradition of the elders', the interpretation of the Torah. He asks 'whether Jesus Christ the "Lord", as the fulfilment of the Law, does not take the place of all Jewish *paradosis*'.[11] It is Jesus

---

[1] O. Cullmann, *The Early Church*, Chapter IV, 'The Tradition'. For tradition in St Paul see also Congar, *La Tradition et Les Traditions*, pp. 20–24. Gerhardsson, *Memory and Manuscript*, cap. 13, agrees with Cullmann.

[2] Cullmann, *Early Church*, p. 62.

[3] Mark 7.8: κρατεῖν τὴν παράδοσιν.

[4] II Thess. 2:15: κρατεῖτε τὰς παραδόσεις.

[5] κατέχειν, I Cor. 11.2; στήκετε, I Cor. 15.1; II Thess. 2.15; παραλαμβάνειν, παραδιδόναι, I Cor. 11.2, 23; 15.3; I Thess. 2.13; II Thess. 2.15; 3.6; Rom. 6.17; Gal. 1.9, 12; Phil. 4.9; Col. 2.6, 8. See Cullmann, *Early Church*, p. 63; Gerhardsson, *Memory and Manuscript*, pp. 288–90.

[6] Cullmann, *Early Church*, pp. 63–64.

[7] I Cor. 11.2; II Thess. 3.6; Rom. 6.17; Phil. 4.9; Col. 2.6.

[8] E.g. I Cor. 15.3 ff.

[9] E.g. I Cor. 11.23. See Cullmann, *Early Church*, p. 64.

[10] *Ibid.* p. 65. Cullmann notes that in I Cor. 7.25 Paul says that he has no instructions from the Lord on the subject of virgins.

[11] Cullmann, *Early Church*, p. 66.

who delivers the *paradosis* through and in the Church. 'The formula of I Cor. 11.23 refers to the Christ who is present, in that he stands behind the transmission of the tradition, that is, he works *in* it.' The words in Col. 2.6, 'You received Christ Jesus the Lord,' mean 'you received as your tradition', in contrast to 'the tradition of men' (Col. 2.8). 'The *Kyrios* appears as the content of the *paradosis*, but he is at one and the same time *its content and its author*.'[1] In short, 'the exalted Christ himself stands as transmitter behind the apostles who transmit his words and works. Paul can place on the same level the revelation on the road to Damascus and the apostolic tradition he has received, because in both Christ is directly at work.'[2] Jesus brings a new interpretation of the Law as the Messiah, rejecting the Rabbinic interpretation. He is the destiny (τέλος) of the Law. The third chapter of II Corinthians expounds Jesus, here identified with the Spirit, as the new Law. The fourth gospel supports this interpretation in its handling of the Spirit, and especially in John 14.26 and 16.13.[3]

H. Riesenfeld, in a paper originally read to the Congress on 'The Four Gospels' in 1957 and since published[4] has made suggestions which in many respects support those of Cullmann. He emphasizes that the language used in the New Testament for the imparting of Christian tradition recalls the terms which usually describe the handing down of traditional teaching in the Rabbinic schools.[5] He suggests that one of the chief functions of the apostles was the preserving of the tradition of the words of Jesus.[6] He conjectures that the place where this tradition was taught and handed down was the regular gatherings of the Christian church for worship; this, he says, is the true *Sitz im Leben* of the tradition.[7] He even outlines the hypothesis that Jesus foresaw that his words would be cherished and formed into a continuing tradition in the community which he had founded, and that this is the reason why he gave so much of his teaching in the enduring and memorable form of poetry.[8]

Cullmann also emphasizes the crucial position of the apostles in handling tradition. It is the apostle, he says, as direct witness (not merely as inheritor of traditional information) and as guided by the Holy Spirit, who is responsible for the *paradosis*. All the apostles do not know all the facts, but only some one, some another (Gal. 1.18; I Cor. 15.3, 11); each

---

[1] *Ibid.* p. 68.   [2] *Ibid.* p. 69.   [3] *Ibid.* pp. 69–71.
[4] *The Gospel Tradition and its Beginnings.*
[5] Riesenfeld, *Gospel Tradition*, pp. 17–20.
[6] *Ibid.* pp. 20–21.   [7] *Ibid.* pp. 22–23.
[8] *Ibid.* pp. 23–30. E. Schweizer (*Church Order in the New Testament*, p. 30, 2k) emphatically rejects Riesenfeld's thesis.

must pass on his testimony to the others. The 'I' of I Cor. 7.10 and 11.23 is significant and emphasizes Paul's apostolic authority. Even where he has no *logion* of the Lord his opinion as an apostle has authority. The Spirit gives to his delivering of the *paradosis* (when he delivers it) the status of revelation, as if the Lord himself were delivering it.[1] The apostle is unique in that he is a direct witness of the Resurrection; Gal. 1.1 and 12 point the contrast between the apostle, who has received his Gospel directly (through revelation, δι' ἀποκαλύψεως) and others who receive it 'through man' (δι' ἀνθρώπου).[2] The fourth gospel distinguishes emphatically between the continuation of Christ's work in the apostles and its continuation in the post-apostolic Church. 'The high-priestly prayer (chap. 17) establishes this line of descent: Christ—the apostles—the post-apostolic Church. The members of the last are described as those who *believe because of the word of the apostles* (John 17.20).'[3] 'Because of the word' in this passage may even refer to the writings of the apostles.[4] E. Hoskyns and N. Davey in their *Commentary on St John's Gospel* had some years before this suggested a very similar explanation of the opening verses of the First Epistle of John.[5] And V. Taylor, in his *The Formation of the Gospel Tradition*, has also stressed the importance of the apostles as eyewitnesses to whose evidence most of the later tradition found in the New Testament must ultimately go back.

Views such as these do not entirely contradict the findings of the exponents of Form Criticism of the gospels, but in some points they are not easy to reconcile with them. Perhaps some material such as the account of the institution of the eucharist and a Passion Narrative may have achieved relative fixity early on, and retained it until it was written down, but can this apply to the greater part of the accounts of the teaching and miracles of Jesus? The Form Critics have pointed to the form in which this particular material appears to have reached the evangelists or editors who first included it in a written document. They confidently draw the conclusion that for the most part the ingredients of this material circulated during the oral period as isolated units, without reliable indication of the context or time in which they first originated. Even if the Church had from an early stage exercised particular care in preserving accounts of the works and words of Jesus as a sacred *paradosis*, they believe that we must accept the evidence of the form in which these

---

[1] Cullmann, *Early Church*, pp. 71–75. Cf. K. Aland, 'The Problem of Anonymity and Pseudonymity in Christian Literature of the First Two Centuries'.
[2] Cullmann, *Early Church*, pp. 77–78.   [3] *Ibid.* p. 79.   [4] *Ibid.* p. 80.
[5] See E. Hoskyns and N. Davey, *Commentary on St John's Gospel*, Vol. I, pp. 45–46, 95–96.

accounts have reached us that they cannot for the most part be regarded as direct statements taken down from the lips of people who had been eyewitnesses of the events recorded shortly after they had taken place. They must have passed through a period of oral transmission between their first utterance, or their first being described by eyewitnesses, and their reaching written form in the gospels, or earlier in the gospels' sources. This is an assumption which is made no less confidently by such scholars as Bornkamm[1] and J. M. Robinson[2] than it was by the older school of Form Critics like Bultmann and R. H. Lightfoot. D. Nineham, indeed, in three recently published articles,[3] denies altogether that the value of eyewitness testimony can be attached in any sense to most of the material to be found in the synoptic gospels. It all, he claims, bears in its form clear evidence of having been transmitted orally for some time and having received impress and colour from the community which transmitted it. He believes that the earliest collectors of material about Jesus, and the evangelists themselves, did not distinguish clearly, as we do, between fact and interpretation. Edification and fact, for them, flowed together into a single whole. After an analysis of the nature of history he concludes that 'what we have, incorporated in the gospels, is the insight into the meaning of the events described which had been given and tested in forty or fifty years of the Church's experience of Jesus as the living Lord,'[4] and that all that the gospels were meant to do was to 'make possible sufficient historical knowledge of the person and ministry of Jesus for us to assure ourselves that the early Christians were not making bricks without straw; and also for us to see the sense in which their interpretations were intended and were legitimate and to set about the task of reformulating them in terms of our own needs and experience.'[5]

Even if we refrain from questioning the exact meaning of that vivid but vague phrase, 'not making bricks without straw', we can still regard this

---

[1] *Jesus of Nazareth.*
[2] *The New Quest for the Historical Jesus.*
[3] 'Eyewitness Testimony and the Gospel Tradition.' An article by C. Evans, 'Bible and Tradition', also suggests that though in the New Testament we have authoritative tradition it must be to some extent Church-shaped tradition.
[4] Nineham, 'Eyewitness Testimony', October 1960, p. 263.
[5] *Ibid.*, p. 264. These articles are full of suggestive and useful remarks, but the author gives surprisingly little evidence to support his fairly drastic views: he quotes, for instance, a passage from Origen, *Comm. on John* 10.4 (*ibid.*, October 1958, p. 248) without giving the least reason why we should take his word that this theologian, steeped in Philonic thought and Hellenistic philosophy, had the same view of historical fact as the synoptic evangelists who lived nearly two hundred years before him; and he asserts that 'probably in some sense most of the New Testament writers thought of themselves as inspired writers of sacred scripture' (*ibid.*, October 1958, p. 250), without attempting to justify this extraordinary idea by any evidence. See below, pp. 212–31.

position as an extreme one. In the first place, it is no consolation to be told that the material in the gospels represents 'the insight into the meaning of events given and tested in forty or fifty years of the Church's experience'. How are we to know that this is the right insight, as, on this assumption, it is not the insight of the apostles? Others can regard this insight as a disastrous misinterpretation of the original message.[1] In the second place, if we accept the arguments of Quispel and others about the significance of the *Gospel of Thomas* (to mention only one of the documents in the Nag Hammadi find), not only have we an independent witness to the substantial accuracy of the evangelists' material, but one of the main assumptions of all the Form Critics (including Nineham) is gravely undermined. It is possible that 'Thomas once and for all disproves the theory that the Evangelists had no more to work upon than "a heap of unstrung pearls".'[2] Even if we do not commit ourselves to the theories of Quispel, it is surely significant that the *Gospel of Thomas* is just such a collection of 'unstrung pearls', i.e. of sayings without context, and that as a form it is quite certainly later than the form represented by the synoptic gospels. If we are going to be strictly logical Form Critics we ought to recognize that this evidence points to the evangelists having received their material at an earlier stage than that represented by the *Logiensammlung*, or collection of sayings without context, and that the oral tradition which transmitted their material possessed 'a greater preserving power than we generally assume'.[3]

Powerful support for this suggestion has recently come from a Swedish scholar, B. Gerhardsson, in his book *Memory and Manuscript*. This is the first really thorough attempt to illuminate the process of transmission of very early Christian tradition by examining the process of transmission of tradition in the Rabbinic schools contemporary with Christianity. M. Dibelius had examined this material already in the hope of finding analogies with the process within early Christianity, but without much success.[4] And Bonsirven had given an interesting picture of the manner in which oral teaching was given in Rabbinic schools at the time of our Lord.[5] But Gerhardsson's researches are altogether more thorough and more fruitful than these. He puts forward a theory that the tradition about Jesus was

---

[1] E.g. M. Werner, *The Formation of Christian Dogma*, p. 64.

[2] R. McL. Wilson, *Studies in the Gospel of Thomas*, p. 86; he is quoting A. M. Hunter, *Interpreting the New Testament*, p. 39. For a fuller treatment of this subject, see below, pp. 231–2.

[3] Bartsch, quoted by Wilson, *Studies*, p. 86.

[4] M. Dibelius, *From Tradition to Gospel*, pp. 133–51. Cf. Y. Congar, *La Tradition*, pp. 15–16.

[5] J. Bonsirven, *Le Judaisme Palestinien au Temps de Jésus-Christ*, p. 292.

in the earliest days of the Church transmitted as authoritative oral tradition, memorized as accurately as the oral Torah or *Mishnah* was memorized and transmitted in contemporary Rabbinic Judaism, and was preserved, taught and commented upon in an halakic manner by the apostles themselves and not least by Paul, in whose letters we can clearly detect a process of this sort taking place. He argues that this 'holy tradition' was passed on in the early Church by careful memorization orally until it gradually came to be written down, at first only in notebooks (codices, not scrolls), in order to aid the memory: by the middle of the second century these 'notebooks' had percolated throughout the Church in the form of gospels and epistles; then began the process of this written *mishnah*, so to speak, becoming recognized as the holy Scriptures, the new sacred Torah, of the Christian Church.[1] He expressly denies some of the most dearly held assumptions of the Form Critics, e.g. that 'the authorities of early Christianity did not formulate the Jesus tradition in order to preserve it for posterity, but merely to proclaim the message of salvation'; on the contrary, he says, 'there lay', in Christianity, as in Jewish and Hellenistic didactic tradition, 'a more or less powerful historical foundation in the authoritative tradition material which was dealt with.'[2] He remarks that 'it seems to be an extremely tenaciously held misapprehension among exegetes that an early Christian author must be *either* a purposeful theologian *or* a fairly reliable historian.'[3] He emphasizes strongly that the apostles were from the beginning thought of as eye-witnesses, and insists that there must have been from the first a demand for some such testimony as the apostles gave.[4]

This work of Gerhardsson's is clearly of the highest importance, and holds out hope that New Testament scholarship will be led out of the vicious circle into which, perhaps unwittingly, Form Criticism has led it. But even if all his suggestions were ultimately to find acceptance in the world of scholarship, it would be necessary to balance them with other considerations. Jesus was indeed, no doubt, a Rabbi, but he was a Rabbi with a difference, a Rabbi who violently attacked the oral tradition of Rabbinic Judaism, or at least part of it, and even repudiated the Torah itself,[5] a Rabbi who also described himself as the Son of Man, and claimed to be the Messiah, and declared that the End-time was arriving with him. And as he could not be fitted into the category of an ordinary Rabbi gathering round him an ordinary Rabbinic school, so it is unlikely

[1] Gerhardsson, *Memory and Manuscript*, cap. 13, and especially pp. 194–207.
[2] *Ibid.* p. 182 n. 1.   [3] *Ibid.* p. 209.   [4] *Ibid.* pp. 280–3.
[5] See W. G. Kümmel, 'Jesus und der jüdische Traditionsgedanke'.

that his followers treated his words precisely as the devout Jews of that day would have treated the words of a Rabbi. This judgement would apply more strongly the further we move away from the years immediately after the Resurrection. Certainly what we can gleam about the appearance of Christian communities at the end of the first and beginning of the second centuries does not suggest that they remained indistinguishable from Jewish Rabbinic colleges. Arguments such as those of Gerhardsson do not necessarily contradict the assumption, which might well be regarded as a safe and natural one, that the longer the period in which the material of early Christian tradition had been circulating in the form of oral tradition the greater must be the uncertainty about the historical reliability of that material.

3. Laws of Tradition

'The history of the tribe is briefly as follows—But we must premise that the tale depends in some degree upon tradition; therefore, excepting when written documents are quoted, it must be considered as in some degree dubious.'

This is the judgement upon oral tradition in general of Walter Scott in the Introduction to his *Rob Roy*. There can be little dispute that as a general judgement this is a wise one.[1] Oral tradition is an uncertain and usually corruptible vehicle of information. But might it not be possible to determine some rules whereby reliable oral tradition can be distinguished from unreliable? The early Form Critics were interested in the search for laws of tradition, in discovering regular and well-demonstrated rules of development or fixed lines of evolution displayed by all orally transmitted tradition in the course of transmission. For instance, would it be possible to say that vivid touches and circumstantial detail tend to disappear from narratives in the course of transmission? Mark, in his account of the Feeding of the Five Thousand, describes how all the multitude sat down 'on the green grass'. But in the reproduction of this account by Matthew and Luke this detail has disappeared;[2] and generally speaking Matthew and Luke in reproducing Mark's narratives tend to

---

[1] Cf. J. Doresse, *Les Livres Secrets des Gnostiques d'Egypte*, p. 286; commenting on the heterogeneity, the fluidity and openness to borrowing of Gnostic ideas, he writes: 'Peut-être en supposant que ces textes ne furent pas toujours transmis par écrit mais circulèrent—comme ce fut le cas si longtemps, en ces mêmes siècles, pour la litterature zoroastrienne—par une tradition orale qui les rendit infiniment, excessivement, malléables.'

[2] Mark 6.31-44; Matt. 14.13-21; Luke 9.10-17.

B

prune and reduce his verbose and apparently circumstantial accounts. Can we not describe this as an universal law applying to all narratives in oral tradition? If we do, however, we shall find ourselves in difficulty over some stories in the apocryphal gospels and in the *agrapha*. The *Gospel according to the Hebrews*, for instance, which gives a version of the story of the Rich Young Ruler, adds the vivid detail that when asked the crucial question by Jesus he scratched his head![1] In its version of the parable of the talents (Matt. 25.14–30) there are three slaves, and one of them spends the money entrusted to him on harlots and flute-girls. A fragment of an unknown gospel in *Egerton Papyrus 2* describes the incident of a leper being healed, reminiscent of similar incidents in the synoptic gospels, and in the middle of it occurs this remarkably vivid and indeed realistic statement by the subject of the healing: 'Master Jesus, because I travelled with lepers and ate together with them in the inn, I contracted leprosy.'[2] And the recently discovered *Gospel of Thomas* has a version of the parable of the Great Supper which is full of interesting additional detail apparently mirroring faithfully life in Palestine contemporary with Jesus. One of the men excusing himself says, 'I have claims against some merchants; they will come to me in the evening; I will go and give them my orders. I pray to be excused from the dinner.' Another says 'I have bought a farm, I go to collect the rent. I shall not be able to come.'[3] This 'gospel' has a parable of a man keeping a great fish out of a haul, and 'without regret' throwing back the rest (cf. Matt. 13.47–50). Its parable of the mustard-seed (Mark 4.30–32) is more elaborate: 'but when it falls on the tilled earth it produces a large branch.' Its version of the parable of the Lost Sheep (Matt. 18.12–13) runs thus: 'The kingdom is like a shepherd who had a hundred sheep. One of them went astray, which was the largest. He left behind ninety-nine, he sought for the one until he found it. Having tired himself out, he said to the sheep: I love thee more than the ninety-nine.'[4] It would be uncritical to decide that because these accounts are more circumstantial than the corresponding ones in the synoptic gospels they are therefore more original than those.

---

[1] Matt. 19.16–26. Further, it describes two rich men instead of one. R. M. Grant and D. N. Freedman (*The Secret Sayings of Jesus*, pp. 37–41) note how many 'vivid details' the Apocryphal *Gospel according to Peter* adds to the synoptic narrative.

[2] *Egerton Papyrus 2*, frag 1, recto, lines 33–35 (*The New Gospel Fragments*, anon., British Museum). Synoptic parallels are Mark 1.40–44; Matt. 8.2–4; Luke 15.12–14 and 17.14.

[3] *The Gospel according to Thomas* (Coptic text established and translated by A. Guillaumont, H.-Ch. Puech, G. Quispel and W. Till and Yassah 'Abd al Masih), Logion 64, lines 15–18 and 27–28. (The numbering of the logia used in this book is that of this edition.) The synoptic parallels are Luke 14.16–24 and Matt. 22.2–10.

[4] *The Gospel according to Thomas*, Logia 8, 20 (cf. 31) and 107.

Vividness and detail alone are not satisfactory criteria.[1] It would be wiser to conclude that oral tradition in the process of transmission may also develop vivid touches and circumstantial detail, interesting but not original. Some scholars have seen in this very inconsistency an evidence of the existence of laws of tradition. 'It is generally recognized,' says Wilson, 'that in oral tradition the tendency of the development is towards a rounding and a conventionalizing of the material, with the elimination of descriptive detail and the omission of personal names. . . . A further stage appears with the attempt to restore some of the detail, to identify the characters and supply the names of the speakers.'[2] It might be wiser to wait until the evidence provided by the *Gospel of Thomas* and similar documents from the Nag Hammadi find has been thoroughly sifted before laws of tradition are confidently inferred for material in this situation.

It is of course possible to explore other situations where tradition is orally transmitted besides the situation in the early Christian Church in the search for laws of tradition. Old Testament scholars have in recent years paid much attention to the operation of oral tradition both in the transmission of the material which was ultimately included in the Pentateuch and in the process of formation of the books of the prophets. In the case of the Pentateuch the long period over which the oral tradition must have accumulated (in some cases over nearly a thousand years), the complexity of the material and the wide range of sources from which it must have come make it virtually impossible for us to draw any confident lessons from it for our study of the early Christian material. In as far as the investigation of oral tradition in the prophets can be of use to our subject, it probably serves to emphasize how much oral tradition can be modified in process of transmission, even by schools of disciples.

In his book *Memory and Manuscript* Gerhardsson repeatedly claims that in the Jewish Rabbinic schools not only was the art of memorization carried to a very high point, but that oral tradition was valued more highly than written tradition (always excepting the immense reverence shown to the written Torah), and that this preference for oral tradition over written can even be seen in the Hellenistic schools of rhetoric. This may well apply to the relatively closed communities of Rabbinic Judaism

---

[1] But this is precisely what J. Jeremias assumes in the case of the version of the incident of the Rich Young Ruler in his book *The Unknown Sayings of Jesus*, p. 35. In this work, however, though we must admire the author's deep knowledge of Rabbinic sources, as we must in all his works, there is more than one passage where the reader is likely to conclude that the author's critical powers have deserted him.

[2] *Studies*, pp. 142–3.

and even to a limited extent to the schools of rhetoric of the world of Greek culture. But that it can be made a law of tradition applying to the transmission of all oral tradition in the ancient world seems a highly precarious conclusion (perhaps Gerhardsson would not wish to draw it). Even within Rabbinic Judaism the result of this preference of oral over written tradition did not in the long run work in favour of a clear distinction between what was historical and what legendary, and we cannot on the strength of it assume that where, for instance, we find Christians in the second century declaring a partiality for oral tradition it follows that that tradition must therefore be regarded as trustworthy. On the contrary, it would be more natural, and more in accordance with the weight of all the evidence, as we shall see, to assume that when written tradition is securely established it tends normally to drive out oral tradition.

Dibelius also investigated the *Vitae Sophistarum* of Philostratus and examined the *chriae*, witty and pointed sayings, attributed to great men. On the whole these suggest that the editor or collector is likely to fill in an incident with vivid detail rather than to reduce it; but on the other hand the more any saying reported in the gospels approximates to the form of a *chria*, the more it is reduced to concentrating on a saying and a saying only, with the bare minimum of introduction.[1] Dibelius went on to examine the collection of *Sayings of the Fathers*, recording the utterances of monks living in Egyptian deserts in the fourth and fifth centuries AD;[2] this field of study provides very little help, except perhaps faintly to confirm the hypothesis that sayings lose the details of place and time originally attached to them in the process of oral transmission. Those who have read *Studies in the Early British Church*, edited by Miss N. K. Chadwick, will find an instructive venture in the art of weighing the value of oral tradition, conducted with consummate skill and sureness of touch by all the contributors. The period which they investigate is one where most of the sources for reconstructing the history consist of legends which circulated in the form of oral tradition for a long time before being written down. It is a fascinating occupation to follow expert historians as they unravel the confused memorials of this period, but one is not in the process inspired with great confidence in the value of oral tradition. Students both of the collection of traditional Welsh legends called the *Mabinogion* and of that superb Icelandic epic known as *Njal's Saga* will find two more fields in which to search for laws governing the oral transmission of tradition. But they will find the search a complicated and perhaps in the end a barren one.

[1] Dibelius, *From Tradition*, pp. 151–64.   [2] *Ibid.* pp. 172–7.

The fact is that the assumption that the oral transmission of tradition proceeds by certain definite laws which apply in every example of such transmission is not yet by any means proved to be a sound one. Circumstances differ in every case, and in every case the trustworthiness of the tradition will be conditioned by the circumstances of transmission. We must not generalize from case to case, but we may in any given case conjecture or even establish what were the factors tending towards a good preservation of the material and what towards a bad. In the case of the Hellenistic mystery-religions, for instance, it is possible that oral tradition might have been preserved intact for a long time, because of the secrecy of the transmission and the care apparently taken over the correct preservation of formulae.[1] Again, it is possible that as long as the Homeric poems about the siege of Troy, or the Norse sagas about the traditional heroes, were recited orally by professional bards, the oral transmission may have been little impaired over a considerable period, though a prose work would presumably be more vulnerable to modification than a verse one. Perhaps some evidence could be produced to show that oral tradition of a simple sort associated with places endures longest and is least liable to corruption. The palace of Minos at Cnossos, with its 'labyrinth', the traditional site of Golgotha and the traditional place of St Peter's burial on the Vatican come to mind to support this point. But one may conjecture with some confidence that in a situation where written tradition and oral tradition on the same subject are circulating simultaneously, oral tradition will suffer. The written word will inevitably appear more permanent, more objective and more authoritative than the oral, and the oral will begin to become more and more modified and less and less reliable. Indeed, it is almost tempting to venture upon something that has been hitherto in this inquiry steadily deprecated, and define a law of tradition: in situations where both written and oral tradition exist, written tradition drives out oral. But the situation of the Church in the years *circa* 60 to *circa* 160 AD is precisely this one, when written and oral tradition are circulating in the Church side by side.

---

[1] The mystery-religions have been adduced as an analogy for the transmission of Christian tradition in the earliest oral period. See Büchsel, *TWNT* II, p. 174, where Plato, *Philebus* 16C, Diodorus Siculus V. 48.4 and Wisdom 14.15 (παρέδωκεν τοῖς ὑποχειρίοις μυστήρια καὶ τελετάς) are cited.

4. Secret Tradition

It is now time that we should turn from the task of estimating the possibilities of the survival intact for an indefinite period of oral tradition to that of inspecting the material for which the claim has been made that it represents this actual intact and genuine oral tradition. There is quite a wide field for our inspection here. In the first place, we must note that in the second half of the second century and the first half of the third Gnostic heretics were laying claim to the possession of secret tradition, not included in the written Scriptures, derived by them from various obscure contact-men who, they claimed, had derived it directly from the apostles. Irenaeus tells us that the heretics, refuted from the Scriptures, attack the Scriptures and say 'that truth cannot be discovered from these by people who do not know the tradition (*traditionem*). For that tradition is not transmitted in documents, but by the living voice (*per vivam vocem*).'[1] We shall hear more of this 'living voice' later, in another context. We learn from Hippolytus that the heretics 'are thought by many to honour God because they are silent and conceal their secret mysteries' and that they 'deliver esoteric mysteries (τὰ ἀπόρρητα μυστήρια) to those who are initiated'.[2] The followers of Valentinus made such a claim. They said that Jesus taught esoterically the fantastic speculations in which they delighted, and that 'these teachings were not spoken of openly, because not everybody could stand the knowledge, but in a mysterious way the information was given by the Saviour in parables to those who could understand'.[3] Tertullian supports this statement, saying that the Valentinians 'take greater care for nothing than to conceal what they preach'.[4] Clement of Alexandria tells us that the contact-man with the apostles claimed by these heretics was a certain Theodas.[5] If, with several scholars, we accept the recently published *Evangelium Veritatis* as the work of Valentinus himself, the master of the heresy can be cited in support of this point, for at the beginning of this work these words appear: 'That then is the Gospel (εὐαγγέλιον) of him whom they seek (and) which he revealed to the perfect, thanks to the clemency of the

---

[1] Irenaeus, *Adversus Haereses* 3.2.1. On this subject see also Turner, *The Pattern of Christian Truth*, pp. 196–200.

[2] Hippolytus, *Elenchos* 1, introd. 1.2.

[3] Irenaeus, *Adv. Haer.* 1.1.5; cf. 1.1.8, where the Valentinians are represented as making a great secret of their cosmogony.

[4] Tertullian, *Adversus Valentinianos* 1.1, and the whole chapter.

[5] Clement of Alexandria, *Stromateis* 7.16.106.4 (PG 9.549). See E. Molland, 'Irenaeus of Lugdunum and the Apostolic Succession', p. 21.

Father, as a hidden mystery (μυστήριον).'[1] The followers of Carpocrates 'allege that Jesus spoke in a mystery (ἐν μυστηρίῳ) privately to his disciples and apostles and required of them that they should hand these doctrines on to those who were fit for them and who were disciples'.[2] Similarly the Ophites taught that in addition to his obvious, simple teaching Jesus 'taught some few from among his disciples whom he knew to be fit for such mysteries'.[3] The Gnostic sect called the Naassenes claimed a contact-girl with the apostles, a certain Mariamne to whom James the brother of the Lord was alleged to have entrusted secret doctrine.[4] And Hippolytus quotes a fragment of a Naassene hymn in which Jesus is represented as saying:

> The hidden things of the Holy Way
> I have called revelation, and I will deliver them.[5]

The same author tells us that the Gnostic Peiratikoi taught that 'their secret mysteries were handed on without (public) speech (ἀλάλως), but that it was proper for the majority to understand by means of things spoken (publicly)'.[6] The Naassenes also, according to Hippolytus, used the *Gospel of Thomas*.[7] Hippolytus also tells us that Basilides, the Alexandrian Gnostic, and his disciple Isidorus asserted that 'Matthias told to them hidden sayings which he heard from the Saviour when he was taught privately.'[8] But Clement of Alexandria says that the contact-man with the apostles for Basilides was a certain Glauceas who was supposed to have known St Peter.[9]

We can support the accuracy of these fathers' statements from other Gnostic sources. The complete *Gospel according to Thomas* is now in our hands, and we can see that it does indeed claim to embody esoteric teaching from Jesus. Its opening words are: 'These are the secret words which the living Jesus spoke and Didymus Judas Thomas wrote.'[10] And it adds, 'Whoever finds the explanation (ἑρμηνεία) of these words will

---

[1] *Evangelium Veritatis*, ed. M. Malinine, H.-Ch. Puech and G. Quispel, f. ix, p. 18.11–15 (90).
[2] Irenaeus, *Adv. Haer.* 1.20.3.   [3] *Ibid.* 1.28.7.
[4] Hippolytus, *Elenchos* 5.7.1: the statement is repeated in 10.9.3.
[5] *Ibid.* 5.10.2: the Greek, in which the metre can clearly be discerned, runs:
τὰ κεκρυμμένα τῆς ἁγίας ὁδοῦ
γνῶσιν καλέσας παραδώσω.
[6] *Ibid.* 5.17.13.
[7] *Ibid.* 5.7.20, 21, 22. This document, he says, supplies them with ὁ ἀπόρρητος αὐτοῖς λόγος καὶ μυστικός.
[8] *Ibid.* 7.20.1; cf. 7.20.5.
[9] Clement of Alexandria, *Strom.* 7.16.106.4 (PG 9.549); see Molland, 'Irenaeus of Lugdunum', p. 21.
[10] *Gospel according to Thomas*, 80.10–12 (3).

not taste death.'[1] We have already encountered the suggestion that the esoteric tradition gives the true interpretation (presumably of the public tradition).[2] The *Gospel according to Thomas* itself might be regarded as a reinterpretation of the public and recognized written tradition in the four gospels (certainly in the first three), partly by an addition of esoteric words to the original sayings and partly by a rearrangement of the sayings themselves. Perhaps Tatian's *Diatessaron* was designed originally as a rearrangement of the four gospels in order to give them a Gnostic interpretation according to the secret tradition. Secondly, the Gnostic *Apocryphon of John*, which probably dates from before 180, for Irenaeus may have used it (*Adv. Haer.* 1.29), represents Christ as appearing to John on the Mount of Olives after the Resurrection and imparting to him all the information contained in this work as secret doctrine, to be given only to Gnostics.[3] Similarly the *Book of Thomas* begins 'The secret words which the Saviour spoke to Judas-Thomas and which I have written, I, Matthias, who . . . heard them while the two were conversing.'[4] Similarly the *Apocryphon of James* (a document from the Nag Hammadi find) purports to be a secret revelation given by the risen Jesus to James (though which James is uncertain) and to Peter, and divulged by James, but only to a few.[5] Another Gnostic writer whose evidence we can use is Ptolemaeus, whose *Letter to Flora* expounding the correct interpretation of the Jewish Law is generally dated about 160. Having given this interpretation to his pupil, Ptolemaeus declares that Flora will later be thought worthy of 'the apostolic tradition which we also have received by succession, while all the time we measure every word (or teaching) by the teaching of the Saviour.'[6] Ptolemaeus was a shrewd and fairly moderate Gnostic, perhaps an ex-Catholic, whose attitude is distinctly reminiscent of the attitude of the authors of the *Gospel of Truth* and the *Gospel according to Thomas* who appear to claim apostolic tradition about how to interpret the truth while preserving carefully the teaching of the Saviour. His words strengthen the impression that what the heretics

---

[1] *Ibid.* 80.13–14 (3); cf. Logion 13 and John 8.51–52.
[2] See above, p. 22, the quotation from Irenaeus, *Adv. Haer.* 3.2.1.
[3] See W. C. Till, 'The Gnostic Apocryphon of John', and J. Doresse, *Les Livres Secrets*, pp. 218–37.
[4] See Doresse, *Les Livres Secrets*, p. 243. The *Book of Thomas* (or *The Secret Words which the Saviour spoke to Judas-Thomas and which were Handed Down by Matthias*) should be distinguished from the *Gospel of Thomas* and from another, later and far less interesting, apocryphal infancy gospel, also called the *Gospel of Thomas*.
[5] W. C. Van Unnik, *Newly Discovered Gnostic Writings*, pp. 80–81.
[6] τῆς ἀποστολικῆς παραδόσεως ἣν ἐκ διαδοχῆς καὶ ἡμεῖς παρειλήφαμεν μετὰ καὶ τοῦ κανονίσαι πάντας τοὺς λόγους τῇ τοῦ Σωτῆρος διδασκαλίᾳ, PG 7.1289D–1292A.

claimed was a secret tradition from our Lord through his apostles designed to interpret the public, and probably written, one.

The orthodox fathers, of course, indignantly refuse to allow the claims of these Gnostics to a secret tradition.[1] Irenaeus denies that the apostles concealed part of their teaching in order to give exoteric doctrine to some groups and esoteric to others.[2] Tertullian rejects this hypothesis just as strongly.[3] 'They have to believe without the support of Scripture', he says, 'so that they can believe against Scripture.'[4] He insists that the rule of faith was plainly and openly taught by the apostles:

> Although they used to converse about some subjects among their intimate friends (inter domesticos), if I may put it like that, we are not to believe that these subjects were any which should impose another rule of faith different from and opposite to that one which they were publicly representing to the catholic Church, so that they should tell of one God in the Church and another at home (in hospitio), that they should describe one nature (substantiam) of Christ openly and another secretly, that they should proclaim one hope of resurrection to the majority but another to the select few.[5]

We should have no hesitation in agreeing that Irenaeus and Tertullian were right here. Even if there were not other grounds for denying this claim of the Gnostics to an oral tradition of genuine esoteric teaching, the new light which has been shed upon second-century Gnosticism by recent archaeological discoveries should make it plain that the content of this esoteric tradition was a number of speculative doctrines and fantasies which it would be ridiculous to consider genuine or original. Doresse, for instance, points out that the elaborate Gnostic pretence of secrecy was a fraud and was mainly designed to confer prestige on mediocre material, and that what the Gnostics really wanted to convey secretly was 'the descriptions of the world above, the names of the beings who were there, the picture and the function of the Saviour, the anti-biblical interpretation of Genesis and of the law of Moses, the revelation of that which should have been the esoteric meaning of Christianity,

---

[1] Irenaeus and Tertullian, says Ellen Flesseman-van Leer, 'deny most decidedly the existence of extra-Scriptural tradition' (*Tradition and Scripture in the Early Church*, p. 191). Cf. Grant and Freedman, *The Secret Sayings*, p. 26.

[2] *Adv. Haer.* 3.5.1; 2.40.3.

[3] *De Praescriptione Haereticorum* 22–27 is devoted to demolishing the proposition *omnia quidem apostolos scisse sed non omnia omnibus tradidisse* (22.2), and *quaedam palam et universis, quaedam secreto et paucis demandasse* (25.2).

[4] *De Praescr. Haer.* 23.5: *credant sine scripturis ut credant adversus scripturas*. Cf. his description of the Church's preaching: *sine ulla significatione alicuius taciti sacramenti* (26.2).

[5] *De Praescr. Haer.* 26.9–10.

finally the declaration to the believer of the superior nature which was in him and the means whereby he might achieve salvation.'[1]

Among all the pre-Nicene fathers of the Church only one claims to possess an esoteric, unwritten, authentic tradition of doctrine independent of Scripture, and that is, significantly enough, Clement of Alexandria.[2] He declares that he is in possession of secret and authentic tradition, unwritten, independent of Scripture, derived by a succession of teachers (among whom we can with some confidence number Pantaenus late in the series and Barnabas early in it) from our Lord and from his apostles.[3] The content of this tradition is not easy to determine, but the arguments recently put forward by Daniélou for concluding that it consisted of speculations and midrash of the type which can be found in the early genre of Christian literature which Daniélou calls 'Judeo-Christian' are very strong.[4] This type of literature often takes an apocalyptic form, is much concerned with angelology, and has in its several elements remarkably like the ingredients of Gnosticism, without necessarily being formally or entirely Gnostic. Clement often calls his tradition γνῶσις,[5] and he regards it as supplying, among its other functions, a symphony or conspectus of the meaning of the whole Bible,[6] much as the author of the Gospel of Thomas regarded his tradition as supplying the true 'interpretation' and Ptolemy put forward his as the proper understanding of the Saviour's words; and Clement identifies it (or rather, confuses it) with the Church's rule of faith.[7] As for the authenticity of Clement's claim, scholars of all traditions are unanimous in agreeing to reject it,

---

[1] Les Livres Secrets, pp. 290–1.

[2] Origen cannot possibly be cited as another example. He does not claim for his secret tradition that it is independent of Scripture nor that it is handed down by a succession of teachers. See D. Van den Eynde, Les Normes de l'Enseignement Chrétien dans la litterature patristique des trois premiers siècles, pp. 231–2, and my Origen's Doctrine of Tradition, cap. V.

[3] Clement of Alexandria, Strom. 1.1.11–12 (PG 8.697–701); 6.7.61 (PG 9.281–4); 6.8.68 (PG 9.289); Eclogae Propheticae 27; Eusebius, HE 6.13.8–9. See Origen's Doctrine of Tradition, cap. IV, where the evidence is set out in full; also J. Daniélou, Théologie de Judéo-Christianisme, pp. 35, 61–63, 122, Message Évangelique et Culture Hellénistique, pp. 144–5, and H. F. Von Campenhausen, Kirchliches Amt und geistliches Vollmacht, pp. 224–6.

[4] Daniélou, Théologie, 62–63, 122, Message Évangelique, pp. 144–5. In Origen's Doctrine of Tradition I had conjectured that speculations borrowed from Philo (who does speak approvingly of unwritten tradition) contributed to this tradition. But it seems to me now that Daniélou's hypothesis is more likely to be correct.

[5] E.g. Strom. 5.10.63.2 (PG 9.96), γνωστικὴ παράδοσις; 6.16.146.3 (9.377) ἀληθὴς γνῶσις; 1.1.11.3 (8.700); 1.12.56.2 (8.753); 6.18.164.4 (9.397); 6.7.61.1 (9.284); 6.15.131.1 (9.356), etc.   [6] Strom. 3.10.70.3 (PG 8.1172); 6.11.88.5 (PG 9.309).

[7] Strom. 7.15.92.3 (PG 9.528); 7.16.105.1 (PG 9.545). For the evidence for this conclusion see Origen's Doctrine of Tradition, pp. 58–61. If, as has already been suggested (pp. 24–25), the Gnostic's claim to a secret tradition of interpretation corresponds to the contemporary church's claim to expound the true rule of faith, this would go far to explain Clement's confusion of the two.

Montdesert, Van den Eynde and Daniélou[1] (who remarks that the affectation of a knowledge of 'so-called revelations made by Jesus to his apostles' is a characteristic of Judeo-Christian literature). Indeed, this pretension of Clement of Alexandria to secret tradition is one more piece of evidence of his close (one might perhaps say suspiciously close) association with Gnostic circles and Gnostic ways of thinking. Secret tradition is characteristic of Gnosticism and not of orthodox Christianity.

It might be suggested that we should make an exception to the last statement in favour of the Church's *disciplina arcani*. This is a subject to which we must now turn. This phrase, first coined in the seventeenth century by J. Daillé, a Calvinist theologian,[2] describes the practice, alleged to have been widespread in the early Church, of deliberately concealing the doctrines and rites of Christianity both to avoid profanation by pagans and to encourage in inquirers and catechumens a healthy curiosity and veneration for things which were so scrupulously veiled. This hypothesis used to be widely employed by apologists for orthodoxy, as a means of accounting for the apparent ignorance on the part of early Christian writers of doctrines developed in the fourth and later centuries. Newman, for instance, applies it frequently in his *Arians of the Fourth Century*.[3] But this method of accounting for the development of Christian doctrine has now been everywhere abandoned. Indeed, Newman himself had abandoned it by the time he came to write his *Development of Christian Doctrine*. The concept of the *disciplina arcani* has, however, recently been defended by Jeremias, as a means of explaining the absence of reference to the institution of the eucharist in the fourth gospel.[4] He produces what at first sight looks like an imposing volume of evidence that 'as early as the first century in various places and increasing measure the tendency to safeguard the holy Eucharist and its words of institution from profanation was making itself felt.'[5] But closer examination suggests that this evidence is not as impressive as it appears to be at first sight. Parallels from Jewish apocalypses, Rabbinic practice, the mystery-religions and the customs of the Essenes may all be irrelevant until it can be shown that the early Christians specifically associated the eucharist

---

[1] C. Montdesert, *Clément d'Alexandrie*, pp. 56, 57; Van den Eynde, *Les Normes*, pp. 220–26, 274–5; Daniélou, *Théologie*, pp. 62–63. Congar, *La Tradition*, p. 65, surprisingly seems to take Clement's claim at its face value.
[2] See the brief but excellent article '*Disciplina Arcani*' in the *Dictionary of the Christian Church*.
[3] J. H. Newman, *Arians of the Fourth Century*, pp. 29–37, 42, 79, 84–85.
[4] J. Jeremias, *The Eucharistic Words of Jesus*, pp. 73–87. Cf. also F. J. Badcock, *History of the Creeds*, pp. 106–7, and F. J. Bethune-Baker, *Introduction to the Early History of Christian Doctrine*, p. 35.
[5] *Eucharistic Words*, p. 86.

with these traditions.[1] The suggestion that Jesus gave some secret tradition to his disciples, not divulged in public, and that this included the celebration of the eucharist[2] seems to be ruled out by the fact, already clearly established,[3] that in the second century no orthodox writer knows of such secret teaching, and the claim to possess it is made only by Gnostics. Indeed, this fact alone should make the existence of a *disciplina arcani* in the first century highly conjectural. St Paul's references to 'mystery' and 'mysteries' cannot possibly be taken to imply the existence of a *disciplina arcani*[4] because he is convinced that, to those who will accept them, these divine mysteries are *open* secrets; they may have been hidden from previous generations, but they are now made known. The fact that he makes no secret of what he means by these mysteries (the resurrection of the body, the admission of Gentiles to salvation, the relation of man and woman in marriage) supports this conclusion. The passage which Jeremias describes as providing 'the clearest evidence'[5] for his theory, Heb. 5.11; 6.8, tends in fact to disprove it. Jeremias assumes that 6.1, 2 give us a list of elementary Christian teaching, including baptism (and perhaps confirmation!), and that this elementary teaching is contrasted with 'perfection', advanced teaching, included in the *disciplina arcani*. It is really impossible to translate the βαπτισμῶν of 6.2 as 'baptism', in view of the fact that precisely the same word, also in the plural, means Jewish purificatory washings in 9.10, and it is asking too much of us to accept laying-on of hands (which in view of the remarkable scarcity of its attestation in the early Church might well be described as a secret doctrine) as an elementary and public piece of teaching. This view is confirmed by 6.4, 5 which goes on to give us a list, not of the esoteric Christian doctrines, but of the main points of Christian doctrine —baptism (illumination), the eucharist (the heavenly gift), the Holy Spirit, the Word of God, the powers of the coming age.[6] That this is a list of Christian doctrines there can be no doubt. But how could a list including the Holy Spirit, the Word of God and the arrival of the Last Age possibly be a list of *esoteric* doctrine? Jeremias' next examples, the account of the Resurrection and the secret number in Rev. 13.18, are no

[1] *Ibid.* pp. 73–78. [2] *Ibid.* pp. 78–79.
[3] See above, pp. 25–26.
[4] Jeremias, *Eucharistic Words*, pp. 80–81.
[5] *Ibid.* p. 80; this misleading interpretation is repeated in *Infant Baptism in the First Four Centuries*, pp. 30–31.
[6] See *Allegory and Event*, pp. 84–85. The earlier list (6.1, 2) is probably an account of the doctrines of Pharisaic Judaism which the recipients of the epistle (who could well be Jewish proselytes later converted to Christianity) were given on encountering Judaism.

less unfortunate.[1] The evangelists do not describe how the Resurrection took place, not because the matter was regarded as a secret, but because in fact there were no witnesses present,[2] a point which, unaccountably, Jeremias seems to have overlooked. It certainly is true that the meaning of the secret number in Rev. 13.18 *is* secret—but then it is so secret that its meaning had been entirely lost as early as the time of Irenaeus, who admits that he is quite in the dark on this point.[3] If this is an example of the *disciplina arcani* in action, it must be a very inefficient discipline! Finally, it is a delicate and perilous operation to explore the description of the eucharist and its institution in the synoptic gospels and the *Didache*[4] in order to show that they do not disclose the full account, when these sources are the only ones we have for determining what the full account should be.[5] In short, Jeremias' attempt to prove that the account of either the institution of the eucharist or its celebration was in the first century treated as esoteric and subject to a *disciplina arcani* falls to pieces when it is closely examined. The view that a *disciplina arcani* existed as early as this is also strongly disputed by J. N. D. Kelly. Writing of Tertullian's time, he says, 'It is improbable that the *disciplina arcani* exercised such an influence at this early date, and Tertullian himself had no hesitation about describing the ceremonies of baptism.'[6] According to this writer, there is no solid evidence for the appearance of a *disciplina arcani* until the second half of the third century, when it develops as a concomitant to the ceremonies of the *traditio et redditio symboli* connected with the creed.[7]

It is, however, worth while looking at those passages in the literature of the first two centuries of the Church's existence which suggest that such a *disciplina arcani* existed. Two of the Apologists use language which might be taken to refer to this custom. Speaking of the Christians, Aristides says 'But they do not publish to the ears of the masses the good

---

[1] Jeremias, *Eucharistic Words*, pp. 80–81.

[2] Unless we take seriously Matthew's story (27.62–66; 28.4) of a watch being set in the tomb, which it is very difficult to do.

[3] *Adv. Haer.* 5.28.2, 3; cf. 2.41.2–3, where Irenaeus argues that there are some things in Scripture whose meaning we cannot know and never shall.

[4] Jeremias, *Eucharistic Words*, pp. 81–86.

[5] The reason why it is so difficult to reconstruct the eucharistic liturgy of the early Church is probably not because it was regarded as an esoteric tradition, but because no fixed and widely accepted liturgy existed at this early date. See my article 'The Liberty of the Bishops to Improvise Prayer in the Eucharist'.

[6] J. N. D. Kelly, *Early Christian Creeds*, p. 87. J. N. Bakhuizen van den Brink, 'Traditio in Theologischen Sinne', pp. 71–73, agrees that the *disciplina arcani* appeared later than Tertullian. Turner, *The Pattern*, p. 316 n. 2, also refuses to recognize the *disciplina arcani* as early as the third century; see also pp. 364–5.

[7] *Ibid.* pp. 100, 168–72.

deeds which they perform, and they take care that no one should become aware of them, and they hide their gifts like a man who finds a treasure and conceals it.'[1] The *Epistle to Diognetus* says, of the Christians, 'But do not expect to be able to learn from man the mystery of their peculiar worship,' and insists that though Christians are recognized as existing in the world, 'yet their worship remains unseen' (ἀόρατος δὲ αὐτῶν ἡ θεοσέβεια μένει), and that 'they are not entrusted with the administration of (purely) human mysteries'.[2] But none of these phrases is definite enough to be sure that it really does refer to a *disciplina arcani*. They might just as well refer to the fact that Christians do not use images in worship or simply signify that Christians do not worship in public. Rather solider evidence is available in Minucius Felix's *Octavius*. In this dialogue, the pagan interlocutor, Caecilius, emphasizes the secrecy of Christians: 'For why do they make strenuous efforts to veil and hide away whatever it is that they worship, since things that are innocent always rejoice in publicity, but crimes are secret? Why do they have no altars, no temples, no recognized images, why do they never speak openly, never meet freely unless what they worship and suppress deserves either punishment or shame?' Earlier he had referred to 'the suspicion that attaches to rites celebrated secretly and by night' (*occultis ac nocturnis sacris adposita suspicio*). Octavius, in his reply to Caecilius, does acknowledge that 'we never preach openly unless we are examined' (*numquam publice nisi interrogati praedicamus*).[3] This certainly makes it clear that Christians were anxious to conceal their worship, a fact which is independently established by the discoveries made in the catacombs of Rome. We cannot be surprised at this, because from at least AD 64 onwards it was formally illegal, and a crime liable to be punished very severely, to be a Christian and to refuse to renounce Christianity. But this does not mean that Christians deliberately withheld their teaching, or part of their teaching, from new Christians on the grounds either that it was too sacred to be divulged or that it was too profound to be easily understood. Besides, Minucius Felix was writing in the late second or early third century, and there are signs that by then Christians are tending to assimilate their language to the language of the mystery-cults, without

---

[1] Aristides, *Apologia* 16.2. The clause 'the good deeds which they perform' could perhaps be translated 'the things which do them good', i.e. the blessings enjoyed by them (Latin, *ea quae bene faciunt*). The exact text of this *Apology* is almost impossible to reconstruct because the Greek fragments extant in the *Life of Barlaam and Joasaph* are not completely trustworthy, and besides these there are only Syriac and Armenian versions; of these latter Goodspeed prints a Latin translation.
[2] *Epistle to Diognetus* 4.6; 6.4; 7.1.
[3] Minucius Felix, *Octavius* X.1; IX.4; XIX.15.

necessarily implying that any of their doctrine is esoteric. Irenaeus makes no mention at all of anything that could correspond to a *disciplina arcani*, but Tertullian has often been quoted as an author who can be shown to have known such a custom. He does indeed write: *ex forma omnibus mysteriis silentii fides debeatur*.[1] But this only means that it is customary to treat with reticence the details of all mystery-religions, among which he for the moment, arguing with pagans, places Christianity; he goes on to adduce the Samothracian and Eleusinian mysteries. In another work he repeats the same words,[2] using the same arguments, but a little later adds: 'Further, how can acquaintance with Christianity come to out-siders, since innocent and lawful mysteries warn off all alien spectators, unless it be that unlawful mysteries are less exclusive?'[3] But shortly afterwards he claims that Christian secrets are in fact no secrets. 'You are aware of the days of our assemblies; consequently we are surrounded and suppressed, and we are arrested even during our secret meetings themselves' (*in ipsis arcanis congregationibus*).[4] And in another work he declares that a pagan husband of a Christian wife will enjoy the power of keeping the *arcana* of his wife continually in peril of being divulged or suppressed.[5] *Arcana* no doubt here means the celebration of the eucharist. This is all the evidence that the works of Tertullian can afford for the existence of a *disciplina arcani*, and it is not enough. It amounts to no more than that the Christians, out of fear of arrest and trial, wor-shipped in secret, and, for the same motive, were not ready to speak openly or readily to pagans about their worship, but that in fact they were not very successful in their efforts after secrecy. That the Church customarily refrained from communicating part of its teaching to its inquirers or catechumens, or to its newly initiated members, on the ground that this teaching was esoteric, there is no hint in Tertullian at all, and the readiness with which in his works he refers to the details of the sacraments of baptism and the eucharist argues strongly against this suggestion.

We are perhaps approaching nearer to the notion of a *disciplina arcani* in the references in Christian funerary inscriptions of the second century to the eucharist. There are the representations of fish, along with bread, on epitaphs in the catacomb of Calixtus and in the catacomb of Priscilla, referring in a veiled manner to Christ as given in the eucharist. There is also the well-known epitaph of Abercius of Hierapolis, which speaks in

[1] Tertullian, *Apologeticus* 7.6.
[2] *Ad Nationes* 1.7.13: *cum vel ex forma ac lege omnium mysteriorum silentii fides debeatur.*
[3] *Ibid.* 1.7.14.   [4] *Ibid.* 1.7.19.   [5] *Ad Uxorem* 2.5.4.

carefully allegorical language of the Christian faith and the Church and Christian worship: 'I am a disciple of the Holy Shepherd who feeds his flocks upon the mountains and in the valleys, whose great eyes are all-seeing. . . . He sent me to Rome to behold a kingdom and a queen robed in gold, wearing golden shoes. But there I saw a people with a radiant sign . . . and there was handed to me everywhere as nourishment the Fish from the Spring, the pure Fish of great size caught by the chaste Virgin. And She continued to hand on this fare to the friends to eat, giving wholesome wine, offering mingled wine and water with bread.' Or there is the epitaph of Pectorius in Gaul, which apparently goes back to the second century: 'Divine race of the heavenly Fish, draw with a pure heart, ye mortals, from the immortal, divine spring-water . . . take the honey-sweet fare of the Redeemer of the Saints, eat, you that are hungry, holding the Fish in the palm of your hands.'[1] In this deliberately symbolical reference to the truths and mysteries of the Christian religion we no doubt have a conscious assimilation of Christianity to the mystery religions, both in order to compete with those religions on their own ground, in a period when they were exercising wide, and perhaps increasing, influence, and as a safeguard against persecution by those who desired to leave memorials of their faith without endangering its adherents. But this does not amount to proof that within the Christian Church some doctrines or some practices were regarded as esoteric, in contrast to public ones.

Towards the end of Hippolytus' *Apostolic Tradition* there is a passage which runs thus:

> And we have delivered to you briefly these things concerning baptism and the oblation because you have already been instructed concerning the resurrection of the flesh ($\sigma\acute{\alpha}\rho\xi$) and the rest according to the Scriptures. But if there is any other matter which ought to be told, let the bishop impart it secretly to those who are communicated. He shall not tell this to any but the faithful and only after they have first been communicated. This is the white stone ($\psi\hat{\eta}\phi o\varsigma$) of which John said that there is a new name written upon it which no man knows except him who receives.[2]

This looks like a genuine example of the *disciplina arcani*, perhaps the first genuine example, though even here there is no question of keeping doctrine or practice secret from the faithful, but only from non-Christians.

---

[1] For all these inscriptions see F. Van der Meer and C. Morhmann, *Atlas of the Early Christian World*, p. 42. Jeremias adduces Abercius' inscription, *Eucharistic Words*, p. 86.

[2] Hippolytus, *Apostolic Tradition* 23.13–14.

It is not clear what the matter delivered through this secret rule was. It obviously could not have had any reference to baptism and eucharist.[1] It has sometimes been suggested that we can find the same doctrine in the Christian Platonists of Alexandria, Clement and Origen. We have already seen[2] that Clement's references to esoteric doctrine must be taken to mean his secret, and unauthentic, tradition of a Gnostic colour. This sort of tradition Origen explicitly disowns. On the phrase 'not to go beyond the things that are written' (I Cor. 4.6), he makes the comment: 'The followers of sects profess to have traditions and say "These are in addition to the things that are written, because our Saviour delivered them in a secret communication (ἐν ἀπορρήτῳ) to the apostles, and the apostles to so-and-so and so-and-so"; and thus by this sort of mythical talk they deceive the minds of the guileless.'[3] But both Clement and Origen do entertain a doctrine of *reserve*, which is allied to the practice of the *disciplina arcani*, that is, they both are convinced that the more difficult doctrines of the Christian faith should not be taught to the simple and uneducated Christian believer, in case they might shock him or upset him or bewilder him, but that they should be reserved for advanced and well-educated believers. This doctrine is much more explicitly and methodically handled in Origen than in Clement, and in Origen it in fact forms his conception of secret tradition.[4] But it must be emphasized that what Origen at least regards as the right subjects for esoteric impartation are not the ordinary doctrines of the Christian faith, not the rule of faith, but the advanced doctrines, in effect the daring and highly philosophical speculations of himself and his friends. For this reason it is necessary to distinguish this concept of secret tradition from a *disciplina arcani*. This is not the official church veiling her regular doctrines and rites in reverent mystery, but a highly intellectual theologian reserving his more far-reaching speculations for those of his students who could understand and appreciate them. There is no solid evidence that Origen regarded the creed or the worship of the church as a suitable subject for esoteric tradition.[5]

[1] B. S. Easton, in his edition of this work, p. 96, suggests that it was the Lord's Prayer.
[2] See above, pp. 26–27.
[3] *Fragments on I Corinthians*, no. XIX, ed. by C. Jenkins (*JTS* 9, p. 357).
[4] For full information on this point the reader is referred to cap. V of *Origen's Doctrine of Tradition*.
[5] The suggestion that in *Contra Celsum* 3.60 Origen's reference to the teaching given privately by Jesus to his true disciples means the symbol of faith and the admission to the sacraments of baptism and holy communion is a quite unnecessary one. Origen, as we shall see (p. 63 below), occasionally mentions the creed, but does not associate it with secret teaching.

C

Two more passages in the literature of this period are relevant. A book called *Testimonias ad Quirinum*, or *Adversus Judaeos*, is included among the works of Cyprian. In fact various reasons make it impossible to regard it as originally composed by Cyprian;[1] he probably edited it for the benefit of his friend Quirinus. It must date from a period not long before Cyprian's, and it must come from a church which had only recently changed from speaking Greek to speaking Latin, probably the church of Rome. In this appears a heading *Sacramentum fidei non esse profanandum* ('The mystery of the faith is not to be profaned'), followed by a quotation from Prov. 23.9 ('Do not speak in the hearing of a fool, for he will despise the wisdom of your words') and Matt. 7.6 ('Give not that which is holy to the dogs, nor throw your pearls before swine').[2] *Sacramentum fidei* here could not possibly mean the eucharist. The warning is probably directed against indiscriminately imparting the doctrines of the Christian faith to pagans. The other passage comes from the *Didascalia Apostolorum*. The passage is a warning against naming a benefactor in private prayer during public worship. All Christian private prayer at that period was liable to be audible, as was even private reading. The passage runs:

> Or it may even chance that one of the faithful, hearing thee, will go out and talk: and it is not expedient that those things which are done or spoken in the church should come abroad and be revealed, for he that divulges and speaks of them disobeys God and becomes a betrayer of the Church.[3]

It is impossible to date this document with certainty. Connolly very diffidently inclines to place it in the first half of the third century and before the persecution of Decius.[4] It is, however, clear that these two passages witness to the growth of a *disciplina arcani* in the first half of the third century, not designed to render some Christian teaching or practice esoteric, in contrast to the rest which was regarded as public, but in order to prevent Christian faith and practice being easily imparted to pagans.

This is almost all the evidence that can be produced in favour of the existence of a *disciplina arcani* in the first two centuries of the Church's existence. It must be admitted that, in view of the relatively large amount of literature and other material available, the evidence is tenuous. We have to put against it the silence of Justin and Irenaeus on this subject, the denial of the existence of esoteric tradition in the Church by Irenaeus, Tertullian and Hippolytus and Origen and the fact that as early as the

---

[1] For a discussion of this work, see Appendix A.
[2] Cyprian, *Testimonia* 3.50.
[3] *Didascalia Apostolorum* XV, p. 143.
[4] *Ibid.* introd. pp. lxxxvii–xci.

decade between 170 and 180 Celsus, the anti-Christian writer, was able to obtain a good deal of information about the Christian Church, much of it accurate, including access to at least one gospel (probably Mark's). A *disciplina arcani* did indeed in the end develop in the Christian Church but it must be made clear that this *disciplina arcani* can have nothing to do with a secret oral tradition independent of the Scriptures and deriving in an authentic transmission from Christ or his apostles. It is obvious from the references to it which we have examined that it can be no such thing. It is only found in the third century. It is in fact only after the Gnostic threat to the Church has become less pressing and the Gnostic claim to secret tradition has been discountenanced that this *disciplina* manifests itself. It is well to recall in this case the dictum of George Salmon about tradition, to the effect that an authentic tradition will become clearer and clearer the nearer it is traced to its source, whereas a spurious tradition may appear strongly and widely attested at a late stage in its history, but will appear more uncertain the further back it can be followed.[1] By this criterion, this *disciplina arcani* cannot be regarded as genuine oral tradition. To do its agents justice, they would probably not have claimed it as such. Its causes were probably various: a safeguard at a time when Christianity was continually liable to persecution; a desire both to emulate and to imitate the impressive reputations of contemporary mystery-religions (manifested perhaps also in the custom of describing the Christian bishop as a priest—ἀρχιερεύς, *sacerdos*—which originated at about the same time); and the increasing stress laid upon the period of instruction preceding baptism, leading, perhaps a little later than the period when this *disciplina arcani* began to be observed, to the ceremonies of *traditio* and *redditio symboli*. However we estimate its causes, we cannot in any case regard it as contributing anything to our search for authentic oral tradition independent of Scripture.

5. *Examples of Oral Tradition*

As we search for reliable oral tradition independent of the Bible current in the early Church, we cannot fail to meet some information attributed to Papias, bishop of Hierapolis, who lived at the end of the first century and the beginning of the second, some more ascribed to Hegesippus, who may have been Papias' contemporary, and yet more to a group of people known as 'the presbyters'. The earliest information

[1] See below, p. 185.

about Papias comes from Irenaeus,[1] who tells us that 'the elders' are recorded as relating that John the beloved disciple described the Lord as envisaging a time when the vines will miraculously multiply ten thousand times and of their own accord call the faithful to come and eat them. He goes on to say that his informant in this case is Papias, whom he describes as 'one who had heard John and had been a friend of Polycarp, a man of the primitive age'.[2] Papias had also told us, Irenaeus adds, that in reply to a sceptical question by the traitor Judas, the Lord had prophesied 'They shall see who shall come into those things' (*Videbunt qui venient in illa*). This is also the time, Irenaeus observes, when the Isaianic prophecy (Isa. 11.6–9; 65.25) of the harmony and harmlessness of animals will be fulfilled. Irenaeus says that he knows that some people interpret these passages of the pacification by the Gospel of people of different savage natures and different occupations, and of their reconciliation with the faithful. But he believes that though this will happen, still the prophecies should be taken literally as well. Irenaeus changed his mind later and opted for the allegorical interpretation.[3] Eusebius is much more informative about Papias.[4] He tells us that Papias' book was in five parts and was called *An Explanation of the Oracles of the Lord* (Λογίων Κυριακῶν Ἐξήγησις).[5] He points out that Papias did not claim to be a hearer of John the apostle, as Irenaeus says he was, but that he received his information from people who had known the apostles. Then he gives a quotation from Papias' work, in which Papias first emphasizes how carefully he had chosen to derive his information from people who were in a position to know the truth. 'If anybody ever arrived who had been in the company of "the presbyters", I enquired for the words of "the presbyters"; what Andrew said or Peter, or Philip or Thomas or James; or what said John or Matthew, or any other of the disciples of the Lord; and the sayings of Aristion or of the presbyter John, the disciples of the Lord. For I did not suppose that statements from books would assist me as much as statements from a living and abiding voice' (τὰ παρὰ ζώσης φωνῆς καὶ μενούσης). Eusebius, while he notes that Papias apparently distinguishes two different Johns, concludes that Papias was a hearer of

---

[1] *Adv. Haer.* 5.33.3, 4.

[2] Ἰωάννου μὲν ἀκουστής, Πολυκάρπου δὲ ἑταῖρος γεγονώς, ἀρχαῖος ἀνήρ. Eusebius has preserved a Greek fragment of Irenaeus in *HE* 3.39.1.

[3] *Demonstration* 61, where he again refers the literalist interpretation to 'the presbyters', again no doubt meaning Papias.

[4] Almost all his information about Papias is to be found in the thirty-ninth chapter of the third book of his *Ecclesiastical History*.

[5] But there is something to be said for the contention of Westcott (*The Canon of the New Testament*, p. 73) that this title should be translated 'An Exposition of Oracles of the Lord' and not 'of *the* Oracles'.

Aristion, one of 'the presbyters', which in fact Papias does not claim for himself in the passage quoted by Eusebius. Then Eusebius adds some more information gleaned from Papias, which he says came to Papias 'apparently by tradition' (ὡς ἂν ἐκ παραδόσεως). Papias stayed with Philip the apostle (whom Eusebius confuses with Philip the evangelist) from whom he received the account of how a dead man had been restored to life by Philip and how Justus who was surnamed Barsabbas (Acts 1.23) had drunk a harmful poison and had sustained no harm through the grace of the Lord. Then Eusebius adds: 'The same writer also sets down other information which apparently came to him from unwritten tradition (ὡς ἐκ παραδόσεως ἀγράφου), and certain odd parables and teachings of the Saviour, and some other legendary material (μυθικώτερα).' Then Eusebius narrates Papias' millenniarist opinions, which he thinks are the consequence of his failing to understand allegorically (μυστικῶς) some information which he received from the apostles; others, says Eusebius, have followed Papias in these opinions, impressed by his primitiveness (ἀρχαιότης), among them Irenaeus. Papias, he adds, has recorded in his work 'other expositions of the words of the Lord (ἄλλας τῶν τοῦ Κυρίου λόγων διηγήσεις) which he learnt from Aristion, and traditions of the presbyter John' (τοῦ πρεσβυτέρου Ἰωάννου παραδόσεις), which Eusebius does not reproduce. He ends his account of Papias by quoting his well-known words about the evangelist Mark, how he had been an interpreter of Peter (ἑρμηνευτὴς Πέτρου) and had put down, 'but not in order' (οὐ μέντοι τάξει) all that he could remember, and his famous and puzzling statement about the evangelist Matthew that 'he recorded the oracles in the Hebrew language. And each man interpreted them as best he could.'[1] Eusebius has already referred to Papias' account of how Mark's Gospel came to be written, relying on the same extract though he has apparently reproduced rather more of it in this passage: the Christians at Rome, he says, 'were not content to be satisfied with having him (Peter) once and no more, nor with the unwritten tradition of the divine teaching' (τῇ ἀγράφῳ τοῦ θείου κηρύγματος διδασκαλίᾳ), and so asked Mark to record what he could remember, and that Peter, who was apparently in Rome while the task was being completed, approved of it.[2]

Different scholars have estimated differently the value of Papias' tradition. It is worth noting that Papias clearly was not one of 'the presbyters', in spite of Irenaeus' assumption that he was, but that,

---

[1] Ματθαῖος μὲν οὖν Ἑβραΐδι διαλέκτῳ τὰ λόγια συνεγράψατο. Ἡρμήνευσε δ' αὐτὰ ὡς ἦν δυνατὸς ἕκαστος.

[2] *HE* 2.15.1, 2. Eusebius tells us that Clement of Alexandria, in his *Hypotyposeis* (now lost), had recorded this tradition also. See below, pp. 47–48.

according to his own account, he made it his aim to glean information from those who had known 'the presbyters' and, if we are to trust Eusebius' account, he had met some of this group personally, Philip (presumably the evangelist) and Aristion. There is no reason to doubt that Eusebius had Papias' book in front of him, and it seems entirely probable that he reproduced in his own work all the information from Papias which he thought trustworthy. It is clear that he did not regard Papias as entirely reliable. He describes him as 'very much limited in intelligence, as can be concluded from the evidence of his own words'.[1] Papias' use of the phrase 'a living and abiding voice' has attracted the attention of several scholars. Van den Eynde regards it as equivalent to Papias' 'affirming the superiority of the oral tradition', and he thinks his remarks about the evangelists Mark and Matthew to mean that though he knew of written documents he positively preferred oral tradition.[2] If this means that Papias expressed a decided preference for oral tradition supposed to be permanently and reliably existing in the Church independent of Scripture at any time and under any circumstances (and this apparently is what Van den Eynde *does* think it means), this is a wholly mistaken idea. The great value of Papias' testimony in the eyes of those who quote him is its early date (ἀρχαιότης); if anyone is looking for witnesses of words or deeds, it is most satisfactory to meet the witnesses themselves and speak to them rather than to rely on other people's written accounts of them; failing that, it is better to meet those who have met the witnesses. This is all that can be squeezed out of Papias' words. The idea that the oral transmission of tradition continues indefinitely to retain a superiority over written transmission cannot be read into Papias' words. Even if it could, every consideration of historical probability compels sober-minded people to reject it. Similarly, when Van den Eynde finds a passage in Irenaeus and another in Tertullian stating that what the apostles first taught orally they later wrote down he seems to assume that this means that Irenaeus and Tertullian imagined that spoken words of the apostles were preserved orally in the Church independently of the written record in the New Testament,[3] and that two separate bodies of tradition issued separately from the two sources, and remained separate, possibly differing and certainly contrasted. There is no justification for this view.[4] Daniélou takes a much more cautious attitude to Papias'

---

[1] σφόδρα σμικρὸς ὢν τὸν νοῦν, ὡς ἂν ἐκ τῶν αὐτοῦ λόγων τεκμηράμενον εἰπεῖν, *HE* 3.39.13.
[2] Van den Eynde, *Les Normes*, pp. 55, 56.
[3] Irenaeus, *Adv. Haer.* 3.1.1; Tertullian, *De Praescr. Haer.* 2.1.3; Van den Eynde, *Les Normes*, pp. 120, 199.
[4] See Flesseman-van Leer, *Tradition and Scripture*, p. 129.

information.[1] His source, he thinks, was not the apostles themselves, but 'the milieu of the first community' (after the apostles).[2] Papias, he notes, associates with the traditions which he reproduces his own 'interpretations' (ἑρμηνείας, Eusebius, HE 3.39.3), which no doubt means his theology. This theology probably included such points as the betrayal of their commission by angels to whom the administration of the world had been committed by God, the millennial kingdom, and some exegesis of the opening chapters of Genesis.[3] In other words, Papias' material was similar in nature (and perhaps one might add, in value) to the 'Judeo-Christian' material reproduced by Clement of Alexandria in his secret tradition,[4] Cullmann is openly sceptical about the value of Papias' tradition. The examples which we can recover of it demonstrate, he thinks, that his recourse to the 'living voice' was futile.[5]

Certainly the examples of Papias' tradition which have survived do not inspire great confidence in it. Part of it at least is, as Eusebius recognized, unmistakably legendary. It is likely, if the conjecture is correct that Eusebius reproduced all of Papias' tradition which he thought at all reliable, that the five parts of Papias' work contained much more legendary material even than Eusebius has hinted at. His statements about Peter's tradition being incorporated into Mark's Gospel have long caused difficulty to students of the synoptic gospels, though it is only fair to add that many scholars have accepted the fact of Petrine influence on Mark. Nobody has ever been able to establish satisfactorily what exactly Papias meant by his cryptic remarks concerning Matthew's Gospel. It would of course be hasty and unwise to rule out a priori the possibility of any of Papias' tradition being authentic; we cannot dogmatically decide against such a possibility. All we can say is that we can be confident that nothing highly significant nor crucially important can have survived in the oral tradition preserved by Papias, and that what has survived is by the very circumstances of its preservation surrounded by an inescapable aura of uncertainty.

Eusebius has preserved a larger body of information from the work of Hegesippus. Eusebius mistakenly imagines that Hegesippus implied that his lifetime had coincided with the lifetime of Antinous, favourite of the Emperor Hadrian, who died in 130;[6] this is why Eusebius can speak of

---

[1] Théologie, pp. 55–64.   [2] Ibid. p. 56.   [3] Ibid. pp. 57, 58.   [4] Ibid. pp. 345–7.
[5] O. Cullmann, The Early Church, p. 89. Cf. p. 96: 'The encounters of Polycarp and Papias with apostolic persons could no longer guarantee a pure transmission of authentic traditions, as is proved by the extant fragments from their writings.'
[6] HE 4.8.2: Hegesippus' words, 'Αντίνοος, ... οὗ καὶ ἀγὼν ἄγεται 'Αντινόειος ἐφ' ἡμῶν γενόμενος, could mean 'Antinous, in whose memory the Antinoean games are celebrated, who lived in our time', but more probably mean 'Antinous, in whose memory are celebrated the games which still are held in our day'.

'Hegesippus, many of whose testimonies we have already used above, on the assumption that by employing his tradition we are presenting some of the material that came from the apostles'.[1] He goes on to tell us that Hegesippus 'in the simplest style of writing recorded in five books the unerring tradition of the apostolic preaching' (τὴν ἀπλανῆ παράδοσιν τοῦ ἀποστολικοῦ κηρύγματος).[2] Elsewhere quotations from Hegesippus himself tell us that he lived in Rome in the days of bishop Anicetus (c. 160–168) who succeeded bishop Pius, and that he spent some time in Corinth, where he made a succession-list of the bishops of that city, and that while he was in Rome he made a succession-list of its bishops up to Anicetus.[3] Eusebius also informs us that Hegesippus' knowledge of Jewish sects and background was such that it is clear that he was a Jewish Christian who knew Hebrew, and that he used the apocryphal gospel according to the Hebrews.[4] This is borne out by the fact that almost all Hegesippus' information is concerned with Jewish Christianity. Eusebius preserves quite a long account of the reputation, the teaching and the martyrdom of James the brother of the Lord, whom he regarded as the first bishop of the Christian community in Jerusalem.[5] It is clearly full of legendary material, though it may also preserve some authentic tradition about James. Hegesippus also related how at the approach of the siege of Jerusalem during the Jewish revolt which broke out in AD 66 the Christians in Jerusalem fled to Pella, and how by that time all the apostles who still remained alive had left Jerusalem in order to preach the gospel to all nations.[6] Most scholars have accepted as reliable this story of the flight of Jerusalem Christians to Pella. Hegesippus also tells how Symeon son of Clopas (who was brother to Joseph) succeeded James as bishop of Jerusalem, and how after the fall of Jerusalem to the Romans Vespasian sought out the Lord's family in order to persecute them.[7] Hegesippus also describes the martyrdom of this Symeon, at the remarkable age of one hundred and twenty, in the reign of Domitian, and he observes at that point that till the time of Symeon the Church had remained a virgin but that from then on owing to the open boldness of sectarians and heretics it had corrupted 'the sound rule of the saving preaching'.[8] Hegesippus elsewhere depicted an interview between

---

[1] Ἡγήσιππος, οὗ πλείσταις ἤδη πρότερον κεχρήμεθα φωναῖς, ὡς ἂν ἐκ τῆς αὐτοῦ παραδόσεως τινα τῶν κατὰ τοὺς ἀποστόλους παρατιθέμενοι (HE 4.8.1).

[2] HE 4.8.1.   [3] HE 4.11.7; 22.3.   [4] HE 4.22.5–7, 8.

[5] HE 2.23.4–18.   [6] HE 3.5.2, 3.

[7] HE 3.11.12; the story of Symeon's succession is mentioned again 4.22.4.

[8] HE 3.32.1–8: 'the sound rule of the saving preaching' is τὸν ὑγιῆ κανόνα τοῦ σωτηρίου κηρύγματος (3.32.7), but it is likely that this interesting reference to the rule of faith is Eusebius', not Hegesippus', as he appears here to be paraphrasing rather than quoting. A similar passage including a similar sentiment ascribed to Hegesippus occurs in 4.22.5–7.

Domitian and the grandsons of Jude the Lord's brother after which the emperor dismissed them as harmless visionaries.[1] They went back, says Hegesippus, and 'ruled the churches' (3.20.6). It is likely too that the statements that Domitian conducted a persecution,[2] that as a result the apostle John was banished to Patmos,[3] and that on Nerva succeeding Domitian John returned to Ephesus[4] all were derived by Eusebius from Hegesippus' *Memoirs*.[5]

We must not describe the whole of Hegesippus' tradition as worthless, but it is difficult to determine which parts are authentic and which legendary. We will perhaps accept the story of the flight to Pella; we will perhaps reject the account of Symeon's martyrdom, and have considerable doubts about an event so scantily supported by other evidence as Domitian's persecution. We could find some basis of truth in the account of Domitian's interview with the grandsons of Jude, but we are likely to find the information about the apostle John difficult to fit into a consistent account of his career. The general impression which Hegesippus gives is of one who is dealing with history, but at so distant a range and after so long a period of oral transmission that facts have begun to fade into fancies before he records them in writing. Once again we are compelled to notice the air of uncertainty which oral tradition in the early Christian centuries assumed after it had circulated for a certain length of time.

We have already[6] found Papias mentioning a group called 'the presbyters', distinct from the apostles but apparently direct successors to them in the function of handing on the original tradition. Irenaeus mentions this group several times. We have seen that he regarded Papias as belonging to it.[7] He also included Polycarp in this group. In his *Letter to Florinus* he declares, speaking of Florinus' opinions, 'The presbyters who were before our time who had associated with the apostles did not deliver (παρέδωκαν) these opinions to you.'[8] Then he goes on to remind Polycarp, as a proof of his statement, that Florinus and he in their youth had listened to Polycarp and learnt from him. Polycarp would describe the miracles and the teaching of the Lord and 'everything consistent with the Scriptures' (20.6). This probably refers to the New Testament, and suggests, not necessarily that Polycarp had additional information to that which was in the New Testament, but that he could confirm, from his acquaintance with the information given him by the apostles whom he had met, that what was in the New Testament

---

[1] *HE* 3.19 and 20.1–6.   [2] *HE* 3.17.   [3] *HE* 3.18.1.   [4] *HE* 3.20.9.
[5] So Lawlor and Oulton argue strongly (*Eusebius*, Vol. II, pp. 90–92).
[6] See above, p. 36.   [7] See above, p. 36.   [8] Eusebius, *HE* 5.20.4.

was authentic. In this passage Irenaeus also calls Polycarp 'the blessed and apostolic presbyter', even though he knew perfectly well that he was a bishop.[1] Similarly, in his *Letter to Pope Victor* on the subject of the Quartodeciman controversy he can refer to 'the presbyters before Soter who presided over the church . . . we mean Anicetus and Pius, Hyginus and Telesphorus and Xystus'.[2] In one passage in his *Adversus Haereses*[3] Irenaeus maintains that our Lord reached the fortieth or fiftieth year of his age during his earthly ministry and that his ministry extended to about ten years, and that 'the presbyters' who knew John the apostle in Asia witnessed that this is what he said, and that John lived to the time of Trajan. He also quotes a piece of teaching which he had heard from 'a certain presbyter who had heard it from those who had seen the apostles and from those who had taught', to the effect that for the righteous men of the Old Testament the correction which is in the Scriptures sufficed; and he instances David and Solomon.[4] This is apparently to explain why they were open to forgiveness and justification when Christ descended into hell; they had experienced their punishment in their earthly life. To 'the presbyters' also he ascribes (as we have seen)[5] the doctrine of the millennial kingdom on an earth endowed with miraculous fertility. 'The presbyters' also taught that at the resurrection of the just different people will be rewarded differently. Some will go direct to heaven, some to Paradise, and some to the millennial city; and this is what our Lord meant when he referred to different people producing various fruits (Matt. 13.8; Mark 4.8). It was in this sense also that 'the presbyters' interpreted the saying 'In my Father's house are many mansions' (John 14.2), the parable of the King's Wedding Feast (Matt. 22.1–14), St Paul's words concerning Christ's subjecting all things to himself (I Cor. 15.25–28, presumably regarded as a reference to the millennial kingdom), and the saying 'I say unto you, I will not again drink of the fruit of the vine until that day when I drink it new with you in the Kingdom of my Father' (Matt. 26.29, another reference, apparently, to the millennial kingdom).[6] Clement of Alexandria also mentions 'the presbyters'. Eusebius tells us that in one of his books Clement showed that 'he was very near to the succession of the apostles' (ὡς ἔγγιστα τῆς τῶν ἀποστόλων γενομένου διαδοχῆς), and that in his book *On the Pascha* (now lost) 'he admits that he was compelled by his friends to

---

[1] *HE* 5.20.7: ὁ μακάριος καὶ ἀποστολικὸς πρεσβύτερος.
[2] *HE* 5.24.14: οἱ πρὸ Σωτῆρος πρεσβύτεροι. οἱ προστάντες τῆς ἐκκλησίας.
[3] 2.33.3.   [4] *Ibid.* 4.42.2.
[5] See above, p. 36; *Adv. Haer.* 5.33.3, 4; cf. 5.35.2.
[6] *Adv. Haer.* 5.5.1; 5.36.

hand down to posterity in writing the traditions (παραδόσεις) which he happened to have heard from the primitive presbyters' (παρὰ τῶν ἀρχαίων πρεσβυτέρων).[1] Clement himself has an interesting passage in which he sets out to explain why 'the presbyters' left no writings. 'They did not want to give time from their responsibility for teaching the tradition (τῆς παραδόσεως) to the responsibility of writing, or to occupy, in writing, their opportunities for meditating upon what they were to speak. And perhaps because they were convinced that to carry through successfully the task of compiling books and to teach were not suitable to the same temperament, they left the task to those who were by nature fitted for it.' He then goes on to point out how useful a written tradition is as 'a written confirmation of the teaching' (ἔγγραφος διδασκαλίας βεβαίωσις).[2] Hippolytus may be referring to the same group of 'the presbyters' when in his *Apostolic Tradition* he remarked of the custom of praying at midnight, 'for those elders too who handed on the tradition taught us thus.'[3] But if this is a reference in Hippolytus to this group, it is the only one, and Van den Eynde may be correct in his conclusion that though Hippolytus refers to predecessors, Justin, Irenaeus, Tatian, Miltiades, and Clement, he does not refer to 'the presbyters';[4] in that case we should have to take the passage in the *Apostolic Tradition* as referring only to immemorial custom in the Church.[5]

What are we to make of this group consisting of 'the presbyters'? Ehrhardt describes them as 'persons of considerable and well-deserved authority, possessing exceptionally good information about the earliest teachings of the Church'.[6] The review of the information derived from them which we have just made suggests that this is an optimistic estimate. Irenaeus associates both Polycarp and Papias with the group, and if we are to accept this as accurate we must envisage the group as more fluid and indefinite than a recognizable body of men formally commissioned by the apostles to maintain the tradition could be. The *First Epistle of Clement*, which speaks of the apostles and their immediate successors,

---

[1] Eusebius, *HE* 6.13.8, 9.

[2] *Eclogae Propheticae* 27. See *Origen's Doctrine of Tradition*, p. 62.

[3] *Apostolic Tradition* 36.12: Latin *nam et hi qui tradiderunt nobis seniores ita nos docuerunt*; it is almost certain that *seniores* translates πρεσβύτεροι.

[4] Van den Eynde, *Les Normes*, p. 215; but see Von Campenhausen, *Kirchliches Amt*, p. 177.

[5] It does not seem at all likely that Daniélou is correct in seeing in an allegorization of the parable of the Good Samaritan attributed to 'one of the presbyters' by Origen a reference to this group of 'the presbyters'. See Origen, *Homilies on Luke* 34, and Daniélou, *Théologie*, p. 59.

[6] Ehrhardt, *The Apostolic Succession*, p. 111. Cf. Van den Eynde, *Les Normes*, pp. 163-4, Gerhardsson, *Memory and Manuscript*, p. 206, and Von Campenhausen, *Kirchliches Amt*, pp. 177-8.

does not seem to know of this group of 'the presbyters',[1] though its author is living at a date nearer to the apostles than the times of Papias or Hegesippus or Irenaeus or Polycarp. Apart from the information derived from these 'presbyters' by Papias (which itself is not unimpeachable), not one tradition ascribed to them by Irenaeus or Clement of Alexandria is at all convincing. It may well be that Daniélou is correct in suggesting that the traditions of 'the presbyters' do not in fact derive from the apostles but are the product of the early 'Judeo-Christian' community.[2] It is quite possible that this group of 'the presbyters' never existed as a formal body, but are the result of an assumption made widely in the Church of the second century that there must have existed such a group in order to bridge the gap between the deaths of the apostles and the universal recognition of their written tradition in the New Testament, much as Rabbinic Judaism believed vaguely in the existence of the men of the Great Synagogue. Irenaeus' statement about Polycarp and Clement of Alexandria's (admittedly rather confused) language about them might be taken to suggest this.[3] Indeed as far as Irenaeus' statements about them go, the phrase could mean no more than 'the men of old'.

Irenaeus refers several times to other predecessors of his from whom he has derived information. He quotes eight very rough iambic lines directed against the heretic Marcus, calling the author 'the divine' or 'the inspired old man' ($\pi\rho\epsilon\sigma\beta\acute{u}\tau\eta s$) and herald of the truth' and 'the godloving old man' ($\acute{o}$ $\theta\epsilon o\phi\iota\lambda\grave{\eta}s$ $\pi\rho\epsilon\sigma\beta\acute{u}\tau\eta s$).[4] He quotes someone whom he calls 'one who lived before us', or possibly 'one greater than we' (*superior nobis*) as saying that the Gnostic 'is lime vilely mixed with the milk of God' (*in Dei lacte gypsum male miscetur*).[5] We are reminded of the sentence of the Muratorian Canon excluding badly attested books on the ground that 'it is not right that gall should be mixed with honey.'[6] He cites with approval the saying of some anonymous predecessor: 'The Son is the measure of the Father because he also embraces him.'[7] Again 'one of those who have gone before' ($\tau\iota s$ $\tau\hat{\omega}\nu$ $\pi\rho o\beta\epsilon\beta\eta\kappa\acute{o}\tau\omega\nu$) said that our Lord's stretching out his arms on the cross brought together the two races (Jew and Gentile).[8] He ascribes also to 'a certain presbyter'

---

[1] *I Clement* 42; 44. It is a most unpromising task to try to see in either the ἕτεροι δεδοκιμασμένοι ἄνδρες of 44.2 or the ἑτέρων ἐλλογίμων ἀνδρῶν of 44.3 an official group of ministers distinct from the ἐπίσκοποι-πρεσβύτεροι of the other passages in the Epistle.
[2] Daniélou, *Théologie*, pp. 27, 55–64.   [3] See above, pp. 42, 43.
[4] *Adv. Haer.* 1.8.17.   [5] *Ibid.* 3.18.3.
[6] Muratorian Canon, lines 66–68.
[7] *Mensura Patris Filius quoniam et capit eum* (*Adv. Haer.* 4.4.6).
[8] *Ibid.* 5.17.4.

a curious conception, found also in the *Gospel of Peter*, that when Christ rose the cross also rose from the tomb.[1] He also tells us that John, author of Revelation, saw his vision, 'not a long time ago, but almost in our generation, towards the end of Domitian's reign', but does not give the source of this tradition.[2] It is highly likely that Daniélou has found the source of all or most of those traditions in the Jewish-Christian milieu to which he also attributes the sayings of 'the presbyters'.[3] Irenaeus also refers in various places to Ignatius[4] and to Justin.[5]

But on other occasions Irenaeus can give the impression that to him miscellaneous tradition outside the New Testament is worth little or nothing. 'This is their doctrine' ($\hat{\upsilon}\pi o\theta\acute{\epsilon}\sigma\epsilon\omega s$), he says, of the heretics, 'which neither the prophets foretold, nor the Lord taught, nor the apostles handed down, which they boast to possess some additional knowledge than the others on the subject of the universe;[6] they discover it by unwritten tradition,[7] and, in the words of the proverb, they are anxious to weave ropes from sand.'[8] After giving a description of the rule of faith and insisting that the same rule is taught everywhere throughout the Church, in Germany, in Gaul, in Spain, in Egypt, in Libya, in the East, he says that Christians use different languages, but the power of the tradition ($\hat{\eta}$ $\delta\acute{\upsilon}\nu\alpha\mu\iota s$ $\tau\hat{\eta}s$ $\pi\alpha\rho\alpha\delta\acute{o}\sigma\epsilon\omega s$) is one and the same. And he ends with the statement, 'Since the faith is one and the same, neither he who can say much about it has said too much nor has he who says only a little about it reduced it.'[9] Similarly, when he deals, very briefly, with Marcion's errors, Irenaeus never hints that he has more material than the Scriptures from which to refute the heretic; his whole complaint is that Marcion mutilates and reduces Scripture:[10] 'We do not know the strategy of our salvation through any other persons than through those through whom the Gospel came to us; this Gospel they then preached, but later through the will of God handed it down to us in the Scriptures, to be the ground and pillar of our faith.'[11] In the third book of his *Adversus Haereses* occurs the famous passage giving the reasons why the gospels had to be four in number, and four only, and he draws the conclusion that nobody has any right to add to or subtract from the quadruple

---

[1] *Ibid.* 4.27.1–2, see Daniélou, *Théologie*, p. 117. [2] *Adv. Haer.* 5.30.3.
[3] See Daniélou, *Théologie*, pp. 58 and 59.
[4] *Adv. Haer.* 5.28.3, where he quotes Ignatius' *Romans* 4 and describes him as *quidam de nostris propter martyrium in Deum adiucatus ad bestias.*
[5] *Ibid.* 4.11.2. [6] Or 'on the whole subject', $\pi\epsilon\rho\grave{\iota}$ $\tau\hat{\omega}\nu$ $\check{o}\lambda\omega\nu$.
[7] $\grave{\epsilon}\xi$ $\grave{\alpha}\gamma\rho\acute{\alpha}\phi\omega\nu$ $\grave{\alpha}\nu\alpha\gamma\iota\nu\acute{\omega}\sigma\kappa o\nu\tau\epsilon s$; Harvey's interpretation 'from writings, but not Scripture' is unlikely, but would not affect the argument here.
[8] *Adv. Haer.* 1.1.15. [9] *Ibid.* 1.3. [10] *Ibid.* 1.25.1, 2.
[11] *Ibid.* 3.1.1; 'strategy of our salvation' translates *dispositionem salutis nostrae*, which almost certainly represents an original $o\grave{\iota}\kappa o\nu o\mu\acute{\iota}\alpha\nu$ $\tau\hat{\eta}s$ $\sigma\omega\tau\eta\rho\acute{\iota}\alpha s$ $\hat{\eta}\mu\hat{\omega}\nu$.

number of the gospels, 'in the one case so that they should appear to have discovered more than the truth, and in the other so that they should reject the dispensation (οἰκονομίας) of God.'[1] In similar vein the Muratorian Canon insists that, though there may be varieties of teaching in the gospels, yet 'all things in all of them are set forth by the single and controlling Spirit.'[2] Yet the writer of this document can reproduce a story, based presumably on oral tradition, of the incident which induced the apostle John to write the fourth gospel.[3] The most probable conclusion from the statements of both these writers is that though they were perfectly ready to reproduce single items of miscellaneous historical information independent of the Bible they do not imagine that any significant or important information about the Christian faith exists in their day outside the Scriptures.

From other writers in the second and third centuries a few more pieces of information presumably resting on oral tradition can be gleaned. Eusebius tells us[4] that Paul was beheaded and Peter crucified by Nero, and that there are two proofs of this: one is 'the attachment of the names of Peter and Paul to the cemeteries there'; and the other is the words of Gaius, who writing in Rome in the time of Pope Zephyrinus (199–217) says that he can demonstrate 'the apostles' *"memoriae"*' (τὰ τρόπαια τῶν ἀποστόλων) to anyone who goes to the Vatican hill or to the Ostian way. In at least one of the cases recent archaeological investigation seems to have confirmed the accuracy of this tradition, which might perhaps be regarded as already witnessed to, though in very general terms, by the words of Clement of Rome.[5] Tertullian also witnesses to this tradition.[6] But it is interesting to note that elsewhere Eusebius tells us that this Gaius rejected the tradition which attributed the fourth gospel and Revelation to John the Apostle, and also that which assigned the Epistle to the Hebrews to Paul.[7]

Tertullian refers to some of his predecessors[8] (though not as 'the presbyters'), but otherwise he reproduces nothing that can go back to oral tradition except the merest legends: the story that Tiberius received from Palestine the news of Christ's resurrection and urged the Senate to acknowledge his divinity, but the Senate refused;[9] and the tale of the Thundering Legion.[10] He refers to Nero as conducting a persecution,[11]

[1] *Ibid.* 3.11.11, 12.   [2] Mur. Canon, ll. 16–20.   [3] *Ibid.* ll. 9–16.
[4] *HE* 2.25.5, 6.   [5] *I Clement* 5.   [6] *Scorpiace* 14.3.
[7] *HE* 6.20.3. See below, p. 222.
[8] Justin, Miltiades, Irenaeus, Proculus: *Adversus Valentinianos* 5.1.
[9] *Apologeticus* 4.1–2.   [10] *Ad Scapulam* 4.6.
[11] *Apologeticus* 4.3; *Ad Nationes* 1.7.8; *Scorpiace* 14.3.

attributes a persecution to Domitian,[1] alleges that the census during which Christ was born was that held 'under Augustus in Judaea by Sentius Saturninus'[2] and attempts separately to date the Nativity and the Crucifixion.[3] But Tertullian recognizes the possibility of the failure or corruption of a merely oral tradition;[4] and he formally refuses to allow the argument that people could have made a certain remark to Jesus simply in order to tempt him, on the grounds that this is a speculation 'outside Scripture'.[5] Hippolytus admits the possibility that somebody in his day might possess genuine unwritten tradition independent of Scripture when he denies this possibility to the heretics: 'they have not ventured upon these doctrines because they have received them from the holy Scriptures nor have they taken this course because they preserved the succession of any holy man' (ἤ τινος ἁγίου διαδοχὴν φυλάξαντες).[6] And elsewhere he says that Justin the Gnostic is entirely inconsistent both with the teaching of the holy Scriptures (i.e. the old Testament), 'and also further with the writing or voice of the blessed evangelists'. But the reading here is uncertain,[7] and otherwise Hippolytus takes little or no notice of the type of oral tradition which we have been considering.[8]

We have already had occasion to consider the origin and value of the oral tradition preserved by Clement of Alexandria, much of it through quotatidns by Eusebius from Clement's lost book *Hypotyposeis*. He alleged that the Lord 'delivered the secret message' (παρέδωκε τὴν γνῶσιν) to James the Just and to Peter, and that they imparted it to Barnabas;[9] this allegation sounds disconcertingly like the spurious historical pedigrees provided by the Gnostics for their secret tradition.[10] Again, Eusebius informs us that a story of James the brother of John

---

[1] *Apologeticus* 4.3.   [2] *Adversus Marcionem* 4.19.10.

[3] *Adversus Iudaeos* 8.11.16; it is not quite certain that this work is by Tertullian, but reasons have been advanced to suggest that at least the first eight chapters are from his hand. In my 'Notes on Tertullian's Interpretation of Scripture' a few additional reasons for this view have been stated.

[4] *De Anima* 28.5, demolishing Pythagoras' claim to have recognized the shield of Euphorbus at Delphi, remembering it from a previous existence: *Quid, si defectae iam traditionis superstes aliquas famae aurulas hausit?*

[5] *De Carne Christi* 7.3: *eo quod nemo prohibebat hic quoque significari temptandi gratia factum, non recipio quod extra scripturam de tuo infers.*

[6] *Elenchos* 1, introd. 8.

[7] *Ibid.* 5.23.1: γραφῇ ἢ φωνῇ is odd, and the suggested emendation ἐγγράφῳ φωνῇ would make better sense.

[8] Perhaps we should make an exception in favour of the legend connected with the name of Simon Magus (*Elenchos* 6.20.2). But Hippolytus may have met some early written version of the story later to be enshrined in the *Clementine Homilies* and *Recognitions*.

[9] *HE* 2.1.4, 5.   [10] See above, pp. 22–24.

converting by his demeanour one of his escort on the way to his execution comes from Clement's *Hypotyposeis* where it is related 'as coming by tradition from those who were before him'.[1] It is not improbable that the tradition that St Mark founded the church in Alexandria came from the same source.[2] Some more information of rather the same sort can be gleaned from the surviving works of Clement (some of it reproduced by Eusebius also). There are a number of stray stories about the apostles, including the words addressed by Peter to his wife on the way to her execution.[3] There is the charming and apparently circumstantial story of the rescue by St John in extreme old age of a robber who in his youth had been a disciple of the apostle's.[4] But at the outset of his narrative Clement says that the young man became John's disciple some time after the death of Nerva (AD 98), and several years must be supposed to have elapsed between the beginning and the end of the narrative. The very least that we can suppose is that John the son of Zebedee, were this an historical incident, was ninety-five or ninety-six at the time (assuming that he was only eighteen at the time of the Crucifixion, and dating the Crucifixion to the year 30), and possibly several years older; his adventures during this story include an active visitation of the churches and a journey on horseback to a robbers' lair in a mountainous region. Much though we might like to believe this story, it must remain highly conjectural. Clement also tells us that the apostle Matthew ate only seeds and berries and vegetables but no meat,[5] and that Barnabas was one of the Seventy,[6] and that Christ is said to have baptized Peter only, but Peter baptized Andrew, Andrew James and John, and these two the rest of the apostles.[7] This last tradition comes from his *Hypotyposeis* and is no doubt an apocryphal supplement to the New Testament designed to remedy what was thought to be the inexplicable absence in it of any reference to the twelve apostles being baptized.

A few similar pieces of information derived from scattered oral traditions can be detected in the works of Origen. The manger where Jesus was laid at his birth, he tells us, was in a cave, and everybody knows this.[8] It is worth recalling that Origen had paid a visit to the Holy Land

---

[1] ὡς ἂν ἐκ παραδόσεως τῶν πρὸ αὐτοῦ, *HE* 2.9.2. The story of how St Mark's Gospel came to be written, which we have already considered (see above, p. 37) was also related by Clement in his *Hypotyposeis*; *HE* 2.15.1, 2.

[2] *HE* 2.16.1.

[3] *Stromateis* 3.4.25 and 3.6.52 f. (PG 8.1129 and 1156 f.); *HE* 3.29 and 30.

[4] *Quis Dives* 42; *HE* 3.23.6-19.   [5] *Paedagogos* 2.1.16.1 (PG 8.404).

[6] *Strom.* 2.20.117.3 (PG 8.1060).

[7] Fragment 6, GCS 3, p. 196. For many of these traditions see *Origen's Doctrine of Tradition*, pp. 132, 133.

[8] *Contra Celsum* 1.56.

in 215, so that he is here probably repeating tradition associated with a particular site. The names of the two disciples whom Jesus met on their journey to Emmaus were, we learn,[1] Simon and Cleopas. Gaius, who is mentioned in Rom. 16.23, was the first bishop of Thessalonica.[2] Of the apostles, Thomas died in Parthia, Andrew in Scythia, and John in Ephesus, and Peter, crucified head downwards, in Rome and Paul also in Rome.[3] The Magi mentioned in St Matthew's Gospel were three in number.[4] Tabor was the mountain upon which the Transfiguration took place, and Hermon the hill upon which was situated the city of Nain,[5] and he tells a story about the death of Zacharias, father of John the Baptist.[6]

We have already had occasion to survey most of the material provided in the first three books of Eusebius' *Ecclesiastical History* which could assist in our search for early oral tradition, but a few more examples may be added. Eusebius quotes Julius Africanus' attempt to harmonize the genealogies of Jesus given in the first and the third gospels; Africanus apparently stated that 'those who were relations of the Saviour according to the flesh . . . handed down this information' (παρέδοσαν καὶ ταῦτα).[7] Eusebius gives us some of the names of the Seventy, under the not very confident rubric 'it is said' and 'they say', but he admits that of these Seventy 'no list is anywhere in circulation'.[8] He also gives us the story of the letter of Abgar, King of Edessa, to Jesus and of Jesus' letter in reply to him, a tradition which would be of the highest importance were it not wholly legendary.[9] He tells us that Simon Magus came to Rome and made such an impression that a statue was put up to him, but he was refuted and discountenanced by Peter.[10] He could have derived this story from Justin Martyr;[11] he rejected as spurious, however, the pseudo-Clementine literature.[12] He tells us that 'the story goes' (λόγος ἔχει) that Philo conversed with St Peter in Rome,[13] and that the destination of the apostles when they left Jerusalem to go to all the nations was, 'as the tradition has it' (ὡς ἡ παράδοσις περιέχει), Thomas to Parthia, Andrew

---

[1] *Ibid.* 2.62, 68; *Hom. on Jeremiah* 20.8.   [2] *Comm. on Romans* 10.41.
[3] Eusebius, *HE* 3.1.1–3, from the third book of Origen's *Comm. on Genesis.*
[4] *Homilies on Genesis* 14.3.
[5] *Comm. on Psalm 89, v. 12* (PG 12.1548).
[6] *Comm. on Matthew*, Comm. Ser. 25; a fragment on Luke 11.51 (PG 17.356); *Comm. on Ephesians* XX. These traditions have been gathered together in *Origen's Doctrine of Tradition*, pp. 45 and 46.
[7] *HE* 1.7.2–15. Africanus does not seem very confident about the trustworthiness of this tradition.
[8] κατάλογος μὲν οὐδεὶς οὐδαμῇ φέρεται, *HE* 1.12.1–3.
[9] *HE* 1.13.1–22.   [10] *HE* 2.14.1–6.   [11] *Apology* 1.26.2; 1.56.1, 2.
[12] *HE* 3.38.5.   [13] *HE* 2.17.1.

D

to Scythia, and John to Asia.[1] And he records a quotation from Polycrates of Ephesus, based no doubt on oral tradition, giving an account of Philip the apostle (whom he has confused with Philip the evangelist) and of John; these statements have for long puzzled scholars of the Johannine literature.[2] No piece of oral tradition can be recovered from the works of Cyprian. As we shall see, this is probably not a coincidence.[3]

6. Conclusions

Our survey in this chapter of the oral tradition independent of the Bible current in the Church for the first two centuries after the Resurrection suggests very strongly that by the middle of the second century this tradition was subject to a growing uncertainty and by the middle of the third it was so faint as to be almost non-existent. This is not to say that among these remains of the oral tradition there may not be preserved some authentic pieces of information. The material will presumably continue to exercise the skill of critical scholarship indefinitely, and each piece must be taken on its merits separately. But it is clear that such oral tradition as did survive was scattered, casual and insignificant. It could not possibly be used as a satisfactory basis for establishing doctrine which was not already witnessed to in the Scriptures. The definition of tradition given by R. M. Grant is worth remembering: 'By "tradition" we mean the older information based sometimes on fact, sometimes on conjecture, and handed down without much, if any, investigation of its sources.'[4]

The insecurity and the unimportance of oral tradition of this sort is well illustrated in the Quartodeciman controversy which broke out during the time of Victor, bishop of Rome, probably at some point between 190 and 195.[5] The point at issue was, which was the correct day on which to celebrate the Paschal Feast, whether on the fourteenth of Nisan (or, to be more accurate, the fourteenth day after the first new moon after the vernal equinox), no matter what day of the week this fell on, or whether on the Sunday after this date. The churches of Asia Minor kept to the former custom, most other churches, including the

[1] *HE* 3.1.1; see above, p. 49.   [2] *HE* 3.31.3.
[3] See below, pp. 99–100, 140–1. The same holds true of the surviving works of Novatian.
[4] *The Earliest Lives of Jesus*, pp. 52–53.
[5] For this controversy see also Turner, *The Pattern*, pp. 332–4, and for an attractive suggestion about the origin of this difference see C. W. Dugmore, 'A Note on the Quartodecimans'.

churches of Rome, of Palestine, of Gaul and of Greece, followed the latter. Eusebius gives us an account of the controversy in the twenty-third to the twenty-fifth chapters of the fifth book of his *Ecclesiastical History*. The point to note is that both sides in the controversy confidently claimed that they were following the tradition handed down to them from the apostles. The side led by Victor of Rome observed their custom 'by an apostolic tradition' and by 'the tradition concerning the Pascha which had come down to them in succession from the apostles'.[1] Polycrates of Ephesus, spokesman for the Asian churches, resolutely maintained not only that their custom had been observed by a long succession of bishops, including men of eminent saintliness, but that it certainly derived from the apostles Philip and John themselves.[2] We cannot help, as we follow this controversy, applauding the wisdom of Irenaeus who, though he agreed with Victor's custom, strongly deprecated that Pope's making this divergence a matter of excommunication, on the ground that the question was one of those unimportant points about which Christians could afford to differ without breaking the bond of unity.[3] Nothing could illustrate more effectively both the uncertainty in which the Church in the late second century was inevitably involved when it came to estimating the value of oral tradition and the fact that such tradition was recognized to be of no fundamental importance. Anyway, nobody who has read the literature of the Christian Church of the first two centuries can avoid the conclusion that eminent Christian writers, whose minds were certainly not formed in the critical mould which has shaped the minds of modern scholars, very readily attributed to apostolic tradition any custom or rite or tradition which they could not find directly referred to in the Bible and which they thought to be older than living memory.

We must therefore conclude that by the beginning of the third century any oral tradition which had not by that time found its way to written form in the New Testament was by an inevitable process suffering badly 'against the wrackful siege of battering days'.

We have yet to examine other possible forms of tradition outside the Bible. But about this particular form, historical information which had not been included in the New Testament and which had remained oral, the judgement of scholarship must be decisive: it is involved in an inevitable mistiness which as the centuries go on thickens into an impenetrable darkness.

---

[1] Eusebius, *HE* 5.23.1; 5.25.   [2] *HE* 5.24.2–7.   [3] *HE* 5.24.9–18.

2

The Creed

1. Early Formal Teaching

WHEN, IN our search for examples of authentic tradition independent of the Bible in the literature and the life of the early Church, we approach the subject of the creed, we are bound first of all to note one salient fact, which is not always properly appreciated by those who champion the sole sufficiency of Scripture as a basis for Christian doctrine. This is that the Church from the earliest moment of its existence was a teaching Church. Christian teaching was given continuously to inquirers and converts from the most primitive ages of Christianity up to the latest point with which our investigation could be concerned, and there is a respectable body of evidence available to give us some idea of what that teaching consisted of, because we can recover from the New Testament and from the writings of the subapostolic age and the age that succeeded it a number of formulae briefly summarizing this teaching and a number of references to it.

Dodd, in his *The Apostolic Preaching and its Developments*, has shown that it is possible to reconstruct an approximate list of the articles of the faith preached by the apostles themselves according to the speeches attributed to them in Acts, and also that this list resembles a similar list which can be reconstructed from those passages in St Paul's epistles where he is, either explicitly or implicitly, repeating the teaching which he himself received when he was converted, and also resembles (*mutatis mutandis*) the brief summary given us by St Mark of the teaching of Jesus himself when he came into Galilee preaching the Gospel of God after the arrest of John the Baptist (Mark 1.14, 15). Others have suggested that there are several other passages in the New Testament where brief formulae summarizing Christian teaching can be discerned. These passages have often been called 'credal' passages; it will later be shown[1]

[1] See below, pp. 64, 65.

how unsatisfactory and inaccurate it is to give them this epithet; for the moment we shall content ourselves with putting the word in question in inverted commas. As examples of these passages (though no attempt is here made to provide an exhaustive list) we may take the following:

Rom. 1.3, 4: '. . . concerning his Son,
   who was born of the seed of David according to the flesh,
   declared the Son of God in power according to the
     Spirit of holiness as a result of the resurrection of the dead,
   Jesus Christ our Lord.'
Rom. 4.24, 25: '. . . him who raised Jesus our Lord from the dead
   who was delivered up for our transgressions
   and was raised for our justification.'
Rom. 8.34: 'It is Christ Jesus who died,
   or rather who was raised,
   who is on the right hand of God,
   who also intercedes for us.'
I Cor. 8.6: 'we have one God, the Father,
   from whom are all things and we are for him;
   and one Lord Jesus Christ,
   through whom are all things and we are through him.'
I Tim. 2.5: 'There is one God,
   and one mediator between God and men,
   the man Christ Jesus,
   who gave himself as a ransom for all,
   a testimony at its own times.'
I Tim. 3.16: 'and, we confess, great is the mystery of godliness;
   who was manifested in flesh,
   was justified in Spirit,
   was seen by angels,
   was preached among Gentiles,
   was believed on in the world,
   was taken up in glory.'
II Tim. 2.8: 'Remember Jesus Christ,
   risen from the dead,
   of the seed of David.'
I Peter 3.18: 'Because Jesus Christ died once for our sins,
   the Just for the unjust,
   that he might bring us near to God,

put to death in the flesh,
but quickened in the Spirit.'[1]

From Ignatius we can recover a few similar formulae:

Ephesians 18.2: 'For our God, Jesus the Christ,
was conceived by Mary from the seed of David and the Holy Spirit;
who was born and was baptized,
in order that he might cleanse the water by his submitting.'

Trallians 9: 'Jesus Christ . . .
of the seed of David, of Mary,
who was really born, ate and drank,
who was really persecuted under Pontius Pilate,
was really crucified and died,
heavenly and earthly and infernal powers looking on,
who also was really raised from the dead,
his Father raising him.'

Smyrneans 1.1, 2: 'Christ . . . who was really of the race of David according to the flesh,
the Son of God according to the will and power of God,
really begotten of a Virgin,
baptized by John in order that all righteousness might be fulfilled by
him,
under Pontius Pilate and Herod the Tetrarch really nailed for us in
the flesh,
and of its fruit are we from his divinely blessed passion,
that he might raise up a standard for the ages through the resurrection
for his holy and faithful ones,
whether among the Jews or among the Gentiles,
in one body of his Church.'[2]

From Polycarp's *Epistle to the Philippians* (2.1) we can recover this:
believing in him who raised the Lord Jesus Christ from the dead,
and gave him glory and a throne at his right hand,

[1] All the examples here given are reproduced in Kelly, *Early Christian Creeds*,
pp. 17–21; other passages which have been described as 'credal' are I Cor. 15.3 ff.;
Phil. 2.5–11; I Tim. 6.13; II Tim. 4.1; and I Peter 1.21. See also Turner, *The Pattern*,
pp. 358–60, and Cullmann, *The Earliest Christian Confessions*, pp. 36–37 and 40, and
E. Stauffer, *New Testament Theology*, pp. 234–57, and A. Richardson, *Creeds in the
Making*, caps. I and II, for further examples; see also Von Campenhausen, *Kirchliches
Amt*, pp. 163–6, and Daniélou, *Message Évangelique*, pp. 132–4.
[2] In *Philadelphians* 8.2 Zahn, Funk and Batiffol were anxious to see a preference
expressed by Ignatius for unwritten over written tradition. Van den Eynde (*Les Normes*,
pp. 30–38) has shown with admirable clarity that this is a most unlikely interpretation
of the passage. For another treatment of it, see *Allegory and Event*, p. 101.

to whom all heavenly and earthly powers were subjected,
whom everything that breathes serves,
who is coming as a judge of living and dead,
whose blood God will require from those who disobey him.[1]

Elsewhere in this letter Polycarp makes a significant reference to contemporary Christian teaching. 'Whoever perverts the oracles of the Lord to his own lusts,' he says, 'is the first-born of Satan,' and he urges his hearers to 'turn to the word delivered to us from the beginning'.[2] Van den Eynde interprets this 'word delivered from the beginning' as 'the doctrine transmitted intact since the beginning,' and suggests that Polycarp is instructing his hearers to interpret the words of the Lord in the light of this doctrine.[3] The translation of this passage is not entirely certain, for it has been suggested that the word translated 'pervert' should really be rendered 'abuse', implying that the people condemned deny the words of the Lord and impugn them as not genuine; and the corollary of this rendering of the passage would be that 'the issue is not at all writing versus tradition, but heretical teaching versus the real tradition of the church'.[4] It is impossible to avoid the conclusion, however, that Polycarp is here referring to teaching given in the Church, whether he conceives it as based on the words of the Lord, or on some other tradition of doctrine. We can also find the author of *II Clement* warning his hearers to pay attention 'while they are being exhorted by the presbyters' (ἐν τῷ νουθετεῖσθαι ὑπὸ τῶν πρεσβυτέρων), though it is clear that the presbyters are basing their teaching on 'the commands of the Lord'.[5] It is remarkable that in *I Clement* though presbyters are frequently mentioned the function of teaching is never attributed to them. *II Clement*, which dates from the middle of the second century, probably marks an advance in the teaching authority ascribed to the regular ministry.[6]

No such formulae can be readily recovered from *I Clement* or from the *Didache* or Hermas or *II Clement*. Not even the *Epistle of Barnabas* gives us a clear idea of what was the content of contemporary Christian teaching. Its emphatic references to 'the knowledge' (γνῶσις) are more likely to mean the peculiar Jewish-Christian speculative method of interpreting

---

[1] The examples from Ignatius and Polycarp are given by Kelly, *Early Christian Creeds*, pp. 65–77.
[2] Polycarp, *Philippians* 7.1, 2: the crucial phrases are ὃς ἂν μεθοδεύῃ τὰ λόγια τοῦ Κυρίου πρὸς τὰς ἰδίας ἐπιθυμίας, and τὸν ἐξ ἀρχῆς ἡμῖν παραδοθέντα λόγον.
[3] Van den Eynde, *Les Normes*, pp. 51, 55.
[4] So Flesseman-van Leer, *Tradition and Scripture*, pp. 45–47.
[5] *II Clement* 17.3–5.
[6] See Van den Eynde, *Les Normes*, p. 65; Flesseman-van Leer, *op. cit.*, pp. 63 and 67.

the Old Testament than to refer to the content of the teaching given to inquirers and converts as their regular diet by the Church.[1] The suggestion that the source entitled 'The Two Ways' which appears in different forms in the *Didache* and in the *Epistle of Barnabas* constitutes part of the original and traditional teaching of the Church handed on by the authors of both these works[2] has become less attractive since the discovery that the literature of the Qumran Covenanters contains a source very like this one. In none of these fathers, as Van den Eynde recognizes, does the word 'tradition' (παράδοσις) have a formal or technical sense.[3] At the same time the conclusion is unavoidable, and indeed is admitted by scholars of all schools of thought, that during this period the Church was delivering its teaching in a continuous and fairly consistent tradition, and it is wholly probable that a number of summaries or formulae such as those which we have already examined were being used.[4] It has already been made clear that the sources of the teaching given during this period must have been both written (Old Testament and to an increasing extent as the period advanced New Testament) and oral. The question of whether these writers subordinated the written sources to the oral sources or subordinated the oral sources to the written sources is an irrelevant, because an anachronistic, one. The teaching given in the Church was assumed by all to be identical with the contents of the Old Testament and with the words of the Lord. To seek narrowly for signs of one being 'subordinated' to the other[5] is to seek for a distinction which was obviously not in the minds of the men of that period. It was during the period beginning with Irenaeus, just after the middle of the second century, that the relation of Scripture, tradition and Church was first, by the force of circumstances, raised, and not before then. During the period of the apostolic fathers doctrinal norms clearly were fluid and little defined. Indeed, one scholar finds in this very indefiniteness one of the reasons for the notorious '*Abfall*' or declension in profundity and grasp of doctrine which is often attributed to this

---

[1] See the useful discussion by Van den Eynde, *Les Normes*, pp. 81–95, of γνῶσις in *I Clement*, Hermas and *Barnabas*, cf. pp. 101–2; see also *Allegory and Event*, pp. 97–101.

[2] Van den Eynde, *Les Normes*, pp. 52–53.

[3] Not even in the tempting phrase ὁ εὐκλεής καὶ σεμνὸς τῆς παραδόσεως ἡμῶν κανών (*I Clement* 7.2), where in fact the teaching of the apostles, Christ and the prophets is intended. See Van den Eynde, *Les Normes*, pp. 51–52.

[4] Van den Eynde, *Les Normes*, pp. 39–67; Flesseman-van Leer, *Tradition and Scripture*, pp. 66–67, and Daniélou, *Théologie*, pp. 320–4, are virtually in agreement here. See also Gerhardsson, *Memory and Manuscript*, pp. 195–6, 203–6.

[5] As Van den Eynde is too often inclined to do; see *Les Normes*, pp. 30, 38, 53–57, 101–2. Flesseman-van Leer justly criticizes Van den Eynde for this misunderstanding, *Tradition and Scripture*, pp. 33, 34.

period. Between the death of the apostles and the widespread recognition of the New Testament as authoritative, doctrine was indefinite and therefore unsatisfactory.[1]

Two apologists, however, afford us rather firmer ground for conjecturing the form or the formulae of Christian teaching in the middle of the second century. The first is Aristides, who probably addressed his *Apology* to Antoninus Pius some time between the year 138, when Antoninus on the death of Hadrian obtained sole control of the Roman Empire, and 147, when he associated Marcus Aurelius with himself in power. It is a delicate business to reconstruct the text of Aristides' *Apology*, and it is impossible to be quite certain about his exact wording, because it survives only in a late and re-handled Greek version and in Syriac and Armenian translations. One passage, however, runs thus:

> Jesus Christ . . . the Son of the most high God . . . who came down in Holy Spirit from heaven; and took flesh from a virgin, and while Son of God dwelt in a daughter of man . . . He was crucified by the Jews and died and was buried, and they affirm that he rose again after three days and ascended to the heavens. [Then his disciples went] into the provinces of the whole world and taught his greatness. [Christians] know God as creator and maker of all things . . . And they do not worship any God except this. They have the commandments of Jesus Christ engraved on their hearts, and they observe these, awaiting a resurrection of the dead and a life of the age to come.[2]

This is not itself a fixed formula, but even allowing for the possibility that the original list of doctrines given by Aristides may have been less developed than this, we would not be unreasonable in conjecturing that this summary of Christian doctrine was based on the teaching of the contemporary Church, and that this teaching could have been presented in a series of articles not unlike these.

The other apologist from whose writings we can reconstruct some outline of the teaching of the contemporary Church is Justin Martyr. We can recover both Trinitarian and Christological formulae from his writings. Here are some examples of Trinitarian forms:

> *Apol.* 1.6.2: 'But we honour and worship that [God] and the Son who came from him and taught us these things, and the host of other

---

[1] Cullmann, *The Early Church*, p. 96.

[2] Aristides, *Apology* 15.1-3. Aristides goes on to describe Christian ethics and practice: the Ten Commandments, just judgements, refusal of idolatry, the Golden Rule, rejection of food offered to idols; care and love for enemies (15.4-5). What Aristides appears to be giving here is the whole Christian tradition, rule of faith and rule of conduct. He says (15.1) that this doctrine is taken from the Gospel.

good angels who follow him and are made like him, and the prophetic Spirit.'

Apol. 1.67.2: 'We bless the maker of all things through his Son Jesus
Christ and through the Holy Spirit.'[1]

Here are some examples of Christological formulae in Justin:

Apol. 1.21.1: 'We say that the Word, who is the first product (γέννημα)
of God was begotten without intercourse, Jesus Christ our teacher,
and that he was crucified and died and rose again and returned to
heaven.'

Apol. 1.42.4: 'According to us Jesus Christ was crucified and died and
rose again, and reigned, returning to heaven, and there is delight
at the good news announced by him through the apostles among
all nations as they expect the immortality announced by him.'

Apol. 1.46.5: 'For which reason a man was conceived by a Virgin by
the power of the Word according to the counsel of God Father and
Master of all, and he was called Jesus and was crucified and died
and rose again and went up into heaven.'

Dial. 85.2: 'For by the name of this same Son of God and first-born
of all creation, who was also generated through a Virgin and who
became a man subject to suffering and was crucified under Pontius
Pilate by your people and died, and rose again from the dead and
went up into heaven, every demon is exorcized and conquered and
subdued.'

Dial. 132.1: 'Jesus, whom also we recognize as Christ the Son of God,
crucified and risen and ascended into the heavens and destined
again to appear as judge of all men without exception even as far as
Adam himself.'[2]

Justin, says Flesseman-van Leer, knows the concept of apostolic tradition
(i.e. of a tradition of formal teaching transmitted continuously in the Church
since the days of the apostles), though he does not use the phrase.[3]
'There are, for Justin, certain points of truth, certain dogmata (though he
does not yet use the word with that meaning) which form a kind of rule
and which constitute, as it were, the essence of the Christian faith.'
These are belief in Jesus the crucified, faith in Christ as Son of God,
belief that he has received judgement over all men, and belief in his
eternal Kingdom (*Dialogue* 46.1).[4] Justin also, it is worth noting, uses

---

[1] Cf. *Apol.* 1.65.3.
[2] Cf. also *Apol.* 1.31.7; *Dial.* 63.1; 126.1. See Kelly, *Early Christian Creeds*, pp. 65–77.
[3] Flesseman-van Leer, *Tradition and Scripture*, p. 83.
[4] *Ibid.* pp. 85–86.

the word 'orthodox'. 'I and any other Christians who are orthodox (ὀρθογνώμονες) at every point,' he says, 'understand that there will be a resurrection of the flesh, and a thousand years in a rebuilt and adorned and enlarged Jerusalem, as the prophets Ezekiel and Isaiah and the rest declare.'[1] But earlier he has said that there are some Christians 'among those who are of pure and pious belief' (τῶν τῆς καθαρᾶς καὶ εὐσεβοῦς γνώμης) who do not believe this doctrine.[2] This suggests that orthodoxy in Justin's day was neither very rigid nor very definite.

2. *The Early Baptismal Creed*

This evidence for the existence of a continuous tradition of teaching within the Church, often expressing itself in formulae which presumably might have attained fixity, suggests that the student has here excellent material for exploring the origins of the creed. But, surprisingly, this suggestion is wrong. It will be demonstrated in the following pages that this material offers us virtually no opportunity of tracing the earliest stages of any creed, though it does allow us to see the beginnings of another form of early Christian tradition, which will be explored in a later chapter, the rule of faith.

It is not within the scope of this work to examine in detail the very large amount of scholarly investigation which has been made during the last fifty or sixty years into the origins of the interrogatory or baptismal creed. It will be enough for our purposes to give a very brief sketch of the conclusions generally agreed to about the origin of one well-known and influential form, the Old Roman creed, the ancestor of the creed known today as the Apostles' Creed. The chief pieces of evidence for reconstructing this creed are a creed which may be recovered from Rufinus of Aquileia's account of the Roman creed of his day, and from the creed given by Marcellus of Ancyra in his apologia to Pope Julius at the Synod of Rome in 340 (given by Epiphanius in his *Panarion*); the creed quoted by Hippolytus in his *Apostolic Tradition*, and a formula which may tentatively be held to underlie Tertullian's references to the rule of faith. It is likely that there survives no single direct ancestor of the Old Roman creed, but that about the year 200 several forms of creed,

---

[1] *Dial*. 80.5. Cf. Athenagoras *On the Resurrection of the Dead* 1, τοὺς εὐγνωμονοῦντας καὶ μετ' εὐνοίας δεχομένους τὴν ἀλήθειαν.

[2] *Dial*. 80.2. For comment on these remarks of Justin see Van den Eynde, *Les Normes*, p. 57, Flesseman-van Leer, *Tradition and Scripture*, p. 85, *Allegory and Event*, p. 344.

all of the same type, were current in the west, none of them officially adopted but all fairly fixed.[1] By 200, says Kelly, 'no one credal formula had apparently yet been granted a monopoly.'[2] Behind the general type discernible about 200 there probably lay an original three-member Trinitarian interrogatory baptismal formula which had had interpolated into its second member a longer Christological formula. The interpolation may have taken place in the time of Pope Victor (189–198), or perhaps a little earlier, some time at least between Justin, who does not betray the Christological insertion, and Hippolytus, who does. The suggestion has been made that this Christological addition was made in opposition to Gnostic Docetism, though we shall see reason later to doubt this.[3] The original Trinitarian formula 'was in all probability a simple, three-clause interrogation modelled on, if slightly fuller than, the Matthaean baptismal formula.'[4]

It is instructive to look at some examples of early forms of the baptismal, interrogatory, creed, which can be reconstructed from the writings of the fathers of the second and third centuries. Perhaps the earliest example of a credal form to be found is represented by the 'noteworthy rejected reading' (as Westcott and Hort designated it) in Acts 8.37, following on from the question of the Ethiopian eunuch to Philip, 'What prevents my being baptized?' 'And Philip said: If you believe with all your heart, it is allowed. And he answered and said: I believe that Jesus Christ is the Son of God.'[5] Next we may see how the creed may have run in Justin's day:

Dost thou believe in the Father and Lord God of the universe?
Dost thou believe in Jesus Christ our Saviour, who was crucified under
Pontius Pilate?
Dost thou believe in the Holy Spirit who spake by the prophets?[6]

---

[1] See Kelly, *Early Christian Creeds*, pp. 100–19. See also *Patrum Apostolicorum Opera*, ed. O. Gebhardt, A. Harnack and T. Zahn, Fasc. 1, Part II, Ed. II (Gebhardt and Harnack), pp. 115–33, for much material for reconstructing this creed, though it is rendered less useful by a failure to distinguish between the Rule of Faith and the creed.

[2] *Ibid.* p. 119.   [3] See below, pp. 65–66, 71.

[4] Kelly, *Early Christian Creeds*, pp. 119–30; the last quotation is from p. 130.

[5] εἶπεν δὲ εἰ πιστεύεις ἐξ ὅλης τῆς καρδίας, ἐξεστίν.
ἀποκριθεὶς δὲ εἶπεν· πιστεύω τὸν υἱὸν τοῦ θεοῦ εἶναι τὸν Ἰησοῦν Χριστόν.

(with some variations). This comes from an early Western MS tradition (429 E 103 it vg[el] sy[h]). J. Jeremias (*Infant Baptism*, p. 72 n. 3) dates the Western text of Acts, following J. H. Ropes (*The Text of Acts*, in *Beginnings of Christianity* I, p. ccxiii) and M. Dibelius (*Studies in the Acts of the Apostles*, p. 90), to 'before the middle of the century'.

[6] This reconstruction is taken from Kelly, *Early Christian Creeds*, p. 73.

This is what the baptismal creed of Irenaeus may have looked like:

Dost thou believe in God the Father?
Dost thou believe in Jesus Christ, the Son of God,
    who was incarnate, and died, and rose again?
Dost thou believe in the Holy Spirit of God?[1]

The *Epistula Apostolorum* is an apocryphal work written some time between 140 and 175, but probably later in that period rather than earlier, designed to supplement the canonical gospels by providing instructions authorized by all eleven apostles and pleasing incidents attributed to the childhood of Jesus. It asks what is the significance of the five loaves left over after the Feeding of the Five Thousand, and answers:

They are the symbol of our faith in the Lord of Christians, even in the Father, the Lord Almighty, and in Jesus Christ our redeemer, in the Holy Ghost the comforter, in the holy Church, and in the remission of sins.[2]

This document gives the first known examples of clauses referring to the Church and to the remission of sins in the baptismal creed. Tertullian never directly transcribes the baptismal creed known to him, but from his words in *De Corona*, 'then we are immersed three times, responding in a rather larger formula than the Lord laid down in the gospel', and in *De Baptismo*, 'there is one baptism and only one for us, [based] as much on the Lord's gospel as on the apostle's letters, because there is one God and one Church in the heavens',[3] we may conclude that he knew of an article professing faith in the Church as well as in the three Persons of the Trinity. We can deduce much the same formula from the statements of Clement of Alexandria, who seems to have known a creed which

---

[1] Kelly, *Early Christian Creeds*, p. 77. Clearly the main passages for reconstructing Irenaeus' creed are *Adv. Haer.* 1.21.3 and *Demonstration* 3, 6 and 7.

[2] *Epistula Apostolorum* 5 (M. R. James, *The Apocryphal New Testament*, p. 487). The dating of this work varies: Altaner (*Patrologie*, p. 61) says between 140 and 170; Dix (*Apostolic Tradition*, introd. p. lxii) says 175. M. R. James places it about 160. It is hard to believe that this work should be dated early, not only in view of the relatively developed state of its creed but because it refers to the New Testament as Scripture (29); and it allegorizes the New Testament, not only the fourth gospel, as in the quotation given here, but also the Matthaean parable of the Wise and Foolish Virgins (43–45). Dr A. Ehrhardt, in an interesting paper read to the Conference, 'The New Testament Today', held in Oxford in September 1961, argues that this work emanates from Egypt and is neither fully orthodox nor rankly Gnostic; he dates it between 150 and 180.

[3] *De Corona* 3.3: *Dehinc ter mergitamur amplius aliquid respondentes quam dominus in evangelio determinavit; De Baptismo* 15.1: *unum omnino baptismum est nobis tam ex domini evangelio quam et apostoli litteris quoniam unus est deus et una ecclesia in caelis.*

included mention of one Father, one Son, one Holy Spirit, and one true Church, and the Christological member of this creed probably contained a reference to the death of Christ. Clement described this as 'the essential things' (τὰ μέγιστα) and as 'the profession' (ὁμολογία).[1]

Hippolytus in his *Apostolic Tradition* and in his *Contra Noetum* gives us fuller material for reconstructing his baptismal creed, though we cannot be sure how far this formula was an official one in the Roman church of Hippolytus' day and how far it represents Hippolytus' idea of what the creed ought to be, just as his account of the liturgy of the church partly consists of traditional material and partly of his own composition. It probably ran thus:[2]

> Dost thou believe in God the Father almighty?
> Dost thou believe in Christ Jesus the Son of God,
> > who was born of the Holy Spirit from Mary the Virgin,
> > and crucified under Pontius Pilate and died,
> > and rose again the third day living from the dead,
> > and ascended into the heavens,
> > and is seated on the right hand of the Father
> > and is coming to judge the living and the dead?
> Dost thou believe the Holy Spirit?
> > and in holy Church?
> > and in resurrection of the flesh?

In his work against Noetus, Hippolytus tells us that the presbyters of the Roman church twice examined Noetus and on the second occasion they taxed him with heterodoxy. He replied that he was only glorifying Christ. To this the presbyters answered: 'We also glorify one God, but as we know him; and we hold to Christ, but as we know him, the Son of God, suffering, as he suffered, and dying, as he died, and rising the third day, . . . and being on the right hand of the Father, and coming to judge the living and the dead. And we repeat this doctrine which we

---

[1] See the evidence set out in *Origen's Doctrine of Tradition*, p. 65, where the work of C. P. Caspari ('Hat die alexandrinische Kirche zur Zeit des Clemens ein Taufbekenntniss besessen, oder nicht?') is largely used. But Caspari's attempt to identify two creeds used in the Alexandrian church, and his conclusion that the Alexandrian church's creed had an anti-Gnostic form, must be rejected.

[2] This formula is based on the reconstructions of Dix (*Apostolic Tradition*, introd. pp. lix–lxi) who gives a Greek version, and claims that this can be reconstructed 'with virtual certainty' and that Connolly, Capelle and Lietzmann 'are agreed on this reconstruction with only the slightest verbal differences' (lix), and of Kelly (*Early Christian Creeds*, p. 91). Though this creed appears as a declaratory 'I believe' form of creed, rather than as an interrogatory 'Dost thou believe' form in the texts of the *Apostolic Tradition*, all authorities are agreed that originally Hippolytus gave it in the interrogatory form in which it appears here. See H. J. Carpenter, 'Creeds and Baptismal Rites in the First Four Centuries', pp. 6–7.

have learnt.' And then, says Hippolytus, 'having refuted this man they thrust him out of the church.'[1]

Traces of the baptismal creed of his day can be discovered in the writings of Origen, though he nowhere gives us a direct transcript of its form. 'It would presumably consist of a Trinitarian formula . . . for certain, and probably a greater or lesser amount of detail under the heading of the second article, including a mention of the Virgin Birth, and conceivably (but here our evidence is tenuous) an article covering the resurrection of the dead.'[2] Surprisingly, there is no evidence in Origen's works for a clause including a profession of belief in the Church, though we ought probably to assume that it was there in his creed, since it appears to have been in Clement's. He describes this creed as 'the great and most important points' (*in magnis et maximis*)[3] and as 'the most important summary of the faith' (τῷ μεγίστῳ τῆς πίστεως κεφαλαίῳ)[4] and as 'public and open articles' (*publicis quidem et manifestis capitulis*)[5] and 'the holy seeds' (τὰ σπέρματα τὰ ἅγια).[6] It is worth noting, too, that Origen does not give a prominent place in his theology to the creed, but appears to regard it as so brief as to be of little use for making an appeal to in teaching. Cyprian tells us something of the baptismal creed that he was used to when, in writing against Novatian, he says:

But if anyone makes this objection and says that Novatian observes the same law as the catholic Church observes, that he baptizes with the same symbol as we baptize, that he knows the same God the Father, the same Son Christ, the same Holy Spirit, and that he can exploit the same power of baptizing for the reason that he appears not to differ from us in the questions at baptism: let anyone who thinks that this objection should be made know first that there is not a common formula of symbol (*symboli legem*) for us and for the schismatics, nor the same questions. For when they say 'Dost thou believe in the forgiveness of sins and in eternal life through holy Church?' (*Credis in remissionem peccatorum et vitam aeternam per sanctam ecclesiam?*), they are mendacious in their questions, since they do not possess the Church.[7]

[1] Hippolytus, *Contra Noetum* 1. The Christological formula runs: ‹καὶ› Χριστὸν ‹ἔχομεν ἀλλ᾽ ὡς› οἴδαμεν, θεοῦ υἱόν, παθόντα καθὼς ἔπαθεν, ἀποθανόντα καθὼς ἀπέθανεν, καὶ ἀναστάντα τῇ τρίτῃ ἡμέρᾳ, . . . καὶ ὄντα ἐν δεξιᾷ τοῦ πατρός, καὶ ἐρχόμενον κρῖναι ζῶντας καὶ νεκρούς. Cf. *ibid.* 17.
[2] *Origen's Doctrine of Tradition*, p. 120. The evidence for his creed is marshalled and discussed pp. 118–20.
[3] *PA* 1, Praef. 2. [4] *Comm. on John* 32.3.
[5] *Comm. on Matthew*, Comm. Ser. 33. [6] *Hom. on Jeremiah* 4.3.
[7] Cyprian, *Epistolae* 69.7.1. He produces a precisely similar argument in *Ep.* 70.2.1, but with the slightly varied formula *Credis in vitam aeternam et remissionem peccatorum per sanctam ecclesiam?* The question of Novatian's creed is a complicated one and cannot profitably be discussed at this point. The reconstruction of his baptismal creed

3. The Baptismal Creed and the Rule of Faith

The first point to be noticed about this account of the origin and development up to the middle of the third century of the baptismal, interrogatory, creed, is that it cannot possibly be an outgrowth or a descendant of the doctrinal formulae which we have noted as occurring in the New Testament, in Ignatius, in Polycarp and in Justin.[1] The earlier formulae are all affirmative, direct statements of doctrine; the credal formulae are all interrogative. The other formulae contain many articles and phrases which are never found in any creed up to 250 and some of which are never found in any creed of any period, such as 'born of the seed of David', 'from whom are all things and we are from him', 'who gave himself as a ransom for all' or 'put to death in the flesh but quickened in the Spirit', 'was seen by angels' or 'heavenly and earthly and infernal powers looking on', 'was preached among the Gentiles' or 'whether among the Jews or among the Gentiles', 'was believed on in the world', a reference to our Lord's baptism, 'to whom all heavenly and earthly powers were subjected', 'whose blood God will require from those who disobey him'. Above all, the interrogatory creed obviously developed slowly and gradually from an original very brief formula, such as 'Dost thou believe that Jesus Christ is the Son of God?' or 'Dost thou believe in God the Father, and in God the Son, and in God the Holy Spirit?'; and even as late as about 170 this formula may have consisted of no more than these three bare questions without the Christological elaboration nor the addition of clauses after the mention of the Holy Spirit. But the other formulae, though they mostly come from a much earlier period than any in which we can with confidence trace even a rudimentary baptismal creed, are already quite full and display several articles. It is against all probability that the baptismal creed should have achieved a fairly full and detailed form by the time of Ignatius, but should by the time of Justin, of Irenacus and of Tertullian have reduced its length and lopped off several details. Finally, the phrases of the baptismal creed are short, lapidary, concise; Hippolytus' 'living from the dead' strikes us at once as uncredal in tone and as due, perhaps, to Hippolytus himself, so little is it congenial to its surroundings. But the language

by his editor (W. Yorke Fausset, Novatian's *De Trinitate*, introd. p. xxvi) is not convincing. It is doubtful whether there is enough material in the *De Trinitate* to recover Novatian's baptismal creed, especially if it is agreed that Novatian is here commenting, not upon the interrogatory creed, but upon part of the rule of faith.

[1] See above, pp. 53–58.

of the other and earlier formulae is fluid and diversified and gives no impression of deliberately aiming at conciseness. It is impossible to believe that the two sets of formulae come from the same tradition. They are obviously independent. We may in fact go further and conclude that in the baptismal interrogatory formulae we have the creed proper; in the other, more fluid, formulae we have the ancestors of the rule of faith. We are therefore inaccurate if we describe the formulae which we have examined in the New Testament, in the apostolic fathers and in Justin as 'credal'; they are in fact creeds neither in embryo nor in a mature form. They are simply doctrinal formulae.

Many scholars in the past have identified the rule of faith with the baptismal creed.[1] A few still do so.[2] But most writers on this subject now recognize that this identification is impossible.[3] It is true that the rule of faith is sometimes associated with baptism in writers of the second and third centuries. Irenaeus, for instance, uses the words, 'Thus he who holds fast in himself unperverted the rule of truth which he has received through baptism':[4] and elsewhere he can write, 'Now this is what faith does for us, as the elders, the disciples of the apostles, have handed down to us. First of all, it admonishes us to remember that we have received baptism', etc.[5] But it is very likely that in passages like these Irenaeus is referring to the rule of faith, not as repeated by the convert as a creed at the rite of baptism, but as taught to him in a course of instruction in preparation for baptism. The rule of faith moreover was (as we shall see) used by writers from about 170 to about 270 primarily as a test of orthodoxy. But it is wholly improbable that the interrogatory, baptismal creed was used as a test of orthodoxy. In the first place, there is some evidence that heretics were quite ready to use an orthodox baptismal creed; what they could not use was an orthodox rule of faith. Hippolytus tells us that the Naasscne Gnostic heretic will say, 'The Spirit is generated there, where the Father and the Son are named, there

---

[1] E.g. Newman, and Harvey who edited Irenaeus.

[2] Apparently Cullmann (*The Earliest Christian Confessions*, pp. 18–47; *The Early Church*, pp. 94–96) and W. Telfer (*The Forgiveness of Sins*, p. 52) do so. For the inaccuracy of this identification see also Kelly, *Early Christian Creeds*, p. 63.

[3] E.g. Van den Eynde, *Les Normes*, pp. 282–9, 296–7; Flesseman-van Leer, *Tradition and Scripture*, pp. 127, 163–5; J. N. D. Kelly, *Early Christian Creeds*, p. 51; Carpenter, 'Creeds and Baptismal Rites', p. 7; V. Ammundsen, 'The Rule of Truth in Irenaeus', p. 578; B. Hägglund, 'Die Bedeutung der "regula fidei" als Grundlage theologische Aussagen', pp. 11–12, 28–29, 31; Turner, *The Pattern*, pp. 350–2.

[4] *Adv. Haer.* 1.1.20: ὁ τὸν κανόνα τῆς ἀληθείας ἀκλινῆ ἐν ἑαυτῷ κατέχων ὃν διὰ τοῦ βαπτίσματος εἴληφε. Cf. 1.9.4.

[5] *Demonstration* 3.

E

out of that Father.'[1] The *Gospel of Philip* has an interesting passage which runs thus: 'There is a rebirth and a symbolic rebirth (εἰκών). It is really necessary that they [the Gnostics] should be reborn through the image . . . It is not right for those who do not receive them [the type and the image] to obtain the Name of the Father, the Son and the Holy Spirit. But they [the Gnostics] have received these [type and image] themselves. If anyone does not receive them the Name will be torn from him.'[2] H. E. W. Turner brings to our notice a passage in which the Gnostic heretic Theodotus refers to the triad of Father, Son and Holy Spirit as 'the three names by whose power the Gnostic is released from the power of corruption', and the one thus baptized is 'sealed through the Father, Son and Holy Spirit', and he reminds us that Marcionite baptism was recognized at Rome.[3]

In the second place, it is clear that even in the developed forms which it achieved by the middle of the third century the interrogatory creed was too bare and austere a summary to be effective as a safeguard against heresy. We are warned against regarding even the development of the rule of faith as greatly influenced by the need to combat particular heresies.[4] This warning applies with double force to the case of the creed.

It is possible that Kelly is right in his conjecture[5] that the rule of faith provided the influence which resulted in the Christological clause in the creed being elaborated towards the end of the second century. But on the whole it seems more likely that the interrogatory creed was regarded by writers from Irenaeus onwards as a minimal summary of the rule of faith, and therefore as in some sense the iron rations or barest essentials of the faith, even though the historical origin of the creed was in fact quite distinct from that of the rule of faith. 'And this is the drawing-up of our faith, the foundation of the building, and the consolidation of a way of life', says Irenaeus,[6] and he goes on to give a slight expansion of the threefold interrogatory creed, containing simply Father, Son and Holy Spirit. 'Drawing-up' here probably means summary or abridge-

---

[1] Hippolytus, *Elenchos* 5.9.4: τὸ δὲ πνεῦμα, φησί, ἐκεῖ, ὅπου καὶ ὁ πατὴρ ὀνομάζεται καὶ ὁ υἱός, ἐκ τούτου τοῦ πατρὸς ἐκεῖ γεννώμενος. Van den Eynde produces more evidence for this point in chapter 5 of his *Les Normes*.

[2] *Gospel of Philip* 67 (115).

[3] *Excerpta ex Theodoto* 80; for Marcionite baptism, Cyprian, *Ep.* 73.4; 74.8; 75.5. See Turner, *The Pattern of Christian Truth*, pp. 154, 158. If the argument of Dr Ehrhardt, mentioned above, p. 61, that the *Epistula Apostolorum* comes from a non-Catholic milieu, were to be accepted, the view put forward here would be greatly strengthened.

[4] Kelly, *Early Christian Creeds*, pp. 64–65, 97–98; Turner, *The Pattern*, pp. 356–8; Hägglund, 'Die Bedeutung', pp. 9–10, 38.

[5] *Ibid.* pp. 145–6.

[6] *Demonstration* 6; Robinson translates 'the order of the rule of faith'.

ment. And at the end of the same work, which is in effect a commentary on the rule of faith and goes far beyond expounding simply the threefold formula, Irenaeus says, 'So error with respect to the three articles of our seal has brought about much wandering away from the truth.'[1] We have already seen[2] that both Clement of Alexandria and Origen use language concerning the baptismal creed which strongly suggests that they regard it as an abridgement or lowest common denominator of the faith; phrases like 'the essential things', 'the most important points' and 'the holy seeds' are significant.

In fact some of the fathers of the period under discussion mention the person undergoing baptism more often as making a promise or taking an oath than as declaring orthodox doctrine or summarizing the faith. This seems to be the aspect of the Christian's response to God in baptism which appeals to them most. Tertullian several times uses for this profession of faith the word *sacramentum*. This is a word which he employs often and in his hands it can mean at least six different things: religion generally, divine activity, prefiguring, mystery, sacrament, and solemn oath. It is in this last meaning that he often applies it to the profession of faith made at baptism.[3] Tertullian also more than once emphasizes the renunciation of the devil and his angels and his pomp which accompanies this profession.[4] Clement of Alexandria called the baptismal response a 'profession' (ὁμολογία),[5] and Origen, recalling the renunciation of Satan, described it as an 'agreement made with God'.[6] Cyprian twice uses the word *symbolum* to mean the interrogatory creed repeated at

---

[1] *Demonstration* 100: Robinson translates 'points' for 'articles'. Earlier (99) Irenaeus has said that heretics distort the teaching about the Father, about the Son and about the Holy Ghost, but he does not suggest that they reject this formula so much as misinterpret it.

[2] See above, pp. 62 and 63. Hägglund, 'Die Bedeutung', p. 4, makes a rather similar suggestion to this one.

[3] *Ad Martyras* 3.1; *Adv. Marcionem* 1.28.2; *De Anima* 1.4; *De Corona* 11.1,7; 13.7; *Scorpiace* 4.5 (twice); *De Idololatria* 19.2. In *De Monogamia* 11.1 it means the obligation laid upon clergy not to remarry; and in *De Ieiunio adversus Psychicos* 10.7 an ordinary military oath. *Adversus Praxean* 30 is doubtful; *sacramentum* here could mean the Christian mystery or doctrine of the Holy Trinity. But E. Evans (p. 331 of his ed. of this work) suggests that it 'apparently means the creed or the *regula fidei*' and compares *De Praescr. Haer.* 20, *eiusdem sacramenti una traditio*. On the whole, though, the meaning 'dispensation' or even 'revelation' would suit the sense better here.

[4] *De Spectaculis* 4 (here he uses the words *cum aquam ingressi Christianam fidem in legis suae verba profitemur*); 24 (the Christian swore enmity against the devil *in signaculo fidei* and by revoking his profession (*rescindendo testimonium*) he unseals the seal (*rescindimus signaculum*)); cf. *De Pudicitia* 9.16 (*fidei pactionem interrogatus obsignat*); *De Anima* 35.3 (*fidei conventio*); *De Idololatria* 6.1, 2 (*sacramentum*); *De Corona* 3.3 (*contestamur renuntiare diabolo*).

[5] *Strom.* 7.15.90.1 (PG 9.525).

[6] *Exhortation to Martyrdom* 17: συνθήκας ἃς ἔθεντο πρὸς τὸν θεόν; cf. *Hom. on Exodus* 8.4 and *Hom. on Numbers* 13.12.

baptism, and he is the first to do so.[1] But he also on several occasions refers to the profession of faith as a solemn oath (*sacramentum*),[2] and at the Great Council of Carthage (Cyprian's seventh Council, held in 256, on the subject of rebaptizing heretics), Caecilius bishop of Biltha and Lucius bishop of Castra Galbae used the same word in the same sense.[3] Dionysius of Alexandria also uses the phrase 'faith and profession' (πίστις καὶ ὁμολογία) for the baptismal responses.[4]

We may sum up our examination of the creed in the search for early tradition outside the Bible by declaring that the interrogatory, baptismal creed will not serve our purpose in the least. Its origins either themselves lay in the New Testament or else were so slight and rudimentary as to make it impossible to claim that they add anything to it, quite apart from the fact that the actual formulae used in the earliest creeds are themselves repeated over and over again in the New Testament. As it is not connected with the doctrinal formulae of the earliest periods which we have examined, it is impossible to claim that its doctrinal content constitutes original authentic tradition. It is regarded as a useful and venerable summary of the Christian faith in the barest possible form, the faith reduced to its lowest possible terms. As such it is used even by heretics, and though it evokes respect from the fathers they do not attribute to it very great importance.

4. Other Forms of Creed

But are there not other sorts of creed besides the interrogatory, baptismal one? The suggestion has been made that there were several other purposes for which creeds were used in the early Church besides at baptisms, and that for these purposes a different form of creed, an affirmative one, beginning 'I believe', not an interrogatory form, was used. The conjecture has been made that the other occasions than the baptismal one on which creeds were used were in the regular cult (liturgy

---

[1] *Ep.* 69.7. See Van den Eynde, *Les Normes*, p. 245, and also Carpenter, 'Creeds and Baptismal Rites', p. 516, where he vindicates this word as referring to an interrogatory and not a declaratory creed. See Blaise, *Dictionnaire Latin-Français des Auteurs Chrétiens*, on this word. Tertullian, *Adv. Marc.* 5.1.2 *quo symbolo susceperis apostolum Paulum* means 'by what token or proof of authority have you accepted the apostle Paul?' and is not an exception.

[2] *Ep.* 10.2.3; 74.4.1; *De Lapsis* 7.13; *Ad Demetrianum* 26. Cyprian, like Tertullian, uses this word in a wide range of meanings: religion, prefiguring, mystery, divine activity, sacrament, and bond of unity, as well as this one.

[3] *Sententiae Episcoporum* 1 and 7. Cf. the expression *foederis pactio* in Pseudo-Cyprian, *De Laude Martyrii* 10 (33).

[4] C. L. Feltoe, *The Letters and other Remains of Dionysius of Alexandria*, p. 56 (*Letters* V.4).

and preaching), as a test of orthodoxy against heretics, by exorcists when dealing with possessed persons, and by Christians accused of the crime of professing Christianity at their trials.[1] Is it not possible that the doctrinal formulae which we have examined and have discovered to be independent of the baptismal creed may have been the direct ancestors of a declaratory type of creed, or even early examples of it? It cannot be disputed that in the early fourth century at latest a declaratory, 'I believe', form of creed was widely, perhaps universally, used both in connection with baptism and as a test of orthodoxy. The suggestion comes readily to hand that this form of creed had existed from the earliest age of Christianity, side by side with the interrogatory form, and had developed along with it.

But this theory encounters the fatal difficulty that there is simply no evidence until the middle of the third century for the existence of anything else besides the baptismal formula that could fairly be called a creed. The other formulae which we have already examined are obviously not credal in character. They vary widely in form and content; they do not have a uniform opening phrase, either 'I believe' or 'We believe'. We can trace no basic affinity between them such as creeds might be expected to display. Their language is not particularly concise nor suggestive of doctrinal definition. They contain several articles which do not appear in declaratory creeds with an 'I believe' form when these do emerge. It would be quite unsound, in the face of these facts, impulsively to identify these as creeds or even as embryo creeds. The earliest example of a declaratory creed which can be found is that quoted by Eusebius of Caesarea at the Council of Nicaea in 325.[2] Failing any earlier evidence of a creed of this form, we are compelled to assume that this form of creed appeared for the first time in the second half of the third century, when Eusebius presumably received it at his baptism in his native city of Caesarea.[3] As we shall see, there is other evidence pointing to the conclusion that this is about the period when declaratory creeds did first appear.

The suggestion that creeds were used by Christians who were facing trial upon the charge of professing Christianity is not supported by satisfactory evidence either. In the Acts which describe these trials the

[1] So Cullmann, *The Earliest Christian Confessions*, pp. 18 ff.
[2] See Kelly, *Early Christian Creeds*, pp. 181, 182.
[3] The only conceivable earlier examples of the occurrence of this form of creed is in the rejected Western reading in Acts 8.37 (which is much too tenuous a foundation upon which to build theories of a declaratory form of creed existing from the beginning) and the creed in Hippolytus' *Apostolic Tradition*, which, it is almost universally agreed, has had its declaratory form imposed upon it in a later recension.

accused either profess their faith in short phrases which could not be taken as formal creeds (as in the *Acts of the Scillitan Martyrs, The Martyrs of Lyons and Vienne*, and the *Martyrdom of Polycarp* and the account of Cyprian's martyrdom), or if they make doctrinal statements these are fluid and varying and lack the conciseness of language which suggests a creed. In the *Acts of Justin and his Companions*, for instance, Justin, on being asked by the prefect Rusticus, 'What is your belief?' (ποῖόν ἐστι δόγμα;) replies,

> The belief which we piously profess in the God of the Christians, whom we regard as one, and this one from the beginning maker and fashioner of the whole creation, visible and invisible, and a Lord Jesus Christ child of God, who also was declared beforehand by the prophets, as destined to dwell with the race of men as a herald of salvation and a teacher of good doctrines.[1]

This is too diffuse and incomplete to be like any known creed, though it could well be an account, expressed in the speaker's own words, of part of the rule of faith. Similarly Pionius, another martyr, in the Decian persecution nearly a century after the martyrdom of Justin, when asked 'What sort of a god do you worship?' replies,

> The almighty God who made heaven and earth and everything in them and us all, who provides everything for us richly, whom we have known through his Word Christ.[2]

Another martyr, Sabina, gives a similar answer, and another, Asclepiades, answers 'The Lord Jesus', and no more, which puzzles the inquisitor.[3] Here again it would be unwise to see in Pionius' answer anything more than a statement in his own language of two essential points of Christian doctrine, perhaps originally taught to him as part of the rule of faith. The fact that we have no accounts at all of exorcisms during this early period, and have very little idea of how they were conducted, precludes

---

[1] *Ausegewählte Märtyrerakten*, ed. D. R. Knopf (revised by G. Krüger), Acts of Justin and his Companions II.4, 5. The Greek runs: (δόγμα) ὅπερ εὐσεβοῦμεν εἰς τὸν τῶν Χριστιάνων θεόν, ὃν ἡγούμεθα ἕνα, τοῦτον ἐξ ἀρχῆς ποιητὴν καὶ δημιουργὸν τῆς πάσης κτίσεως, ὁρατῆς τε καὶ ἀοράτου, καὶ Κύριον Ἰησοῦν Χριστὸν παῖδα θεοῦ, ὃς καὶ προκεκήρυκται ὑπὸ τῶν προφητῶν, μέλλων παραγίνεσθαι τῷ γένει τῶν ἀνθρώπων σωτηρίας κῆρυξ καὶ διδάσκαλος καλῶν μαθημάτων. It is worth noting that Paion, one of the martyrs, calls his religion τὴν καλὴν ταύτην ὁμολογίαν (IV.6), and that the same noun is used by the writer of the Acts to describe the confession of the martyrs at their death (VI.1).

[2] Knopf, *op. cit.*, The Martyrdom of Pionius VIII.3. The Greek runs: τὸν θεὸν τὸν παντοκράτορα τὸν ποιήσαντα τὸν οὐρανὸν καὶ τὴν γῆν καὶ πάντα τὰ ἐν αὐτοῖς καὶ πάντας ἡμᾶς, ὃς παρέχει ἡμῖν πάντα πλουσίως, ὃν ἐγνώκαμεν διὰ τοῦ λόγου αὐτοῦ Χριστοῦ.

[3] *Ibid.* IX.6, 8. The expression describing a Christian under torture *libertatis suae dominum ac salutis auctorem repetita saepius voce profiteri*, in the third-century *De Laude Martyris* 8 (31) ascribed to Cyprian, can hardly refer to a creed.

us from formulating any theories about the use of creeds at them.[1] To reconstruct exorcists' creeds for the first two centuries of the Church's history would be to act on the principle of *obscurum per obscurius*. The references of Origen at least to exorcizing suggest that on these occasions it was the power of names (of Christ, or of the Holy Trinity, or even of Old Testament worthies) which was all-important, and not the doctrinal content of the formula used.[2] There is no evidence whatever for the use of a *creed* in liturgy other than the interrogatory baptismal creed during the period with which we are concerned, nor can we find any trace of such a use in preaching. Once we have established the distinction both in origin and in function between the creed and the rule of faith, evidence for the existence of early creeds other than interrogatory baptismal ones simply disappears.[3]

The use of creeds as tests of orthodoxy is also very poorly evidenced during this period. The nearest approach to such a use is found in the passage which we have already examined[4] in which Hippolytus describes the interview which the presbyters of Rome had with Noetus. But it is far from certain whether the creed (and it clearly is the baptismal creed) is being here used as a test of orthodoxy. We are not told that Noetus refused to assent to it, nor even that he was asked to assent; and it is very likely that had he been asked to do so he could have assented with a clear conscience, interpreting it according to his own modalistic monarchianism. It is much more likely that the presbyters on this occasion expressed their conviction that Noetus' teaching was contrary to their traditional baptismal creed and without giving him an opportunity to assent to it or to dissent incontinently excommunicated him. If they regarded the creed as an abridgement of the rule of faith (which Noetus probably *would* find difficulty in accepting), this conduct would be all the more intelligible. Kelly says that between this incident and the eighth canon of the Council of Arles there is no example of a creed being used as a test of orthodoxy.[5] In fact one further example coming

---

[1] The evidence adduced by Cullmann (*The Earliest Christian Confessions*, pp. 23-25) for the use of creeds during exorcism is virtually confined to Justin, *Dialogue*, 30.3; 76.6; 85.1, 2 and Acts 3.6. We have already seen one of these passages (see above, p. 58); they are all useful for suggesting material which may have formed an early *rule of faith*, but are altogether too fluid to provide satisfactory evidence for a *creed* at exorcisms. Acts 3.6 tells us that healings were performed 'in the name' of Jesus Christ, and nothing more.

[2] See *Allegory and Event*, pp. 205-7.

[3] The question of how far we can assume the existence of an early Christian liturgy is touched upon below, pp. 62-3.

[4] See above, pp. 168-74.

[5] *Early Christian Creeds*, p. 206. The Council of Arles was held in 314, and the eighth canon ordained that the authorities when they meet someone anxious to return

from near the middle of the third century has recently been discovered, and was published at almost the same time as Kelly published his book. This is the creed-like statement made in the *Conversation with Heracleides*, the account of a conference held between Origen and some bishops in an unknown place in Arabia probably in the year 246, on points of doctrine about which the unsoundness of these men was causing uneasiness. Heracleides, the bishop chiefly suspect of heterodoxy, apparently on the subject of the distinction between the Father and the Son, volunteered this creed-like statement. The relevant passage runs thus:

> When discussion was raging among the bishops who were present about the belief of bishop Heracleides, in order that he might profess in the presence of all of them what his belief was, and as each person was saying what occurred to him and asking questions, bishop Heracleides said: 'I too believe what the Holy Scriptures say [and here he quotes John 1.1-3, as far as 'was not anything made']. You can see therefore that we agree on the faith as expressed here also, and
> we believe that Christ took flesh
> that he was begotten
> that he went up to the heavens in the flesh in which he had risen,
> that he sits on the right hand of the Father
> destined to come from there and to judge living and dead,
> God and man.[1]

This is more like part of a declaratory creed than any other statement we have so far met coming from the second or the third centuries, though even this formula has some features (such as the last clause of all and the phrase 'in the flesh in which he had risen') which suggest the rule of faith rather than the creed. It opens up the interesting conjecture that here we have a formula halfway between a statement of the rule of faith and a declaratory creed, and that the declaratory creed may have evolved out of the rule of faith about the middle of the third century. It certainly does represent an example of a creed, or a doctrinal formula, used to test orthodoxy, or rather volunteered by one suspected of heterodoxy for such a test. We may perhaps find some support for the conjecture that about the middle of the third century the rule of faith was in process of becoming a stereotyped declaratory creed in Novatian's *De Trinitate*. This work is in effect a commentary on three articles, God the Father

---

from heresy to the Catholic Church *interrogent eum symbolum* (i.e. ask him to repeat the interrogatory creed he repeated at baptism); if he professes the Trinitarian formula, then *manus ei tantum imponatur ut accipiat Spiritum Sanctum* (F. Lauchert, *Die Kanones der Wichtigsten Altkirklichen Concilien*, Council of Arles, VIII).

[1] *Entretien d'Origène avec Héraclide et les Evêques ses Collègues sur le Père, le Fils et l'Âme*, ed. J. Scherer, pp. 118-20 of the text.

(caps. 1–8), God the Son (caps. 9–28) and God the Spirit (cap. 29); these articles could be articles of the baptismal creed, of course, but they could just as well be articles of the rule of faith, and Novatian's language suggests decisively that this is just how he regarded them. He begins 'The rule of truth demands that first of all we should believe . . . ',[1] and in several other passages he refers to this rule;[2] in one of these he says, 'it is not my intention so much to speak against this heresy as to expound briefly the rule of truth about the person of Christ.'[3] His attention to points of Christology throughout the work is so careful and he is so much on the watch to confute contemporary heresies that the impression is irresistible that the subject of his exposition is that which was thought to be in a peculiar way the Church's defence against heresy, the rule of faith. It is significant, therefore, when in two passages we find him speaking of the rule of truth as if it were a fixed formula. In one of these[4] he is contending against the view which regarded Christ as a mere man. 'If Christ is only a man', he says, 'why did he lay down a rule of belief for us like this in which he says, But this is life eternal that they should know thee the one and true God, and Jesus Christ whom thou hast sent? (John 17.3) . . . therefore we must believe, according to the fixed rule, in the Lord, one true God, and consequently in him whom he sent, Jesus Christ . . . and he associated himself with God rightly in order to lay down a formula of his deity for those who were to believe.' Now, the 'fixed rule' here might mean simply the words of our Lord in Scripture. But it could equally well mean a fixed form of words defining belief. This impression is strengthened by the second passage, which forms the opening words of his chapter treating of the Holy Spirit: 'But the logical order and the authority of the faith based on the sayings and Scriptures of the Lord properly ordered warns us next to believe also in the Holy Spirit, once only promised to the Church but at determined crises of the times given.'[5] This certainly refers to some fixed, traditional formula

---

[1] Novatian, *De Trinitate* 1, p. 1, lines 1–2: *regula exigit veritatis ut primo omnium credamus . . .*

[2] E.g. 9, p. 28, ll. 4–6; 11, p. 38, l. 21–p. 39, l. 3; 17, p. 58, ll. 12–15; 21, p. 76, ll. 4–6; 26, p. 95, ll. 20–21; 29, p. 110, ll. 7, 8.

[3] 21, p. 76, ll. 4–6: *non tam mihi contra hanc haeresim propositum est dicere quam breviter circa personam Christi regulam veritatis aperire.*

[4] 16, p. 56, ll. 5–7, 13–15, 21, 22: *si homo tantummodo Christus, quare credendi nobis talem regulam posuit quo diceret . . . est ergo credendum secundum praescriptam regulam, in dominum unum verum deum, et in eum quam misit Iesum Christum consequenter . . . et deo se iungit merito ut credituris divinitatis suae formulam poneret.*

[5] 29, p. 105, l. 10–p. 106, l. 1: *sed etiam ordo rationis et fidei auctoritas digestis vocibus et litteris domini admonet nos post haec credere etiam in Spiritum Sanctum, olim ecclesiae repromissum, sed statutis temporum opportunitatibus redditum. Ordo rationis* could mean 'the order of our intended task', for *ratio* in Tertullian (and therefore

regarded as giving a summary of the teaching of the Lord recorded in Scripture. These words apply much more appropriately to the rule of faith than they do to the baptismal creed.[1] It is therefore quite possible that Novatian knew of a fixed form of the rule of faith, and if he did, the Roman church of his day was obviously well on the way to evolving a declaratory creed.

Kelly is quite confident that the declaratory creed is not an original part of Christian tradition and cannot be found anywhere before the second half of the third century,[2] though he is willing to concede that the rule of faith as known to Tertullian was based on formulae which 'had attained a fair measure of fixity'.[3] And he conjectures that when the declaratory creed did appear it was simultaneous with the ceremony of *traditio* and *redditio symboli* undergone by catechumens under instruction for baptism, and that this probably first developed at Rome.[4] It is very likely that these ceremonies did assist the development of the declaratory creed, but the evidence we have just surveyed suggests that the declaratory creed was developing in other places as well as in Rome in the middle of the third century. Carpenter believes that there did not exist a declaratory creed anywhere till the middle of the third century, but he has advanced the thesis that 'for a period lasting well into the third century, there were current in the same locality a number of more or less stereotyped forms of summaries of the faith, outlines rather than formulae, which were used as the basis of instruction, but not regarded as sacred formulae to be imparted and retained by the catechumens with verbal exactness.'[5] This thesis would explain several of the facts which we have surveyed in this chapter, the absence of any solid evidence for a creed other than the interrogatory one, and the presence of a number of outlines or statements of the faith which are similar but not precisely alike. It only remains to add to Carpenter's theory that these outlines or forms of summaries of the faith were no more or less than that enigmatic phenomenon which we must now turn to examine thoroughly—the rule of faith.

---

probably in Novatian) can mean 'purport' or 'intention'. Fausset *in loc.* translates *digestis vocibus et litteris domini* literally as 'by the words and Scriptures of the Lord set forth in due order', and paraphrases it as 'in an orderly statement of the teaching of the Lord, by His Word written and spoken'. *Vocibus et litteris* probably means gospels and epistles.

[1] Cf. V. Ammundsen, 'The Rule of Truth in Irenaeus': he concludes that the rule of truth in Novatian does not exactly mean a creed, but to define the contents of the rule he uses a creed, 'not as identical with, but as a means of arranging the description of the *Rule of Truth*' (p. 579). H ecites *De Cib. Iud.* 7 and *De Trinitate* 1, 9, 16, 17, 21, 26, 29.

[2] *Early Christian Creeds*, pp. 30–49, 95.   [3] *Ibid.* p. 88.   [4] *Ibid.* pp. 49–52.

[5] Carpenter, 'Creeds and Baptismal Rites', pp. 8–9.

3

The Rule of Faith

1. References in the Fathers to the Rule of Faith

THE EARLIEST reference to the rule of faith is to be found in the works of Irenaeus. We cannot be quite sure of the vocabulary which Irenaeus used to express this concept because most of his work does not survive in the original Greek. He certainly used the phrase 'rule of truth' (κανὼν τῆς ἀληθείας) among his other expressions, for this phrase survives in one Greek fragment.[1] But he also used the words 'preaching' (κήρυγμα) and 'the faith' (ἡ πίστις),[2] and 'tradition' (παράδοσις) to express the same thing, and also the word 'construction' (ὑπόθεσις).[3] Irenaeus' translator seems regularly to have translated all words used for the rule of faith by the phrase 'rule of truth' (regula veritatis).[4] Irenaeus also refers to the rule of faith in the opening of his *Demonstration*,[5] where the fact that this work survives only in an Armenian version makes it impossible for us to determine his exact words in Greek. Athenagoras, a contemporary of Irenaeus, uses a phrase which may indicate the rule of faith. He says that the detractors of truth have left nothing uncontaminated, 'neither the existence of God, nor the knowledge of him, nor his activity, nor the consequences which follow these things and which indicate to us the doctrine of piety' (τὸν τῆς εὐσεβείας λόγον).[6] Polycrates bishop of Ephesus, writing in the last decade of the second century to Victor bishop of Rome, on the subject of the Quartodeciman controversy, gives a list of the departed worthies who had handed on the faith

---

[1] *Adv. Haer.* 1.1.20.   [2] *Ibid.* 1.3.
[3] *Ibid.* 1.1.20. For full accounts of Irenaeus' vocabulary on this subject see Flesseman-van Leer, *Tradition and Scripture*, p. 126 n. 2. Van den Eynde gives very full information about the vocabulary used by the fathers in the period dealt with in this chapter for the rule of faith in the seventh chapter of his *Les Normes*. See also Ammundsen, 'The Rule of Faith in Irenaeus', pp. 578, 579, and Turner, *The Pattern*, pp. 348–56.
[4] Irenaeus also calls the systems of the heretics 'rules' regularly throughout his second and third books of the *Adversus Haereses*.
[5] *Demonstration* 3.
[6] Athenagoras, *On the Resurrection of the Dead* 1.

in the province of Asia, and says 'All these observed Easter on the four-teenth day, making no deviation according to the Gospel but following according to the rule of faith' (κατὰ τὸν κανόνα τῆς πίστεως). Here the phrase 'rule of faith' must include practice, though Polycrates may have thought that doctrine was involved also. In order to justify his keeping of this custom, Polycrates adds that he is acting in accordance with his seven predecessors in his see, he is sixty-five years old (in the Lord) and in agreement with 'the brethren from the whole world' and he has 'gone through every holy writing' (πᾶσαν ἁγίαν γραφὴν διεληλυθώς).[1] An anonymous writer against the school of the Theodoti, favourers of peculiar views about the relation of the Son to the Father, some time in the reign of Pope Zephyrinus (198–217), accuses his opponents of violating the rule of faith. 'They have shamelessly played fast and loose with divine Scriptures,' he says, 'they have set aside the rule of primitive faith (πίστεως ἀρχαίας κανόνα), they have not known Christ, nor investigated what the divine Scriptures say . . . deserting the holy Scriptures of God they devote themselves to the study of geometry.'[2] It is evident that to these writers the rule of faith is closely connected with the Scriptures. The author of the *Acts of Paul and Thecla*, attempting in the second half of the second century to imitate Paul's style, represents him as saying: 'And whoso receiveth [abideth in] the rule which he has received by the blessed prophets and the holy gospel shall receive a recompense from the Lord.'[3] This may be a reference to the rule of faith conceived as found in the Bible, and as giving the gist of the Bible's teaching.

Hippolytus uses the phrase 'the definition of truth' (ὅρος). He says that he has expounded 'the definition of truth in the manner in which it exists, without safeguard or ornament', and later he says of this 'definition', 'we have often written apologetic works (ἀπόδειξεις) about it, and have sufficiently and abundantly expounded the rule of truth (τὸν τῆς ἀληθείας κανόνα) to those who desire it.'[4] Elsewhere he uses the word *horos* (defini-tion) to mean an ecclesiastical rule or decree governing the admission of sinners to communion.[5] He can also use the expression 'the preaching of the truth' (τὸ τῆς ἀληθείας κήρυγμα)[6] and 'the word' (λόγος) con-

---

[1] Eusebius, *HE* 5.24.6, 7.

[2] *Ibid.* 5.28.13. The same writer had used the phrase τοῦ ἐκκλησιαστικοῦ κανόνος of the Church's Christology (Eusebius, *HE* 5.28.6). See below, p. 207.

[3] *The Acts of Paul* VII.3.36 (M. R. James, *The Apocryphal New Testament*, p. 291). Only Latin, Armenian and Coptic versions of what was certainly a Greek original survive for this work.

[4] *Elenchos* 10.5.1, 2. In 9.10.1 he describes Zephyrinus as ἀνδρὰ ἰδιώτην καὶ ἀγράμματον καὶ ἄπειρον τῶν ἐκκλησιαστικῶν ὅρων.

[5] *Ibid.* 9.12.21.   [6] *Ibid.* 7.32.6.

cerning truth.[1] Clement of Alexandria uses the word *canon* for the rule of faith on several occasions.[2] He employs it in several different expressions: 'the ecclesiastical rule' (ἐκκλησιαστικὸς κανών),[3] 'the *canon* of the Church'(ὁ κανὼν τῆς ἐκκλησίας),[4] 'the rule of truth' (ὁ κανὼν τῆς ἀληθείας),[5] and 'the rule of faith' (ὁ κανὼν τῆς πίστεως).[6] We have already noticed that he identified, or confused, this rule of faith with his secret, and spurious, tradition.[7]

Tertullian frequently refers to the rule of faith, usually using the expression *regula fidei*.[8] As we shall see, he gives us an account of the contents of this rule on one or two occasions. He also uses 'rule of God' (*dei regula*).[9] He is fond of associating with this concept the word *disciplina* meaning traditional Christian ethics as well as traditional Christian doctrine.[10] He says that Paul went up to Jerusalem after his conversion to compare 'the rule of his Gospel' (*evangelii sui regulam*) with that of the other apostles.[11] And he can accuse the heretic Valentinus of having broken off 'from the Church of the genuine rule' (*de ecclesia authenticae regulae*).[12]

A document known as the *Epistola Clementis* prefixed to the pseudo-Clementine literature (the *Clementine Homilies and Recognitions*) mentions the *canon* of the church. This purports to be a letter of Clement of Rome describing the circumstances of his appointment by Peter as his successor. Peter is quoted as saying of Clement 'for he will bind what ought to be bound and he will loose what ought to be loosed, as one who knows the rule of the Church' (τὸν κανόνα τῆς ἐκκλησίας).[13] This letter was probably

---

[1] *Ibid.* 9.31.2; cf. 10.34.1.

[2] For an analysis of Clement's uses of the word κανών see *Origen's Doctrine of Tradition*, pp. 59–61.

[3] *Strom.* 7.7.41.3 (PG 9.457); 6.15.125.3 (PG 9.349); 6.18.165.1 (PG 9.397).

[4] *Ibid.* 1.19.96.1 (PG 8.813), where the phrase obviously refers to practice, for Clement says that some heretics used bread and water at the eucharist against the Church's *canon*; 7.16.105.5 (PG 9.545).

[5] *Ibid.* 7.16.94.5 (PG 9.532); 6.16.124.5 (PG 9.348).

[6] *Ibid.* 4.15.98.3 (PG 8.1305).

[7] See above, pp. 26–7, and *Origen's Doctrine of Tradition*, pp. 53–61. Hägglund, in his discussion of Clement's conception of the rule of faith ('Die Bedeutung', pp. 31–34), has not taken sufficient account of this identification.

[8] For full statistics on Tertullian's use of the word *regula*, see Flesseman-van Leer, *Tradition and Scripture*, p. 126 n. 2, and for her discussion of the meaning of this concept in Tertullian, see pp. 161–70. See also Hägglund, 'Die Bedeutung', p. 23.

[9] *Adv. Marc.* 1.21.4.

[10] *Apologeticus* 46.17: *regula disciplinae*; cf. *De Monogamia* 2.3: *regulam fidei . . . ordinem disciplinae*; *De Resurr. Mort.* 21.3: *fides tota . . . disciplina*; *Ad Nationes* 1.10.1; *disciplina* means the Christian religion; cf. *De Test. Animae* 2.2; *De Praescr. Haer.* 6.4.

[11] *Adv. Marc.* 5.3.1.

[12] *Adv. Valentinianos* 4.1. But *regula fidei* in *Adv. Marc.* 4.36.12 means the exercise of faith in Jesus like that of Bartimaeus.

[13] *Ep. Clem.* 2.4 (Rehm's text in GCS).

not composed specially for the pseudo-Clementine literature, but was used by its author or authors, and dates from some fairly early date in the third century (the limits are after Irenaeus and before Cyprian).[1] It is not easy to determine the exact meaning of the phrase 'canon of the Church' in this context. It could mean 'the rule for the Church laid down in the gospel according to St Matthew', just as the fifteenth canon of the Council of Neocaesarea, when it says that deacons in a church must be seven in number 'according to the canon' (κατὰ τὸν κανόνα), means, as it goes on to explain, the rule laid down in the book of Acts. It could mean the tradition of the Church, though there is no precise parallel for this use of the phrase. It could mean the rule of faith; but the context makes this meaning very unlikely. Perhaps 'long-standing rule' is the best interpretation to take of the phrase here. We have already seen examples of canon being used to refer to ecclesiastical practice.[2] It is possible that there is one reference to the rule of faith in the Didascalia Apostolorum, where in one passage the Syriac version runs: 'But if you follow and conform to the truth of the Church and the power of the Gospel, your hope in the Lord shall not be frustrated.'[3] For 'the truth of the Church and the power of the Gospel' the Latin version (which is extant here) has 'the ecclesiastical rule and the evangelical form' (ecclesiasticam regulam et evangelicam formam). But we cannot be sure whether this phrase is not due to later adaptation by a translator or editor. However the Didascalia, as we shall see, supplies us elsewhere with some material for determining the contents of the rule of faith.[4]

Origen refers often to the rule of faith.[5] His most frequent word for it is canon (κανών). He can speak of 'the rule prevalent among the majority of the Church',[6] or of 'the ecclesiastical rule' (ὁ κανὼν ὁ ἐκκλησιαστικός),[7] and he can identify the canon with 'the purport of sound teaching' (τὴν πρόθεσιν τῆς ὑγιοῦς διδασκαλίας).[8] He speaks of 'the canon of the churches',[9] and mentions one who 'is outside the faith and the Church's canon and the Scripture',[10] and of 'the canon of Jesus Christ's heavenly

[1] See W. Ullmann, 'The Significance of the Epistola Clementis in the Pseudo-Clementines'.

[2] See above, pp. 76, 77.

[3] Didascalia XXVI, p. 240; the Latin version is given on p. 241. Earlier in the same passage (also p. 241) Connolly has suggested an emendation of norma or forma evangelica for a corrupt nomine evangelico, and this might point to a conception of the rule of faith. But the passage is very uncertain.

[4] See below, p. 89.

[5] Cap. 6, cf. Origen's Doctrine of Tradition, deals fully with this subject.

[6] Comm. on John 13.16.   [7] Comm. on I Corinthians LXXXIV.

[8] Hom. on Jeremiah 5.4.   [9] Comm. on Matthew, Comm. Ser. 28.

[10] ὁ μὲν ἔξω τῆς πίστεως καὶ τοῦ τῆς ἐκκλησίας κανόνος καὶ τῆς γραφῆς. Comm. on Matthew, Comm. Ser. 46.

Church according to the succession of the apostles.'[1] It is clear that he links this canon closely with the Scripture; for instance, in the *Conversation with Heracleides*, at one point, moving from one subject to another, he says: 'If any doubtful point concerning the rule (κανόνος) remains, mention it; we shall continue to give a commentary on Scripture.'[2] But Origen also uses other words for the rule of faith. He mentions 'the ecclesiastical principle' (ὁ ἐκκλησιαστικὸς λόγος),[3] 'the mind of the Church' (γνώμη ἐκκλησιαστική),[4] 'Church instruction and teaching' (κατήχησιν ἐκκλησιαστικὴν καὶ διδασκαλίαν),[5] and 'the foundation-doctrines of the Church' (τὰ ὑποβεβηκότα δόγματα τῆς ἐκκλησίας),[6] and 'the Church's intention' (βούλημα).[7] He also refers to the 'preaching' (κήρυγμα) of the Church, and can say, 'in the preaching it is handed down that angels and powers exist'.[8] We shall examine later on the contents of this rule of faith, for Origen gives us a list of them.[9]

The statement that Cyprian never mentions the rule of faith[10] is indeed formally correct. But, as we shall see,[11] he produces a formula which looks like part of the rule of faith, and he has one phrase, *tenor fidei*, which may refer to the rule. He associates *tenor fidei* in one passage with 'fear of God' and 'the precepts of Christ',[12] and in the other he is referring to perseverance in faith;[13] it would perhaps therefore be better to take this as referring to tenacity of faith rather than to continuity in faith. But the bishops of the North African church in council under Cyprian at Carthage in the year 255 (the fifth Council of Carthage under Cyprian,

---

[1] τοῦ κανόνος τῆς Ἰησοῦ Χριστοῦ κατὰ διαδοχὴν τῶν ἀποστόλων οὐρανίου ἐκκλησίας, *PA* 4.2.2.

[2] *Conv. with Heracleides*, text p. 144.

[3] *Hom. on Jeremiah* 5.14; *Comm. on Matthew* 11.17; 13.2; 17.35; *Frag. on Exodus* (PG 12.287); *Comm. on I Corinthians* XXXVII.

[4] *Comm. on Ps.* 48.12 (PG 12.1441).   [5] *Comm. on Matthew* 15.7; cf. 10.14.

[6] *Comm. on Ps.* 27.5 (PG 12.1280): the doctrine of the Trinity is one of these. Cf. *Frag. on Proverbs* 24.6 and a *Fragment on Song of Solomon* 4.3, 4 (PG 17.225 and 272) and *Comm. on Matthew* 13.1.

[7] *Contra Celsum* 5.22.

[8] *PA*, Origen's Preface 10, ἐν τῷ κηρύγματι καὶ τὸ εἶναί τινας ἀγγέλους καὶ δυνάμεις ... παραδέδοται; cf. *PA* 3.1.1 for the same phrase, and (in Latin version) 2.10.1.

[9] See below, p. 90.

[10] So Van den Eynde, *Les Normes*, p. 298; in *Ep.* 59.8.1 Cyprian says that the insults of abandoned men should not affect us *quominus a via recta et a certa regula non recedamus*; but it is not clear what the 'definite rule' is here. It is not likely that Van den Brink is correct in his suggestion that the phrase *secundum fidem nostram et divinae praedicationis datam formam* (*Ep.* 55.27.3) is equivalent to a reference to the *regula* ('Traditio', p. 76).

[11] See below, p. 90.

[12] *Ep.* 74.9.1 *Quod si est apud nos, frater dilectissime, Dei timor, si tenor praevalet fidei, si custodimus Christi praecepta*; Bayard paraphrases the passage so much in his translation that it is impossible to determine exactly how he thought this phrase should be translated.

[13] *Ep.* 76.1.3 *custoditae fidei tenore viguistis*; Bayard 'une foi vigoureuse et ferme'.

the first on the subject of baptism), addressing a group of bishops who had asked about schismatic baptism, employ the expression 'although you yourselves hold the truth and the solidity of the catholic rule on this point',[1] which probably includes both faith and practice. This expression no doubt had the approval of Cyprian and may even have been drafted by him. Similarly during the last Council of Carthage over which Cyprian presided (the seventh under him, the third on baptism) in 256, Eucratius bishop of Thenae referred to the 'rule of ecclesiastical law' (legis ecclesiasticae regulam), but made it clear that both law and rule were to be found in the Scriptures;[2] and Vincentius bishop of Thibari delivered his opinion of the heretics thus: 'if they are converted and want to come to the Lord, they have of course the rule of truth (regulam veritatis) which the Lord in a divine precept entrusted to his apostles, saying: Go, in my name lay on hands, cast out demons. And in another place: go and teach the nations baptizing them in the name of the Father and of the Son and of the Holy Spirit.'[3] It is interesting to find Eucratius and Vincentius seeing the rule of faith actually laid down in the words of Scripture; we shall see that Novatian has the same conception.[4] Firmilian, bishop of Caesarea in Cappadocia, whose letter to Cyprian on the baptismal controversy, translated into very Cyprianic Latin, is included in the collection of Cyprian's correspondence, refers twice to the rule of faith. He congratulates Cyprian that 'you have dealt with this point about which a controversy now exists according to the rule of truth and the wisdom of Christ',[5] and, reproaching Stephen of Rome, he says, 'Nor were the exhortations of the apostle able to conform you to the rule of truth and of peace.'[6] There is no reason to doubt that Firmilian intended by his use of 'the rule of truth' the same meaning as would have been attached to it by, for instance, his friend Origen, and not the more narrowly biblical meaning in vogue in North Africa at the time. Firmilian can also use the phrase 'ecclesiastical rule' (ecclesiastica regula) of the customary form and formula of baptizing.[7] Here we may suspect a canon in the original Greek. Novatian, as we have seen, on several occasions refers to the 'rule of truth' (regula veritatis), and, as we

[1] Ep. 70.1.2 quamquam et ipsi illic veritatem et firmitatem catholicae regulae teneatis.
[2] Sent. Episc. 29.
[3] Ibid. 37. The bishop's quotations appear to come from Mark 16.17 and from Matt. 28.19.
[4] See below, pp. 115–16.
[5] secundum regulam veritatis et sapientiam Christi hoc de quo nunc quaeritur disposueritis, Ep. 75.3.1.
[6] Nec te informare ad regulam veritatis et pacis apostoli praecepta potuerunt, Ep. 75.24.3.
[7] Ep. 75.10.5.

shall see, allows us to conjecture something about its contents.[1] At this point we can most appropriately look at one revealing little appearance of the concept of the rule of faith. The earliest prologue to the second epistle to Timothy in the Latin New Testament runs thus:

He likewise writes to Timothy about exhortation concerning martyrdom and concerning all the rule of truth and what will happen at the last times and about his passion.[2]

It is highly likely that this mention of the 'rule of truth' is a reference to II Tim. 1.13, where the writer of the epistle refers to 'the pattern of sound words which you have received from me'. The author of this prologue clearly thinks that Paul passed on to Timothy some form of the rule as he knew it in his day. As this would suggest a conception of the rule as nearly stereotyped we may find here an additional support for Souter's conjecture that this prologue comes from the middle of the third century, perhaps it would be more accurate to say, in the second half rather than the first.[3] The phrase *regula veritatis* does not seem to occur in Latin writers of the fourth century.[4]

Pope Cornelius, writing about the year 251 on the subject of Novatian's lack of full Christian initiation because he had been baptized on what had been thought to be his death-bed, says: 'Even when he recovered from the disease he did not receive any of the other things which it is necessary to partake of according to the Church's rule (κατὰ τὸν τῆς ἐκκλησίας κανόνα), nor of the sealing by the bishop.'[5] Here the *canon* clearly refers to the Church's traditional practice rather than the Church's traditional doctrine. As we shall see, Dionysius of Alexandria gives evidence of knowing a form like the rule of faith.[6] He also uses the phrase 'we have received a formula, and rule (τύπον καὶ κανόνα) from the men of old (πρεσβυτέρων) who were before us,' to set out the proper manner

---

[1] See above, pp. 72–3, and below, p. 90.

[2] *Item Timotheo scribit de exhortatione martyrii et omnis regulae veritatis et quid futurum sit temporibus novissimis et de sua passione.*

[3] A. Souter, *Text and Canon of the New Testament*, p. 190. This prologue is not a Marcionite one. All the earliest prologues, Marcionite or Catholic, can be found printed in *Novum Testamentum Domini Nostri Jesu Christi Latine*; an account of them is given in *Partis Secundae Fasciculus Primus* (1913), p. 41. The text is also available in Souter, *Text and Canon*, p. 190, and in D. de Bruyne, 'Prologues Bibliques d'Origine Marcionite'; it was de Bruyne who first pointed out that most of them were Marcionite.

[4] No occurrence of the phrase is listed in Blaise, *Dictionnaire Latin-Français des Auteurs Chrétiens*, between Novatian and Augustine. The Rev. Prof. S. L. Greenslade, D.D., in a private communication, expresses himself as inclined to agree with this judgement.

[5] Eusebius, *HE* 6.43.15; cf. the contemporary author of *De Singularitate Clericorum* who refers to *regulam disciplinae* 1 (173), and the phrase *disciplinam traditam* in Ps.-Cyprian, *De Laude Martyrii* 9 (32).

[6] See below, p. 91.

F

in which to end the great prayer in the eucharist.[1] This obviously refers to traditional liturgical practice in the Church. Dionysius of Rome, his contemporary and at one point his opponent in a controversy about orthodoxy, uses the phrases 'the most solemn preaching of the Church of God, the unity' (of God), and 'the holy preaching of the unity'.[2] We are reminded of Origen's use of 'preaching' to denote the rule of faith.

The Synod of Antioch, held at intervals between 264 and 268, which examined the orthodoxy of Paul of Samosata and finally condemned and inflicted formal deposition on him, has left us three examples of the use of the word *canon*. The word was, as far as we can gather from the fragmentary remains available, used at least twice in the final synodical letter of the Council. Eusebius quotes one sentence which says of Paul, 'but when leaving the *canon* he changed to false and spurious teachings';[3] and another fragment condemns one notion of Paul's on the grounds that 'the catholic and ecclesiastical canons do not approve of this'.[4] It is not easy to determine why the *canons* should be in the plural; perhaps this is a sign that by this time the conception of a single, generally agreed rule of faith is beginning to be stereotyped into a number of formal definitions, or even creeds, made by councils; or perhaps the wording has suffered from alteration to fit the conditions of a later day. The third occurrence of *canon* occurs in the *Letter of Hymenaeus* (also called the *Letter of the Six Bishops*). This is a document purporting to be addressed by six bishops of sees in Palestine or its neighbourhood, headed by Hymenaeus bishop of Jerusalem, addressed to somebody from whom it crisply demands a decision, whether he will subscribe to their Christological doctrine or not. It sets out quite elaborately a doctrine of the relation of the Son to the Father which has obvious affinities with the teaching of Origen.[5] Several eminent scholars have either rejected it as a forgery or relegated it to the controversies of the fourth century,[6] mainly because the language of the letter recalls in various places passages in Eusebius'

---

[1] Feltoe, p. 198 (Dionysius of Alexandria's *Refutation and Defence* 14, quoted in Basil *De Spiritu Sancto* XXIX [73]).

[2] τὸ σεμνότατον κήρυγμα τῆς ἐκκλησίας τοῦ θεοῦ, τὴν μοναρχίαν and τὸ ἅγιον κήρυγμα τῆς μοναρχίας, Feltoe, pp. 177 and 182 (from Athanasius, *De Decretis* 26).

[3] ὅπου ἀποστὰς τοῦ κανόνος ἐπὶ κίβδηλα καὶ νόθα διδάγματα μετελήλυθεν, Eusebius, *HE* 7.30.7.

[4] τοῦτο δὲ οὐκ ἀξιοῦσιν οἱ καθολικοὶ καὶ ἐκκλησιαστικοὶ κανόνες, H. de Riedmatten, *Les Actes du Procès de Paul de Samosate*, p. 144, frag. 16 (from Severus of Antioch's *Contra Grammaticum*).

[5] For the text of the Letter see Mansi, *Sacrorum Conciliorum Nova et Amplissima Collectio*, Vol. I, pp. 1033–40; Routh, *Reliquiae Sacrae*, Vol. III, pp. 289–99; G. Bardy, *Paul de Samosate*, pp. 13–19. For discussions of the genuineness of the letter see C. Raven, *Apollinarianism*, pp. 60–63, Bardy, *Paul de Samosate*, pp. 9–34; de Riedmatten, *Les Actes*, pp. 121–34.

[6] E.g. Dorner, Hefele, Bardenhewer and Schwarz.

work against Marcellus, in the third creed produced at the Synod of Antioch ('the Creed of the Dedication') held in 341, and in the slightly later creed called the Macrostich (the fifth Antiochene creed, 344). But all these documents, as well as condemning Marcellus of Ancyra, associate with him Paul of Samosata, and this could well explain the resemblance of language. An impressive list of scholars have accepted this *Letter of Hymenaeus* as genuine.[1] It contains in fact nothing that is not perfectly appropriate for a document drawn up by a group of Origenist theologians in the middle of the third century in order to serve as a test of Christological doctrine,[2] as Bardy and de Riedmatten have shown. The signatories of the letter do not present Paul with a creed;[3] it is much more likely that they are facing him with their own commentary on the relevant portion of the rule of faith. Their opening words suggest this:

> We have decided to set out in a written form the faith (τὴν πίστιν) which we have received from the beginning and we possess handed down and preserved in the catholic and holy Church by succession until the present day, preached by the blessed apostles who also were eyewitnesses and ministers of the word, from the law and the prophets and the New Testament.[4]

Then they proceed to set out this faith, as far as the Christological point under discussion is concerned, with copious quotations from the law and the prophets and the New Testament. They are anxious to prove their rule of faith from Scripture.[5] During the course of the letter, they declare that if anyone says that the Son did not exist before the foundation of the world 'this man we regard as a stranger to the ecclesiastical rule, and all the catholic churches agree with us.'[6] There can be no doubt that this is a reference to the rule of faith. Very similar to this document is the *Profession of Faith according to Revelation of Gregory Bishop of Neocaesarea*, included by Gregory of Nyssa in his Life of Gregory. It is not a creed,

---

[1] Kattenbusch, Harnack, Loofs, Bardy, Raven and de Riedmatten.

[2] Particularly impressive as evidence for its mid-third-century date is the sentence (Bardy, §9, Routh, p. 299, ll. 11–12) οὕτω καὶ καθὸ Χριστὸς ἐν καὶ τὸ αὐτὸ ὢν τῇ οὐσίᾳ, εἰ καὶ τὰ μάλιστα πολλαῖς ἐπινοίαις ἐπινοεῖται. This use of ἐπίνοιαι is peculiarly Origenistic and is not likely to have survived as long as a century after his day. See F. Bertrand, *Mystique de Jésus chez Origène*, p. 21; H. Koch, *Pronoia und Paideusis*, pp. 65–74; W. Völker, *Das Vollkommenheitsideal des Origenes*, p. 99, and *Allegory and Event*, pp. 272–7.

[3] See Bardy, *Paul de Samosate*, p. 19.

[4] Bardy, §1, Routh, p. 289, l. 15–p. 290, l. 6.

[5] See Bardy, *Paul de Samosate*, p. 21.

[6] τοῦτον ἀλλότριον τοῦ ἐκκλησιαστικοῦ κανόνος ἡγούμεθα, καὶ πᾶσαι αἱ καθολικαὶ ἐκκλησίαι συμφωνοῦσιν ἡμῖν (Bardy, §3, Routh, p. 291, ll. 3–5, 6–7). Bardy (*Paul de Samosate*, p. 23) makes surprisingly heavy weather over the phrase ἐκκλησιαστικὸς κανών, but we have already found this identical phrase used by Clement of Alexandria and by Origen (see below, pp. 77–8).

and does not include any word for creed or statement of faith; it is neither interrogatory nor declaratory; it is a brief but careful theological statement of the respective natures and functions of the Persons of the Trinity, couched in Origenistic terms. It is clear that statements such as these were becoming increasingly common in the second half of the third century.[1]

We can recover a few instances of the use of *canon* to mean rule of faith in Eusebius' *Ecclesiastical History*, where he is not quoting the words of earlier writers but giving his own opinion. Paraphrasing the words of Hegesippus, he says that up to the reign of Trajan nobody had seriously corrupted 'the sound rule of the saving preaching',[2] and it is much more likely that he is here giving us his own words and not those of Hegesippus. Again, he says that Beryllus bishop of Bostra, whom Origen reclaimed for orthodoxy about the year 243, had perverted 'the ecclesiastical *canon*'.[3] And one more mention of this 'ecclesiastical *canon*' is very probably a reference to the rule of faith rather than to the canon of Scripture, though the two meanings approach each other in this passage.[4] One gains the impression that in Eusebius' day the word *canon* and its Latin equivalent *regula* were being employed in so wide a variety of uses that the time was passing when the phrase *canon* would be convenient for referring to the rule of faith.[5] The time was dawning, too, when the declaratory creed was, as the conciliar creed, to take over from the rule of faith the function of defining and summarizing the teaching of the Church.[6]

---

[1] See A. Hahn, *Bibliothek der Symbole und Glaubensregeln der Alter Kirche*, pp. 253–5. The authenticity of this document was much disputed in the past, but Hahn and Harnack accepted it, convinced by Caspari's full defence of it, and so apparently does B. Altaner (*Patrologie*, p. 176). Gregory of Nyssa said that the Christian folk of Neocaesarea were still instructed in it in his day, and that they still in his day preserved Gregory's signature.

[2] τὸν ὑγιῆ κανόνα τοῦ σωτηρίου κηρύγματος, *HE* 3.32.7.

[3] *HE* 6.33.1; cf. *ibid.* 4.23.4: πολεμῶν τῷ τῆς ἀληθείας κανόνι.

[4] *HE* 6.25.3: τὸν ἐκκλησιαστικὸν φυλάττων κανόνα. If this is a reference to the canon of Scripture, it is the earliest use of κανών in this meaning, but it is most unlikely that anybody used κανών in this sense before Athanasius. See H. Oppel, 'ΚΑΝΩΝ, zur Bedeutungsgeschichte des Wortes und seiner lateinischer Entsprechungen (Regula–Norma)', pp. 70, 71.

[5] The Council of Arles, for instance, meeting in 314, uses the phrase *ecclesiastica regula* (13) to mean a rule that false accusations shall not be brought against clergy. The Council of Ancyra (314) uses both κανών and ὅρος to mean a local church rule about diet and similar matters (14, 24, 19, 21). And every time a Greek-speaking Council met, it produced κανόνες.

[6] Neither the Ἔκθεσις τῆς κατὰ μέρος πίστεως, attributed in Migne, PG 10.1103–24 to Gregory Thaumaturgus, nor the Ἐξήγησις ἀποστολικοῦ κηρύγματος found in the *Apostolic Constitutions* VI.11 has been included in this list. The first by internal evidence plainly betrays its origin from the Arian controversy; the second is printed with underlining by F. X. Funk, *Didascalia et Constitutiones Apostolorum*, Vol. I, pp. 325–7, who thereby indicates that it was not part of the *Didascalia Apostolorum*, though Hahn (*Bibliothek*, pp. 13–14) prints it as a mid-third-century creed. Its date is uncertain; it is not exactly a creed, but a short commentary upon some points of Christian faith and practice.

2. *The Contents of the Rule of Faith*

We can with some confidence determine the contents of the rule of faith. Irenaeus and Tertullian each gives us three separate lists, and Origen in the Preface to his *Peri Archon* carefully analyses the contents of the rule. And we can find in Hippolytus, in the *Didascalia Apostolorum*, in Cyprian, in Novatian and in Dionysius of Alexandria passages which appear to give us the rule in part or in whole. The results of a comparison of these texts are here set out in tabular form.

IRENAEUS[1]

Adv. Haer. 1.2	Adv. Haer. 3.4.1	Adv. Haer. 4.53.1
One God, Father Almighty, who made heaven, earth, seas and their contents. One Christ Jesus, Son of God, who was made flesh for our salvation. Holy Spirit who through the prophets announced the dispensations and the advents and the birth from a virgin and the passion and the rising from the dead and the assumption of the Beloved, Christ Jesus our Lord, in flesh, into the heavens, and his appearance from the heavens in the glory of the Father to sum up all things, and to raise all flesh of all humanity in order that every knee should bow . . . to Christ Jesus our Lord . . . and that he should exercise righteous judgement over all, and send evil angels and wicked men into eternal fire and give life and glory to the righteous and holy.	One God, Maker of heaven and of earth their contents. Jesus Christ the Son of God, through whom creation took place, who was born of a virgin, himself uniting himself, a man, to God, suffered under Pontius Pilate, rose again, was received in glory, is destined to come as Saviour of those who are saved and Judge of those who are condemned and will send to eternal fire those who distort the truth.	One God, Father Almighty from whom are all things, The Son of God, Jesus Christ our Lord, through whom are all things, and his dispensations, through which the Son of God became a man. The Spirit of God, who supplies knowledge of the truth, who expounded the dispensations of the Father and the Son, according to which he dwelt with the human race in the manner in which the Father wills.

---

[1] Irenaeus gives a list of the rule of faith in *Adversus Haereses* 1.2; 3.4.1 and 4.53.1. In 1.15 he refers to the rule of truth and quotes with great emphasis its teaching that there is only one God who made the world and that through his Word and Spirit, but does not cite the rule any further. The last few lines of the first example have been a little abridged and paraphrased in order to fit it into the same page as the others. See also Hägglund, 'Die Bedeutung', pp. 17–19.

TERTULLIAN[1]

Adv. Praxean 2	*De Praescr. Haer.* 13.1–6	*De Virg. Vel.* 1.3
We believe in a single God, under, however, this condition, which we call 'economy', that There is a Son of the single God, his own Word who proceeds from him, through whom all things were made and without whom nothing was made; this Son sent into a virgin and born of her, man and God, Son of man and Son of God, and called Jesus Christ; this Son suffered, this Son died and was buried according to the Scriptures, and was raised by the Father and assumed into heaven, and sits on the right hand of the Father and will come to judge living and dead.	There is only one God and no other beside the Founder of the world who produced everything from nothing through his Word who was sent out first of all things. This Word called his Son was seen under the title of God in various ways by the patriarchs, was continually heard in the prophets, finally was conveyed by the Spirit of God the Father and by power into the virgin Mary, was made flesh in her womb and was born of her and lived as Jesus Christ; next he preached a new law and a new promise of the Kingdom of heaven, did miracles, was crucified, rose again the third day, was snatched up into the heavens and sat on the right hand of the Father.	The Rule of Faith is that of believing In a single almighty God, Founder of the world And in his Son Jesus Christ, who was born of the Virgin Mary, crucified under Pontius Pilate, raised from the dead the third day, received into the heavens, now sits at the right hand of the Father, will come to judge the living and the dead.

We believe in a single God, under, however, this condition, which we call 'economy', that There is a Son of the single God, his own Word who proceeds from him, through whom all things were made and without whom nothing was made; this Son sent into a virgin and born of her, man and God, Son of man and Son of God, and called Jesus Christ; this Son suffered, this Son died and was buried according to the Scriptures, and was raised by the Father and assumed into heaven, and sits on the right hand of the Father and will come to judge living and dead.

Next he sent according to his promise from the Father the Holy Spirit, the Paraclete, the sanctifier of the faith of those who believe in the Father and the Son and the Holy Spirit.

He sent the plenipotentiary power of the Holy Spirit to animate believers

He will come with glory to take the saints into the enjoyment of eternal life and heavenly promises, and to judge the profane with unending fire.

A resurrection of both parties will take place accompanied by the restoration of the flesh.

---

[1] These three lists are found in *Adversus Praxean* 2; *De Praescriptione Haereticorum* 13.1–6; and *De Virginibus Velandis* 1.3. All three are set out in parallel columns in E. Evans, *Tertullian's Treatise against Praxeas*, pp. 189–92. See also Hägglund, 'Die Bedeutung', p. 29.

HIPPOLYTUS[1]

Let us believe therefore, blessed brethren, according to the tradition (παράδοσις) of the apostles, that God the Word came down from heaven to the holy Virgin Mary, that taking flesh from her, including a human rational soul, he might become wholly man, without sin. The word of truth (ἀληθείας λόγος) shows us that there is one Father, whose Word he is, through whom he made everything. He was predicted by the law and the prophets and had a heavenly part from the Father and an earthly part, when he was incarnate from Adam. He showed that he was human by enduring human experiences, sleep, weariness, arrest, insult, and finally crucifixion, death and burial. He roused the dead and the third day was raised by the Father. He had been witnessed to as the Son of God during his ministry and had performed miracles and at his death portents occurred. He breathed on his disciples and gave them the Spirit and entered through closed doors. In the sight of his disciples he was taken up into heaven and sits at the right hand of the Father and is due to come as judge of living and dead. This is God, who became man for us.

[1] *Contra Noetum* 17 and 18, a long passage, ending the discourse, in carefully composed style using a series of contrasting clauses, reminiscent of Melito's *Homily on the Passion* and *Epistle to Diognetus* 11 and 12, of which only the main points are presented here in paraphrase.

'DIDASCALIA APOSTOLORUM'[1]

XV, pp. 132–3	XXVI, p. 258
Righteousness (i.e. how to achieve justification) Faith in God Refutation of idols and the unity of God Punishment and reward (or perhaps rest, refreshment) The Kingdom of the name of Christ His dispensation How our Lord clothed himself in a body The passion of Christ	Now to him who is able to open the ears of your hearts to receive the incisive[2] words of the Lord through the Gospel and the teaching of Jesus Christ the Nazarene who was crucified in the days of Pontius Pilate, and slept, that he might announce to Abraham, to Isaac and to Jacob and to all his saints the end of the world and the resurrection that is to be for the dead, and rose from the dead, that he might show and give to us, that we might know him,[3] a pledge of his resurrection, and was taken up into heaven by the power of God his Father and of the Holy Spirit, and sat on the right hand of the throne of God Almighty upon the cherubim, to him who cometh with power and glory to judge both the dead and the living, to him be dominion and glory, etc.

[1] Two passages, the first defining what a widow is to teach and the articles of faith which (presumably because of her lack of education and authority) she is not to teach; the second comprising the final ascription which includes a Christological formula. The first is given in précis, the second in direct quotation.

[2] διηκονημένα (*Ap. Const.*): either from δακονάω (to sharpen), which is how the Syriac took it, or from δακονέω (to minister), which is how the Latin (*quae ministrata sunt*, p. 259) interpreted it; the second is the more likely meaning.

[3] So the Syriac; ἡμῖν alone *Ap. Const.*; *notis suis* Latin (p. 259).

ORIGEN[1]

One God, the creator, God of the Old Testament.

Jesus Christ, the Son of God, who was incarnate, who was born of a Virgin Birth, who suffered, died, rose again, and is now glorified.

The Holy Spirit, who inspired the men of the Old Testament and the New Testament.

The future life and the resurrection from the dead.

Free will and the struggle against sin (but the manner of the soul's generation is not stated).

The existence of the devil and his angels (but how the devil became the devil is not clearly stated).

The creatureliness and final destruction of the world.

That the Holy Scriptures are inspired by the Holy Spirit and have two meanings, the second only intelligible to those who have wisdom and knowledge from the Holy Spirit; and that there is a 'spiritual law'.

The existence of angels (but their creation, and other details, are not in the 'preaching'; and whether the heavenly bodies have rational souls or not is not stated).

CYPRIAN[2]

Surely [Marcion] does not affirm the same God as Father and Creator as we do? Does he know the same Son Christ born of the Virgin Mary, who as Word was made flesh, who carried our sins, who conquered death by dying, who first inaugurated the resurrection of the flesh in his own person and manifested to his disciples that he had risen in the same flesh?

NOVATIAN[3]

The Virginal Conception of Jesus
His Miracles of healing
The four gospels
The Gentiles are to believe in him

[1] *PA*, Origen's Preface, 4–10: a list of the things which Christ and his apostles preached as necessary; here given in précis, as in *Origen's Doctrine of Tradition*, p. 116.

[2] *Ep.* 73.5.2, translated unabridged.

[3] *De Trinitate* 9, pp. 29–30, where Novatian is giving a list of prophecies about Christ made by Isaiah and other prophets. The list is abstracted from Novatian's presentation of it. The list is limited by the necessity of finding proof-texts in the prophets for each article, but it looks like the Christological part of a rule of faith.

His passion
The injuries and blows inflicted on him
His humility
The unbelief of the Jews
His resurrection from the dead
The time of this resurrection
His sitting at the right hand of the Father
He is the possessor of all things
He is judge of all men

DIONYSIUS OF ALEXANDRIA[1]

On points, however, of prime importance and great weight we must insist. For if anyone utters impiety about God, as do those who say that he is without mercy; or if anyone introduces the worship of strange gods, such an one the law had commanded us to stone. But we with the vigorous words of our faith will stone them. Or[2] if a man receive not all the mystery of Christ, or alter or distort [saying] that he is not God, or that he did not become a man, or that he did not die, or that he did not rise, or that he will not come again to judge the quick and the dead—or preach anything else apart from what we preached, let him be a curse, says Paul. Or if so be he have wronged the word concerning the resurrection of the flesh, let him be already reckoned with the dead.

*　　　*　　　*

The comparison of these examples of the rule of faith suggests a number of interesting conclusions. It is obvious that a writer's expression of the rule varied with his own interests and predilections or those of his local church. Irenaeus introduces into his rule his characteristic doctrine of 'recapitulation' when he says that Christ came 'to sum up all things' (ἀνακεφαλαιώσασθαι). Tertullian expresses a perculiarly Montanist tenet when he lists in his rule of faith that Jesus Christ 'preached a new law'

[1] This passage is taken partly from an article by F. C. Conybeare, 'Newly-discovered Letters of Dionysius of Alexandria to Popes Stephen and Xystus' translated from the Armenian version of a refutation of the Tome of Leo published by Timothy Ailurus (Monophysite Patriarch of Alexandria about 460), where the letters are cited (pp. 112–13 of the article); and partly from a translation from the Syriac of this letter, by N. McLean, printed by Feltoe, *Dionysius of Alexandria, Letters* V (2), p. 47. This letter is to Stephen of Rome, and in it Dionysius is distinguishing between divergences which Christians can permit between themselves, and those which they cannot permit. 'Our faith' in line 5 might refer to the rule of faith.

[2] Here begins the part translated from the Syriac.

(*nova lex*), and when he includes the fine phrase (coined, no doubt, by Tertullian himself) 'the plenipotentiary power' (*vicaria vis*) of the Holy Spirit. We are struck by Hippolytus' doctrinal elaboration concerning the heavenly part and the earthly part in Christ. Origen's rule of faith is strongly Alexandrian, indeed Origenistic, with its mention of two meanings to Scripture (i.e. Origenistic allegory, based on Philo's) and of the 'spiritual law', and its formidable list of subjects additional to the conventional ones, such as the speculative minds of Alexandrian churchmen would find interesting. It is most surprising to find no mention at all of the Church as an article in any of these lists, though it is virtually certain that the Church figured in Tertullian's baptismal creed, probably in Clement of Alexandria's, and quite certainly in that of Hippolytus. The position in these lists of the article concerning the resurrection of the dead varies remarkably. In Irenaeus' first example it appears in a long Christological statement which has itself been tacked on to the article concerning the Holy Spirit, in a way which suggests that the Christological statement was originally separate and perhaps confirms Kelly's conjecture that it was under the influence of the rule of faith that the Christological member in the interrogatory creed was enlarged and elaborated. In Tertullian's first and third examples no mention appears of the resurrection of the dead, but in his second example it comes last of all along with the article on judgement, outside both Christological and Pneumatological sections. It takes a rather similar position in Origen's account. In the *Didascalia* and in Cyprian's fragment it is included in the Christological section, but in the passage from Dionysius of Alexandria it appears at the end of the list. In the extracts from Hippolytus and from Novatian it does not appear at all. Hippolytus, however, with his clause 'he roused the dead' (ὁ τοὺς νέκρους ἐγείρων) is the first author to include the Descent into Hell in the rule of faith, and the writer of the *Didascalia Apostolorum* perhaps the next. Tertullian's second example is obviously controlled by a desire to exclude Gnostics, as is Dionysius of Alexandria's by the need to exclude adoptianist and modalist monarchianism. This suggests that whereas the interrogatory creed was of little use for excluding heresies, the rule of faith could include this among its functions. All the points which we have noticed weigh against the theory that the rule of faith could have been regarded as in any sense a creed, though they do not exclude the possibility of the rule having some relation to the creed, perhaps as a list of the material which was reduced to its barest essentials in the creed. The only example which really looks like a creed among all those which have just been set out is Tertullian's third example, from the *De Virginibus Velandis*. It may well be that Tertullian was here quoting a creed, simply as a convenient and quick summary of the rule of faith, even though he calls it the rule of faith. His citing of the rule in this context is not an important step in his argument; he does so merely to show the immutability of the rule of faith in contrast to the possibility, which he believes was always open to the Holy Spirit, of alteration or adjustment in Christian discipline and ethics; a summary of the rule would have sufficed for his argument. Of course he does not give the whole rule, nor, for that matter, the whole creed, here; he does not mention the Holy Spirit. The suggestion has been made[1] that Tertullian's Montanist convictions came into play here, and that he omitted the Holy Spirit in order to suggest that the advent of the Spirit came later than Pentecost. But this seems far-fetched. After all, Irenaeus in his second example does not mention the Spirit; neither does Novatian; neither does Dionysius.

If a conjecture is to be made based on the evidence so far reviewed, as to what the rule of faith was, if it was not a creed, and if it was not a mere list of proof-texts, the suggestion presents itself very strongly that the rule of faith was simply an account, divided into subjects, of the content of the preaching and teaching of the Church contemporary with the writer who mentions or quotes the rule of faith. This would account for the fact that while the rule preserves a general similarity everywhere it varies in details from place to place and from writer to writer; it would explain why the rule tends to run into doctrinal or speculative elaboration with some fathers, and why it looks like material used for teaching, perhaps for catechetical teaching before baptism, rather than a cut-and-dried formula used at the rite of baptism itself. Above all, it would explain why the rule can be used against heretics, and why, though it is closely associated with Scripture, and often proved from Scripture (as is clear already, and will become clearer), it is not regarded as in form precisely the same as Scripture. This theory might explain also why the rule never during this period quite becomes a fixed and stereotyped formula and why the ingredients of the rule sometimes vary in their order and often in their expression as the Church in this formative period deals flexibly and in some instances even fluidly with her doctrine. Origen tells us[2] that the truths of the rule of faith have to be worked into a system 'either by the evidence to be found in the sacred Scriptures, or by that to be discovered by the investigation of the logical consequences of the

[1] E.g. by E. Evans, in his edition of *Adversus Praxean*, pp. 189–92.
[2] *PA*, Origen's Preface, 10. See *Origen's Doctrine of Tradition*, p. 116.

Scriptures and adherence to accuracy.' This philosophically minded theologian takes as the material of his theology the faith as it is preached by the church of his day, divided at this point conveniently into headings, and works it into a speculative system, proving it and supporting it at each step by evidence taken from the Bible.

3. *The Rule of Faith as Tradition*

Between the years 180 and 300, Van den Eynde tells us, the word 'tradition' (παράδοσις) meant three things: (*i*) the teaching of the apostles in contrast to the preaching of the prophets and the words of Christ; (*ii*) the doctrine handed down by succession in the churches, beginning with the apostles, in contrast with the Scriptures; (*iii*) the rites of the cult and other ecclesiastical practices which are handed on by custom. And he adds that 'tradition' to the fathers of this period always means the object handed on and not the organ handing it on.[1] It is with the second of these three meanings that we are now concerned, for we must now turn to consider the evidence that several early fathers describe the rule of faith expressly as tradition or use language about it which suggests that they regard it as tradition.

Irenaeus is the first of these fathers to claim our attention. He ends his succession-list of the bishops of the Roman church with the words: 'In the same order and by the same succession both the tradition from the apostles in the Church and the preaching of the truth has reached us.'[2] Later he declares that if there is any dispute about anything, recourse should be had to the oldest churches among which the apostles had moved: 'Why, even if the apostles had not left the Scriptures to us, would it not be right to follow the pattern of tradition (*ordinem traditionis*) which they handed down to those to whom they entrusted the churches?' Many races of the barbarians agree to this pattern (*ordinationi*)

---

[1] *Les Normes*, p. 158. This is a beautifully clear and accurate definition. Dix describes tradition in the Introduction (pp. xliii–xliv) of his edition of Hippolytus' *Apostolic Tradition*, but his account is far from clear and not entirely accurate: in a footnote he says that the phrase 'Scripture and tradition' 'comes from the earliest age of the church'; in fact, it is doubtful if this precise phrase can be found anywhere in any early father. The nearest approach is the 'Scripture *or* tradition' of Tertullian; see below, p. 136. G. L. Prestige in *Fathers and Heretics* has a chapter on tradition which is, like all Prestige's work, full of light and learning, though it is not certain that statistics of the vocabulary used for tradition in the fathers would support his generalizations about it. See also J. N. D. Kelly, *Early Christian Doctrines*, cap. II, and H. E. W. Turner, *The Pattern of Christian Truth*, pp. 309–78, Y. Congar, *La Tradition*, pp. 41–122, and Daniélou, *Message Évangelique*, pp. 135–45.

[2] *Adv. Haer.* 3.3.3: 'succession' is διαδοχή (Harvey's emendation for διδαχή); 'tradition' is παράδοσις; 'preaching of the truth' is τὸ τῆς ἀληθείας κήρυγμα.

who are Christians without reading the Scriptures (*sine charta et atramento*),[1] because they follow the original tradition.[2] Then Irenaeus goes on to give the tradition, in the form of the rule of faith, which we have already seen, as Irenaeus' second example of the rule.[3] Elsewhere, emphasizing that the whole Church everywhere, in Gaul, Spain, Egypt, Libya, the East, even the churches in Germany, teaches the rule of faith, neither more nor less, he directly describes this rule as 'tradition' (παράδοσις);[4] and he is clearly referring to the rule of faith in another passage, where he speaks of 'that tradition, which is from the apostles, which is preserved through the successions of presbyters in the churches'.[5] The fullest account of the rule of faith as tradition occurs in a passage which has given its interpreters considerable difficulty. It may be rendered thus:

> The true knowledge, the teaching of the apostles, and the primitive structure of the Church throughout all the world, and the nature [character] of the body of Christ according to the successions of the bishops to whom they entrusted the Church which is in every place; this teaching has come down to us, having been preserved without any use of forged writings, by being handled in its complete fulness, neither receiving addition nor suffering curtailment; and reading without falsification, and honest and steady exposition of the Scriptures without either danger or blasphemy; and the special gift of love which is more precious than knowledge, and, further, more glorious than prophecy, and also superior to all the other sacred gifts (*charismatibus*).[6]

In a later passage Irenaeus returns to his favourite theme that the teaching of the Church is everywhere the same 'because it has a sure tradition (*traditionem*) from the apostles, and allows us to see that one and the same

---

[1] Either because they could not read, one presumes, or because the Scriptures were not translated into their language.

[2] *Adv. Haer.* 3.4.1.

[3] See above, p. 86.

[4] *Adv. Haer.* 1.3. Is this mention of Egypt the first concrete evidence for the existence of Christianity in Alexandria, and is not his silence about churches in Britain significant?

[5] *Ibid.* 3.2.2.

[6] *Ibid.* 4.53.2 The translation suggested by E. Molland ('Irenaeus of Lugdunum and the Apostolic Succession', pp. 18–20) is here adopted for the opening lines, which in a Greek fragment run: γνῶσις ἀληθής ἡ τῶν ἀποστόλων διδαχὴ καὶ τὸ ἀρχαῖον τῆς ἐκκλησίας σύστημα κατὰ παντὸς τοῦ κόσμου, but in the Latin translation: *agnitio vera est apostolorum doctrina et antiquus ecclesiae status in universo mundo.* Molland's rendering has also been followed in translating the difficult clause *custodita sine fictione scripturarum tractatione plenissima.* Van den Eynde (*Les Normes*, p. 138) gives a translation based upon an Armenian version of the passage given by Merk in 'Der armenische Irenaeus Adversus Haereses' in *Zeitschrift für Katholische Theologie*, 50, 1926, pp. 384, 397–8. But this differs in so many respects from the Latin that it seems unwise to rely upon it. For this passage see also below, p. 160.

faith is that of all.' Then he gives a list of this tradition, which comprises these contents:

All teach one and the same God as Father
and believe the same economy (*dispositionem*) of the incarnation of the Son of God
and know the same gift of the Spirit
and take to heart the same commandments
and preserve the same shape of that ordinance (*figuram ordinationis*) which is towards the Church
and wait for the same coming of the Lord
and uphold the same salvation of the whole man, that is of soul and body.[1]

Though it is not clear what exactly Irenaeus (or his translator) means by 'the shape of that ordinance which is towards the Church', it is sufficiently obvious that Irenaeus regards the rule of faith, or possibly the creed considered as a summary of the rule of faith, as part of the whole inheritance which might be called traditional Christianity. For Irenaeus, says Flesseman-van Leer, 'tradition is the living *kerygma* of the church in its full identity with the revelation of Jesus Christ given to the apostles.'[2] We have already seen that Ptolemaeus the Gnostic at least, and probably other Gnostics too, had much the same view of tradition, only substituting for the rule of faith of the Church his own peculiar interpretation of Scripture, which he called 'the apostolic tradition which we have received by succession.'[3] Similarly the unknown author of the last two chapters of the *Epistle to Diognetus* (who is not the writer of the first ten chapters) declares 'I am a disciple of the apostles, and I am a teacher of the Gentiles; I minister properly the traditional teaching (τὰ παραδοθέντα) to those who are the disciples of truth,'[4] and later, in a rhapsodical passage he exclaims: 'Then the fear of the law is hymned and the grace of the prophets is recognized and the faithfulness of the gospels is established and the tradition (παράδοσις) of the apostles is preserved and the grace of the Church dances.'[5]

Tertullian, as the whole argument of his work *De Praescriptione Haereticorum* makes clear, had precisely the same conception of the rule

[1] *Adv. Haer.* 5.20.1.
[2] *Tradition and Scripture*, p. 103.
[3] See above, p. 24.
[4] *Ep. to Diognetus* 11.1–2.
[5] *Ibid.* 11.6; but we should probably see the first of Van den Eynde's meanings of παράδοσις here; see above, p. 94. There is an odd parallel for the last phrase of this sentence, ἐκκλησίας χάρις σκιρτᾷ, in the apocryphal *Acts of John* 95 (M. R. James, p. 253) where a Gnostic hymn contains the expression 'grace dances'.

of faith as tradition, that is to say as the original teaching of the apostles handed on in the Church and preached and taught in his own day. But he is much less likely to call this 'tradition' because he has two separate concepts of tradition to which he attaches very different values.[1] The first is this conception of the rule of faith as the authentic content of original Christian doctrine. The second is the concept of tradition as 'long-continued customs carried on in the life of the Church'[2] and to this he attaches far less value than to the other. He can speak of single marriage (i.e. marriage of only one partner and none other even after that partner's death) as 'catholic tradition',[3] and he can accept as a proper regulation 'that observances are attached to this faith by the Scriptures or by the tradition of the men of old and that no sort of observance is to be added because of the unlawfulness of innovation.'[4] But he is uneasy about this attitude, and later calls it 'overworking tradition' (*exercendo traditionem*).[5] And earlier he had laid down the rule, 'we are all the more bound to produce a proper reason for the things which are observed by tradition the more they lack the authority of Scripture, until they may be either confirmed or corrected by some heavenly inspiration.'[6] And there are plenty of examples of Tertullian seeking support in Scripture for customs prevalent in the Church.[7]

Enough has been said already about the identification or confusion between secret tradition and the rule of faith of the Church evident in the pages of Clement of Alexandria to make it clear that he certainly regarded the rule in the light of tradition.[8] He frequently uses the word 'tradition' (παράδοσις) for it. He speaks of 'the true tradition of the blessed teaching',[9] 'the secret traditions of the true knowledge',[10] 'the unwritten tradition of the written work',[11] and of one who 'kicks away the ecclesiastical tradition',[12] of the concern of 'the elders' for teaching 'the tradition',[13] and in

---

[1] Flesseman-van Leer brings out this distinction with admirable clarity in *Tradition and Scripture*, p. 147. She gives a full list of the different meanings of *traditio* and *tradere* in Tertullian on pp. 146–50.

[2] Flesseman-van Leer, *Tradition and Scripture*, p. 147.

[3] *catholicam traditionem*, De Monogamia 2.2; cf. *rationes traditionum*, referring to baptism, De Baptismo 1.1.

[4] *constituta esse sollemnia huic fidei scripturis vel traditione maiorum nihilque observationis amplius adiciendum ob illicitum innovationis*, De Ieiuniis adversus Psychicos 13.1.

[5] *Ibid.* 13.2.

[6] *eorum quae ex traditione observantur tanto magis dignam rationem adferre debemus quanto carent scripturae auctoritate, donec aliquo caelesti charismate aut confirmentur aut corrigantur*, ibid. 10.5.

[7] E.g. De Oratione 15.2; 16.1–6; De Ieiun. adv. Psych. 10.6. The treatment of custom in Tertullian is discussed more fully below, pp. 131–7.

[8] See above, pp. 26–7, 77. [9] Strom. 1.1.11.3 (PG 8.700). [10] *Ibid.* 1.12.56.2 (PG 8.753).

[11] *Ibid.* 6.15.131.5 (PG 9.356), ἡ τῆς ἐγγράφου ἄγραφος παράδοσις, a phrase strikingly reminiscent of Ptolemaeus' concept. [12] *Ibid.* 7.16.94.5 (PG 9.532). [13] Eclogae Propheticae 27.

G

one particularly interesting passage says: 'for just as the teaching of all the apostles was one, so is the tradition'.[1] Similarly Hippolytus prefaces the long recapitulation of the rule of faith which we have already noted[2] with the phrase 'let us therefore believe . . . according to the tradition (παράδοσις) of the apostles.'[3] That Hippolytus believed in a tradition of rite and custom deriving from the apostles is evidenced by the very existence of his work, the *Apostolic Tradition*. But in several references to this tradition he appears to include doctrine within it. He ends this work by words of exhortation: 'I counsel thee that all these things be observed by all who rightly understand. For upon all who hearken to the apostolic tradition (παράδοσις) no heretic will prevail to deceive . . . and thus many heresies increased because those who were at the head (προιστάναι) would not learn the purpose (προαίρεσις) of the apostles, but according to their own pleasure would do what they choose and not what is fitting.'[4] Elsewhere he says of the Quartodecimans, 'In all other respects these people agree with all the things handed down (τὰ παρα-δεδομένα) to the Church by the apostles.'[5]

Origen does not use 'tradition' (παράδοσις) of the rule of faith,[6] but he certainly did regard it as traditionally handed down in the Church. He speaks of 'the rule of Jesus Christ's heavenly Church according to the succession of the apostles',[7] and says elsewhere, 'In the preaching (κήρυγμα) it is handed down (παραδέδοται) that some angels and powers exist.'[8] And it is quite clear that for Origen 'the Church has the right to decide what is genuine Scripture, and what is not, but has no right to complement or mutilate Scripture once it has decided that it is Scripture proper.'[9] And he accuses the heretics on the ground that 'even in the allegorical interpretation they do not preserve the rule of apostolic truth.'[10] But as Origen never despaired of refuting the heretics from Scripture and, unlike Clement, laid no claim to secret tradition deriving

---

[1] *Strom.* 7.17.108.1 (PG 9.552). This could refer to the oral teaching and the written teaching of the apostles, but it is more likely to refer to the original teaching of the apostles and the teaching of the Church of Clement's day.   [2] See above, p. 88.
[3] *Contra Noetum* 17. In the *Apostolic Tradition* 21 Hippolytus uses the phrase 'the παράδοσις of holy baptism', meaning its conferring, which is the first example that we have encountered of the word used in the sense of *traditio activa*.
[4] *Apostolic Tradition* 38.2 and 3b.
[5] *Elenchos* 8.18.2; cf. 9.12.26, where he says that Callistus' school still continues, φυλάσσων τὰ ἔθη καὶ τὴν παράδοσιν, where he no doubt means Callistus' morals and Callistus' doctrine.
[6] For statistics of Origen's use of παράδοσις see *Origen's Doctrine of Tradition*, pp. 73–4.
[7] *PA* 4.2.2: τοῦ κανόνος τῆς Ἰησοῦ Χριστοῦ κατὰ διαδοχὴν τῶν ἀποστόλων οὐρανίου ἐκκλησίας.
[8] *Ibid.*, Origen's Preface, 10.
[9] *Origen's Doctrine of Tradition*, p. 100. See also pp. 97–99 and 101.
[10] *apostolicae regulam veritatis*, *Homily IV on Psalm 37.1* (PG 12.1351).

from the apostles, on the whole he lays less stress than other fathers on the aspect of the rule of faith as tradition.

Cyprian, whose references to the rule of faith are so faint and so few, also distinguishes himself from the other fathers whom we have been considering by confining doctrinal tradition entirely to the Bible; tradition as custom he, like Tertullian, regards as far less important.[1] In one of his letters he sets out for us in a characteristically trenchant and lucid way his concept of doctrinal tradition:

> For if ever we turn to the fountain and source of divine tradition, human error ceases and, once the purport of the heavenly mysteries is perceived, whatever was lying hid under a fog and cloud of darkness is brought out into the light of truth.[2]

Then follows the illustration of an aqueduct in which the water is failing; the way to repair it is to trace the break back towards the source. Then he applies this parable:

> This is what the priests of God should now do as they observe the divine commandments, so that if truth should have faltered and wavered in any point, we should return to the dominical source and to the evangelical and apostolic tradition, and the reason for our action should derive from where its order and origin arose.[3]

In accordance with these convictions, every single use of the *traditio* of the Church in Cyprian's works refers to some doctrine or practice which is taken, or which he clearly thinks is taken, directly from the Bible.[4] In one passage he refers to the Novatianist party having set up a bishop 'against the mystery of the divine ordinance once delivered', and to his own agents' recognizing Pope Cornelius 'according to what the holiness and no less the truth of divine tradition and of the institution of the Church was requiring',[5] but it is altogether probable that his words in

---

[1] See below, pp. 140–2.

[2] *Ep.* 74.10.2: *nam si ad divinae traditionis caput et originem revertamur, cessat error humanus et sacramentorum caelestium ratione perspecta quidquid sub caligine ac nube tenebrarum obscurum latebat in lucem veritatis aperitur.*

[3] *Quod et nunc facere oportet Dei sacerdotes praecepta divina servantes, ut si in aliquo nutaverit et vacillaverit, et ad originem dominicam et ad evangelicam atque apostolicam traditionem revertamur et inde surgat actus nostri ratio unde et ordo et origo surrexit.*

[4] Cf. *Epp.* 4.1, 2; 63.1.1 and 19; 69.3.2; 73.15.2; *De Unitate Ecclesiae* 19; *De Lapsis* 2; *De Dominica Oratione* 2. In *Ep.* 43.6.1 the word refers to heretical tradition.

[5] *contra sacramentum semel traditum divinae dispositionis . . . secundum quod divinae traditionis et ecclesiae institutionis sanctitas pariter et veritas exigebat, Ep.* 45.1.2; cf., of the same situation, *contra Dei dispositionem* (the election of Cornelius), *contra evangelicam legem* (Matt. 16.18, 19), *contra institutionis catholicae unitatem alium episcopum fieri consensisse, Ep.* 46.1.2.

both instances mean the Lord's words to Peter in Matt. 16.18, 19 interpreted in Cyprian's special way to apply to all properly constituted bishops.

Novatian speaks of the Christian faith, by which he probably means the rule of faith, in terms of tradition also. In his *De Trinitate* he declares that 'the heretics are wont to carry on a controversy with the pure tradition and catholic faith,' and goes on to say that he holds himself bound to ensure 'that no impediment may befall the truth of Scripture, nor yet our faith in which one God is set forth through the Scriptures also and is adhered to and believed by us.'[1] Elsewhere Novatian appears to distinguish between tradition (probably meaning inherited ethics and customs) and doctrine, when he uses the phrase 'you hold simply to the tradition and the doctrine of Christ.'[2] Dionysius of Alexandria, in attempting to determine the precise time at which the Easter (or, as we would say, Lenten) fast is to end, does not attach any authority to custom, even the custom of the Roman church (though he notes it) but he tries to decide the matter by Scripture and by common sense, while allowing that the Scriptural evidence is inadequate for the purpose.[3] And in writing to Pope Xystus he describes baptism in the threefold Name as 'the sure and immovable teaching and tradition begun by our Lord after his resurrection from the dead.'[4] But though here he proves himself anxious to read tradition into Scripture, we have already seen him accepting Church practice of long standing as a *canon* which he must respect.[5]

It is easy to see why so many fathers regard the rule of faith as tradition. The rule of faith was the doctrine which the Church of their day was preaching, and they were convinced that the Church had always been preaching the same doctrine; this was one of their great points against the heretics. It is also beyond dispute that the Church had been teaching doctrine continuously since the beginning, before the New Testament was written. The appeal to the rule of faith as a traditional and original constant in the Christian religion had obviously much to commend it. We can also readily understand why the rule of faith was often associated with, or extended to cover, ethics, custom or practice of long continuance in the Church. If appeal is made to one traditional factor, the rule of faith,

---

[1] *De Trinitate* 30, p. 112, ll. 1–2, 6–8: *haeretici sincerae traditionis et catholicae fidei controversiam solent trahere . . . ut non impediat scripturae veritatem, sed nec nostram fidem, qua unus deus et per scripturas promitur, et a nobis tenetur et creditur.*

[2] *De Cibis Iudaicis* i (PL 3.983A), *traditionem solam Christi doctrinamque teneatis.*

[3] Feltoe, *Dionysius of Alexandria*, Letters XIV (from the Letter to Basilides), pp. 95–96.

[4] Conybeare, 'Newly-discovered letters of Dionysius of Alexandria', p. 113 the second letter, the first to Xystus).   [5] See above, pp. 81–2.

it is logical to appeal to another, the rule of custom. It is remarkable, in fact, that this second appeal was not made more frequently by these fathers than it apparently was. Traditional faith shades simply into traditional practice. But there was evidently in the third century some uneasiness on this point.

J. N. Bakhuizen van den Brink, in two remarkable articles,[1] has pointed out that all the fathers of the early Church regarded the whole Christian revelation as in one sense a divine tradition. The Christian faith had been delivered from God to Christ, from Christ to the apostles and from the apostles to the Church, and as each Christian receives the faith so he receives the divine tradition. This tradition, though given once and for all by Christ, necessarily continues to be delivered anew in the Church as each generation succeeds the last. This concept is not only to be found in Irenaeus[2] and in Tertullian,[3] but also even in Cyprian,[4] and before any of these *I Clement*, Ignatius, the *Epistle to Diognetus* and Justin all speak of revelation in terms of tradition.[5] This tradition, which is to be distinguished sharply from traditions made by men and subject to men's judgement, is self-authenticating, and cannot be judged or compared with anything else. 'The truth is sovereign and alone explains itself.'[6] In this sense, *regula* and *traditio* are really the same thing, 'the *traditio* conceived as the living totality of the whole revelation, or of the kingdom of truth'.[7] In the fathers' conception of tradition, there is no attempt to distinguish between *traditio activa* (the agent delivering or the process of delivery) and *traditio passiva* (the thing delivered), because 'the former is only the life and movement of the latter. They can be distinguished but not separated. If we interpret the expression "tradition" in the fathers as far as possible by "revelation", we understand better the faith and the life of the primitive Church.'[8] This is not tradition in an historical, but in a theological sense. Tradition in a theological sense means for the fathers 'the content of the divine revelation which has come to them by tradition but was exalted above all traditions and was appointed to judge them and to be a norm for them'.[9]

Valuable though the points made in these articles are, they do not seriously affect our theme, because we are concerned with tradition in an historical sense, or, to put it in another way, we are investigating how

[1] 'La Tradition dans l'Église primitive et au xvie siècle' and 'Traditio in Theologischen Sinne.' The author acknowledges his indebtedness to Hägglund's article, 'Die Bedeutung'.   [2] 'La Tradition', p. 276, 'Traditio', pp. 74–76.
[3] 'La Tradition', p. 274, 'Traditio', pp. 70–73, 76–77.
[4] 'Traditio', pp. 65–67, 69, 79.   [5] 'Traditio', pp. 73–74.   [6] 'Traditio', p. 78.
[7] 'Traditio', p. 75; cf. 'La Tradition', p. 276.
[8] 'La Tradition', p. 280.   [9] 'Traditio', p. 78.

exactly this theologically conceived divine tradition is to be apprehended concretely by men living in history. What actual apprehensible forms did the fathers envisage this divine tradition as taking? It may have been possible for the writers of the first Christian centuries not to distinguish strictly between one form of tradition and another, but we today stand at the end of a long historical development during which the forms and sources of Christian tradition have been put seriously in question. We cannot adopt their innocent attitude. We must ask, what is the evidence for the ways in which they received the Christian tradition? We must inquire how far their appeal to the continuity of Christian doctrinal tradition can be allowed. One great stream of contemporary theology bases all its authority and all its claim to exclusive superiority on precisely this tradition. On the other hand, there are some who entirely deny the validity of this claim. Werner regards the appeal as 'a gross fiction'.[1] In the last chapter we reviewed enough evidence to leave the impression strongly in our minds that at least from the time of Ignatius a pattern of church teaching had existed which would fairly be regarded as an ancestor of the later rule of faith. On the other hand, we must remember that almost all the fathers of the second and third centuries were devoid of critical insight when they attempted to look back to the early years of the Church's history, and that it is impossible to take seriously their conviction that Christian teaching as they knew it in their own day had always existed precisely in that form from the very beginning. They were unable to appreciate, except to a very small extent, the development of Christian doctrine. But when we have made full allowance for this fact, we cannot entirely reject the claim for the continuity of Christian doctrine. Some continuity there must have been; the rule of faith was not a gross fiction. The Church had always been conscious of its responsibility to teach a coherent message; it was never wholly irresponsible towards this obligation. There were reasons, as we shall see, why the confident appeal to the rule of faith as genuine tradition could not remain valid much longer, but in making this appeal the Church of the second and third centuries was not deceiving itself.

4. *The Relation of the Rule of Faith to Scripture*

We have already had occasion to notice[2] that Irenaeus claims that even if the apostles had not bequeathed the Scriptures to the Church, the rule

---

[1] *The Formation of Christian Dogma*, p. 67; he erroneously imagines the rule to be an expansion of the baptismal *symbolum*.

[2] See above, pp. 94–5, where *Adv. Haer.* 3.4.1 was quoted.

of faith would have sufficed as a body of doctrine, and that barbarians were becoming Christians without reading the Scriptures by following this rule. He also says that St Paul preached to the Gentiles 'without the Scriptures', that is, without being able to appeal to Scriptures (as he would do when preaching to the Jews), for the Gentiles would not recognize the Old Testament Scriptures;[1] and he clearly distinguishes the rule of truth from the Scriptures (though it may be a distinction without a difference) when he says that everybody who followed the witness which St Luke gave concerning the action and teaching of the apostles, and who kept the rule of truth unadulterated, could be saved.[2] Ammundsen suggests that the cases in which Irenaeus approved of reliance on tradition apart from Scripture are not important; they cover the churches outside the Greek-Latin world, who have no translations of the Bible in their tongue, and smaller questions as to which the Bible gives no certain evidence, and here the case applies to all Christians.[3] Tertullian is far more emphatic about the independence of the rule of faith from Scripture. This is, indeed, the theme of his *De Praescriptione Haereticorum*, and he alludes to the argument of this book on six other occasions.[4] Having quoted the rule of faith, in the form which we have already seen as the second example of the rule in Tertullian,[5] he goes on to explain its function: 'Your faith, [Christ] says, has made you whole, not your exposition of the Scriptures. The faith has been enshrined in the rule, it has a law and a salvation coming from keeping of the law. But exposition consists in inquisitiveness and has its only glory in concern for expertise.'[6] He goes on to argue that it is vain to dispute with heretics; they have no right to the Scriptures, and anyway they will simply deny what the Catholic affirms, and *vice versa*, and the resulting uncertainty will merely disturb and not edify the faithful.[7] The question first to be determined is the truth of the Christian religion, and when this has been

---

[1] *Adv. Haer.* 4.38.2. Tertullian also emphasizes St Paul's independence of the Scriptures, inasmuch as he points out that he went up to Jerusalem to consult Peter and the others in order to see that his *regula fidei* was the same as theirs; *Adv. Marcionem* 4.2.5; cf. 5.3.1.

[2] *Adv. Haer.* 3.15.1.

[3] Ammundsen, 'The Rule of Truth in Irenaeus', p. 576. Van den Eynde appears to share this view, *Les Normes*, p. 122, though he takes a different attitude on p. 262.

[4] *Apologeticus* 47.10; *Adv. Marcionem* 1.1.6; 3.1.2; 5.19.1; *Adversus Hermogenem* 1.1; *De Carne Christi* 2.3.5. For Flesseman-van Leer's treatment of this point see *Tradition and Scripture*, pp. 177-8.

[5] See above, p. 87.

[6] *De Praescr. Haer.* 14.3, 4: *fides, inquit, tua te salvum fecit, non exercitatio scripturarum. Fides in regula posita est, habet legem et salutem de observatione legis. Exercitatio autem in curiositate consistit habens gloriam solam de peritiae studio.*

[7] *Ibid.* 15-18.

determined it is possible to decide where lies the truth of what is genuine Scripture and what not, and which is the genuine interpretation of Scripture, and the genuineness of anything else handed down as traditional.[1] The apostles founded the Church which was to be the bearer of this authentic tradition. Second-generation churches inherited from the first ones 'the transmission of faith and the seeds of doctrine' (*traducem fidei et semina doctrinae*).[2] So all churches today have the same single faith deriving from the apostles. Their unity is proved by 'peaceful intercommunion, the title of brotherhood, and the masonic fellowship of hospitality'.[3] The principle which controls these practices is 'the single tradition of the same mystery'.[4] Later he unfolds the argument that the Church taught what it now teaches even before the heresiarchs arose; it can be summed up in two of Tertullian's trenchant sentences: 'we must take our stand on the primitiveness of truth and the later development of falsehood';[5] 'that is from the Lord and is true which was delivered earlier, but that is foreign and false which was introduced later.'[6] By this ingenious proof Tertullian imagines that he has precluded an appeal to the Scriptures by the heretics 'whom we prove without the aid of the Scriptures to have no right to the Scriptures'.[7] It is possible that Clement of Alexandria's confusion between the rule of faith and his secret tradition may have arisen partly from an appreciation of the weight of this argument for the autonomy of the rule of faith.

But this argument is much more weighty in appearance than in fact. The position taken by Tertullian in the *De Praescriptione Haereticorum*, says Van den Eynde, was 'so lofty and so radical' that it was bound to evoke challenge, and he had in the end to abandon it and write a series of treatises in which he did argue with heretics about Scripture (e.g. *Adversus Marcionem*, *Adversus Praxean*, *Adversus Hermogenem*).[8] Flesseman-van Leer states that 'for Tertullian Scripture is the only means for refuting or validating a doctrine as regards its content, and the so-called prescription proof is no equivalent for it.'[9] One might add that

---

[1] *Ibid*. 19.2, 3: *quibus competat fides ipsa cuius sunt scripturae, a quo et per quos et quando et quibus sit tradita disciplina qua fiunt Christiani, ubi enim apparuerit esse veritatem disciplinae et fidei christianae, illic erit veritas scripturarum et expositionum et omnium traditionum Christianarum.*   [2] *Ibid*. 20.5.

[3] *communicatio pacis et appellatio fraternitatis et contesseratio hospitalitatis, ibid*. 20.8.

[4] *eiusdem sacramenti una traditio, ibid*. 20.9.

[5] *ad principalitatem veritatis et posteritatem mendacitatis disputandum, ibid*. 31.1.

[6] *id esse dominicum et verum quod sit prius traditum, id autem extraneum et falsum quod sit posterius inmissum, ibid*. 31.3.

[7] *quos sine scripturis probamus ad scripturas non pertinere, ibid*. 37.1.

[8] Van den Eynde, *Les Normes*, p. 124.

[9] *Tradition and Scripture*, p. 184; she is referring particularly to *Adv. Marcionem* 1.22. Hägglund, 'Die Bedeutung', pp. 23–7, discusses this doctrine of Tertullian's too.

Tertullian's argument might be formally countered by pointing out that it is only because of Scripture that we know that our Lord gave the command to his apostles to go out into the world and preach the gospel, upon which the whole of Tertullian's argument in fact rests. His argument, if followed logically, would mean an acceptance by Christians of the Scriptures purely on the authority of the Church without examination of them; the Church professes to derive its authority from the apostles and the apostles from Christ. On what authority do we accept the existence of Christ and his empowering of the apostles? To answer, from the Church, would be to argue in a circle. One suspects that both Tertullian and his opponents were united in unconsciously acknowledging the authority of the Scriptures in witnessing to Christ and his apostles. Anyway, Tertullian's method was followed in practice neither by Tertullian himself, nor by any other of the fathers of the first three centuries, all of whom appeal constantly and confidently to the Scriptures against the arguments of heretics. In the *De Praescriptione Haereticorum* Tertullian, following up a hint dropped *en passant* by Irenaeus, produced a *tour de force*, typical of his brilliance and of his malevolence, designed to irritate rather than to refute the heretics.

It must, however, be acknowledged that though the appeal to the rule of faith as an autonomous authority independent of the Bible among the fathers is only rarely and unconvincingly made, many fathers speak of the rule of faith as a way of interpreting the Bible. Irenaeus frequently stresses this point. The heretics, he says, 'override the order and structure of the Scriptures' (τὴν μὲν τάξιν καὶ τὸν εἱρμὸν τῶν γραφῶν ὑπερβαίνοντες), and, as far as they can, dissolve the limbs of the truth, as if somebody were to take to pieces a mosaic portrait of the Emperor and reassemble it to make a picture of a dog or a fox.[1] 'They indulge in spurious fantasies', he says elsewhere, 'and by their inventions they destroy the proper construction (ὑπόθεσιν) of the Scriptures . . . but the man who maintains undistorted in his own mind the rule of truth which he has received through baptism will recognize the words and the passages and the parables from Scripture, but he will not recognize this blasphemous construction.'[2] We must, he says in another passage, 'take refuge in the Church and be brought up in its bosom, and be nourished with the Scriptures of the Lord. For the Church is planted as a Paradise in this world. You will therefore eat food from every tree of Paradise, says the Spirit of God, that is, eat from every Scripture of the Lord.'[3] This conceit of the Church as a Paradise is found in several other places in

---

[1] *Adv. Haer.* 1.1.15.   [2] *Ibid.* 1.1.20.   [3] *Ibid.* 5.20.2.

early Christian literature.[1] The corollary of this is that only among Christians, and only in the Church, can the Bible be properly interpreted.[2] There is, in fact, no salvation outside the Church, a sentiment voiced first by Irenaeus, then repeated by Origen, but put into its classic form only by Cyprian.[3] The preaching (*praedicatio*, probably translating κήρυγμα) has been entrusted to the Church, which is everywhere the same and has continued so and has been witnessed to by the prophets, the apostles and all the disciples and by 'the whole strategy of God and that serious activity directed towards the salvation of man, which is our faith', i.e. Christianity considered as a consistent system and as something which can be seen everywhere working in practice. The Church alone has this faith, 'For where the Church is, there is also the Spirit of God; and where the Spirit of God is, there is the Church and all grace; but the Spirit is truth.'[4] There are, however, limits to the Church's interpretation of Scripture. Irenaeus confesses that there are some things in the Bible whose meaning we cannot know and never shall.[5] He has, for instance, no tradition of the Church about the interpretation of the number of the Beast (Rev. 13.14–18), as his long discussion and ingenious suggestions about this point betray.[6]

In a similar vein Tertullian can write that looking for truth means 'going into the inquiry as far as is possible without abandoning the rule of faith'.[7] And he accuses heretics of interpreting parables arbitrarily in a manner unconnected with the rule of truth.[8] But he does not emphasize this point nearly as strongly as does Irenaeus. The Christian Platonists of Alexandria, on the other hand, frequently insist that the Scriptures can only be interpreted according to the rule of faith of the Church.[9] Clement of Alexandria says that 'the law together with the prophets, along with the Gospel are brought together into a single interpretation' (γνῶσιν),[10] and he speaks of 'the Church's harmony, of the law together with the prophets, and of the apostles with the Gospel',[11] of 'a deposit entrusted by God, the interpretation and practice according to the

[1] See *Ep. Diognetus* 12.1–3; Tertullian, *Adv. Marcionem* 2.4.4; Cyprian, *Epp.* 73.10.1 and 75.15.1 (Firmilian of Cappadocia); Cyril of Jerusalem, *Mystagogical Catechesis* 1.9 (in a baptismal context) and the inscription over the baptistery of the small, fourth-century Christian church in Ostia, *In Christo Geon Fison Tigris Eufrata Christianorum sumite fontes.*   [2] *Adv. Haer.* 4.40.2.
[3] Cyprian, *Ep.* 4.4.3 *nemini salus esse nisi in ecclesia possit*; 73.21.2 *salus extra ecclesiam non est.*   [4] *Adv. Haer.* 3.38.1.   [5] *Ibid.* 2.41.1–3.
[6] *Ibid.* 5.28.2, 3; 30.1–3. Hippolytus' very tentative opinions about the same point, *De Antichristo* 50, suggest the same conclusion.
[7] *idque dumtaxat quod salva regula fidei potest in quaestionem devenire*, *De Praescr. Haer.* 12.5.   [8] *De Pudicitia* 8.12.
[9] See the whole of caps. IV and VI in *Origen's Doctrine of Tradition.*
[10] *Strom.* 3.10.70.3 (PG 8.1172).   [11] *Ibid.* 6.11.88.5 (PG 9.309).

teaching of the Lord through his apostles of the godly tradition' (θεοσεβοῦς παραδόσεως).[1] Heretics 'adulterate the truth' and 'steal the Church's canon' in misinterpreting the Scriptures, and they will always err 'unless they receive the rule of truth from the truth itself, and hold it fast',[2] and they have not learnt 'the mysteries of the ecclesiastical interpretation' (γνώσεως).[3] It is our duty to hand on the right interpretation of the Scriptures 'according to the rule of truth'; our Lord spoke all things in parables, and the law and the prophets are not easy parables to interpret. But understanding minds can interpret them who carefully expound the Scriptures 'according to the ecclesiastical *canon*'; and he adds: 'The ecclesiastical *canon* is the harmony and concert of the law and the prophets with the dispensation delivered at the coming of the Lord.'[4] Origen is quite as emphatic as Clement in commending the Church's interpretation of the Bible according to the rule of faith. The various classes of people who hold errors about Scripture do so because they understand the Scriptures literally, not spiritually. The errors would be corrected if students of the Bible would 'hold fast to the rule of Jesus Christ's heavenly Church according to the succession of the apostles'.[5] When heretics try to produce their doctrines from acknowledged Scriptures, then they are saying, 'Behold, he is in the inner chambers' (Matt. 24.26); but the Church alone has the right to interpret Scripture; it only does not add to nor subtract from the word and the meaning of Scripture.[6] But this sentiment is so much a commonplace in Origen's writings that it is unnecessary to cite more texts. 'Origen did regard the Church's rule of faith as separate from Scripture, but not entirely dissociated from it. The Church's rule of faith was in fact the Church's handling and interpretation of Scripture.'[7] The Christian Platonists of Alexandria, however, differ from the other fathers in their insistence that the interpretation of the Scriptures by their characteristically Philonic type of allegory, which is virtually unknown in the Church before their day, is a part of the rule of faith. This is an illusion peculiar to Clement of Alexandria and Origen.[8]

To some, this conviction displayed by these fathers that the Scriptures must be interpreted according to the rule of faith of the Church means that they are in effect 'subordinating' the authority of Scripture to the

---

[1] *Ibid.* 6.15.124.4 (PG 9.348).
[2] *Ibid.* 7.16.105.5 (PG 9.545) and 7.16.94.5 (9.532): 'the truth itself' clearly means the Bible.   [3] *Ibid.* 7.16.97.4 (PG 9.536).   [4] *Ibid.* 6.15.125.3 (PG 9.349).
[5] *PA* 4.2.2.   [6] *Comm. on Matthew*, Comm. Ser. 46 and 47.
[7] *Origen's Doctrine of Tradition*, p. 100.
[8] See *Origen's Doctrine of Tradition*, pp. 59 and 101–5, and *Allegory and Event*, caps. 2–4 and 9. Newman, when he wrote his *Arians of the Fourth Century*, appears to have accepted this estimate of allegory as true; see p. 32 of that work.

tradition of the Church. Van den Eynde, for instance, strongly presses this point.[1] But language such as this rests upon a misunderstanding. These fathers envisage the Church from the very beginning interpreting both the Old Testament Scriptures and the Gospel of the new dispensation which was entrusted to it orally, and later interpreting the Scriptures both of the Old and New Testaments, and in the course of this process of interpretation both retaining the shape of the original oral Gospel and finding this Gospel supported and illuminated in Scripture. Scripture was for them, so to speak, the crystallization in written form of the original unwritten Gospel. If they speak of interpreting Scripture according to the rule of faith this does not mean that they regard Scripture as a dark mass of obscurities and the rule of faith as an independent norm to which Scripture must somehow be made to fit. To interpret a mass of documents is not necessarily to 'subordinate' them to anything. If a judge interprets a code of law when he delivers a judgement, he does not 'subordinate' the law to any external norm except logic and common sense, or if he does his judgement will be quickly reversed by an appeal court. When Irenaeus in his *Demonstration* writes a commentary on the rule of faith, he is not thereby 'subordinating' the rule of faith to anything. Language such as this smacks of a later day when the whole subject was viewed in the light of later controversies. Again, as we shall see,[2] all of these fathers are anxious to prove the rule of faith from Scripture; nothing could show more clearly that any idea of 'subordinating' Scripture to the rule of faith was absent from their minds. The only writer who tries to reverse the process, and to prove the validity of Scripture from the rule of faith, was Tertullian, and, as we have seen, his attempt was neither a successful nor a happy one. Flesseman-van Leer emphasizes strongly that both Irenaeus and Tertullian believed in the *perspicuitas*, the transparence, of Scripture. Irenaeus believes that what the Church teaches is the genuine content of Scripture; but he does not exalt this into a formal principle of exegesis. He never believed that the Scriptures without the authoritative exegesis of the Church are incomprehensible.[3] Tertullian does in three places appeal to the rule as a principle of exegesis; but elsewhere he insists upon interpreting Scripture by itself, or by viewing one passage in the light of the whole. He can do this because he regarded the content of the rule as identical with the content of Scripture. Because of this identity of content it is inappropriate

---

[1] *Les Normes*, pp. 267–74.   [2] See below, pp. 112–14.

[3] *Tradition and Scripture*, pp. 133–9; for the *perspicuitas* of Scripture in Tertullian, see p. 176. Hägglund also denies that the *regula* is a norm for interpreting the Scriptures ('Die Bedeutung', pp. 4–5).

to regard either as superior to or subordinate to the other.[1] The whole purpose of Irenaeus, at least, as we can reliably collect it from the prefaces and endings of each of the books of *Adversus Haereses*, was to refute the Gnostics from Scripture. The digression on apostolic tradition in Book 3 is only a digression, necessitated by the fact that the Gnostics appeal to their own oral tradition, and the oral tradition of the Church must then be brought forward against it.[2] The whole point of this third book is to bring forward proofs from the Gospel writings; they will defend and vindicate the faith which the Church has received from the apostles.[3] In short 'If Irenaeus wants to prove the truth of a doctrine materially, he turns to Scripture, because therein the teaching of the apostles is objectively accessible. Proof from tradition and from Scripture serve one and the same end: to identify the teaching of the Church as the original apostolic teaching. The first establishes that the teaching of the Church is the apostolic teaching, and the second, what this apostolic teaching is.'[4] Prestige, after a long and interesting discussion of the concept of tradition in the fathers, asks the question whether the fathers were not, in dealing with this subject, arguing in a circle: 'They interpreted the Bible by the tradition, and yet expounded the tradition out of the Bible.' He answers this question by saying that the fathers in fact identified tradition with a part of the Bible, with the content of the gospels. 'The appeal was really from the Bible as a whole to the Gospel.'[5] Ammundsen similarly points out that Irenaeus speaks of harmonizing the expressions of the Scriptures to 'the main body of truth'.[6] Flesseman-van Leer makes the interesting suggestion that the interpretation of Scripture according to the rule in Irenaeus and Tertullian (and, one might add, in Clement and Origen) was equivalent to that which the Reformers of the sixteenth century meant by their expression 'the analogy of faith', because 'in neither case is meant a formal principle outside of Scripture, but the purport, intention, of Scripture itself.'[7]

[1] *Ibid.* pp. 178–80. The three passages are *De Praescr. Haer.* 12; *De Pudicitia* 8 and *Adv. Praxean* 20.

[2] *Traditione igitur quae est ab apostolis sic se habente in ecclesia et permanente apud nos, revertamur ad eam quae est ex Scripturis ostensionem eorum qui et evangelium conscripserunt apostolorum ex quibus conscripserunt de Deo sententiam ostendentes quoniam Dominus noster Jesus Christus veritas est et mendacium in eo non est, Adv. Haer.* 3.5.1. Ammundsen had made the same point earlier ('The Rule of Faith in Irenaeus', pp. 576-7). See also Hägglund, 'Die Bedeutung', pp. 14–17.

[3] The arguments here summarized will be found in Flesseman-van Leer, *Tradition and Scripture*, pp. 139–44. [4] *Ibid.* p. 144. [5] *Fathers and Heretics*, p. 44.

[6] 'The Rule of Faith in Irenaeus', p. 575, quoting *Adv. Haer.* 1.9.4, προσαρμόσας τῷ τῆς ἀληθείας σωματίῳ; Ammundsen points out that σωμάτιον means 'main body', and not summary. Hägglund ('Die Bedeutung', pp. 6–9) discusses the same passage.

[7] *Tradition and Scripture*, p. 194.

Certainly there is evidence in abundance that the very fathers of the second and third centuries who wrote most frequently of the rule of faith as interpreting Scripture regarded the content of the Scriptures as materially identical with the content of the rule of faith, or professed to draw all their doctrine from Scripture. We have already seen that Irenaeus claimed that the Church allowed neither addition to nor subtraction from the Scriptures.[1] He also can write 'but we, who follow the one and only true God as teacher and have as the rule of truth his words always teach the same doctrine about those words'.[2] Elsewhere he says that John the apostle, 'anxious . . . to set up the rule of truth in the Church,' wrote John 1.1–5, 10–11.[3] 'The idea of separating Scripture from the Church does not occur to Irenaeus,' says Ammundsen; for him, the same truth can be found outside Scripture in tradition, 'for materially Scripture coincides with tradition.'[4] 'The *regula veritatis* and the tradition of the Church are not an addition to the content of the Scriptures. The apostolic doctrine is found in the Scriptures, and this doctrine is preached by the Church.'[5] It is in this sense, and only in this, that the statement of Daniélou is correct that for Irenaeus 'this tradition is written and oral at the same time'.[6] Passages from Tertullian to the same effect can be quoted quite as freely. 'What we are', he says in one of his epigrammatic remarks, 'this is what the Scriptures are from its beginning. We are from them, before anything was different from what we are.'[7] Elsewhere he has occasion to compare the four gospels with each other. Matthew and John, he says, were apostles, Luke and Mark were apostolic men who bore the apostles' authority. All four of them 'based themselves on the same rules of faith, as far as concerns one God the Creator and his Christ born of a virgin, the fulfilment of the law and the prophets. It is a man's own business if the order of the accounts has been changed, as long as he agrees on the summary of the faith, on which there is no agreement in the case of Marcion.'[8] Again:

[1] *Adv. Haer.* 4.53.2; see above, p. 95.   [2] *Ibid.* 4.7.4.
[3] *Ibid.* 3.11.7, cf. his statement (*Adv. Haer.* 3.25.1) that in the matter of whether the 'young woman' of Isa. 7.10–17 is a virgin or not the translation of the seventy *consonat apostolorum traditioni*, because Matthew and Luke wrote an account of the Virgin Birth.
[4] 'The Rule of Truth in Irenaeus', p. 579.
[5] Molland, 'Irenaeus of Lugdunum and the Apostolic Succession', p. 20.
[6] *Théologie*, p. 56.
[7] *De Praescr. Haer.* 38.5: *quod sumus, hoc sunt scripturae ab initio suo. Ex illis sumus, antequam nihil aliter fuit quam sumus.*
[8] *Adv. Marcionem* 4.2.1, 2: the Latin of the passage quoted runs: *iisdem regulis exorsi, quantum ad unum deum attinet creatorem et Christum eius natum ex virgine, subplementum legis et prophetarum. Viderit enim, si narrationum dispositio variavit, dummodo de capite fidei conveniat, de quo cum Marcione non convenit.*

In short: if it is agreed that that is truer which is earlier, and that is earlier which is there from the beginning, and that is from the beginning which is from the apostles, then it will of course equally be agreed that that has been handed down from the apostles which will have been reverently preserved among the churches of the apostles. Let us inspect the milk which the Corinthians drank from Paul, the rule by which the Galatians were set right, what the Philippians, the Thessalonians, the Ephesians say, what even the Romans next pronounce, to whom both Peter and Paul bequeathed the Gospel marked also by their own blood.[1]

No language could demonstrate more vividly that to Tertullian the contents of the rule of faith and of the Bible were identical.[2] Clement of Alexandria, when for a moment he forgets his predilection for an esoteric source of doctrine independent of Scripture, can speak warmly of the sufficiency of Scripture. We have, he says, the Lord given to us in the Scriptures as 'the beginning of the teaching', and since, if you ask for a standard of judgement of 'the beginning' it ceases to be the beginning', the Scriptures must be the standard of judgement of the Scriptures.[3] He does not find this at all incompatible with insisting in the same passage that the Scriptures must be interpreted according to the true belief of the Church. Origen has many passages to the same effect. He says that Christ, 'when he discoursed about God, declared the facts about God to his true disciples; and because we find traces of this teaching in the written books, we possess the foundations of our own theology.'[4] He refuses a theory of some Greek philosophers about the body: 'The faith of the Church does not accept it,' he says, and for two reasons: first, it cannot be found in Holy Scripture, and second, the circumstances themselves forbid us to accept it.[5] He reveals to us the sources of his doctrine

---

[1] *Ibid.* 4.5.1: '*In summa: si constat id verius quod prius, id prius quod ab initio, id ab initio quod ab apostolis, pariter utique constabit id esse ab apostolis traditum quod apud ecclesias apostolorum fuerit sacrosanctum. Videamus quod lac a Paulo Corinthii hauserunt, ad quam regulam Galatae sint recorrecti, quid legant Philipenses, Thesalonicenses, Ephesii, quid etiam Romani de proximo sonent, quibus evangelium et Petrus et Paulus sanguine quoque suo signatum relinquerunt.*

[2] Van den Eynde, realizing this, admits in Tertullian's view 'the identity of Christian doctrine with the teaching, real and entire, of the Scriptures', though the case is not that the faith could not exist without them, but only that it cannot exist where the text or meaning of Scripture is altered (*Les Normes*, p. 123). It is hard to see how the first idea can fail to be involved in the second. Later he concludes that all the writers within the limits of his period imagined that all doctrine could be found in Scripture. He seems to think this evidence of an immature and undeveloped phase in the Church's life (*Les Normes*, p. 320).

[3] *Strom.* 7.16.95.3–5 (PG 9.532).

[4] *Contra Celsum* 2.71.

[5] *PA* 3.6.6.

in several passages in the *Contra Celsum*. The Christians expound to those under instruction, he says, what Christ was, 'both from the prophecies about him (and they are many), and from those things which have been carefully handed down to those who can hearken with an understanding mind to the gospels and to the words of the apostles.'[1] Teaching concerning God's judgement is to be found partly in the Scriptures and partly from common sense.[2] Later he says that 'there are certain secret and inexplicable systems and logical trains of argument about the dispensation of different destinies to different souls,' and for these and similar arguments 'the educated man will need to calculate the principles of the doctrine by various sorts of explanations both from the inspired writings and from the logical development of the principles themselves.'[3] This double appeal to Scripture and common sense reappears in the *Peri Archon*. The teaching of the Church, he there says, is based upon 'either the evidence to be found in the sacred Scriptures, or that to be discovered by the investigation of the logical consequences of the Scriptures and adherence to accuracy'.[4] And in the same work he professes to refute an heretical opinion 'from the authority of the Scriptures', but he also adds some arguments taken 'from the logic of reason itself'.[5]

This sort of language used by Origen can prepare us well for a closer look at one fact of considerable importance to the relation of the rule of faith to Scripture, and that is that the great majority of the writers of the period under discussion show themselves anxious to prove the rule of faith from Scripture. According to Irenaeus, says Flesseman-van Leer, 'Scripture is the instrument with which to refute the heretics, and, what is even more important, the tradition of the Church (*fides quae creditur*) should be defended and proved through Scripture.'[6] This is particularly true of Irenaeus' later work, the *Demonstration of the Apostolic Preaching*. The reader finds as he makes his way through it that it is no more or less than an exposition of the rule of faith, supported by copious quotations from the Bible which demonstrate that this rule is grounded upon Scripture. If we accept the view that Irenaeus regarded the baptismal creed

---

[1] 3.15.   [2] 3.16.

[3] 4.8.9; cf. Athenagoras, *De Resurrectione* 24: τοῦτό που καὶ τῆς κοινῆς πάντων ἐννοίας ἐκδιδασκούσης καὶ τῶν ἐν ὀφθαλμοῖς στρεφομένων ἐπιμαρτυρούντων.

[4] Origen's Preface, 10.

[5] 2.5.3. Prestige (*Fathers and Heretics*, p. 30) has commented upon the practice, widespread in the fathers, of appealing to reason as well as to Scripture, but to no other material source. For language of Clement and Origen suggesting the sole sufficiency of Scripture, see *Origen's Doctrine of Tradition*, cap. III.

[6] *Tradition and Scripture*, p. 142 n. 6; she quotes Reynders, *Paradosis*, p. 179, as describing the *Adversus Haereses* and the *Demonstration* as 'une démonstration de la Tradition apostolique par l'Écriture'; cf. *Tradition and Scripture*, p. 130.

as a convenient summary of the rule of faith, we can find several references to the rule of faith in this work,[1] and one particularly revealing passage:

This, beloved, is the preaching of the truth, and this is the manner of our salvation, and this is the way of life, announced by the prophets and ratified by Christ and handed over by the apostles and handed down by the Church in the whole world to her children.[2]

Tertullian follows exactly the same course when, as a preliminary to attacking Praxeas' doctrine, he seeks to establish his own Trinitarian position. His own doctrine he calls the rule of faith.[3] The fact of the separate existence of Father and Son establishes itself, he says, 'by the Scriptures and by the interpretations of them'[4] Then, having in masterly way stated his doctrine of the Trinity, and having exhibited the unreasonableness of his opponents' doctrine of God, he addresses himself to the task of proving his doctrine and disproving theirs from the Scriptures.[5] In particular, he discusses the question of whether we find two gods and two lords in the Old Testament and in the New Testament, and shows that both the New Testament and the logical consequences of his own Trinitarian doctrine demand that we should call Christ God.[6] And later he proceeds to examine the New Testament for those texts alleged to support their view by the heretics, 'who refuse to examine the rest of the Bible, though it supports the rule without damaging the unity of the Godhead and the permanence of the monarchy.'[7] He is convinced, as we have seen, that the Bible is not obscure: 'then it is not likely that that sort of mystery to which faith commits itself entirely, for whose sake self-control exerts itself, should appear declared uncertainly and represented obscurely, although the hope of resurrection could not convert anyone, particularly to this sort of religion, exposed to public hatred and hostile defamation, unless it was quite clear about the danger and the reward.'[8] He does not use tradition to supplement or develop the scriptural material for his doctrine of the next life,[9] nor for his conviction about the resurrection of the body,[10] though he readily allows alleged

---

[1] *Demonstration* 3, 6, 7, 86, 99, 100.   [2] 98.   [3] *Adversus Praxean* 2, 3, 9.
[4] *Ibid.* 5, *scripturis et interpretationibus earum.*   [5] *Ibid.* 11 ff.   [6] *Ibid.* 13.
[7] *Ibid.* 20: *cetera nolentes intueri quae et ipsa regulam servant et quidem salvo unione divinitatis et monarchiae statu.*
[8] *De Resurrectione Mortuorum* 21.3: *tunc quod verisimile non est, ut ea species sacramenti, in quam fides tota committitur, in quam disciplina conititur, ambigue adnuntiata et obscure proposita videatur, quando spes resurrectionis, nisi manifesta de periculo et praemio, neminem ad huiusmodi praesertim religionem, publico odio et hostili elogio obnoxiam, persuaderet.*
[9] *De Anima* 58.8.
[10] *De Resurr. Mort.* 63.9.

H

revelations from the Spirit to inspired Montanists to perform this function. The bases of his religion are: Scripture, nature, morality,[1] and he makes it clear that he draws his morality from Scripture when he says that Christianity draws all its being from heaven, 'both nature through the bath of regeneration, and morality through the documents of the message, and conviction through the judgements declared in each Testament.'[2] Even Clement of Alexandria can point out how useful a written tradition is 'as a written confirmation of the teaching'.[3] It is instructive to see, in order to illustrate this point, how Hippolytus refutes Noetus. First he quotes the proof-texts which Noetus used to support his doctrine;[4] then he asserts that the Scriptures themselves refute Noetus' doctrine, and 'even if Noetus does not understand them, the Scriptures are not for that reason to be rejected. For who will not say that there is one God? Yet he will not destroy the economy (i.e. the doctrine of the Trinity). In fact it is necessary therefore first that the proof-texts should be disproved in his interpretation of them, and should be proved according to the true interpretation.'[5] This Hippolytus then proceeds to do. Later he declares, 'There is one God whom we do not know from any other source, brethren, except the Scriptures. Just as if anyone wants to practise the wisdom of this world, he will not be able to find this unless he encounters the opinions of the philosophers, in the same way people such as we who desire to practise true religion will not practise it from any other source than from the oracles of God.'[6] No doubt his ending the work with a reproduction in rhapsodical form of the rule of faith was in order to show that this rule was the true meaning of Scripture, upon which it was based.[7]

We have already seen unmistakable evidence that Origen regarded the Church as taking its doctrine from Scripture and appealing to Scripture to commend its rule of faith.[8] One remarkable and unusual trait in Origen confirms the impression that, if we are to speak of 'subordination' in connection with this subject, Origen 'subordinated' the rule of faith to Scripture; this is that he occasionally encourages his pupils to ignore or transcend the rule of faith, but never dreams of suggesting that they should ignore the Bible or go beyond it.[9] In his *Commentary on John* he interprets the mountain referred to in John 4.21 as the pretended know-

---

[1] *De Virginibus Velandis* 16.1, 2, *scriptura, natura, disciplina.*
[2] *De Pudicitia* 1.5: *et naturam per lavacrum regenerationis, et disciplinam per instrumentum praedicationis, et censuram per indicia ex utroque testamento.*
[3] *Eclogae Propheticae* 27.   [4] *Contra Noetum* 2.   [5] *Ibid.* 3.
[6] *Ibid.* 9.   [7] See above, p. 88, n.1.   [8] See above, pp. 111–12.
[9] This point is discussed more fully in *Origen's Doctrine of Tradition*, pp. 105–9.

ledge of the heretics, and Jerusalem as 'the rule of faith (κανών) prevalent among the majority of the Church', and teaches that this rule can be transcended by the man who is 'perfect' and 'holy'.[1] He distinguishes between 'the doctrines which are kept in reserve' (τὰ σιωπώμενα δόγματα) and 'the doctrines generally believed' (τὰ πεπιστευμένα δόγματα).[2] He will occasionally reject the interpretation of a passage which an ordinary churchman (ὁ ἐκκλησιαστικός) would give.[3] Particularly on the subject of the resurrection of the body he refuses to be guided by the rule of faith. The rule held that Christians should believe in the resurrection of the *flesh* (σαρκός); Origen, Platonist as he was, could not possibly believe this, but was convinced (with some justice) that the New Testament taught the resurrection of the *body* (σώματος). Consequently on this point he parted company with the rule of faith.[4] There is no question of Cyprian proving the rule of faith from the Bible, because, as we have seen, he gives virtually no formal authority to the rule of faith at all,[5] and attempts to derive authority for doctrine and morals and practice from Scripture and Scripture alone. For Cyprian Christianity is, as it was for Tertullian, gospel and practice and law, all to be derived direct from the Bible.[6] He describes himself, in desiring to preserve ecclesiastical discipline, as determined 'not to abandon the evangelical and apostolic traditions'.[7] An almost exaggerated reverence for Scripture, amounting to bibliolatry, seems to have been characteristic of the North African church of Cyprian's day, for at Cyprian's last Council of Carthage Leucius bishop of Thebeste used the phrase 'the holy and adorable words of the Scriptures'.[8] Novatian in his *De Trinitate* makes it absolutely clear that he regards the rule of faith as based on Scripture, as capable of being proved from Scripture; indeed, the whole work might be regarded as a commentary on t͡ three main articles of the rule of faith, proving them from Scripture.⁹ ᴀͭ͡ ͭͬ contending that to take one particular view of our Lord's divinity woula

---

[1] *Comm. on John* 13.16: τὸν δὲ κανόνα κατὰ τοὺς πολλοὺς τῆς ἐκκλησίας, ὃν καὶ αὐτὸν ὁ τέλειος καὶ ἅγιος ὑπεραναβήσεται.

[2] *Fragment on Song of Solomon* 4.3, 4, PG 17.272.

[3] As in *Comm. on John* 13.44.

[4] *Contra Celsum* 5.18–24; *Comm. on Matthew*, Comm. Ser. 29. For Origen's views on the resurrection of the body see *Allegory and Event*, pp. 346–8.

[5] See above, pp. 79–80.

[6] *cum evangelio Christi et cum observatione eius et lege non stantes*, *De Unitate Ecclesiae* 3.

[7] *ab evangelicis et apostolicis traditionibus non recedere* (quoting Jer. 3.15; Wisd. 3.11 and Ps. 2.12), *Ep.* 4.1.2.

[8] *sancta et adorabilia scripturarum verba*, *Sententiae Episcoporum* 31. Cf. the expression *scripturis deificis* in the anonymous author, writing some time shortly before 240, of the treatise *De Montibus Sina et Sion* 1 (104–5) and 11 (1161).

[9] See especially 21, p. 76, ll. 4–6: *non tam mihi contra hanc haeresim propositum est dicere quam breviter circa personam Christi regulam veritatis aperire.*

be to overset 'the rule of truth',[1] he goes on, 'Why therefore should we be doubtful about saying what the Scripture is not doubtful about saying? Why will the truth of faith hesitate where the authority of Scripture has never hesitated?'[2] We have already seen that Novatian envisaged Christ as speaking the rule of truth in the gospels;[3] he thinks similarly of Moses.[4] Later he says 'since the purport and gist of the heavenly Scriptures show Christ to be God, but as Son of God, and, once the Son of man also has been assumed by God, to be believed also to be man'.[5] By 'purport and gist' Novatian means what Irenaeus meant by 'the main body of truth' to which the Scriptures were to be harmonized and what Athanasius meant by 'drift',[6] and Prestige by the Gospel by which the Scripture was to be interpreted, and what the Reformers, according to Flesseman-van Leer, meant by the 'analogy of faith'. Elsewhere he writes that 'since the whole Old and New Testament can be produced as a proof that the true faith is expressed thus',[7] and 'since the heretics are wont to carry on a controversy with the pure tradition and true faith', he is bound to ensure 'that no impediment should be put in the way of the truth of Scripture, nor of our faith either, by which one God is set forth through the Scriptures, and is held and believed by us.'[8] Between 'tradition' and 'faith' on the one hand and 'the truth of Scripture' on the other there appears to be a distinction without a difference. Finally there is this statement:

> But the way in which we hold and declare and believe this doctrine should be by ignoring no part of the heavenly Scriptures; simply because we ought by no means to reject even those signs of Christ's divinity which are placed in the Scriptures, in case by destroying the authority of the Scriptures we should be held to have destroyed the wholeness of the holy faith.[9]

Dionysius of Alexandria similarly, in his account of the debate at Arsinoe

[1] *De Trinitate* 11, p. 38, l. 21–p. 39, l. 3.

[2] *Ibid.* 12, p. 39, ll. 1–3: *Cur ergo dubitemus dicere quod scriptura non dubitat exprimere? cur haesitabit fidei veritas in quo scripturae numquam haesitavit auctoritas?*

[3] See above, p. 73, where the passage in *De Trinitate* 16 is quoted; cf. 26, p. 95, ll. 20–21.   [4] *De Trinitate* 17, p. 58, ll. 12–15.

[5] *Ibid.* 23, p. 85, ll. 11–13; *ratio et temperamentum* is the Latin behind 'purport and gist'; Fausset's 'proportion and reserve' seems to me inaccurate. *Ratio* in Tertullian often means 'purport'.   [6] σκοπός, see below, pp. 180–1.

[7] *De Trinitate* 30, p. 111, ll. 13–15: *quandoquidem ad testimonium quod ita se habeat fides vera totum vetus et novum testamentum possit adduci.*

[8] *Ibid.* 30, p. 112, ll. 1–2 and 6–8: *quia haeretici sincerae traditionis et catholicae fidei controversiam solent trahere . . . ut non inpediat scripturae veritatem, sed nec nostram fidem, qua unus deus et per scripturas promitur, et a nobis tenetur.*

[9] *Ibid.* 30, p. 113, l. 24–p. 114, l. 5: *sed quo modo hoc tenemus et legimus et credimus, sic scripturarum caelestium nullam partem praeterire debemus; quippe cum etiam illa quae in Scripturis sunt posita Christi divinitatis insignia nullo modo debemus recusare, ne scripturarum auctoritatem corrumpendo integritatem fidei sanctae corrupisse teneamur.*

about the book of Nepos *Against the Allegorizers*, leaves the clear impression that Scripture was the only authority adduced on both sides.[1] Elsewhere he tells us that we argue with unbelievers 'from secular arguments and common assumptions and reasonings', but that we ourselves rely 'on the divine oracles'.[2] We have already seen enough of the *Epistle of Hymenaeus* to be sure that it represents a development of the Christological part of the rule of faith by a number of Origenist-minded bishops, who are very careful to justify every step of their development by an appeal to Scripture.[3] The third-century work *Adversus Iudaeos* declares that if Jews were to ask a Christian of any sort, a boy, a child, an old woman, a widow, a rustic, then 'he would expound the Scriptures to them, illiterate though he be'.[4] This statement forms an interesting contrast to Irenaeus' claim that barbarians who do not have the Scriptures learn Christianity from the rule of faith.[5] During the years that separate these two writers the claim that the rule of faith had autonomous authority had quietly been abandoned.

5. *The Formation of Doctrine*

The necessity for doctrine to develop was recognized, though rather reluctantly, by the two fathers who did most at the end of the second and beginning of the third centuries to develop doctrine themselves in a healthy direction: Irenaeus and Tertullian. But before the time of Irenaeus there was no serious recognition of this necessity. Among some of the apologists for Christianity in the second century there was, on the contrary, a tendency which was, if not anti-intellectualist, at least anti-philosophic. The author of the *Epistle to Diognetus* described the theories of pagan philosophers as 'those empty and nonsensical theories of the respectable philosophers', and as 'wonder-working and trickery of the magicians'.[6] Tatian begins his *Oratio ad Graecos* with a coarse tirade against philosophers as well as believers in the pagan religions with which however there are mingled some shrewd criticisms,[7] and he is, as far as

---

[1] Feltoe, *Dionysius of Alexandria, On the Gospels* 2, pp. 111–14. Dionysius refers once to orthodoxy, when he says εἰ καὶ μὴ φαίνοιντο ὀρθῶς ἔχοντα (p. 112), but he regards as the material for discussion τὰ ταῖς ἀποδείξεσι καὶ διδασκαλίαις τῶν ἁγίων γραφῶν συνιστανόμενα.

[2] *Ibid., Miscellaneous Fragments* VIII 2 (p. 257): ἀπὸ τῶν ἔξωθεν καὶ τῶν κοινῶν ἐννοιῶν and ἐκ τῶν θείων λόγων.

[3] See above, pp. 82–3, and Bardy, *Paul de Samosate*, p. 21.

[4] Ps.-Cyprian, *Adversus Iudaeos* 10 (143), *sine litteris disserit scripturas eis.*

[5] See above, pp. 94–5, 102–3.

[6] τοὺς κενοὺς καὶ ληρώδεις ἐκείνων λόγους τῶν ἀξιοπίστων φιλοσόφων ... τερατεία καὶ πλάνη τῶν γοήτων, *Ep. Diog.* 8.2, 4.

[7] *Oratio ad Graecos* 1–3.

we know, the first Christian to reproduce the theory, invented by Alexandrian Judaism, that the Greek philosophers knew the works of Moses; he thinks that they misunderstood the sacred books and misrepresented their doctrines in the process of borrowing them, in order to make their readers believe that Moses' ideas were worthless legends and theirs the truth.[1] Hermias adopts the view that pagan philosophy results from the revolt of the fallen angels, and spends almost the whole of his short work deriding each contemporary form of philosophy in turn.[2] This is not to say, of course, that second-century writers did not in fact take advantage of contemporary philosophy to express their ideas. They certainly did, as can be seen from a reading of Justin, Tatian, Theophilus and Athenagoras (especially in the *De Resurrectione* of the last-named author). But they saw no need consciously to reckon with the formation of doctrine. The nearest approach to development or speculation before Irenaeus is the *gnosis*, or speculative and often fantastic interpretation of Scripture, to be found in the *Epistle of Barnabas*, in chapter 12 of the *Epistle to Diognetus* and in the literature of that genre which Daniélou calls Judeo-Christian.

Irenaeus, on the other hand, not only himself contributed to the formation of doctrine, but recognizes consciously that, within strict limits, such a formation is right and proper. The limits are strict because he always has in mind the unlimited licence to speculate wildly which his Gnostic opponents usually allowed themselves. In a famous passage[3] he gives us a list of the subjects on which he thinks it is legitimate to formulate Christian doctrine; it will be observed that none of them can be precisely identified as the ingredients of the rule of faith:

> But if some of us possess a certain knowledge[4] to a greater or lesser extent, this is not to be accounted for by our altering the whole construction[5] itself, and contriving some other God than the Creator and Maker and Sustainer of all, as if he were not sufficient, or another Christ, or another only begotten. It is accounted for by the process of working out the truth of those things which are spoken in parables, and assimilating it to the rule of faith; and by the exposition of that enterprise and dispensation of God undertaken towards the human race; and by the instruction about God's patience both at the rebellion of angels who sinned, and at man's disobedience, and by the imparting of reasons for one and the same God having made some things temporary and some things eternal, some things heavenly and some earthly; and by the understanding of why, even though he is invisible,

---

[1] *Ibid.* 40.1.   [2] Hermias, *Irrisio Gentilium Philosophorum* 1, *et passim*.
[3] *Adv. Haer.* 1.4.   [4] κατὰ σύνεσιν εἰδέναι.   [5] ὑπόθεσις, i.e. the rule of faith.

God appeared to the prophets, not in one unvarying form, but differently to different men; and by explaining why several covenants with the human race were instituted, and the character of each covenant; and by investigating why God shut up all under sin that he might have mercy upon all; and by establishing[1] why the Word became flesh and suffered, and by explaining why at the end of the times the incarnation of the Son of God took place, that is, the beginning took place in the end, and by expounding the end and the things to come, and such things as those found in the Scriptures, and by not concealing the reason for God's having made the Gentiles who had no hope fellow-heirs and fellow-members of the Body and equal sharers in the holy things; and by teaching how this mortal flesh shall put on immortality and this corruptible incorruptibility, and by declaring how he shall say, That which was not a people is a people and she who was not beloved is beloved, and how the children of her who was barren are more than those of her who has a husband.

This list is much less like (to use Prestige's phrase) 'the accumulating wisdom of philosophically-grounded Christianity'[2] than an exposition of various mysterious or contentious points in the Bible which are not included in the rule of faith, though it should be noted that these points are not, according to Irenaeus, to be treated in a way which contradicts the rule of faith. Beyond subjects like these Irenaeus will allow no speculation at all. He will not allow philosophizing on the question of what God was doing before he created the world, even though this philosophizing may be, or may profess to be, based on Scripture.[3] Nor will he permit the development of a theory of how the Son was generated by the Father: 'If anyone says to us, how then has the Son been produced by the Father?, we shall reply that this production, or revelation, or, in short, this indescribable generation, whatever name you like to call it, nobody knows, not Valentinus, not Marcion, not Saturninus, not Basilides, not the angels, nor the archangels, nor the principalities, nor the powers, but only the Father who has begotten the Son who is born.'[4] Irenaeus will allow Scripture alone as his source of information about God, and if Scripture tells us nothing, then we can know nothing.

Tertullian, though in his own individual way, has exactly the same attitude to development of doctrine as has Irenaeus: within limits it is proper and permissible, but the limits are strict. On the one hand one can point to his famous *Quid ergo Athenis et Hierosolymis?* in the *De*

---

[1] Allowing Harvey's παριστᾶν for εὐχαριστεῖν.
[2] *Fathers and Heretics*, p. 12.　　　　　[3] *Adv. Haer.* 2.41.4.
[4] *Ibid.* 2.42.4. Van den Eynde treats of the extent and the limits of Irenaeus' speculation, *Les Normes*, pp. 135-7.

Praescriptione Haereticorum. This passage comes as the climax of a violent denunciation of every type of philosophy, in the strain of Tatian and Hermias:

> What therefore have Athens and Jerusalem in common? What have the Academy and the Church, heretics and Christians, in common? Our education comes from the school of Solomon who himself had delivered that the Lord was to be sought in singleness of heart. Let those who introduce a Christianity that is Stoic or Platonist or dialectical go their own way. We have no need of speculation after Christ Jesus nor of research after the Gospel. When we believe, we want to believe nothing further. For our belief rests on the belief that nothing exists which we ought to believe further.[1]

This is noble writing, exhibiting Tertullian at his most condensed, using his sinewy, epigrammatic style to great rhetorical effect. But an honest expositor of his thought is bound to point out that, in a more humdrum mood, Tertullian can considerably modify this attitude (the *De Praescriptione Haereticorum* is full of extreme positions), and that, whether he is conscious of it or not, Tertullian was deeply indebted to contemporary philosophy, particularly Stoicism, as a reading of the *De Anima* alone will show. He prefaces his own exposition of Trinitarian doctrine against Praxeas by saying 'a place for discussion also must be allowed on every point so that some may be taught and provided with a defence',[2] and a little later he calls the doctrine he is about to formulate 'expositions' (*tractatus*). Towards the end of his *De Anima* he remarks: 'We have encountered, I think, every human opinion about the soul from the viewpoint of the teaching of faith and have done justice at least to right and necessary research.'[3] In another work he allows cautiously philosophical arguments a certain restricted and peripheral relevance: 'It is allowable to speculate about innate ideas in theology, but only as a proof to support the truth, not as an aid to falsehood, which should be according to and not contrary to the divine economy. For certain truths are known even by nature, such as the immortality of the soul in many people's convictions

---

[1] *De Praescr. Haer.* 7.9.13: *Quid ergo Athenis cum Hierosolymis? Quid academiae et ecclesiae? quid haereticis et christianis? Nostra institutio de porticu Solomonis est qui et ipse tradiderat Dominum in simplicitate cordis esse quaerendum. Viderint qui Stoicum et Platonicum et dialecticum christianismum protulerunt. Nobis curiositate opus non est post Christum Iesum nec inquisitione post evangelium. Cum credimus nihil desideramus ultra credere. Hoc enim prius credimus non esse quod ultra credere debeamus.*

[2] *Adv. Praxean* 2: *ubique tamen propter instructionem et munitionem quorundam dandus et etiam retractatibus locus*; cf. the passage from *De Praescr. Haer.* 12.5, quoted above, p. 106.

[3] *De Anima* 58.9: *ad omnem, ut arbitror, humanam super anima opinionem ex doctrina fidei congressi iustae dumtaxat ac necessariae curiositati satisfecimus.*

and the existence of our God in the conviction of all.'[1] Later he prohibits the heretics from using such arguments: 'In short, remove from the heretics the wisdom which they share with the heathen, so that they should hold their discussions simply about the Scriptures, and they cannot stand. Argument from general consensus of opinion or from innate ideas (*communes sensus*, κοιναὶ ἔννοιαι) will do for ordinary superficial argument, but the divine meaning is in the centre, not on the surface, and often contradicts the superficial appearance.'[2]

Hippolytus refuses to speculate about the generation of the Son quite as intransigently as Irenaeus: 'Is it not enough for you to learn that the Son of God was manifested for your benefit for salvation?'[3] But at the end of his later and more elaborate *Elenchos* Hippolytus himself indulges in quite a detailed formulation of doctrine which goes well beyond the limits of the rule of faith, and includes the nature and generation of the Word, the creation, the nature and destiny of man, freewill, the incarnation and the earthly career of the Word, final judgement, hellfire, everlasting life, and a reference to the Atonement.[4] This is a developed form of the old second-century apologists' pattern of argument, improved by a knowledge of Irenaeus' thought. The theological activity that was going on around him, both of the Gnostics and of the various theorists in the direction of Monarchianism, whether private individuals like the Theodoti, Noetus and Praxeas, or respectable officers of the Church like Zephyrinus and Callistus, had forced Hippolytus to abandon his prejudices against the formation of doctrine. Cyprian, as might be expected, leaves no room in his thought for speculation or development of doctrine at all, as far as his explicit statements go, though he was in fact responsible for some important doctrinal developments which had a far-reaching effect. Not only was his mind not of a fundamentally intellectual bent, but he had apparently been educated (as far as he received any education in Christianity) in an anti-intellectualist school. Among the headings to the material in the *Testimonia* (which Cyprian inherited rather than composed, and which represents some church at a time a little before Cyprian's day, perhaps the church of Rome about 220), one runs thus: 'It is not possible for the secrets of God to be peered into, and therefore our faith

---

[1] *De Resurr. Mort.* 3.1: *est quidem et de communibus sensibus sapere in dei rebus, sed in testimonium veri, non in adiutorium falsi, quod sit secundum divinam dispositionem. Quaedam enim et naturaliter nota sunt, ut immortalitas animae penes plures, ut deus noster penes omnes.*

[2] *Ibid.* 3.6; the Latin for the last sentence runs: *ratio autem divina in medulla est, non in superficie, et plerumque aemula manifestis.*

[3] *Contra Noetum* 16: ἢ οὐκ αὐταρκές σοί ἐστιν μαθεῖν ὅτι υἱὸς θεοῦ σοι ἐφανερώθη εἰς σωτηρίαν;

[4] *Elenchos* 10.32–34.

ought to be simple.'[1] This accords both with the reverence which Cyprian is known to have paid to Tertullian's works and also with the Puritan or 'Protestant' strain which many scholars have seen in Cyprian's thought.

Most of the writers whom we have been considering hitherto acknowledged explicitly or in effect that the formation of doctrine was a right and proper activity, but were suspicious of pagan philosophy and of theological speculation based upon it. The Christian Platonists of Alexandria, however, took up, as is well known, an entirely different attitude to this subject. Clement of Alexandria is ready to believe the old story that the Greek philosophers had read the works of Moses and had stolen and misrepresented his doctrines, and that the fallen angels initiated the tradition of philosophy by illicitly repeating to the mortal women with whom they were united some heavenly truths.[2] But, far from being suspicious of pagan philosophy, he welcomes it with open arms. There was 'a certain primitive kinship of men with heaven', and this, in spite of being darkened and uncertain, pagan philosophy has preserved.[3] Philosophy he can describe as 'the clear image of truth, given as a divine gift to the Greeks';[4] it was the Greeks' Old Testament;[5] God was known 'in a heathen way by the Greeks, in a Jewish way by the Jews, but freshly and spiritually by us'.[6] Plato in particular he admires, calling him 'the admirer of Moses',[7] and 'the philosopher of the Hebrews'.[8] The appetite for philosophy is even stronger in Origen, and all the more so because his is the profounder, the abler and the more sophisticated mind. We have already seen that he recognized the rule of faith, and even formulated a list of its contents.[9] The truths which this rule contains must, he tells us, be worked into a system (*seriem quandam et corpus*) 'either by the evidence to be found in the sacred Scriptures, or by that to be discovered by the investigation of the logical consequences of the Scriptures and adherence to accuracy'.[10] This presumably is no more than the process of forming

---

[1] *Testimonia* 3.53: *Dei arcana perspici non posse et ideo fidem nostram simplicem esse debere*; two other sections in the same third book of this work, 69 and 87, express the same sentiment.

[2] For Clement's attitude to philosophy see R. B. Tollinton, *Clement of Alexandria*, Vol. II, p. 233; Molland, *The Conception of the Gospel in Alexandrian Theology*, caps. 5 and 6; *Origen's Doctrine of Tradition*, pp. 157–62, and E. F. Osborn, *The Philosophy of Clement of Alexandria*.

[3] *Proptreptikos* 2.25.3 (PG 8.93): ἦν δέ τις ἔμφυτος ἀρχαία πρὸς οὐρανὸν ἀνθρώποις κοινωνία.

[4] *Strom.* 1.2.20.1 (PG 8.709; *Origen's Doctrine of Tradition*, p. 160).

[5] *Ibid.* 1.5.28.2–3 (PG 8.717; *Origen's Doctrine of Tradition*, p. 161); cf. 6.8.67.1 and 6.17.159.9 (PG 9.288 and 392; *Origen's Doctrine of Tradition*, p. 161).

[6] *Ibid.* 6.5.41.7 (PG 9.261; *Origen's Doctrine of Tradition*, p. 161).

[7] *Paidagogos* 3.11.54.2 (PG 8.628; *Origen's Doctrine of Tradition*, p. 161).

[8] *Strom.* 1.1.10.2 (PG 8.696; *Origen's Doctrine of Tradition*, p. 162).[9] See above, p.90.

[10] *PA*, Origen's Preface, 10. For Origen's speculative scope see *Origen's Doctrine of Tradition*, cap. VII.

doctrine which inevitably results from the exposition of the rule of faith, such as Irenaeus would call 'working out the truth of those things which are spoken in parables,' and Tertullian would call *tractatus*. But in fact, as is well known, Origen in the course of his theological works went very much farther than this, and quite clearly recognized that he had done so. It is highly significant that Origen, alone of the writers whom we have been considering, tells us what the rule of faith did *not* pronounce upon, as well as giving us its positive content. He wanted to leave himself room to speculate. Beyond the elaboration of the rule there was, for him, a further stage of theological speculation founded on philosophy; it was a stage from which Irenaeus, Tertullian and Hippolytus shrank, but one upon which Origen gladly embarked; he called it his 'secret' tradition, reserved for the intellectual *élite*, the perfection and climax of Christian life and thought. He certainly did not shrink from speculation, as can easily be realized if we consider some of his more daring flights: the eternal existence of the spiritual world; the pre-mundane fall; universal salvation; the virtual dissolution of eschatology; the wholesale application of non-historical allegorization to the Bible. A list of the points upon which he felt himself free to speculate can be compiled.[1] It was because Origen felt himself entirely at home in pagan philosophy that he was able to launch out so confidently into such speculation. His confidence made a permanent impression on the history of Christian thought. Neither Dionysius of Alexandria nor the authors of the *Epistle of Hymenaeus* show any mistrust in elaborating or developing the rule of faith for what they think are the proper purposes. After Origen, Christian theology was never again to be timid about using philosophy in order to develop doctrine.

We may therefore safely allow that, as far as they gave the matter any thought, most of the Christian fathers of the period which we are considering did leave a place for the formation of doctrine. Apart from the Alexandrians, Clement and Origen, they were willing to see an elaboration of the doctrine which was already taught according to the rule of faith, but were suspicious of any development which threatened to go farther than that. They did not want to become involved with contemporary philosophy. It clearly did not occur to them that they themselves might be modifying or adding to the rule of faith. The Alexandrians, however, perhaps because by their day, or in their intellectual milieu, the threat of

---

[1] It has been, in *Origen's Doctrine of Tradition*, p. 122. Lebreton, 'Les Degrés de la Connaissance Religieuse d'après Origène', p. 280, and Van den Eynde, *Les Normes*, pp. 153–5, would like to include the doctrine of the Holy Trinity among the subjects upon which Origen felt himself free to speculate.

Gnosticism had receded, welcomed philosophy as an aid to Christianity, and were not averse to speculation, provided that it did not contradict the rule of faith, but only filled in its gaps, so to speak. Origen, however, though he would never have consciously contradicted the rule of faith, expected his pupils to transcend it, to go beyond it, as they advanced in the speculative theology which was peculiarly his.

6. *Conclusions*

At first sight it looks as if in the rule of faith we have at last met the elusive object of the search with which this book began—the survival of original, authentic tradition within the Christian Church outside the Bible. The fathers claim that the rule of faith is the contemporary form of what the Church has always taught, handed on from the beginning without break of continuity in the Church from the apostles themselves. Irenaeus says that there are circumstances in which the rule can be a substitute for the Bible, and Tertullian maintains stoutly that the rule of truth can stand on its own feet, by its own authority, without making any appeal to the Bible. Several fathers speak as if the rule of faith were a body of doctrine or a principle by which the Bible is to be interpreted. Before we decide whether we here have found the object of our search, we should decide whether we can define the rule of faith and determine what exactly it was.[1] It is not a creed; it is not any sort of universally agreed formula exchanged between churches as a token of orthodoxy; it is not a doctrinal confession like the Augsburg or Westminster Confessions; it is not even a principle nor a universally received regulation for interpreting Scripture. It alters and develops. It is not an exact mirror of the faith as taught and preached in the first century. It varies from writer to writer and from place to place. The early formulae which precede the rule in Ignatius and Justin are not precisely the same rule as that to be found in the *Didascalia Apostolorum* or in the pages of Dionysius of Alexandria; and Origen's presentation of the rule is markedly different from that of Hippolytus or of Irenaeus. There may be continuity between the earliest form of the Gospel and the rule of faith of the second or third century. There is not identity. The definition of it which will cover more of the uses of it than any other is that which regards it as an account of the teaching of the Church as it is known to the writer who uses the concept of the rule, believed to be continuous and virtually identical with

---

[1] For definitions of it see Ammundsen, 'The Rule of Faith in Irenaeus', pp. 578–9, and Van den Eynde, *Les Normes*, pp. 104, 312–13.

the teaching which the Church has been giving from the very beginning, from the time of the apostles. Even this definition will not cover all uses of the phrase, for some writers, such as Polycrates and Cornelius, employ it to mean the immemorial practice of the Church, and not its doctrine. But this definition is the one which comes nearest to expressing the real meaning of the rule of faith.

Can we take seriously, then, its claims to originality? Can we regard it as a separate source of Christian doctrine, owing nothing of its authority and deriving none of its contents directly from the Bible? If the rule of faith included in its contents any doctrines which are clearly non-biblical, though not necessarily in conflict with biblical doctrines, this question would be easier to answer. Daniélou thinks that it does, that the doctrine of the Descent into Hell 'constitutes a dogmatic development which will be accepted by the common tradition and finally included in the creed'; he believes, with several scholars, that the New Testament does not evince a knowledge of the doctrine later known as the Descent into Hell, but that the language which is usually taken in the New Testament to refer to this doctrine really refers to Christ's descent from heaven to earth, the earth being regarded as the abode of devils, not the under-world.[1] But this is in fact nothing but a speculation. In the first place, it is only by the exercise of ingenious academic self-deception that such a passage as I Peter 4.6 can be held to refer to anything else than to Christ's activity among souls in the next world. In the second place, though some modern scholars may be able to see no reference to the Descent into Hell in the New Testament, it is impossible to prove (and it is wholly improbable in fact) that the early Christian fathers did not imagine this passage, and several others, to refer to this doctrine. Daniélou's contention can only be upheld if it could be shown that this doctrine derived directly from Christ or his apostles independently of the Bible, and was not an interpretation of the Bible (perhaps a rather 'mythical' one) current in the early Church, which was gradually adopted into the rule of faith, and so, after considerable hesitation, into the creed. But such a theory has no solid support in evidence; it is simply a theory, and no more.

It is at any rate certain that all the fathers believed that the rule of faith was in its contents identical with the contents of the Bible, and that they all regarded the rule as open to being proved from the Bible, but, with two doubtful exceptions, none of them regarded the Bible as open to being supported in its authority by the rule. The two doubtful excep-

[1] *Théologie*, p .257.

tions are Tertullian, whose attempt to make the rule stand on its own feet independently of the Bible rested upon a *petitio principii* and proved impracticable, and Clement of Alexandria, whose confusion of the rule with an esoteric tradition must be regarded by everybody as an error. We could perhaps make a third exception of Origen, because he regarded the rule as representing rather less than the contents of the Bible, though for most purposes he thought it representative enough. At least we can confidently conclude that no father with whom we have had to do would have imagined for a moment that the Church had authority to add any doctrine to the rule of faith which it could not show clearly to be well evidenced in the Bible. The idea of the rule of faith as supplementing or complementing, or indeed adding anything whatever to, the Bible, is wholly absent from their thoughts; indeed, such an idea would be in complete contradiction to their conception of the relation of rule to Bible.

It is of course true that several of the fathers of the period under discussion, notably Irenaeus and Hippolytus, regard the rule as the doctrinal part of the whole nexus which they had inherited as traditional Christianity—worship, faith, morals, practice, orders, Church, discipline, love, ethos, ecclesiastical law, in short everything that can be covered by the word Christianity. The ease with which rule as traditional doctrine can melt into rule as traditional practice facilitates such a way of looking at the rule. But to assume that this view gives the rule of faith an autonomy over against Scripture would be to beg the question under discussion. *Did* they assume that tradition in this its broadest sense which we have just outlined guaranteed the rule of faith independently of Scripture? Once again we must answer, No. Irenaeus and Hippolytus were particularly aware of the traditional nature of the rule of faith, of its continuity with the teaching of the Church from time immemorial, but they did not regard it as immune from the necessity of being proved by Scripture. Again other writers as different from each other as Tertullian, Origen and Cyprian, show no inclination at all to identify the rule of faith with tradition in its broadest sense, and Tertullian and Cyprian at least are aware of the ambiguity of this word 'tradition', and of the need for caution in claiming its support.

One more consideration must be added to this discussion. The rule of faith, if it is an example of tradition, is plainly an oral tradition. There is no solid evidence that there was such a thing as a written formula circulating widely in the Church at this period known as the rule of faith. The very variety of its expression, even within the works of a single writer, should assure us of this. As oral tradition, therefore, it is subject to the laws of history. It cannot continue preserved indefinitely in oral form in the Church without succumbing to corruption and distortion. This is particularly true of a formula which is necessarily compared with written Scriptures. It was inevitable that the rule of faith should either disappear or achieve permanent and stereotyped written form. Reasons have been shown earlier in this book[1] for thinking that the rule of faith suffered the second of these two alternatives, and developed in fact into the declaratory creed, a formula which was avowedly and unmistakably based upon the Scriptures and an interpretation of them. If the appeal to the rule of faith is an appeal to a 'collective historical memory'[2] (which is another way of putting the concept of an oral tradition preserved in the Church), then with time that memory must fade. The suggestion that it could be a sound and reliable memory as late as the end of the second century is possible, but not very likely; the suggestion that the memory could still be functioning satisfactorily by the middle of the third century is only a remote possibility. The theory that it could be still functioning reliably when centuries, when nearly two millennia, have passed, is one that brings us into a dream-world of fantasy and self-deception. This fading of the historical memory is mirrored perhaps in the attitude towards the rule taken by different fathers within our period as the decades move on. Polycrates and Irenaeus can appeal to the rule as tradition deriving from Christians of the primitive age which is not so very far from their own. Tertullian protests so much about the independence of the rule as to make us suspicious. Clement of Alexandria in order to support the rule's independence has to produce an impossible notion about esoteric tradition. Origen, Novatian and Cyprian are fervent advocates of the sole sufficiency of Scripture for Christian doctrine, and nobody after their day imagines that the rule of faith is anything but an interpretation of Scripture by the Church. The law of history was between 150 and 250 having its ineluctable effect upon the rule of faith.

We cannot therefore allow that the rule of faith is really an example of what we set out to search for. The case for the rule of faith as original, authentic tradition independent of the Bible breaks down. But this should not prevent us from recognizing it for what it is—a graph of the interpretation of the Bible by the Church in the second and third centuries. We have already argued that to regard it in this light is not to submit the Bible to the control of the Church, and that nobody in the

[1] See above, pp. 72–4.
[2] Flesseman-van Leer, pp. 188–9. She has clearly seen this point.

second and third centuries imagined that this could be so.[1] As we look at the examples of the rule of faith which can be collected from the memorials of this period, we have a guide to the mind of the Church as it selects its material for teaching and preaching, as it wrestles with the deep truths and encounters the difficulties and grasps the drift of Scripture. We can see that the doctrines which were in the next two or three centuries to occupy the main attention and to form dogmas are already well to the fore, the doctrine of the Trinity, the relation of Godhead and manhood in Christ; even the Christian doctrine of man is represented, and the doctrine of the Holy Spirit is present, though not in a developed or prominent way. There are some surprising absences; there is nothing whatever about the eucharist or about the Church, though the minds of Christian theologians were occupying themselves about these subjects at the time. Perhaps this is because the rule of faith was a traditional list, and those who witness to it would be likely to be conservative rather than innovators in giving their account of it.

Perhaps the most important aspect of the rule of faith is that it gives us what the Church conceived to be 'the main body of truth' (to use Irenaeus' phrase). The Scriptures are, after all, a body of documents testifying to God's activity towards men in Christ. They are not a rule of faith, nor a list of doctrines, nor a manual of the articles of a Christian man's belief. In the rule of faith we have a key to what the Church thought the Scriptures came to, where it was, so to speak, that their weight fell, what was their drift. This interpretation of their drift was itself a tradition, a way of handling the Scriptures, a way of living in them and being exposed to their effect, which, while not an original part of the Christian Gospel, not itself the *paradosis par excellence*, had been developed from the Gospel itself, from its heart, under the guidance of the Holy Spirit as an essential part of the existence of the Christian faith in history. 'The canon of truth', says Flesseman-van Leer, 'cannot be anything but the real purport of Scripture . . . it is not a formal principle of exegesis, brought to the Bible from outside, but the real teaching of the Bible, that is, the revelation embedded in Scripture.'[2] Materially, the rule is identical with revelation, but not formally, because 'the rule of faith is apostolic, is mediate revelation'.[3] She also suggests that the rule of faith can be reduced to 'the *regula* behind the *regula*', that is, the same thing as is expressed in Barth's definition of 'the Dogma': 'it is that which the dogmas try to express, the innermost meaning of all dogmatic sen-

---

[1] See above, p. 108. [2] *Tradition and Scripture*, p. 127.

[3] *Ibid.* p. 127.

tences.'[1] We cannot recognize the rule of faith as original tradition, going back by oral continuity independently of Scripture to Christ and his apostles. But we can recognize it as the tradition in which the Church was interpreting Scripture under the guidance of the Holy Spirit, and as such claim it as an essential ingredient of historical Christianity.

[1] Flesseman-van Leer, *Tradition and Scripture*, p. 167 (cf. p. 165). The phrase 'the *regula* behind the *regula*' is one originally coined by Bakhuizen van den Brink. The reference to Barth paraphrases his *Die Kirchliche Dogmatik*, 5th ed., 1947, I/1, p. 283; cf. *Church Dogmatics* I.1, *The Doctrine of the Word of God*, ET, 1936, p. 307.

I

4

Custom and Rite

1. *Traditional Custom*

WE HAVE already had occasion to observe that the concept 'tradition' for Christians living between 180 and 300 could include the rites of the cult and other ecclesiastical practices which were handed on by custom,[1] and that Irenaeus includes in his concept of 'tradition' not only the rule of faith but also such not directly doctrinal ingredients as the structure of the Church, the gift of love, and the commandments.[2] Van den Eynde points out that according to Irenaeus the apostles handed down in the Church, as well as a doctrinal rule, also precepts, an organization, Scriptures and various customs.[3] Ordinary common sense anyway ought to convince us that no institution as enduring, as influential and as, in some respects, closely knit as the Church could have existed for even fifty years, far less for centuries, without producing or discovering a tradition of morals and a tradition of practice, as well as a tradition of doctrine. Studies of the moral exhortations in the New Testament epistles have suggested that the primitive Church used a relatively uniform pattern of ethical behaviour and injunction which owed much to contemporary Jewish practice and something to Stoic ethical ideas as well as deriving from the words of our Lord and the moral standards enjoined in the Bible generally.[4] But it can scarcely be denied that the moral standards and teaching about good behaviour prevalent in the Church must have been formally and officially based upon the Old Testament (one has only to read *I Clement* to be aware of this) and in the early period upon the known words of the Lord and, later on, upon the New Testament when it became widely recognized. The fathers show no more inclination to

---

[1] See the reference to Van den Eynde, *Les Normes* (p. 158), above, p. 94.
[2] See above, p. 96; see also Turner, *The Pattern*, pp. 310–12.
[3] *Les Normes*, p. 160.
[4] See P. Carrington, *The Primitive Christian Catechism*; E. G. Selwyn, *The First Epistle of Peter*. For an account of the beginnings of ecclesiastical law see Harnack, *Constitution and Law of the Church*, pp. 144–9.

find their morality outside the Bible than they do their doctrine. But long-standing practice and custom is a rather different question, and it was a subject which had by the end of the second century become an observable phenomenon in the life of the Church, as Irenaeus' words witness.

We have already seen that Tertullian distinguished between tradition meaning the traditional doctrine of the Church as taught in his day and (so he presumed) as it had always been taught from the time of the apostles, and tradition meaning long-continued custom or observance in the Church.[1] The second form of tradition, which he calls *observatio* or *consuetudo*, causes him a good deal of trouble. Generally, he likes to find biblical authority in order to decide questions of practice or custom if he possibly can, e.g. whether Christians should attend the games or not,[2] or whether Christians should marry again after their first partner has died,[3] whether virgins should be veiled during public prayer,[4] what times of the day should Christians use for prayer,[5] whether Christians should pray with their outer garment on,[6] whether supererogatory fasts (*stationes*) should be extended to a later hour than was conventional.[7] Generally his rule is the essentially Puritan one, 'what Scripture does not commend it in effect disapproves of.'[8] And, as we have seen, even where he allows some force to custom, he does so only uneasily.[9] But there are two of Tertullian's works which discuss this subject more largely than any of his other books, and they appear to represent him as coming to two incompatible conclusions. These are the *De Corona* and the *De Virginibus Velandis*. The subject of *De Corona* is whether it is legitimate for Christians to wear crowns of leaves or flowers, as was the custom among pagans of that day, on occasions of festival, rejoicing or celebration. A Christian soldier had recently been put to death after a trial which resulted from his refusal to wear a crown on the occasion of a military review in honour of an imperial anniversary. Tertullian sympathizes wholeheartedly with the soldier. He contends that the custom of refusing to wear a crown, even without consideration being taken of the peculiar temptations of wearing it on a military occasion, has been universally

---

[1] See above, pp. 96–7. J. N. Bakhuizen van den Brink, in both his articles already quoted, emphasizes this distinction more than once. See 'La Tradition', p. 273, 'Traditio', pp. 65–67, 77–78, 85. Turner deals with Tertullian's account of tradition, *The Pattern*, pp. 312–14.

[2] *De Spectaculis* 3 and 18.   [3] *De Monogamia* 4.2.   [4] *De Oratione* 22.1.

[5] *Ibid.* 25.   [6] *Ibid.* 15.2.   [7] *De Ieiun. adv. Psychicos* 10.6.

[8] *De Corona* 2.4: '*Sed quod non prohibetur, ultro permissum est?' Immo prohibetur quod non ultro est permissum. De Exhort. Castitatis* 4.2: *quod a Domino permissum non invenitur, id agnoscitur interdictum. De Monogamia* 4.4: *Negat Scriptura quod non notat.*

[9] See above, p. 97.

observed among Christians. Therefore no Christian has a right to abandon it, even though he may question the custom. If he has abandoned this custom of refusing the crown, he has no right to question the custom.[1] He admits that there is no guidance on this subject in Scripture.[2] He is unwilling to initiate a see-saw argument, for and against, on the question of support by Scripture or lack of support,[3] and goes directly to the point:

> If no Scripture has decided this point, assuredly custom has confirmed what doubtless derived from tradition. For how can anything become practised if it had not been previously handed down in tradition? 'But written authority is to be required even where tradition is alleged,' you say. Therefore let us inquire whether tradition should not be accepted unless it is written. Obviously we shall deny that it can be accepted if there are no examples to influence us of other observances which we can support without any appeal to the text of Scripture, in the category of tradition alone and consequently by the authority of custom.[4]

Then Tertullian proceeds to give a series of examples to prove that traditional custom unsupported by Scripture was in many cases regarded as a sufficient justification. These are: at the rite of baptism, the renunciation of the devil; the *threefold* immersion and the words of the baptismal creed which go beyond what the Lord laid down in the Gospel; afterwards the tasting of milk and honey and the avoidance of a bath for a week after being baptized; the celebration of the eucharist early in the morning, and by a bishop and a bishop only; offering prayers at the eucharist for the dead, and celebrating the eucharist on the anniversary of the deaths of martyrs; abstinence from fasting and from praying in a kneeling position on Sundays, and prolonging this observance from Easter till Whitsunday; care taken to prevent any part of the bread and wine consecrated at the eucharist falling to the ground; making the sign of the cross on the forehead on a number of different occasions occurring in every day's routine.[5] Tertullian then comments:

---

[1] *De Corona* 2.1–3; the word that Tertullian here uses for custom is *observatio*. J. Quasten has devoted a useful note to this passage in 'Tertullian and "Traditio" '.
[2] *Ibid.* 2.4.
[3] 'See-saw argument' is a translation, using another metaphor, of *per hanc lineam serram reciprocabimus, ibid.* 3.1.
[4] *Ibid.* 3.1–2: *hanc si nulla scriptura determinavit, certe consuetudo corroboravit quae sine dubio de traditione manavit. Quomodo enim usurpari quid potest si traditum prius non est? 'Etiam in traditionis obtentu exigenda est', inquis, 'auctoritas scripta.' Ergo quaeramus an et traditio nisi scripta non debeat recipi. Plane negabimus recipiendam si nulla exempla praeiudicent aliarum observationum quas sine ullius scripturae instrumento, solius traditionis titulo et exinde consuetudinis patrocinio vindicamus.*
[5] *Ibid.* 3.2–4.

If you demand a biblical rule for these observances and others of the same sort, you will find none written. Tradition will be alleged to you as the authority and custom to support them and faith to practise them. You yourself will either see the reason which supports the tradition and the custom and the faith, or you will learn it from someone who will have seen it. Meanwhile you will believe it to be not lacking in authority to which obedience should be owed.[1]

A little later he develops the subject of finding a reason for traditional observances. 'If I find a rule nowhere, it follows that tradition gave to custom its moral support, which was designed to possess indefinitely the authority of an apostle, as reason interprets the case. It was later on to be decided that even tradition which was not written could, relying on these examples, be defended in the case of practice; the tradition would be supported by custom acting as an appropriate witness of a tradition in this case approved by the long continuance of the practice'.[2] He concludes that, in affairs where no precept of the Lord survives, the Christian has to use his own initiative in discovering the reason for a custom.[3] But in one or two places even in this work he hankers after scriptural authority for the prohibition of wearing crowns.[4] By *traditio* in this case Tertullian clearly means something originally imparted by one of the apostles and preserved continuously in the Church ever since. If some practice not found explicitly commended in Scripture has apparently the support of immemorial antiquity, it is legitimate to suppose that it derived from the apostles and to find some appropriate reason for the apostles having originated it.

But in a work which is generally allowed to be a later one than the *De Corona*, the *De Virginibus Velandis*, Tertullian takes an entirely different line on the subject of custom. The subject of this work is whether women who have taken a private vow of perpetual virginity should wear

[1] *Harum et aliarum eiusmodi disciplinarum si legem expostules scripturarum, nullam leges. Traditio tibi praetendetur auctrix et consuetudo confirmatrix et fides observatrix. Rationem traditioni et consuetudini et fidei patrocinaturam aut ipse perspicies aut ab aliquo qui perspexerit disces. Interim non nullam esse credes cui debeatur obsequium. Ibid. 4.1.*
[2] *Ibid. 4.4: Si legem nusquam reperio, sequitur ut traditio consuetudini morem hunc dederit, habiturum quandoque apostoli auctoritatem ex interpretatione rationis. His igitur exemplis renuntiatum erit posse etiam non scriptam traditionem in observatione defendi, confirmatam consuetudine, idonea teste probatae tunc traditionis ex perseverantia obser-vationis*; the verb *renuntio* has here been translated to mean 'announce' or 'declare', which is a perfectly possible meaning for it, though Tertullian also uses it often to mean 'renounce'; if we were to take it to mean 'renounce' in this passage we would have to make the sentence an interrogation, and translate 'will the theory have to be abandoned that even tradition which was not written, etc.?'
[3] *Ibid. 4.5, 6.*
[4] E.g. *ibid. 9.1–4.*

veils in public, and especially in public worship, or not. The custom on this point prevailing in the North African church of Tertullian's day was evidently that they should not; Tertullian disagrees violently with this custom, so he sets out to discredit the authority of custom. He refers to the possibility of exception or privilege conferred by lapse of time, by the importance of persons, or by local considerations, and then proceeds:

> By means of these exceptions custom gains a starting-point because of ignorance or simple-mindedness and then is strengthened in use by continuance, and so is justified in spite of the truth. But our Lord Christ called himself truth, not custom.[1]

His argument seems to be, not that the veiling of virgins is commanded in Scripture, but that the Paraclete (newly apprehended by the Montanists) has commanded it. Faith (i.e. doctrine) is unalterable, but the Holy Spirit can bring about alteration and reformation in practice, morals or customs (*disciplina*).[2] Those who listen to the Paraclete 'put truth before custom', and veil their virgins.[3] However, later in the work, Tertullian characteristically attempts to have the best of both sides of the argument by pointing out that some churches do have the custom of veiling virgins; some churches in Greece and some among the barbarians follow this custom, but also some 'which apostles or apostolic men founded'.[4] So what are we to decide? he asks. We may not condemn those who belong to the same Church as ourselves and are brothers in Christ, who share 'the right of intercommunion and the name of brotherhood' (*ius pacis et nomen fraternitatis*) and who have the same baptism.[5] So 'as is the usage in all matters where variety of practice and doubt and uncertainty prevails, we had to institute an inquiry as to which of two so different customs better agrees with the discipline of God.'[6] In former times virgins who were unveiled and those who were veiled were equally in communion and the decision was left to the choice of each. 'Truth was satisfied to make an agreement with custom, so that it should at least partially express itself under the heading of custom.'[7] But this permission has now been abused.[8] It is now time for truth to vindicate itself against

---

[1] *De Virg. Vel.* 1.1: *ex his enim consuetudo initium ab aliqua ignorantia vel simplicitate sortita in usum per successionem corroboratur et ita adversus veritatem vindicatur. Sed dominus noster Christus veritatem se, non consuetudinem cognominavit.* Compare the words of Libosus of Vaga, quoted below (p. 141), which echo this sentence.

[2] *Ibid.* 1.3–5. [3] *Ibid.* 1.7. [4] *Ibid.* 2.1. [5] *Ibid.* 2.2.

[6] *Ibid.* 2.3: *sicut in omnibus varie institutis et dubiis et incertis fieri solet, adhibenda fuit examinatio, quae magis ex duabus tam diversis consuetudinibus disciplinae dei conveniret.*

[7] *Ibid.* 3.1: *contenta erat veritas pacisci cum consuetudine, ut tacite sub consuetudinis nomine frueretur se vel ex parte.*

[8] *Ibid.* 3.2–4.

custom; and he apostrophizes truth: 'Thyself interpret thy Scriptures which custom does not understand!'[1] By this Tertullian means, as he explains later, that the Paraclete is now through his Montanist devotees expounding to the Church the passage in I Corinthians (11.2–16) dealing with women covering their heads in church in such a sense that it is to be taken as a command to virgins to veil themselves.[2] He concludes the whole matter by a marshalling of Scripture, nature, and morality to overwhelm custom:

> This is where the defence of our viewpoint lies, according to Scripture, according to nature, according to morality. Scripture laid down the rule, nature witnesses to it, morality demands it. What use can opinion based on custom be to any of these, or what the illusion of a different viewpoint? Scripture is God's, nature is God's, morality is God's. Whatever is contrary to these is not of God. If Scripture is uncertain, nature is obvious, and Scripture cannot be doubtful about the witness of nature. If there is doubt about nature, morality demonstrates what is more definitely determined by God.[3]

And he clinches this argument by a vision vouchsafed to a Montanist sister in a dream.[4]

This suggests an almost complete contradiction between the attitude to custom in the *De Corona* and that in the *De Virginibus Velandis*. But if there is a contradiction, it can be easily accounted for. In the *De Virginibus Velandis* Tertullian is in a thoroughly Montanist frame of mind. We must not easily assume that by the time he wrote this work Tertullian had left the communion of the Catholic Church in order to join a separate sect of Montanists. It is on the whole more likely that he remained for some time formally in communion with the great Church, but representing a strongly Montanist school within it; even when he wrote his violently Montanist work, *De Ieiunio adversus Psychicos*, he may still have been formally within the Catholic fold. It is only when he wrote his very late book *De Pudicitia* (perhaps as late as 217 or 218) that we can be sure that he is wholly and formally a Montanist schismatic. But in the *De Virginibus Velandis* we certainly find a Tertullian who is deeply influenced by

---

[1] *Ibid.* 3.5: *ipsa scripturas tuas interpretare quas consuetudo non novit.*
[2] *Ibid.* 8.4.
[3] *Ibid.* 16.1, 2: *in his consistit defensio nostri opinionis secundum scripturam, secundum naturam, secundum disciplinam. Scriptura legem condit, natura contestatur, disciplina exigit. Cui ex his consuetudo opinionis prodest, vel qui diversae sententiae color? Dei est scriptura, dei est natura, dei est disciplina. Quicquid contrarium est istis dei non est. Si scriptura incerta est, natura manifesta est, et de eius testimonio scriptura incerta non potest esse. Si de natura dubitatur, disciplina quid magis deo ratum sit ostendit.*
[4] *Ibid.* 17.3.

Montanist ideas, and consequently the work presents us with Tertullian at his worst, Tertullian the misogynist, Tertullian the Puritan, Tertullian the legalist. The *De Corona* is much more likely to represent the conventional contemporary view on custom than the other book. It seems clear from this work that it was the practice at the end of the second century to allow long-continued custom as proper and as possibly apostolic if it was concerned with some matter upon which the Bible did not throw clear light. It is, however, clear too that each church was entitled to make and to follow its own customs, and even to regard them as apostolic if it liked. This is evident from the records of the Quartodeciman controversy,[1] and from some of the passages which we have already examined in the *De Virginibus Velandis*.[2] It is also reflected in a passage in Tertullian's *De Ieiunio adversus Psychicos*, where he states (as far as can be ascertained, fairly) the orthodox attitude to fasting, which he intends to demolish in this book: only the days on which the bridegroom was taken away are obligatory days of fasting (presumably Fridays); legal ordinances and the ancient prophetic injunctions have been abolished. Fasting on other days is simply a matter of individual choice; there has been no imposition of a new discipline; each acts according to circumstances and seasons. This is what the apostles observed, imposing no other common universal obligatory fast.[3] Tertullian describes this as based on 'Scripture or tradition of the elders'.[4] He himself believes that the situation has been changed by inspired messages given from the Paraclete to Montanists,[5] but he also does his best to show that the different Montanist practice in regard to fasting has good scriptural foundation.[6]

From this complicated situation, in which the issues were obscured by Tertullian's Montanist propensities, we may infer that in his day it was generally agreed that, if it were possible, justification for the observance of customs and practices within the life of the Church should be found in Scripture, but if Scripture were silent on any point customs of immemorial antiquity could be regarded as deriving from the apostles and as supported by what was expressly called tradition.[7] We can find a good example of this in the anonymous writer of a treatise against the Montanists written about the year 192, who protests against the Montanist prophets' practice of delivering messages and uttering cries while

---

[1] See above, pp. 50-1.   [2] *De Virg. Vel.* 2.1, 2, 3; 3.1; see above, pp. 133-5.
[3] *De Ieiun. adv. Psychicos* 2.1-3; cf. 14.3.
[4] *Scripturis vel traditione maiorum, ibid.* 13.1.
[5] *Ibid.* 8.4; 10.5; 14.1-2; 16.1-4.   [6] *Ibid.* 10.6.
[7] Augustine explicitly formulates this theory as the proper assumption for Christians to make, *De Baptismo contra Donatistas* IV. 6.9; II. 7.12.

in a trance. What he objects to is not their prophesying, which apparently he did not regard as unusual, but their prophesying *while in a trance*. This he describes as 'against the custom of the Church supported by tradition and by long continuance'.[1] But it would be wholly misleading to conclude from this agreement that tradition was in any serious sense regarded as a second source of Christian truth beside Scripture; tradition of this sort was clearly regarded as a matter of secondary importance in which divergence and diversity between different Christian churches could easily be tolerated. This tradition did not cover doctrine; it did not even interpret Scripture; far less was Scripture 'subordinated' to it. It supplements Scripture only in as far as in certain practical matters Scripture is silent, and here tradition presumed to emanate from the apostles is allowed to speak. Whether of course tradition in each case really did emanate from the apostles was a matter of guess-work. And, as we have seen, the conjectures of the second-century Church were not always reliable.

Clement of Alexandria also recognizes that in matters of practice and custom the Church may sanction or ordain things which are not specifically mentioned in Scripture. He speaks of heretics 'using bread and water in the eucharist against the rule (κανών) of the Church',[2] and he refers in the course of his work to a number of customs in the Church, such as the celebration of the Agape,[3] the giving of the holy kiss,[4] the practice of turning east for prayer,[5] and the distribution of the consecrated elements at the eucharist so that it was left open to anyone not to communicate if he liked.[6] How far he associated the observance of such customs in the Church with his esoteric tradition is uncertain; but it is unlikely that he saw no connection between the two. Hippolytus of course believed that the practice and indeed the ritual of the Church of his day had descended more or less intact from the days of the apostles. It was to emphasize the fact that the leaders of the Church of his day were departing from this tradition that he wrote his *Apostolic Tradition*. The subject of it is 'the tradition which is proper for the churches . . . the tradition which has continued until now'.[7] He believes that the Holy Spirit makes

---

[1] Eusebius, *HE* 5.16.7: παρὰ τὸ κατὰ παράδοσιν καὶ κατὰ διαδοχὴν ἄνωθεν τῆς ἐκκλησίας ἔθος.
[2] *Strom.* 1.19.96.1 (PG 8.813); see also Turner, *The Pattern*, pp. 314–16.
[3] *Paedagogos* 2.1.4–5 (PG 8.384–5).
[4] *Ibid.* 3.11.81.2–4 (PG 8.660–1).
[5] *Strom.* 7.7.43.6 (PG 9.461).
[6] *Strom.* 1.1.5.1 (PG 8.692). This is one of the very few places in the pre-Nicene fathers where even the possibility of non-communicating attendance at the eucharist is suggested.
[7] *Apostolic Tradition* 1.2, 3.

it possible that 'those who believe rightly may know how those who are at the head of the Church should teach the tradition and maintain it in all things.'[1] Towards the end of his work he declares that it is necessary to pray at midnight, and adds, 'and truly those men of holy memory who handed on the tradition taught us thus.'[2] A little earlier, concluding his account of the way to celebrate the sacraments of baptism and the eucharist, he had said, 'And we have delivered to you briefly these things concerning baptism and the oblation because you have already been instructed concerning the resurrection of the flesh and the rest according to the Scriptures';[3] he professes apparently to be delivering the tradition of practice, in contrast to the tradition of doctrine. The conclusion to the *Apostolic Tradition* contains these words: 'I counsel that all these things be observed by all who rightly understand. For upon all who hearken to the apostolic tradition no heretic will prevail to deceive . . . and thus many heresies increased because those who were at the head would not learn the purpose of the apostles but according to their own pleasure do what they choose and not what is fitting.'[4] We may sympathize with Hippolytus' rather archaistic desire for preserving custom and rite just as they had been when he was young, but we cannot allow his contention that they had always been so, unaltered from the time of the apostles. It is evident that a great deal of the custom and ritual and ceremonial which he describes represents a development made during the course of the second century; custom and rite had not stood still since the middle of the first century, as he uncritically assumed. And if we want to know how far they have developed, we cannot avoid comparing Hippolytus' evidence with the evidence of the earliest documents of Christianity which we possess—the books of the New Testament. This is not a tradition which we can confidently regard as preserved intact independently of the Bible. Again, the fact that we can today only tentatively reconstruct Hippolytus' *Apostolic Tradition* from a mass of later accretions, interpolations and distortions speaks for itself; this was a tradition which the Church felt at liberty to tamper with; but the Church did not dare to tamper with the Bible.

Origen, in the course of the considerable volume of his work which has been preserved for us in the original Greek or in Latin translations, refers several times, as might be expected, to Christian customs and practices and rites.[5] He mentions prayers and intercessions, the eucharist, baptism, the authority of bishops, presbyters and deacons, fasting for the

---

[1] *Ibid.* 1.5.   [2] *Ibid.* 36.12.   [3] *Ibid.* 23.13.   [4] *Ibid.* 38.2, 3b.
[5] See *Origen's Doctrine of Tradition*, pp. 176–81; Turner, *The Pattern*, pp. 317–18.

sake of mortification, and several other such matters. It is not difficult
to find passages where he evinces a regard for Christian customs and
institutions as a source of authoritative tradition. He mentions baptism
in water and the receiving of chrism and the power and understanding
(*virtus et ratio*) which accompanied these ceremonies in St Paul's day,
and adds, 'For this reason the Church also accepted from the apostles
the tradition of giving baptism even to infants.'[1] He discourages the
taking literally of our Lord's command to his disciples to wash each
other's feet on the grounds that nobody in the Church of his day takes
it literally.[2] In an important passage he mentions several Church customs,
turning to the east for prayer, kneeling to pray, the manner of celebrating
the eucharist, and the words, actions, questions and replies in baptism,
and remarks that many of those who observe them do not know the
reason for them; all the same these customs are practised, 'according to the
way in which they have been handed down and entrusted by the great
High Priest and his sons' (a reference, probably, to Christ and his
bishops).[3] In another passage, commenting on Prov. 1.8 ('My son, hear
the instruction of thy father, and forsake not the law of thy mother'), he
says: 'We hear the words of our father the Scripture, but the unwritten
traditions (τὰς ἀγράφους παραδόσεις) of our mother the Church, such as
fasting on Fridays, and other such practices.'[4] Then in the *Conversation
with Heracleides* (the report of a conference which Origen held with some
heterodox bishops and others in a town in Arabia about 246) Origen is
represented as urging the bishops present when they were praying at the
eucharist to 'keep to the conventions'.[5] It is clear that he greatly respected
church custom and long-standing tradition in things ritual. But Origen is
also an unusually strict devotee of biblical Christianity (or at least of what
he thinks is biblical Christianity), and he prefers if he can to ground
church customs on biblical support. He may call the necessity of baptism
'an ecclesiastical rule', but he bases it on John 3.5;[6] and he may describe
the giving of the holy kiss as 'handed down as the Church's custom', but
he clearly regards this custom as deriving its authority from Rom. 16.16.[7]

---

[1] *Comm. on Romans* 5.8, 9. Other passages referring to the same tradition are *Hom.
on Luke* 14, on Luke 2.22a, and *Hom. on Leviticus* 8.3. See also Jeremias, *Infant Baptism
in the First Four Centuries*, pp. 65–66.
[2] *Hom. on Isaiah* 6.3.
[3] *Hom. on Numbers* 5.1.
[4] Frag. from a catena, PG 17.157. Cf. *Contra Celsum* 6.6, where Origen declares
that Jesus spoke some things privately to his disciples and some things which he then
spoke have not been written.
[5] ἐμμένειν ταῖς συνθήκαις, *Conv. with Heracleides*, pp. 129–30 of Scherer's text; cf.
'The Liberty of the Bishops to Improvise Prayer', p. 222.
[6] *Comm. on Romans* 2.7.   [7] *Ibid.* 10.33.

The most remarkable example of this 'biblicism' of Origen is perhaps displayed in his little *Treatise on Prayer*. In this he takes every single example of prayer from the Bible and never once appeals to Christian tradition in his suggestions about prayer. Further, he positively contradicts Christian tradition (if by this we mean contemporary practice in the Church which must have been known to be of considerable antiquity) when he discourages prayer directly addressed to Christ, and not to the Father through Christ; he condemns it as 'an eccentric error arising from utter simple-mindedness committed because of their lack of power to examine and criticize by those who pray to the Son, either along with the Father or without the Father'.[1] Generally, however, it is accurate to describe Origen as taking much the same attitude to customs and rites in the Church as did most of the other fathers of his period. He assumed broadly that any custom or practice which existed in the Church of his day and had existed for some time before that and which could not find clear justification from Scripture probably derived from the apostles. But he liked to find support in the Bible for such matters, and he regarded them as of secondary importance. It did not enter his head that they could constitute a second source of Christian truth beside or comparable with Scripture.

Van den Eynde notes that Cyprian subordinated tradition, in every sense in which this scholar uses the word, to Scripture.[2] This judgement is in essentials accurate, but we can detect in Cyprian's work some authority given to custom and traditional usage; he frequently refers to the decisions or practice of his predecessors in the see of Carthage and he defends his action in requiring letters from the ordaining bishops at Pope Cornelius' consecration before he could formally recognize him as Pope by referring to 'ancient custom'.[3] In almost every other case, however, he endeavours to find justification for ecclesiastical practice in the Bible, without appealing to a tradition of practice deriving independently of the Bible from the apostles. He justifies, for instance, the practice of aspersion rather than total immersion in baptism by reference to several passages in the book of Numbers.[4] He refuses to allow local customs in churches to prevail on the grounds that they may conflict with God's truth (to be found in the Bible).[5] The issue of custom (*consuetudo*) versus

---

[1] *PE* 16.1: ἰδιωτικὴν ἁμαρτίαν κατὰ πολλὴν ἀκεραιότητα διὰ τὸ ἀβασάνιστον καὶ ἀνεξέταστον ἁμαρτανόντων τῶν προσευχομένων τῷ υἱῷ, εἴτε μετὰ τοῦ πατρὸς εἴτε χωρὶς τοῦ πατρός. Cf. 15.1. He may be concerned about this point too in the passage from the *Conversation with Heracleides* which we have just noticed.
[2] *Les Normes*, pp. 241–2, 244, 246–51.   [3] *veteres mores*, *Ep.* 45.3.1.
[4] *Ep.* 69.12.3; the passages are Num. 19.8, 12, 13 and 8.5–7 and 19.9.
[5] *Ep.* 69.14.12.

truth (*veritas*) seemed to him (as it seemed to Firmilian of Cappadocia) to be brought to a head by the action of Stephen, bishop of Rome, in readmitting already baptized heretics to the Church without rebaptizing them. Over and over again during the course of this controversy Cyprian refused to admit that the force of custom unsupported by Scripture constituted any argument at all in favour of a practice. 'We are not here making rules about custom, but vindicating the right by reason.'[1] Some people, he says, allege custom as a support for rebaptizing: 'As if custom were greater than truth! . . . And let nobody say "We follow that which we have received from the apostles" '; for Cyprian 'evangelical authority' and 'apostolic tradition' are to be found in the New Testament.[2] 'And custom, which has crept into the practice of some people, should not prevent truth prevailing and conquering. For custom unsupported by truth is merely antiquity in error.'[3] Those faithful henchmen of Cyprian, the bishops at his last Council of Carthage, echo this sentiment. 'The Lord in the gospel,' says Libosus bishop of Vaga, 'says I am the truth. He did not say, I am custom, and so once the truth has been revealed custom must give way to truth, so that even if in the past anybody used not to baptize heretics in the church, now he must begin to baptize them.'[4] And Felix bishop of Buslacenae declared: 'No one should prefer custom to reason and truth by readmitting heretics without the Church's baptism, because reason and truth always cancel out custom.'[5] Bayard, the editor of Cyprian's letters, makes the comment upon Cyprian's epigram *consuetudo sine veritate vetustas erroris est* that 'Unhappily for the train of argument of St Cyprian, the Pope's opinion had on its side truth as well as custom.'[6] The sentiment of Christian posterity has certainly supported the practice of Stephen against the practice of Cyprian.[7] But this is a side-issue. Cyprian thought that he had Scripture on his side. Stephen apparently, as we shall see,[8] thought that he had tradition continued intact from the apostles on his. What concerns our

---

[1] *Ep.* 71.3.1: *Non est autem de consuetudine praescribendum sed ratione vincendum.*
[2] *Ep.* 73.13.1, 3; 15.2.
[3] *Ep.* 74.9.1: *nec consuetudo quae apud quosdam obrepserat impedire debet quo minus veritas praevaleat et vincat. Nam consuetudo sine veritate vetustas erroris est.* Compare our examination of Cyprian's conception of tradition in doctrine above, pp. 99–100.
[4] *Sententiae Episcoporum* 30: *in evangelio Dominus ego sum, inquit, veritas. Non dixit, ego sum consuetudo; itaque veritate manifestata cedat consuetudo veritati, ut etsi in praeteritum quis in ecclesia haereticos non baptizabat, nunc baptizare incipiat.*
[5] *Sent. Ep.* 63: *in haereticis sine ecclesiae baptismo admittendis nemo consuetudinem rationi et veritati praeponat, quia consuetudinem ratio et veritas semper excludit.* Cf. 28 and 77.   [6] Bayard on *Ep.* 74.9.2, *in loc.*
[7] The Roman Catholic church today formally agrees with Stephen's judgement, but in practice it bewilders non-Roman Catholics by apparently supporting Cyprian.
[8] See below, pp. 152–3.

theme is not, was Cyprian right in seeing rebaptism ordained in Scripture, nor, was Stephen right in imagining that his practice went back to the apostles; it is in fact highly likely that both these judgements were wrong. The question is, supposing that there were in this case a clash between tradition and Scripture, was Cyprian right in preferring Scripture to tradition? Stephen may not have seen the affair as a clash between Scripture and tradition, but Cyprian certainly did. In view of the attitude towards tradition which we have found prevailing already in this period, it is difficult to deny that Cyprian and Firmilian, once they were convinced that this affair involved a clash between Scripture and tradition, took the right line. As an authority for Christian truth, tradition simply cannot compare with Scripture, though tradition may have its own authority within its own limited sphere. It is quite possible that, in a calmer moment, Cyprian would have admitted this last proposition, as (in one of his rare moments of calm) Tertullian did.

Cyprian's opponent and contemporary, the anonymous author of *De Rebaptismate*, expresses himself several times on the subject of the strength of custom. He declares that the practice of not rebaptizing those who return to the Church from heresy is done 'by very old custom and ecclesiastical tradition';[1] he goes on to suggest as a wise counsel that if any practice is in dispute, it should be rejected 'if it be judged against the primitive and memorable and most venerable practice of all the saints and faithful who have run their course'.[2] He proposes that the disputants should, without disturbing current custom, come together to discuss the matter 'so that we may introduce a manner of acting in the church and a most wholesome practice and one that shall bring harmony to all the brethren'.[3] To disturb the long-standing custom of the Church would be 'the greatest inconvenience and loss for our most holy mother the Church'.[4] He argues strenuously from Scripture in order to support his position, but adds finally 'although this custom even by itself ought to occupy a special position in the minds of men who have the fear of God and are humble'.[5] Language such as this is quite consistent with the general attitude to custom which we have found in the fathers and wholly incompatible with the theory that unwritten custom from the

---

[1] *vetustissima consuetudine ac traditione ecclesiastica, De Rebapt.* 1(69).

[2] *si contra priscam et memorabilem cunctorum emeritorum sanctorum et fidelium solemnissimam observationem indicatur, ibid.* 1(70).

[3] *ut agendi in ecclesia formam et consuetudinem saluberrimam atque pacificam universis fratribus insinuemus, ibid.* 1(71).

[4] *maximum incommodum et dispendium sanctissimae matris ecclesiae, ibid.* 6(77).

[5] *quamquam haec consuetudo etiam sola deberet apud homines timorem Dei habentes et humiles praecipuum locum obtinere, ibid.* 19(92); cf. 15(89).

apostles (the author of *De Rebaptismate* does not claim apostolic authority for the practice which he favours) is binding on all as part of the original deposit of equal value with Scripture.

Novatian, though, as we have seen,[1] he does not envisage the rule of faith as in any sense independent of Scripture, once in the comparatively short compass of his extant works appeals to ecclesiastical practice. 'If Christ is only a man,' he says, 'why is a man invoked as a mediator in prayers, since the invocation of a man must be deemed useless for supplying salvation?'[2] We have seen already how Pope Cornelius invoked the custom (κανών) of the Church against the integrity of Novatian's initiation into Christianity,[3] and that the anonymous author of the *Epistola Clementis* used the same concept.[4] Dionysius of Alexandria, as we have also seen,[5] described as a 'formula and rule received from the men of old' the form of words which he used to end the great prayer in the eucharist. He uses exactly the same phrase in a different order ('rule and formula') for the precedent which he inherited from Heraclas, his predecessor in the see of Alexandria[6] in dealing with perverts to heresy who ask to return to the Church. We have seen how he proceeded in attempting to determine from Scripture and from common sense, but without reference to long-standing custom, the point at which the Lenten fast should end.[7] In one of his letters to Stephen, which have survived only in an Armenian version, he throws a little more light upon his attitude to this subject. It is evident that he sided against the Pope in the controversy about rebaptism, though not very violently. He argues that human customs can and do change. But any custom that had its origin with the apostles must be observed by the Church today. Later customs should be ignored.[8] Apparently Dionysius was not impressed by Stephen's claim that his practice of not rebaptizing returning heretics

---

[1] See above, pp. 72–3, 90.
[2] *De Trinitate* 14, p. 46, l. 23–p. 47, l. 2: *si homo tantummodo Christus, cur homo in orationibus mediator invocatur, cum invocatio hominis ad praestandam salutem inefficax iudicetur?* This incidentally seems to rule out the invocation of saints.
[3] See above, p. 81.
[4] See above, pp. 77–8.
[5] See above, pp. 81–2.
[6] Feltoe, *Dionysius of Alexandria, Letters* V 2, p. 53.
[7] See above, p. 100.
[8] F. C. Conybeare, 'Newly discovered letters of Dionysius of Alexandria', p. 112. The second letter reproduced by Conybeare (p. 113), which is to Stephen's successor, Xystus, suggests that the controversy ended in a compromise, whereby Dionysius conceded that returning heretics were only to have hands laid upon them, but were not to be rebaptized, and Xystus conceded that those who had been baptized only in the name of the Son should be rebaptized with a full formula; Stephen probably held that these last were properly baptized. Van den Eynde has some remarks about Dionysius' attitude to ecclesiastical customs, *Les Normes*, pp. 256–7.

went back to the apostles. Dionysius therefore does not seem to have differed markedly from the other fathers of the period on the question of custom and rite. If a tradition on these matters believed to derive from the apostles existed, it was to be followed; in other cases, each church could please itself. But the tradition of custom and rite was clearly to him an entirely secondary concern.[1]

2. The Tradition of the See of Rome

There is one particular example among all the instances of the observance of traditional customs in the early Church which demands special attention, even though the subject is intensely controversial, and that is the tradition of the see of Rome. There can be no doubt that from a very early period, certainly as early as the time of Irenaeus and probably from a much earlier period, a special respect was accorded to the church of Rome by Christians in the west, and probably by many Christians in the east too. The subject of this investigation precludes us from entering upon the very difficult and delicate topic of the authority or the jurisdiction of the Roman church during the period with which we are concerned, except in as far as this topic involves the main subject with which we are concerned; this is, the possibility of the Roman church's having preserved during this period some original, authentic tradition, either of doctrine or of practice, independent of the Bible, but deriving from our Lord or his apostles.

We know that Irenaeus regarded the church of Jerusalem as the original mother-church of all other churches, and as having thereby a peculiar authority, for in one place, after quoting extensively from the first four chapters of Acts, he says, 'These are the utterances of the church from which every other church had its origin; these are the utterances of the citizens of the metropolis of the new covenant.'[2] But he refers several times also to the church of Rome with great respect. There is one passage above all others to which the attention of scholars has been attracted and round which discussion has raged. We must give it in full:

> It is therefore open to all who want to see the truth to observe in every church the tradition of the apostles manifested in the whole world, and we can enumerate those who were set up by the apostles as bishops in the churches and their succession-lists (*successiones*) down to our-

[1] Turner comes to a very similar conclusion, *The Pattern*, pp. 319–20.

[2] *Adv. Haer.* 3.12.5: αὗται φωναὶ τῆς ἐκκλησίας ἐξ ἧς πᾶσα ἔσχηκεν ἐκκλησία τὴν ἀρχήν· αὗται φωναὶ τῆς μητροπόλεως τῶν τῆς καινῆς διαθήκης πολιτῶν. This point is taken by P. Nautin, 'Irenée "Adv. Haer." III 3.2, église de Rome ou église universelle?', p. 55.

selves. . . . Indeed, if the apostles had known hidden mysteries which they were in the habit of teaching to the perfect separately and clandestinely from the rest, they would have delivered them above all to the men to whom they were also committing the churches themselves. . . . But because it is a very long task to retail the succession-lists of all the churches in a book of this size, we will set down the tradition of the very great and very ancient church, known to all, founded and ordered by the two very glorious apostles, Peter and Paul, the church of Rome; this tradition it has from the apostles, and this faith has been declared to men by the successions of bishops and has come down to us. Thereby we shall refute all those who for any reason at all, for evil self-satisfaction, for empty glory, or because of blindness and wrong opinion, believe otherwise than as they should. For the whole Church, that is, those who are everywhere believers, cannot fail to agree with that church, on account of its commanding position of leadership, in which the tradition which derives from the apostles is perpetually preserved by those who come from all quarters.[1]

For Irenaeus, the church of Rome is a good church for those who want to discover the true tradition because it is very ancient and was founded by two apostles, Peter and Paul, and because in its commanding position it can collect the different accounts of tradition held by all the other churches. Irenaeus consistently speaks of both Peter and Paul as founding the Roman church and never connects the importance of the Roman church with our Lord's words to Peter recorded in the gospels. Directly after this passage he gives the succession-list of the bishops of Rome.[2] It is evident that the church of Rome is judged to be sound in doctrine because it preserves the tradition collected from the whole Church, and not *vice versa*; the words 'cannot fail to agree' (*necesse est . . . convenire*) in the passage just quoted express a necessity of logic and not of law. Shortly afterwards[3] Irenaeus adduces Polycarp of Smyrna as another witness to the true apostolic tradition, in notable opposition to the Gnostics, parallel with but independent of the Roman church.

A noteworthy attempt, however, to quench the whole controversy over this passage *pulveris exigui iactu* has recently been made in a remarkable article by P. Nautin, already referred to. He would translate the last sentence of the passage which has just been quoted thus:

For the whole Church, that is the faithful who are everywhere, must because of its pre-eminent authority agree with that Church in which

---

[1] See Appendix B for a discussion of this passage, *Adv. Haer.* 3.3.1.
[2] *Adv. Haer.* 3.3.2, 3. [3] *Ibid.* 3.3.4.

K

the tradition which comes from the apostles is preserved by those who come from everywhere.

In other words, Nautin believes that Irenaeus is not appealing to the tradition of the church of Rome, but to the tradition of the whole Church, in contrast to the partial and corrupt tradition of heretical sects. This is an appeal which Irenaeus makes over and over again.[1] The reason why Irenaeus gives the succession-list of the Roman church and no other was because this was the only succession-list which he knew. He could not have given the lists of Ephesus, nor of Antioch, nor of Smyrna; but he had Hegesippus' Roman list.[2] Nautin expressly denies that Irenaeus saw each church as holding the unity of the faith simply by reason of its unity with the church of Rome; its unity in the faith was guaranteed only because it could trace its institution back to the apostles.[3] His argument in a word is this: 'The demonstrative power of the Roman episcopal succession does not come to it from its being Roman, but from its being an *episcopal succession which goes back to the apostles*, as is the case with others; and what Irenaeus is looking for in it is an *example* illustrating *the preservation of the tradition of the apostles in the universal church*.'[4] It may well be that this interesting suggestion is the right one, and that Irenaeus in this much-debated passage is not after all saying anything whatever about the value of the tradition of the church of Rome.

It must of course also be remembered that the limitation which we have already observed as inevitable for all oral tradition applies just as strongly to the tradition of the Roman church in Irenaeus' day. It is subject to the advance of time. It is impossible to assume that if this tradition remained permanently unwritten the laws of history ceased to operate in its case in such a way that it was immune from the threat of corruption and uncertainty to which every decade added weight. The tradition of which Irenaeus was writing in the passage which we have just examined was a doctrinal one. We have already seen, in glancing at the Quartodeciman controversy,[5] how much weight Irenaeus attached to the tradition of custom or rite in the Roman church. He regarded the Roman church as having preserved the correct manner of deciding on what day the Easter festival should be celebrated, but he thought that matters such as these were of such secondary importance that each church could afford to observe different customs without disturbing the bond of intercommunion; in other words, he took the normal attitude of the Church of his day towards custom, and apparently made no exception in the case of the

---

[1] Nautin, 'Irenée', pp. 37–40.   [2] *Ibid.* p. 54.   [3] *Ibid.* p. 55.
[4] *Ibid.* p. 59.   [5] See above, pp. 50–1.

church of Rome. But we may conjecture that in the action of Pope Victor in threatening to excommunicate those who disagreed with him[1] on this point we have the first known example in history of the bishop of Rome attempting to compel other churches to accept the tradition of his church just because it is the church of Rome, a church founded by Peter and Paul.[2] It is significant that such an attempt should have been made; it is equally significant that the attempt was resisted.

Tertullian in the course of his works makes several references to the church of Rome. Reproducing Irenaeus' example of appealing to the succession of bishops in the various churches as a guarantee of the genuine derivation of their doctrine from the apostles, he instances Polycarp of Smyrna who was appointed bishop by the apostle John (an error, for Polycarp did not claim to have been appointed directly by John) and Clement, who was ordained bishop of the Romans by Peter (a statement no less doubtful);[3] earlier he has mentioned Peter as called a rock for the sake of building the Church and given the keys of the kingdom of heaven and the power of loosing and binding both in heaven and on earth, and has paralleled with him John who was given the privilege of leaning on Jesus' breast, of first recognizing Judas as the traitor and of stepping into the place of Jesus as the son of Mary.[4] Elsewhere he similarly parallels the church of the Romans, founded by Peter and Paul, with the churches founded by John.[5] In another place he writes, 'For although you may think that heaven has hitherto been closed, remember that the Lord bequeathed its keys here to Peter and through him to the Church, these keys which everybody who here survives prosecution and confession will carry with him.'[6] The same thought of Peter as the channel through whom example or privilege was given to the whole Church occurs in a very elliptical and concentrated passage, where Tertullian says, of Peter, 'I presume that he was only once married because of the Church in which Christ was destined to establish on him all grades of ordained persons taken from the singly married';[7] the

---

[1] Eusebius, *HE* 5.24.9–18.
[2] For Van den Eynde's views about Victor, see *Les Normes*, pp. 191–2.
[3] *De Praescr. Haer.* 32.2.
[4] *Ibid.* 22.4, 5.
[5] *Adv. Marcionem* 4.5.1, 2; in 4.13.6 he refers to Peter again, but the passage is irrelevant to our theme.
[6] *Scorpiace* 10.8: *nam etsi adhuc clausum putas caelum, memento claves eius hic dominum Petro et per eum ecclesiae reliquisse, quas hic unusquisque interrogatus atque confessus feret secum.* Compare Tertullian's tremendous words addressed to the Christian: *tota paradisi clavis tuus sanguis est, De Anima* 55.4.5.
[7] *De Monogamia* 8.3: *monogamum praesumo per ecclesiam qua super illum omnem gradum ordinis de monogamis erat collocaturus.*

Church, and therefore the clergy, were founded on Peter; but only the singly married could be ordained; therefore Peter must have been singly married. He can say of Valentinus 'he broke off from the Church of the true rule',[1] but there is no reason to think that the Roman church (which was the part of the Church from which Valentinus broke off, though Tertullian does not say so in this passage) was in Tertullian's eyes in any peculiar or privileged way the church of the true rule; presumably other orthodox churches were equally churches, or part of the Church, of the true rule. But Tertullian's most significant reference to the church of Rome occurs in the *De Praescriptione Haereticorum*. He bids the reader look at the churches where the apostles actually taught and to which they wrote letters which are now read there, first Corinth, then Philippi, then Ephesus, and then:

> But if you are near Italy, you have Rome, from which authority is available for us also.[2] How happy is that church for which the apostles poured out all their teaching as they poured out their blood, where Peter was put on a level with the Lord in his suffering,[3] where Paul was crowned with the same death as John,[4] where the apostle John after he had been plunged in boiling oil and had endured no harm was banished to an island![5]

Tertullian then gives a brief summary of the teaching of the church of Rome—one God, Creator of the universe, Christ Jesus from the Virgin Mary the Son of the Creator God, the resurrection of the flesh, the law and the prophets with the evangelical literature—all of it deliberately anti-Gnostic. Then he says:

> From this source it drinks its religion; this religion it marks with water, clothes with the Holy Spirit, feeds with the eucharist, exhorts to martyrdom.[6]

---

[1] *Adv. Valentinianos* 4: *de ecclesia authenticae regulae abrupit.*
[2] I.e. for Christians in North Africa.
[3] I.e. was crucified, as the Lord was.
[4] I.e. was beheaded, as was John the Baptist.
[5] *De Praescr. Haer.* 36.2, 3: *si autem Italiae adiaces, habes Romam unde nobis quoque auctoritas praesto est. ista quam felix ecclesia cui totam doctrinam apostoli cum sanguine suo profuderunt, ubi Petrus passioni dominicae adaequatur, ubi Paulus Johannis exitu coronatur, ubi apostolus Johannes posteaquam in oleum igneum demersus nihil passus est, in insulam relegatur.*
[6] *De Praescr. Haer.* 36.5: *inde potat fidem; eam aqua signat, sancto spiritu vestit, eucharistia pascit, martyrium exhortatur.* In this passage *fides* must virtually mean 'faithful believers'. I have printed *exhortatur* here, encouraged to do so by that expert Tertullianist the Rev. Dr E. Evans, who points out in a private communication that Oehler and Refoulé (in the edition du Cerf 1957) adopt this reading. But Refoulé in the *Corpus Christianorum* edition of this book and Bakhuizen van den Brink (Vol. II of *Scriptores Primaevi* [*sic*]) inexplicably allow *exhorbatur* in their texts.

This is only to say that Tertullian takes in most of his work exactly the same viewpoint as Irenaeus on the church of Rome, saving that he does not speak of its *potentior principalitas*. The advantages enjoyed by it are, of course, historical, not dogmatic; and legend has already begun to be busy about its history.

But, as is well known, in his latest work, the *De Pudicitia*, Tertullian betrays a marked antipathy towards some bishop, and most scholars appear to allow that this bishop was Callistus, bishop of Rome from 217 to 222. Some[1] have adopted the view that this object of Tertullian's intense dislike was the current bishop of Carthage, perhaps Agrippinus, who is known to have held a council in Carthage about the year 220. But at one point in this work Tertullian accuses his victim of 'alleging false witness about *his* apostle';[2] the apostle is certainly Peter, so the bishop is probably Peter's successor, Callistus. Again, Tertullian is particularly indignant that the target of his invective should have appealed to Hermas' *Shepherd* in order to support the offending policy,[3] and it is rather more likely that a bishop of Rome should appeal to a work which was written for and in the church of Rome than that a bishop of Carthage should. Further, Tertullian calls his opponent 'apostolic man' sarcastically, a gibe which would have been rather pointless applied to the bishop of Carthage;[4] there are also references to confessors, and particularly confessors in mines, being supposed to have the power to forgive sins, and Tertullian sneers at the shabby and shady character of some confessors.[5] This suggests Callistus' experience as a confessor in the mines of Sardinia, and also his unfortunate financial vicissitudes.[6] Finally, we know that Callistus did institute a new policy of admitting to communion (after a proper period of penance) people guilty of fornication and adultery, and it is very clear that this is in Tertullian's eyes the offence of the bishop against whom his vilification is directed. If we may assume that this conjecture is correct, then we can draw some tentative conclusions about the claims that Callistus was making as bishop of Rome.[7] Tertullian

[1] E.g. E. W. Benson, *Cyprian, His Life, His Times, His Work*, pp. 30–31, Esser in 1908 (see D'Alès, *L'Édit de Calliste*, p. 229 n.), W. Telfer, *The Forgiveness of Sins*, pp. 62 and 67, and Von Campenhausen, *Kirchliches Amt*, pp. 251, 259 n. 5.

[2] *De Pudicitia* 16.22: *ut falsum testimonium recitet de apostolo eius.* But the *eius* could refer to the Holy Spirit who has just been mentioned.

[3] *Ibid.* 10.12; cf. 13.7. In his early period Tertullian had referred to this book without loss of equanimity (*De Oratione* 16).

[4] *Ibid.* 21.5.

[5] *Ibid.* 22.1, 2, 3.

[6] See Hippolytus, *Elenchos* 9.10–21, and the chapter on Callistus in Prestige, *Fathers and Heretics*.

[7] The question of whether Callistus was *innovating* in admitting people who had committed sins of this grave category to communion after penance is a much disputed

calls him 'chief pontiff and bishop of bishops',[1] but it is wholly unlikely that Callistus was claiming these titles for himself; after all, Tertullian also claimed ironically that his opponent was a praetor, a claim which is certainly not a serious one. But when we find Tertullian saying that the apostles had both power of discipline (*disciplina*) and special authority (*potestas*), we may be nearer our mark; this special authority enabled them to do exceptional things, such as raising the dead, restoring the sick and bringing on inflictions. But in Tertullian's view the bishops who succeeded the apostles have power of discipline but no special authority.[2] Next, Tertullian argues that the Lord's words to St Peter in Matt. 16.18–19 conferred power on Peter personally and on him alone, that he exercised this power, and that it did not extend to 'irremissible' sins: 'I now inquire about your view, and ask how you have stolen the Church's right. Is it because the Lord said to Peter [here he quotes the Lord's words to Peter recorded in Matt. 16.18 f.] ... for that reason you assume that the power of loosing and binding has descended to you, *id est ad omnem ecclesiam Petri propinquam?*'[3] The last words can be taken to mean a number of different things.[4] It could mean the Roman church (Harnack), or every church deriving its apostolicity through Rome, and not through other apostolic foundations such as Ephesus or Jerusalem (Caspar), or the whole Church as connected with or attached to Peter (Koch). Van den Eynde chooses the third alternative, and deduces from it that Callistus was at that time claiming to be 'the first bishop of the Church', and was appealing to Scripture to support this profession.[5] If Callistus did so, he was not the first to connect the church of Rome with the passage Matt. 16.18–19; Tertullian himself had already done so.[6] But the phrase *id est ad omnem ecclesiam Petri propinquam* sounds very like Tertullian's own theory that powers were given to Peter as a symbol or token that they were given to the whole Church; it is therefore more

one. D'Alès, in his book *L'Édit de Calliste*, argued as strongly as he could that he was not innovating but was only implementing what had always been the Catholic policy on this subject, or at the most officially recognizing a long-standing unofficial traditional practice. The chief argument in favour of his case is that Hermas' *Shepherd* certainly does allow one repentance after baptism for grave sins, the chief point against him that Hippolytus explicitly accuses Callistus of innovating, and Hippolytus cannot be dismissed as influenced by Montanism. D'Alès has a considerable weight of scholarship against him, including the opinions of Prestige and Turner.

[1] *pontifex maximus et episcopus episcoporum, ibid.* 1.6.
[2] *Ibid.* 21.1–4, 6.
[3] *Ibid.* 21.9.
[4] See Van den Eynde, *Les Normes*, pp. 204–9. For Flesseman-van Leer's views on this passage see *Tradition and Scripture*, pp. 153–4.
[5] *Op. cit.* p. 206.
[6] *De Praescr. Haer.* 22.4 and *Scorpiace* 10; Van den Eynde points this out, *Les Normes*, pp. 203–4.

probable that Tertullian is here trying to show the absurdity of Callistus'
claim: 'You claim that the power of loosing and binding was given by
descent to you? You must therefore be the whole Church, which comes
next to Peter in receiving these powers!' Earlier[1] he has said that the
Church, and not a single bishop, has the right to remit sins. This would
relieve us of the necessity of making the improbable assumption that
Callistus was claiming jurisdiction over the whole Church. It therefore
seems reasonable to assume that Callistus admitted fornicators and
adulterers, after they had done penance, to communion, alleging that as
a successor of the apostle Peter he had special authority (*potestas*) to do
this within the limits of his own see, because Peter had been given
authority to bind and loose by the Lord, and perhaps as an additional
justification for exercising this right putting forward as a pretext his own
experience as a confessor in the mines of Sardinia. Tertullian of course
violently rejected this claim; and there can be little doubt that, if Callistus
made it, Hippolytus rejected it too. Our conclusions about what exactly
Callistus claimed must, however, be only tentative because of the obscurity of the evidence. Perhaps it is significant that the *Epistola Clementis*,
which may date from about this time, appears to be making a similar
claim concerning binding and loosing for Clement as a successor of
Peter and therefore conceivably for Clement's successors as bishops of
Rome also.[2] The author of this work may, by his reference to 'the *canon*
of the Church', have intended to appeal to the traditional custom of the
Roman church. It ought to be remembered that this document was a
conscious forgery, perhaps the first *conscious* forgery in the history of
orthodox Christianity.[3]

Clement of Alexandria and Origen never make even the most passing
reference to the tradition of the Roman church. It was apparently a subject which they did not regard as important in any sense. Indeed, Origen
appears to have spent the last twenty years or so of his life formally out of
communion with the church of Rome without suffering inconvenience
or anxiety thereby.

The next situation from which we can learn something about what was
thought of the tradition of the Roman church by various parties is the
controversy over the rebaptism of heretics, which we have already had
occasion to glance at.[4] This controversy took place between the years

---

[1] *De Pudicitia* 21.7.   [2] See above, p. 77.
[3] We can acquit the author of the *Acts of Paul and Thecla* of this charge, with a little
charity, if we take the view outlined in K. Aland's article. See below, pp. 242–3.
[4] See above, pp. 140–2. For a conspectus of the controversy which has been carried
on over this subject, see N. Sykes, *Man As Churchman*, pp. 43–59.

255 and 257 and engaged the attention as leaders of it on different sides of Cyprian bishop of Carthage and Stephen bishop of Rome. Cyprian conducted the controversy on his side with admirable courtesy and restraint, qualities which are conspicuously lacking in the one letter which has survived of Firmilian, bishop of Caesarea in Cappadocia, a violent partisan of Cyprian's view. It happens that we have to reconstruct the views and expressions of Stephen entirely from the statements of his opponents, and this means that we must be careful not to exaggerate them. It is clear that he believed that if anybody had been baptized by a proper formula even outside the catholic Church, on seeking re-entry they need not be rebaptized, but only have hands laid on them, and that he reckoned baptism into the name of Jesus Christ alone as a proper formula, though presumably he would have preferred baptism into the name of the Holy Trinity.[1] Stephen appears to have appealed to custom (*consuetudo*)[2] and supported his appeal with phrases such as 'We are following what we have received from the apostles'[3] and 'There should be no alteration of what has been handed down'; once[4] Cyprian quotes what appears to be a fragment of Stephen's letter:

If therefore people in the future come to you from any heresy at all, there should be no alteration of what has been handed down, so that they should be received with the laying-on of hands after penance, since the heretics themselves on their side especially do not baptize those who come to them, but only admit them to communion.[5]

Stephen believed that the apostles themselves had forbidden the rebaptism of those who joined the Church from heresies.[6] He broke off communion, or threatened to break off communion, with those who disagreed with his view;[7] he refused to receive or see the bishops sent as the representatives of the African church to him,[8] and called Cyprian 'a false Christ, and a false apostle, and a deceitful agitator'.[9] Firmilian, who in his

[1] Cyprian, *Ep.* 73.4.1; 73.16.1, 2. This is a letter of Cyprian to bishop Iubaianus, but it seems not unlikely that this bishop had been attracted by the views of the opposite party in the controversy to Cyprian's; 73.26.1, 2 suggest that Cyprian knows that he is contending against Stephen's views. But 74.7.3 makes it quite clear that Stephen did hold this opinion.
[2] *Ep.* 73.13.1; 75.19.1.
[3] *quod accepimus ab apostolis hoc sequimur, Ep.* 73.13.3.
[4] *nihil innovetur nisi quod traditum est, Ep.* 74.2.2.
[5] *si qui ergo a quacunque haeresi venient ad vos, nihil innovetur nisi quod traditum est, ut manus illis inponatur in paenitentiam, cum ipsi haeretici proprie alterutrum ad se venientes non baptizent, sed communicent tantum, Ep.* 74.1.2.
[6] *Ep.* 75.5.2.
[7] *Ep.* 75.6.2.
[8] *Ep.* 75.25.1.
[9] *Ep.* 75.25.4: *pseudochristum et pseudoapostolum et dolosum operarium.*

indignant letter shows that he can match Stephen in ecclesiastical vitu-peration,[1] speaks of Stephen 'who boasts so much about the position of his see and claims that he holds the succession of Peter upon whom the foundations of the Church are laid',[2] and 'who announces that he has the chair of Peter by succession'.[3] It seems clear therefore that Stephen was following in the footsteps of Victor in claiming that his knowledge of the traditional custom of the Roman church justified him in excommunicating those who disagreed with him, and imitating Callistus in appealing for scriptural support in his policy to the words of Christ to Peter in Matt. 16.18–19. There is really no reason at all for thinking that Stephen claimed jurisdiction over the whole Church in any form. It is wholly likely that, had he done so, Cyprian or Firmilian would have mentioned the fact.[4]

It is not directly relevant to our theme to discuss Cyprian's general attitude to the see of Rome. The most important passage is of course *De Unitate Ecclesiae* 4, where the question of whether we have here to deal with a later interpolation or a second draft from Cyprian's own hand must, after the researches of Benevot, be left an open question.[5] There is the famous passage in Cyprian's fifty-ninth letter where he describes the church of Rome as 'the chair of Peter and the leading church whence priestly unity has been derived', and the Romans as those 'whose faith is praised by the apostle's declaration, to whom treachery could not have entry'.[6] This passage is probably to be explained by his attitude to the apostle Peter in the *De Unitate Ecclesiae*, where he regards Peter as first endowed with authority by the Lord (Matt. 16.18–19) in order to empha-size the necessity of the church's unity, and the other apostles as given equal authority later. The founding of the Church on Peter was the symbol of the unity of the whole church, and thus though he can regard

---

[1] Stephen is accused of *inhumanitas* and compared to Judas (75.2.3), charged with *audacia* and *insolentia* and *res improbe gestae* (75.3.1), arraigned for *stultitia* (75.17.1) and incompetence and unjustified anger (75.24.1, 2) and finally *mendacium* is attributed to him (75.25.5).

[2] *qui sic de episcopatus sui loco gloriatur et se successionem Petri tenere contendit super quam fundamenta ecclesiae collocata sunt, Ep.* 75.17.1.

[3] *qui per successionem cathedram Petri habere se praedicat, Ep.* 75.17.2.

[4] For Van den Eynde's treatment of Stephen, see *Les Normes*, pp. 252–3.

[5] For the main points in this much-discussed question very fairly stated see M. Benevot, *St Cyprian: The Lapsed: The Unity of the Catholic Church*, translated and annotated (Ancient Christian Writers, No. 25), pp. 6–8 (introduction) and pp. 46–48 (text), with his notes on pp. 75–76 and pp. 102–8. For an earlier statement of the question, where a rather truculent line is taken, see E. W. Benson, *Cyprian*, pp. 202–18. See also Von Campenhausen, *Kirchliches Amt*, p. 304 n. 3.

[6] *Petri cathedram adque ecclesiam principalem unde unitas sacerdotalis exorta est . . . Romanos quorum fides apostolo praedicante laudata est, ad quos perfidia non possit habere accessum, Ep.* 59.14.1.

the apostles (and the bishops who succeeded them) as autonomous in their own sees, yet he can speak of their authority as deriving its origin from Peter.[1] In the very next section of this fifty-ninth letter he maintains uncompromisingly the right of the North African church to order its own affairs unhindered by appeals to the see of Rome.[2] He can also exhort some of his own flock who are about to sail from Carthage to Rome to 'recognize and hold fast to the womb and root of the catholic Church',[3] but the context makes it clear that what he means is, not 'be sure to go to church when you are in Rome' (which would be a pointless exhortation to third-century Christian travellers, however relevant it might be to twentieth-century ones), but 'attach yourself to the Catholic party in Rome' (i.e. to Cornelius' church, which in Rome represents the catholic Church, and not to Novatian's).

On the question of the value of the tradition of the Roman church, however, there can be no doubt of Cyprian's attitude. While, like Irenaeus, he regarded the church of Rome as the leading church, and (unlike Irenaeus) he believed that this leading position had been given to it by Christ's words to Peter, and not (or not only) because St Peter and St Paul had founded it, he attached very little value to its unwritten tradition. The quotation from Stephen defining Stephen's attitude to the question of rebaptizing heretics, which we have already examined,[4] Cyprian classed among 'arrogant, irrelevant or contradictory remarks which he wrote in an unskilled and unconsidered way'.[5] In the same letter he expressly denies the value and accuracy of Stephen's alleged tradition:

'There should be no alteration,' he says, 'of what has been handed down.' Where does this tradition come from? Does it derive from the authority of the Lord and the gospels or does it come from the ordinances and letters of the apostles? . . . If therefore it is either enjoined in the gospel or included in the letters or Acts of the Apostles that 'those who come from any heresy at all' are not to be baptized, 'but only that they should receive the laying-on of hands after penance', then let this be followed as a divine and holy tradition.[6]

---

[1] This seems a reasonable statement of his views, whatever attitude we take to *De Unitate Ecclesiae* 4.   [2] *Ep.* 59.14.2.

[3] *ut ecclesiae catholicae matricem et radicem agnoscerent et tenerent, Ep.* 48.3.1.

[4] See above, pp. 152–3. See also Turner, *The Pattern*, pp. 334–6, on this controversy.

[5] *inter cetera vel superba vel ad rem non pertinentia vel sibi ipsi contraria quae inperite adque inprovide scripsit, Ep.* 74.1.2.

[6] *Ep.* 74.2.2, 3: '*Nihil innovetur*', inquit, '*nisi quod traditum est*'. *Unde est ista traditio? Utrumne de dominica et evangelica auctoritate descendens an de apostolorum mandatis adque epistulis veniens? . . . Si ergo aut in evangelio praecipitur aut in apostolorum epistulis vel actis continetur ut 'a quacunque haeresi venientes' non baptizentur, 'sed tantum manus inponatur in paenitentiam', observetur divina haec et sancta traditio.*

Then, a little later:

How great is that obstinacy and that audacity which prefers men's tradition to the divine ordering and does not notice that God is indignant and angry whenever men's tradition dissolves and disregards the divine commandments![1]

It is only in sarcasm that he can refer to 'that truly famous and lawful tradition which is put forward by the teaching of our brother Stephen!'[2] We have already seen that, on the positive side, Cyprian held a doctrine of tradition which precluded the possibility of the unwritten tradition of the Roman church being of any serious force.[3]

Firmilian of Caesarea in Cappadocia, in his letter written to Cyprian which has been preserved among Cyprian's correspondence, follows precisely the same line as Cyprian, only more emphatically. He accuses Stephen of betraying the Church[4] and of virtually opening communion indiscriminately to heretics.[5] He wholly rejects *consuetudo* when it clashes with truth.[6] He directly refuses the claim that Roman tradition has any value *per se*: 'we unite custom to truth and to the custom of the Romans we oppose custom, but the custom of truth, holding from the beginning what was handed down by Christ and by the apostles.'[7] He expressly denies the theory that communion with Rome constitutes the touchstone of catholicity:

But how great a sin have you heaped up for yourself when you have separated yourself from so many flocks. You yourself have separated yourself—make no mistake—if he really is a schismatic who makes himself an apostate from the communion of the church's unity. For while you think that everybody can be excommunicated from you, you have simply excommunicated yourself from everybody.[8]

Both Cyprian and Firmilian allow that each church may follow its own customs, without having the right to insist that others must adopt them.

---

[1] *Ep.* 74.3.1: *quae ista obstinatio est quaeve praesumptio humanam traditionem divinae dispositioni anteponere nec animadvertere indignari et irasci Deum quotiens divina praecepta solvit et praeterit humana traditio!*

[2] *Ep.* 74.4.1: *praeclara plane ac legitima traditio Stephano fratre nostro docente proponitur!*

[3] See above, pp. 99–100, 140–2.   [4] *Ep.* 75.17.1.   [5] *Ep.* 75.17.2.   [6] *Ep.* 75.19.1.

[7] *Ep.* 75.19.3: *nos veritati et consuetudinem iungimus et consuetudini Romanorum consuetudinem sed veritatis opponimus, ab initio hoc tenentes quod a Christo et ab apostolis traditum est.*

[8] *Ep.* 75.24.2: *peccatum vero quam magnum tibi exaggerasti, quando te a tot gregibus scidisti. Scidisti enim te ipsum, noli te fallere, si quidem ille est vere schismaticus qui se a communione ecclesiasticae unitatis apostatam fecerit. Dum enim putas omnes a te abstineri posse, solum te ab omnibus abstinuisti.* He immediately goes on to correct the bishop of Rome by referring him to the rule of truth, accusing him of violating it. Cf. 75.25.1, 2.

Cyprian held most passionately that it was a gravely wrong policy to admit heretics to the Church without rebaptizing them; but he was prepared to allow Stephen to continue in what was, in Cyprian's eyes, a disastrously false custom. Modern theologians who find it difficult to envisage reunion with people of different ecclesiastical traditions would do well to consider this. 'In this matter we are not coercing anybody nor laying down the law, since every prelate has the free choice of his own decision in the administration of the Church, and will give an account of his act to the Lord.'[1] Or again he refuses to judge brother bishops who think differently from him: 'Let a loving disposition be preserved patiently and mildly by us, and the honour of the bench, the bond of faith, the harmony of the priesthood.'[2] Similarly Firmilian will not allow that anything universally binding in the way of unwritten tradition can have been handed down from the apostles;[3] anybody can see that different Christians in Rome celebrate Easter at different times and are at variance in many other sacred observances, and do not even keep everything uniformly as they are kept at Jerusalem, as if Jerusalem was (as it well might be) the fountain-head of tradition in this respect.[4]

It ought now to be clear that the controversy over rebaptizing which took place in the middle of the third century is less interesting for the central question which agitated the parties concerned in it than for the secondary question which rose out of it, that is, whether the church of Rome could legitimately claim the possession of a genuine tradition of practice upon the central subject handed down in unbroken continuity from the apostles. On the point of doctrine almost all Christians now agree that Cyprian and Firmilian were wrong. But on the point of history, the secondary point, can we as readily condemn them? They explicitly and formally denied the accuracy of the Roman church's claim to this tradition, and they suggested that any tradition of this sort in any church was of minor importance and should never be a matter of excommunication. It is a point in their favour that they were maintaining precisely the viewpoint of Irenaeus in his letter to Victor some sixty years previously, the viewpoint which, our investigation has suggested, was the prevailing, normal one in the Church of their day. And if we apply the test of modern

---

[1] *Ep.* 72.3.2: *Qua in re nec nos vim cuiquam facimus aut legem damus, quando habeat in ecclesiae administratione voluntatis suae arbitrium liberum unusquisque praepositus, rationem actus sui Domino redditurus.*

[2] *Ep.* 73.26.1, 2: *servatur a nobis patienter et leniter caritas animi, collegii honor, vinculum fidei, concordia sacerdotii.*

[3] *Ep.* 75.6.1: *eos autem qui Romae sunt non ea in omnibus observare quae sint ab origine tradita et frustra apostolorum auctoritatem praetendere scire quis etiam inde potest . . .*

[4] *Ep.* 75.6.1.

critical judgement, it is very difficult not to agree that, on the point of history, Cyprian and Firmilian were entirely justified. Did St Peter or St Paul explicitly lay down a rule while they were in Rome that those who returned to the Church from heresy should not be rebaptized but should be admitted only by imposition of hands after penance? And was this rule carefully observed in continuous tradition ever since that time up to the episcopate of Stephen? We cannot possibly give an affirmative answer to this question without a gross violation of historical probability. Modern historical scholarship does not conceive the relationship of these apostles to the church of Rome (whatever it was) to have been such that they are remotely likely to have laid down ordinances to regulate the church at the considerably later stage before such words as 'heresy', 'penance' and 'imposition of hands' could have had any meaning. Cyprian and Firmilian may have been rigorist on the question of doctrine. But on the question of history Stephen was romantic.

3. *Apostolic Succession*

We have had many occasions of noting that the fathers will sometimes appeal to the succession of bishops in the great sees as a manifestation of tradition, guaranteeing that what was taught by the Church was in genuine continuity with what had been taught by the apostles. Hegesippus must have been the first who regularly collected succession-lists of bishops; it was probably upon his list for the bishops of Rome that Irenaeus relied when he quoted it in the interests of genuine tradition.[1] He sums up this appeal in one sentence when he says, 'For all these [i.e. the heretics] are much later than the bishops to whom the apostles handed over the churches.'[2] But occasionally he refers to the succession of presbyters rather than of bishops.[3] Tertullian has the conception of the apostolic succession of bishops, though he does not make as much of it as Irenaeus does. 'Let them [the heretics] therefore produce the pedigrees of their churches, let them unfold the succession-list of their bishops, which should so descend by succession from the beginning that the first

---

[1] *Adv. Haer.* 3.3.2, 3; 1.27 in a Greek fragment quoted by Eusebius, *HE* 4.11.1, places Hyginus ninth; but the Latin translation at this point reads *octavus* and this is confirmed by *Adv. Haer.* 3.4.3 where Anicetus is again listed as tenth.

[2] *Adv. Haer.* 5.20.1: *omnes enim ii valde posteriores sunt quam episcopi quibus apostoli tradiderunt ecclesias.*

[3] *Adv. Haer.* 3.2.2; 4.40.1; Letter to Florinus (Eusebius, *HE* 5.20.4); Letter to Pope Victor (Eusebius, *HE* 5.24.14). Molland ('Irenaeus of Lugdunum', pp. 22–23) calls attention to these passages, and remarks of Irenaeus, 'He does not take any interest in the question of hierarchical degrees.'

bishop, whoever he is, should have as originator and predecessor somebody from among the apostles or the men who are only apostolic but still will have continually associated with the apostles.'[1] It is evident that with Tertullian, as with Irenaeus, the succession is one of tradition, not of ordination. But Tertullian on the whole sees the succession as that of apostolic churches rather than of apostolic bishops. Jesus Christ, he says, sent the disciples to teach and baptize in the threefold Name; this they did:[2] 'and at the same time they founded churches in every town, from which other churches in turn borrowed the transmission of faith and the seeds of doctrine and every day they are borrowing them so that they become churches. And this is why they too are reckoned apostolic, as the offspring of apostolic churches.'[3] For Tertullian, says Flesseman-van Leer, apostolic succession consists in 'the succession of one church generation to the next', and not in episcopal succession, even though he believes that monarchical bishops were directly instituted by the apostles.[4] 'So apparently, to Tertullian, the Spirit guides the churches to transmit and understand rightly the apostolic tradition, without any special reference to the bishops.'[5]

The Christian Platonists of Alexandria emphasize apostolic succession of this sort very little; indeed, the concept can scarcely be found in Clement of Alexandria. The nearest Clement comes to the concept is when he describes his secret tradition as 'handed down unwritten to a small group by succession from the apostles'.[6] It is characteristic of him to substitute the succession of specially gifted teachers for the succession of bishops. Van den Eynde, in noting this omission, suggests that it was caused, not by Clement's lack of interest in the subject, but because he took it so much for granted that he forbore to mention it.[7] But it is much more likely that Clement simply saw no value in this appeal to apostolic succession; and indeed, after Tertullian, the appeal seems to have gradually faded out of Christian apologetics, as did the appeal to the rule of

---

[1] De Praescr. Haer. 32.1: edant ergo origines ecclesiarum suarum, evolvant ordinem episcoporum suorum, ita per successionem ab initio decurrentem ut primus ille episcopus aliquam ex apostolis vel apostolicis viris, qui tamen cum apostolis perseveraverint, habuerit auctorem et antecessorem.
[2] Ibid. 20.1–4.
[3] Ibid. 20.5–6: et perinde ecclesias apud unamquamque civitatem condiderunt, a quibus traducem fidei et semina doctrinae ceterae exinde ecclesiae mutuatae sunt et cottidie mutuantur ut ecclesiae fiant. Ac per hoc et ipsae apostolicae deputabuntur ut suboles apostolicarum ecclesiarum.
[4] Tradition and Scripture, p. 152.
[5] Ibid. p. 155.
[6] Strom. 6.7.61.3 (PG 9.284).
[7] Les Normes, p. 220.

faith as independent of Scripture. Hippolytus seldom makes the appeal to apostolic succession, and Origen very rarely. He refers to 'the rule of Jesus Christ's heavenly church according to the succession of the apostles',[1] but he never quotes a succession-list of bishops. Cyprian certainly believes in apostolic succession inasmuch as he believes that monarchical bishops, with all their appurtenances and prerogatives as he knew them in the middle of the third century, were directly instituted by Christ in the persons of the apostles who ordained bishops to succeed them in all their essential functions and powers.[2] But he never appeals to this succession to guarantee the soundness of his doctrine nor of his tradition because he sees no necessity to produce authority for his doctrine from any source except the Bible and because he does not believe in the existence of any tradition outside the Bible. The practice of commending Christianity by quoting episcopal succession-lists seems to have died out with Tertullian. This is natural enough, because the force of this appeal, like the force of the appeal to the rule of faith as independent of Scripture, is diminished by the advance of time.[3] The relatively short succession-lists which Hegesippus could produce in the middle of the second century would by the middle of the third century have doubled in length and would consequently look far less convincing as evidence of oral tradition independent of the Bible.

One remark of Irenaeus, however, on the subject of bishops deserves special attention. He is contending that Christians alone can interpret Scripture properly:

> For this reason it is right to obey those presbyters who are in the churches, those who have succession from the apostles, as we have shown; for they with the succession of the episcopate have received a certain sacred gift of truth according to the Father's goodwill.[4]

A little later, he has a rather similar passage:

> Therefore where the sacred gifts of the Lord are located there we ought to learn truth, with those among whom is the succession of that

---

[1] *PA* 4.2.2.

[2] Cf. *Ep.* 33.1.1: *inde per temporum et successionum vices episcoporum ordinatio et ecclesiae ratio decurrit ut ecclesia super episcopos constituatur et omnis actus ecclesiae per eosdem praepositos gubernetur*: 66.4.1: *omnes praepositos qui apostolis vicaria ordinatione succedunt*. Cf. 45.1.2. Firmilian uses precisely the same sort of expressions, 75.16.2.

[3] Turner (*The Pattern*, pp. 325–6) recognizes that the appeal to 'the continuity of testimony' would 'tend to dwindle with the lapse of time.'

[4] *Adv. Haer.* 4.40.2: *quapropter eis qui in ecclesia sunt presbyteris obaudire oportet, his qui successionem habent ab apostolis, sicut ostendimus; qui cum episcopatus successione charisma veritatis certum secundum placitum Patris acceperunt*. There can be little doubt that the phrase originally used by Irenaeus was χάρισμα ἀληθείας.

Church which is from the apostles, and there exists sound and unblam-
able behaviour and the word is undiluted and uncorrupted.[1]

There is also the long list of the benefits and graces enjoyed by the
Church, which we have already examined,[2] that ends with the words,
'and the special gift of love which is more precious than knowledge and
further more glorious than prophecy, and also superior to all other sacred
gifts'.[3] The conception of bishops possessing a sacred gift of truth is an
unusual but not quite unprecedented one. Hippolytus at the beginning
of his *Elenchos* says that what will refute the heretics will be 'the Holy
Spirit handed down in the Church, which the original apostles received
and imparted to those who believed rightly ($\dot{o}\rho\theta\hat{\omega}s$); we are their successors
and share the same grace ($\chi\acute{a}\rho\iota\tau os$) and high priesthood ($\dot{a}\rho\chi\iota\epsilon\rho a\tau\epsilon\acute{\iota}as$)
and teaching and are reckoned the guardians of the Church.'[4] But the
use of *charisma* in the sense attached to it in the first three of these
quotations from Irenaeus appears to be unique. *Charisma* is a word
which Tertullian uses untranslated; at one point he quotes Eph. 4.8
('he gave gifts unto men') and glosses this 'that is gratuities (*donativa*)
which we call *charismata*';[5] and he equates these on the one hand with the
sevenfold gifts of wisdom enumerated in Isa. 11.2–3 and on the other
with the gifts of the Spirit enumerated in I Cor. 12.8–10, but not with
ordination.[6] Often Tertullian seems to have regarded *charisma* as equivalent to a gift of prophecy.[7] Frequently too he uses the word to denote
some inspired message given to Montanists as the peculiar receptacles
of the Spirit's activity.[8] It is most unlikely, anyway, that Tertullian
would have subscribed to any view that appeared to render bishops
infallible, for he held that bishops could only function effectively within
certain limits: if they behaved immorally they ceased (as all clergy
ceased) to be clergy at all;[9] and there were certain sins which they could

---

[1] *Ibid.* 4.42.1: *ubi igitur charismata Domini posita sunt ibi discere oportet veritatem,
apud quos est ea quae est ab apostolis ecclesiae successio, et id quod estsanum et irreprobabile
conversationis et inadulteratum et incorruptibile sermonis constat.*
[2] See above, p. 95.
[3] *Ibid.* 4.53.2: *et praecipuum dilectionis munus quod est pretiosius quam agnitio,
gloriosius autem quam prophetia, omnibus autem reliquis charismatibus supereminens.*
[4] *Elenchos* 1, introd. 6. This is one of those rare passages in Hippolytus where
apostolic succession is mentioned. Hippolytus certainly knew Irenaeus' work.
[5] *Adv. Marcionem* 5.8.5.   [6] *Ibid.* 5.8.8, 9.
[7] E.g. *De Praescr. Haer.* 29.3; *Adv. Valentinianos* 4.4; *De Ieiun. adv. Psych.* 8.4;
16.8. It is remarkable that *Adv. Iudaeos* 8.14 should say that *baptizato Christo . . .
omnis plenitudo spiritalium retro charismatum in Christo cessavit*; is this a very early
stage in Tertullian's career, or is this passage not from Tertullian's hand?
[8] E.g. *De Monogamia* 1.2; *De Anima* 58.8; *Adv. Praxean* 1; *De Ieiun. ad Psych.* 5.
[9] *De Fuga in Persecutione* 10.3; on fleeing during a persecution, clergy cease auto-
matically to be clergy: *qui enim talem pastorem malum pronuntiat, utique damnavit;
omne autem quod damnatur illicitum factum est sine dubio.*

not forgive.[1] Hippolytus also associates *charismata* with the inspired utterances of the Montanists;[2] and he regards the power of healing possessed by a Christian layman as a *charisma*.[3] Here the word certainly means an unofficial gift, not conferred by ordination. Origen uses the word *charisma* several times, but never in any sense that suggests either the grace of ordination or a special endowment for teaching the truth.[4] He certainly did not believe either in the automatic competence of bishops to teach truly, nor in their impeccability.[5] He held as strongly as Tertullian or Hippolytus that bishops had no power to forgive idolatry or adultery or fornication,[6] and, like Tertullian, he believes that the bishop's powers are limited by his moral and religious character.[7] Cyprian, as is well known, in spite of his very high regard for the office of a bishop, held that immoral behaviour in a bishop rendered his functions void, and on more than one occasion counselled the people of an offending prelate to withdraw their allegiance from him.[8] Novatian also transcribes the word *charismata*, using it in much the same sense as Tertullian did in his pre-Montanist phase.[9] The author of *De Singularitate Clericorum*, who is probably a contemporary of Cyprian, uses the phrase *de charismatibus ecclesiasticis* to denote the various gifts of the spirit granted to individuals in the Church in a conventional way.[10]

If therefore we are to regard *charisma* in the passage under discussion as meaning a power conferred by ordination of teaching infallibly, we shall be using *charisma* in a way otherwise without example, and expressing an idea which does not occur precisely like this in any other writer of the period. This is the sense, however, in which Van den Eynde takes it.[11] Ehrhardt regards this remark of Irenaeus as an ingenious device whereby he included within the function of the official, ordained, ministry a function—that of prophecy—hitherto attributed only to the less official

[1] *De Pudicitia* 21.9–15.
[2] *Elenchos* 8.19.2; cf. 10.25.
[3] *Apostolic Tradition* 15; the healer is expressly forbidden ordination.
[4] Many examples of Origen's use of *charisma* can be culled from *Origen and the Doctrine of Grace*, by B. Drewery, on pp. 18–19, 20, 22, 27, 29, 31, 32, 40, 41, 45–46, 47 and 64.
[5] See *Contra Celsum* 3.9, 30; *Comm. on Matthew*, Comm. Ser. 12; *Hom. on Lev.* 12.3; *Hom. on Ezekiel* 12.2; Cadiou, *Commentaires Inédits des Psaumes*, 118, 9a, p. 103; 119, 161a, p. 118; 142, 4d, p. 130.
[6] *PE* 28.10.
[7] *Comm. on Matthew* 20.14. For Origen's attitude to bishops, see *Allegory and Event*, pp. 330–1.
[8] *Ep.* 65.2.1 and 4.1; 67.3.1, 2. In practice also it is clear that Cyprian held that the bishop was bound on occasion to defer, even against his better judgement, to the opinion of the *plebs* and the presbyters; cf. *Ep.* 59.15.2–4.
[9] *De Trinitate* 29, p. 108, l. 2.
[10] 22 (99).   [11] *Les Normes*, pp. 181–7, and especially p. 187.

L

Christian prophet.[1] Molland denies that the expression here can mean a gift of infallibility, and suggests that its real meaning is 'the true doctrine according to the right tradition, the deposit of faith committed to the Church',[2] a use for which there is certainly no parallel in contemporary writers. Flesseman-van Leer has a more attractive suggestion than any other when she says that what Irenaeus means is that bishops are always chosen by God from among the *charismatici*, men who have the gift for expounding truth: 'God makes those men bishops in the apostolic succession to whom he commits the gift of his *kerygma*.' She insists strongly on this, and maintains that Irenaeus' ideas are incompatible with the view that bishops are given the *charisma* by virtue of being bishops. Irenaeus, she believes, held that unworthy men, though they might appear to be bishops, in fact were no bishops at all, and she can speak of 'the "Donatism" of Irenaeus, and, in fact, of all ancient Christian writers'. She believes that Tertullian, Cyprian and Origen were not alone in this view; Irenaeus' doctrine was that 'a real bishop, in the full sense of the word, is only he who has the gift of the Spirit, he whom God has made bishop: the Church in appointing him is only recognizing God's appointment.'[3] If we remember that Cyprian emphasizes very strongly that the divine decision must play a part in the choice and consecration of a bishop, and that this decision can only be shown by the bishop's later career, we shall probably conclude that Van den Eynde's explanation is an attempt to read into Irenaeus' words a much later concept both of ordination and of infallibility, and agree that Flesseman-van Leer's account is the more probable, as more in keeping with the ideas of the second and third centuries.

The appeal to the succession of bishops in the major sees was a fair and effective way of proving that the Church as an institution had existed well before the Gnostic sects such as those of Marcion and Valentinus. It constituted, as Van den Eynde points out, the external and historical side of the appeal to the rule of faith; it was really only another way of stating that appeal.[4] It was also an appeal to public tradition in contrast

---

[1] *The Apostolic Succession*, pp. 113–14.

[2] 'Irenaeus of Lugdunum', pp. 25–26. Von Campenhausen (*Kirchliches Amt*, p. 188) takes it in much the same sense.

[3] *Tradition and Scripture*, pp. 119–22; the first quotation comes from p. 119 and the next two from p. 120. On this point of the *charisma veritatis* see also Turner, *The Pattern*, pp. 327–8. Harnack, *Constitution and Law of the Church*, p. 214, calls attention in this context to Clement of Alexandria, *Quis Dives* 42: κλήρῳ ἕνα γέ τινα κληρώσων τῶν ὑπὸ τοῦ πνεύματος σημαινομένων. E. Schweizer believes that all Christian ministry was originally thought of as charismatic in this sense; see *Church Order in the New Testament*, p. 102 (7m) and *passim*.

[4] *Les Normes*, p. 196.

to the heretics' form of appeal to history, which was in effect an appeal
to secret tradition.[1] But it suffered from two defects. It rested upon a
schematization of history about whose accuracy we cannot be confident;
and it did not really, even taken *au pied de la lettre*, guarantee the purity
of the tradition. It assumed that in all the great sees to whose tradition
it appealed the apostles had instituted monarchical bishops of the kind
known to the writers of the second and third centuries who made this
appeal, and that they, consciously charged to preserve the tradition, had
handed it on to their successors. The origins of the monarchical bishop
are plunged in obscurity, but very few scholars of any tradition would
today maintain with confidence that the monarchical bishop owes his
origin to the direct institution of the apostles.[2] The last full-scale attempt
to support this thesis was the volume called *The Apostolic Ministry*,
edited by the late K. E. Kirk, a work which, despite the learning and
ingenuity of its authors, has certainly not met with widespread agreement.[3] Clement of Rome, who according to the succession-lists, was one
of the early monarchical bishops of the see of Rome, in the *First Epistle
of Clement*, which is attributed to him by the judgement of the great
majority of scholars, does not claim to be a monarchical bishop at all,
and quite clearly assumes the identification between bishop (*episcopus*)
and presbyter which is made by the New Testament itself.[4] He is convinced that there has been a succession of ecclesiastical officials from the
apostles, but he equally clearly regards them as presbyters, or perhaps
we should say presbyter-episcopi.[5] Ignatius, who witnesses unmistakably
to the existence of monarchical bishops in his own see (which he calls
'Syria', not simply Antioch) and in several other places,[6] makes no reference at all to the monarchical bishop as standing in any line of succession
(indeed, it is the council of the presbyters whom he compares to the
apostles, not the bishop, whose prototype is Christ himself),[7] and in
writing to the church of Rome he does not even name a bishop. In writing

---

[1] See above, pp. 22–5.
[2] Neither Van den Eynde nor Congar make this claim without qualification.
[3] See the trenchant criticism of it in Ehrhardt's *Apostolic Succession*, pp. 11–20
See also A. T. Hanson, *The Pioneer Ministry*, cap. 7, and the account of Harnack,
Constitution and Law of the Church, pp. 126–8. On the subject of the relation of bishops
to apostles see also Harnack, *ibid.*, pp. 193, 245; O. Linton, *Das Problem der Urkirche*,
pp. 31–46, 54–55, 69–112; Von Campenhausen, *Kirchliches Amt*, cap. 7 and especially
pp. 173–6; E. Schweizer, *Church Order in the New Testament*, pp. 70–71 (5i), and
B. Reicke in *The Scrolls and the New Testament*, pp. 154–6.
[4] See *I Clement* 42.4, 5. Turner, *The Pattern*, pp. 325–6, rejects the idea that *I Clement*
intends to establish any single theory of transmission.
[5] *Ibid.* 42.1–5; 44.1–4.
[6] *Romans* 2.2; cf. *Magnesians* 14; *Trallians* 13.
[7] *Magnesians* 6; *Philadelphians* 5.

to the church of Ephesus he makes no mention of a connection of the church with John, but calls them 'brother masons with Paul'.[1] A glance at the succession-lists cited by Eusebius in his *Ecclesiastical History* will show the uncertainty surrounding the early succession-lists. Eusebius, whose aim is not of course that of Irenaeus and Tertullian, to substantiate the trustworthiness of the rule of faith, at intervals throughout his work quotes the succession-lists of four great sees, adding to them as he advances through the history of the periods which he is chronicling, the sees of Rome, of Jerusalem, of Alexandria and of Antioch. For the list of the bishops of Rome up to Pontianus (230–235) it is likely that he is relying upon a very early recension of the Liberian catalogue of the Popes which itself used the list given in Hippolytus' *Chronica* (now lost) of the Popes up to Pontianus.[2] It is almost certain that this list of Hippolytus did not have the dates of the Popes' reigns attached to their names, but only the number of years, and perhaps months, that they had reigned. It is quite possible that the earliest succession-lists were simply lists of names without either dates of accessions or length of reigns attached to them. It may be that Hippolytus himself attempted to calculate the lengths of the reigns of the Popes in his list; it is very likely that Eusebius added to the list which he inherited the dates of the Popes' accessions from the *Chronicle* of Julius Africanus, which he knew and used. Irenaeus' succession-list, probably reproducing that of Hegesippus, may constitute an independent confirmation of that of Hippolytus. Certainly it is difficult to impugn the accuracy of Hegesippus' list at least as far back as Hegesippus is likely to have known from his own experience, as far back perhaps as Pope Telesphorus (*c.* 125–130). In the very earliest names on the Roman succession-list there are some variations. The second name is sometimes Anencletus and sometimes Cletus, and the Liberian catalogue makes him into two persons, Anacletus and Cletus; and there is a tendency sometimes to regard Clement, who comes third in the list, as the first Pope proper, his two apparent predecessors, Linus and Anencletus (Cletus), being merely co-bishops with Peter but not inheriting, as Clement did, rights or jurisdiction as direct successors of Peter. Ullmann has shown that this was the argument of the *Epistola Clementis*.[3] Anyway, the story of Peter founding the church of Rome and setting up a monarchical bishop to succeed him there is rendered altogether improbable

---

[1] Παύλου συμμύσται (*Ephesians* 12).
[2] For a full and able recent discussion of this complicated subject, see H. J. Lawlor and J. E. L. Oulton, *Eusebius*, Vol. II, pp. 40–46. The matter is also very lucidly expounded by Turner, *The Pattern*, pp. 338–43 and 379–86.
[3] 'The Significance of the *Epistola Clementis* in the Pseudo-Clementines.'

by the evidence of St Paul's epistle to the Romans, which witnesses to
the existence of a flourishing church in Rome, apparently doing very well
without the assistance of a monarchical bishop, before either St Peter
(who is not mentioned in the letter) or St Paul set foot in the city. The
succession-list of the bishops of the Roman church is almost useless as a
guide to the shape and government of the Roman church in its very
earliest days. It amounts to little more than a list of people who may have
been prominent in some capacity (but we do not know in what) in the
early days of the Church; some of the names may have been imported
from the New Testament.[1] The evidence available in the succession-list
of bishops of Jerusalem is even more untrustworthy.[2] It is probable, but
not certain, that Eusebius derived all his information on this subject
from Hegesippus' *Memoirs* (then extant, though perhaps in a corrupted
form, in the archives of the church of Aelia Capitolina). According to the
list which Eusebius supplies there were fourteen bishops (counting
James, the Lord's brother) before the interruption of the succession of
Jewish Christian bishops during the revolt of Bar-Cochbha in 135, and
fourteen bishops between 135 and the episcopate of Narcissus who was
bishop of Jerusalem when Hegesippus was writing. This is odd enough,
but Symeon, according to this account the second bishop, is recorded as
dying about the year 107; this makes the situation even odder, for it
necessitates a succession of no less than twenty-seven bishops between
about 107 and about 180! The probability is that Hegesippus' list of
bishops from 135 to 180 has been interpolated and meddled with; there
are two examples of Gaius and two of Julianus in it—an unlikely coincidence. Turner regards the authenticity of this list as indefensible, writing
of a 'plethora of unwanted names' and of 'the embarrassing richness of
names'.[3] The list of Jewish Christian bishops up to 135 is probably
uninterpolated but may well contain some names which are not names of
bishops but of local worthies, or these names may represent presbyter-
episcopi (or the more eminent among them) holding office simultaneously
with others. Ehrhardt's theory, argued with great ingenuity and erudition,
that the idea of the apostolic succession of monarchical bishops was 'the
continuation of the sacerdotal succession under the Old Covenant by the
episcopal succession under the New, as expressed by the imitation of

[1] Clement appears in Phil. 4.3; Linus in II Tim. 4.21; Anencletus just might have
been conjured out of Titus 1.6, 7. Turner (*The Pattern*, pp. 338–43) cautiously concludes that this is a list of bishops, but what sort of bishops they are he does not like
to say.
[2] See Lawlor and Oulton, *Eusebius*, Vol. II, pp. 167–70.
[3] *The Pattern*, pp. 343–4.

the Jewish succession-lists of High Priests in the Christian episcopal lists',[1] entails the hypothesis that the church of Jerusalem virtually invented the idea of apostolic succession, and that every other church gradually copied it. But this theory is not convincing, mainly because it is difficult to conceive, even in a Christianized form, and even if we discount the influence against the idea of the Epistle to the Hebrews, of more than one High Priest like the Jewish High Priest holding office at the same time; far more difficult is it to conceive of High Priests dotted all over the Roman Empire. Again, Ehrhardt can produce no evidence of monarchical bishops being called High Priests before the time of Tertullian. Even then we are not bound to translate either *archiereus* or *sacerdos* as 'High Priest'; either word could mean (and in fact is more likely to mean) 'chief priest', not necessarily denoting *the* High Priest; but with this translation most of Ehrhardt's theory falls to the ground, though much of his incidental research is of value. Eusebius' succession-list for the church of Alexandria is open to criticism also. He records, but in a phrase that he often employs to denote a statement based on vague legend, that Mark founded the church of Alexandria,[2] and a little later on records that in the year 62 'Annianus first after Mark the evangelist received the sacred charge of the see in Alexandria',[3] a phrase which some have thought to be carefully devised to avoid saying that there was a bishop in Alexandria; there is some evidence for the view that proper episcopal consecration was not practised in the church of Alexandria for a long time, but that the custom of the presbyters of the church choosing, on the death of their bishop, one of their number and ordaining him bishop long prevailed.[4] Anyway, it is very difficult to accept the origin of the church in Alexandria from St Mark in 62. If St Mark, as Eusebius, following Papias, records elsewhere,[5] really was in Rome with St Peter and wrote his gospel there either during Peter's lifetime or shortly after his martyrdom, then it is impossible that he should have been founding a church in Alexandria some considerable time before the year 62. Further, there is an extraordinary absence of evidence for the existence of Christianity at all in Alexandria until well into the second century, and even

---

[1] *The Apostolic Succession*, p. 107. Turner (*The Pattern*, pp. 385–6) has penetratingly criticized Ehrhardt's theory.

[2] *HE* 2.16. 'They say' (φασί) is the rubric which introduces this story.

[3] *HE* 2.24: πρῶτος μετὰ Μάρκον τὸν εὐαγγελιστὴν τῆς ἐν 'Αλεξανδρείᾳ παροικίας 'Αννιανὸς τὴν λειτουργίαν διαδέχεται.

[4] See W. Telfer, 'Episcopal Succession in Egypt'. Earlier treatments of the same subject were C. Gore, 'On the Ordination of the Early Bishops of Alexandria', and E. W. Brooks, 'The Ordination of the Early Bishops of Alexandria'.

[5] See above, p. 37.

then it is tenuous and indirect. *Egerton Papyrus 2*, a fragment of an unknown gospel from Egypt containing unmistakable echoes both of the synoptic gospels and of the fourth gospel, dating from some time before 150,[1] is probably the first, faint, witness of Christianity in Alexandria, if we grant that, were there Christianity anywhere in Egypt, it would be in Alexandria; then we can note the existence of two Christian Gnostics, Basilides, who taught Gnostic Christianity in Alexandria about 130, and Valentinus, who came from Egypt (but not necessarily as a Christian) and was an orthodox member of the church of Rome at about 140, and later a Gnostic; and then there is one statement by Irenaeus that there were Christian churches in Egypt,[2] and then references to the orthodox teacher Pantaenus, one of the masters of Clement of Alexandria. A yawning darkness of about seventy years has to be crossed by the frail bridge of Eusebius' succession-list, one end of which almost certainly is built on a legend.[3] Eusebius gives one name as bishop of Antioch before Ignatius, that of Euodios;[4] but do the book of Acts and the epistles of St Paul encourage us to think that either Peter or Paul, or any other apostle, really set up a succession of monarchical bishops in Antioch? These documents tell us quite a lot about the state of the church in Antioch, but not that monepiscopacy was established there by the apostles. In short, the earliest names in the succession-lists of monarchical bishops, whether derived from Hegesippus or from Hippolytus or from any other source, must be regarded with grave suspicion and suggest a schematization of history rather than an accurate record of tradition-bearing bishops succeeding each other regularly.

But even if we were to accept the episcopal succession-lists of the great sees provided by the historians of the ancient Christian Church at their face value, they would not provide certain authentication of the version of the Christian faith as orally delivered by the Church of the late second and early third centuries. We cannot ignore the fallibility of human mediation in oral tradition. Irenaeus assumed that faith and succession

---

[1] See *Fragments of an Unknown Gospel*, edited by H. I. Bell and J. C. Skeat.
[2] *Adv. Haer.* 1.3. See above, p. 95.
[3] It cannot be claimed with confidence that the influence of Alexandrian Jewish-Hellenistic thought visible in the works of the authors of the Epistle to the Hebrews and the *Epistle of Barnabas* proves that they originated in a Christian community in Alexandria. If we could trust the accuracy of Codex Bezae at Acts 18.25, we could be sure that Apollos had heard the word 'in his own country', but we cannot be sure here either. For different views on this question, see Westcott, *Canon of the New Testament*, pp. 59 and 348, J. N. Sanders, *The Fourth Gospel in the Early Church*, pp. 55–57, W. Telfer, 'Episcopal Succession in Egypt', p. 1, Van Unnik, *Newly Discovered Gnostic Writings*, p. 188, and Turner, *The Pattern*, pp. 343–4.
[4] *HE* 3.22.

coincided; but that assumption was not beyond question. Tertullian made the same assumption, but it is possible that before the end of his career he 'had a dim awareness of the possibility that revelatory truth and rightful succession could fall apart and in that case one had to choose between them.'[1] To accept wholeheartedly the argument from apostolic succession as advanced by Irenaeus would be almost to identify the apostolate with the episcopate.[2] Bishops in succession to the apostles are not the immediate bearers of revelation, nor even the first witnesses to it; they are, at the most, authorized guardians of revelation as it makes its continuing impact upon history. The authorized witness to revelation which has now taken the place of the apostles is the New Testament, not the bishops; or rather, two apostolic functions have now separated. The apostles witnessed to what they knew of the revelation from God in Christ given in the history through which they had lived; this function is now performed by the New Testament.[3] They also interpreted and taught that revelation and applied it in the fields of prayer, or worship, of practice and of ethics; this is the function now performed by the bishops (at least for those who accept episcopacy as the proper form of Church government). Apostolic doctrine today (as in Irenaeus' time) should mean, not the doctrine taught by the men who are successors of the apostles, whatever they teach, but the doctrine of the essentially apostolic book, the New Testament.[4]

4. Traditional Rites

We have already had occasion more than once to observe that when the fathers give examples of unwritten tradition in the form of customs or practices within the life of the Church they usually include some rite or ceremony connected with the sacraments in their examples. Tertullian is one obvious example[5] and Hippolytus another,[6] Origen a third,[7] and Basil of Caesarea[8] will presently afford us a fourth. It is beyond question that the sacraments of baptism and of the eucharist at least had their origins before a word of the New Testament was written, from the very

---

[1] Flesseman-van Leer, *Tradition and Scripture*, p. 190.
[2] Though Flesseman-van Leer (*op. cit.*, pp. 114–15) believes that Irenaeus did not in fact do this.
[3] See Von Campenhausen, *Kirchliches Amt*, p. 25.
[4] Much of this thought is well expressed in Flesseman-van Leer, *op. cit.*, pp. 114–15.
[5] *De Corona* 3.2–4; see above, p. 132.
[6] *Apostolic Tradition* 1.2, 3, 5; 23.13, *et passim*; see above, pp. 137–8.
[7] See above, pp. 138–9.
[8] *On the Holy Spirit*, XXVII. 66.188a–189. See below, pp. 181–3.

institution of our Lord himself in the days of his flesh. Formally at least they constitute early and authentic Christian tradition which antedates the New Testament.[1] May there not be traces of a genuine tradition independent of Scripture connected with these? Are there any remains, for instance, of early liturgies?

There are of course early descriptions of the rite and ceremonies of Christian baptism by Justin,[2] by Tertullian,[3] and by Hippolytus.[4] But these are all much later than even the latest documents of the New Testament. A very recent book in English by Whitaker,[5] in a section entitled 'Documents of the Ante-Nicene Church', gives all extracts thought relevant by the author from the *Didache*, from Justin's *First Apology*, from Hippolytus, from Tertullian, from the *Didascalia Apostolorum*, the *Acts of Judas Thomas* and the *Acts of Xanthippe and Polyxena*.[6] The only evidence that one can collect from all this material for a traditional rite or a traditional formula is the rite of immersion in water and the formula of invocation of the Father, of the Son and of the Holy Spirit, things which can hardly be described as independent of the New Testament. There are in fact one or two hints of traditional formulae or even of a liturgy in the pre-Nicene fathers not noticed by Whitaker. Cyprian in one of his letters has a sentence concerned with unction with oil after baptism where there occurs the archaistic or stylized, perhaps even Semitic, phrase 'creature of oil';[7] such a phrase strongly suggests a sterotyped liturgical formula. Again, Firmilian of Cappadocia in his letter to Cyprian tells the story of a woman in his part of the world who set herself up as a Church leader and, among other activities, administered baptism and 'borrowed the customary and lawful words of interrogation';[8] this suggests a stereotyped form of baptismal profession. If this form was stereotyped, the rest of the rite may have been so also. The anonymous author of *De Rebaptismate* confirms this impression when he refers to unskilled bishops who when administering the rite of baptism 'speak in their conferring of the sacrament otherwise than they should' and 'either put questions or when they have put the questions accept from those

---

[1] Büchsel (παράδοσις in *TWNT* V) notes that Paul does not use παράδοσις nor παραδοῦναι of sacraments. But later of course sacraments were freely included in the *paradosis*; cf. Tertullian, *De Baptismo* 1.1: *non exploratis rationibus traditionum*, of those who have not investigated the reasons for baptism.

[2] *Apology* 1.61.9.

[3] *De Baptismo* 6–8.

[4] *Apostolic Tradition* 21–22.

[5] E. C. Whitaker, *The Documents of the Baptismal Liturgy*.

[6] Whitaker, *Documents*, pp. 1–17.

[7] *creaturam olei*, *Ep.* 70.2.1.

[8] *usurpans usitata et legitima verba interrogationis*, *Ep.* 75.10.5.

who are replying answers which are anything but what such questions and answers ought to be.'[1] Again Jeremias, in his *Infant Baptism in the First Four Centuries*, institutes[2] a close comparison between Matt. 18.3, Mark 10.15 (=Luke 18.17), John 3.5 (and 3), Justin *Apology* 1.61.4 and *Apostolic Constitutions* VI.15.5, designed to show that 'all five formularies have to do with one and the same saying' (p. 51). Justin's version of the saying resembles the saying in John 3.5 only in the use of one verb, and for the rest is more like Matthew's version, indeed in the last eight words actually reproduces it.[3] The saying in Justin is commonly reckoned a quotation from John 3.5, especially as the following sentence makes an allusion to John 3.4. But Justin's words reappear exactly in Clement of Alexandria *Protreptikos* 9.82 and in the *Clementine Homilies* 11.26.2 and *Clementine Recognitions* 6.9. Jeremias concludes that Justin's saying must have circulated independently, and he comments: 'Although he knew the Nicodemus story, he follows in his wording . . . the oral tradition.'[4] But even so this was presumably oral tradition based on the Matthaean saying as applied to Christian baptism; or at least we can only conjecture the existence of this oral tradition because we know of the Matthaean saying. Next, Jeremias shows[5] how strong is the evidence for the view originally proposed by Cullmann[6] that a formula inquiring 'What hinders?' was used just before the administration of baptism in the primitive Church, at least at the period when the Book of Acts was written, but possibly earlier too, to ensure that there were no impediments to baptism. Cullmann relied for his evidence on Mark 10.14; Matt. 19.14; Luke 18.16; Acts 8.36; 10.47; 11.17. He added Matt. 3.14 and Epiphanius *Haer.* 30.13.8 (a fragment of an Ebionite gospel). But Jeremias adds further evidence: an analogous procedure in receiving a Gentile into Judaism; *Clementine Homilies* 13.5.1 (the 'What hinders?' formula) and 13.11.2 (the last two examples adduced by Molland), and the same 'What hinders?' formula to be found in 'the Syriac version of the Irene legend' (p. 53). But the material unearthed by researches such as these is very small and very fragmentary, and itself can only be discovered because we

---

[1] *aliter quam oportet in traditione baptismi locuti . . . aut interrogantes a respondentibus audierint quod minime ita interrogari aut responderi debet*, *De Rebapt.* 10 (81); cf. 16 (90).

[2] pp. 51–55.

[3] Justin's ἂν μὴ ἀναγεννηθῆτε οὐ μὴ εἰσέλθητε εἰς τὴν βασιλείαν τῶν οὐρανῶν is like John 3.5 only in the use of the verb ἀναγεννάω, but otherwise is very like Matthew's ἐὰν μὴ . . . γένησθε ὡς τὰ παιδία, οὐ μὴ εἰσέλθητε εἰς τὴν βασιλείαν τῶν οὐρανῶν.

[4] *Infant Baptism*, p. 52.

[5] *Ibid.* pp. 53–55. Even Westcott, who quotes Ephraem Syrus *De Paenitentia* 3 and *Apostolic Constitutions* VI.15 as reproducing this form of saying, cannot be confident that it derives directly from the fourth gospel (*Canon of the NT*, pp. 153–6).

[6] In *Baptism in the New Testament*, pp. 71–80.

have already have the New Testament to compare with it. The scantiness
of the material only serves to emphasize how early are the documents
of the New Testament and how quickly they became influential enough
to drive almost every other early source off the field.

The same situation holds for eucharistic liturgies or eucharistic material
of any sort. The witness of the New Testament to the institution of the
eucharist and its meaning to and use in the early Church stands immovably
in the position of earliest evidence. There are early prayers to be found
in *I Clement*[1] and Irenaeus[2] and in the *Martyrdom of Polycarp*,[3] but we
cannot be sure that they are all (or any of them) eucharistic prayers.
There are descriptions of the eucharist in Justin[4] and in Hippolytus,[5]
and there are a great many incidental pieces of information to be gleaned
about it from early patristic works. But there is a remarkable lack of early
liturgies, and the man who speaks readily about 'the early liturgies of the
Church' is either referring to post-Nicene authorities or does not know
what he is talking about. Hippolytus in his *Apostolic Tradition* gives us
the outline of the eucharistic liturgy in Rome of his day, with some
prayers, but nothing like a full liturgy, and it is not easy to determine
how much is genuinely traditional material and how much composed by
Hippolytus himself. The earliest full liturgy which we possess is the
so-called Clementine Liturgy in the *Apostolic Constitutions*, a work composed in the second half of the fourth century, and though (like most of
the *Apostolic Constitutions*) it contains early material, it has been worked
over and rehandled by an author who rather fancied himself as a liturgio-
logist. Again, there is considerable question as to whether there ever
was such a thing as an early liturgy. The picture of early Christian
worship given in I Cor. 11.17-34 and 14.1-40 does not suggest a liturgical
service. There are strong reasons for believing that from at least 150-250,
and very probably for a long time before 150, even since the beginning
of the Church, the celebrant in the eucharist had the privilege of composing his own prayer of the anaphora if he chose, though within limits
imposed by a conventional range of subjects.[6] A rite in which the

---

[1] 59.3-61.3.   [2] *Adv. Haer.* 3.6.3.   [3] *Mart. Polyc.* 14.1-3.
[4] *Apology* 1.66, 67.   [5] *Apostolic Tradition*, pp. 6-9, 40-43.
[6] See my article, 'The Liberty of the Bishop to Improvise Prayer in the Eucharist'.
To the evidence there given we may add the brief examples of prayers made at the
celebration of the eucharist given in the apocryphal Acts of the second and third
centuries. These prayers are often not dominated by Gnostic motifs, and can consequently be regarded as typical examples of contemporary eucharistic prayers. They
show no sign of taking a fixed form, but all vary, and are sometimes attractive examples
of the art of free prayer. See *Acts of John* (James, pp. 228-70) 85 and 109; *Acts of
Thomas* (James, pp. 364-438) 49 and 158. Another example of the same liberty may
be found in *Didache* 10.7: τοῖς δὲ προφήταις ἐπιτρέπετε εὐχαριστεῖν ὅσα θέλουσιν.

celebrant has the option of composing his own prayer in the central part of the service is not one which we may expect to produce full liturgical forms at an early period. The search for the early liturgy of the Church may well, therefore, be a search for a mare's nest, though it can hardly be denied that the early Christians, since their religion came from a Jewish matrix, must have been used to the employment of liturgical forms and even at their most spontaneous they can hardly have had far from their minds conventional formulae both from the Old Testament and from Jewish worship.

The *Didache* presents a special problem. The interpretation of its significance depends upon the date of the work, and conversely the dating of the work must be influenced by our estimate of its contents.[1] As far as early attestation and evidence of the manuscripts go, the signs are all in favour of a relatively late date, in the third or late second century. The earliest certain attestation comes from the third-century *Didascalia Apostolorum*. It is certainly a composite document and the Greek version at least (the one which is usually printed in textbooks) is only preserved in an eleventh-century manuscript. But there are also two Latin versions, some fragments of an earlier Greek version, a Georgian version and a Coptic version; and two later works, the *Church Ordinances* (beginning of fourth century, written in Egypt, in Greek) and the *Apostolic Constitutions*, reproduce parts of it. The affair is complicated by the appearance in the *Epistle of Barnabas* of a source known as the 'Two Ways' extremely like most of the matter in *Didache* 1–6. This, indeed, appears to be the document translated in one of the Latin versions of the *Didache*, the *Doctrina Apostolorum*, edited by Schlecht, which extends no further than *Didache* 1–5. The relation between all these documents is a highly complex and much disputed subject. It is generally agreed that the Manual of Discipline among the Dead Sea Scrolls preserves a wholly Jewish, pre-Christian version of this 'Two Ways' source, which is however not necessarily the direct ancestor of any form of this source which we possess. Some of the material in the *Didache*, at least, bears marks of coming from a very early period. Some scholars have consequently regarded it as a work of the late first or early second century; others have inclined to place it late in the second century and to describe it as a deliberately archaizing work or as one emanating from some community in a backwater whose ideas had for long remained static. One of the latest

---

[1] For a finely conducted account and discussion of the state of scholarship on the subject up to 1938, conducted in English, see *The Riddle of the Didache* by F. E. Vokes.

studies, that of Audet,[1] suggests that part at least of the *Didache* (1.1–11.2) derives from a period even before the appearance of written gospels (in Antioch, between 50 and 70), and that the rest (11.2–16.8) represents a correction or modification of the earlier part by the same author in the light of the publication of the first gospel. As the *Didache* has a quantity of material both on baptism and on the eucharist, this would mean that in it we have what we are looking for, tradition about these sacraments deriving from before the New Testament was written. The weakest part of this thesis is the attempt to show that *Did.* 1.1–11.2 was for the most part written before the appearance of any written gospel. It depends ultimately upon the argument that the phrase

as the Lord ordered in his gospel (8.2)

must have been written before the appearance of a written gospel, whereas the phrase

as you have in the gospel of our Lord (15.3)[2]

must have been written after the appearance of a written gospel, and that even this gospel was 'an evangelical tradition closely related to' St Matthew's Gospel.[3] This is a far from self-evident proposition. The further difficulty has to be encountered of explaining the existence of St Mark's Gospel, which Audet leaves out of his argument altogether, apparently assuming, against an impressive weight of scholarship with a long tradition behind it, the priority of Matthew. There is also the extreme improbability that such a document as *Didache* 1.1–11.2 should have circulated in a written form among Christian communities before any written gospel, or any written source of a gospel, did. There is no really solid argument in Audet's book to prevent our dating the *Didache* between 70 and 100. Recent studies by B. C. Butler have tended to show that the *Didache* is after all dependent upon the synoptic tradition, and even dependent for its 'Two Ways' source on the *Epistle of Barnabas*, a work which certainly cannot be dated as early as 70–80.[4] In spite of the admiration which the ingenuity, the freshness and the scholarship of Audet's book must evoke, we are not justified in following him in such a large-scale reconstruction of the relations and the dates of early Christian

[1] See J. P. Audet, *La Didaché*, especially pp. 112–219.
[2] ὡς ἐκέλευσεν ὁ κύριος ἐν τῷ εὐαγγελίῳ and ὡς ἔχετε ἐν τῷ εὐαγγελίῳ τοῦ κυρίου ἡμῶν. The other rubrics, *Did.* 9.5 and 11.3, do not affect this argument.
[3] Audet, *La Didaché*, p. 182.
[4] 'The Literary Relations of *Didache* Ch. XVI' and 'The "Two Ways" in the Didache'.

sources. The *Didache*, at least in the present state of scholarly opinion, is hardly firm enough ground upon which to undertake building operations as extensive as these. Even on Audet's premises, it is surely significant that the *Didache* was deliberately altered to accord with St Matthew's Gospel; so influential was the authority of the gospels once they were published.

It is of course true that the sacraments of baptism and of the eucharist do historically antedate the writings of the New Testament. But in order to see how little advantage this fact is for us in our search for genuine tradition independent of the New Testament, we have only to ask, how much would we know of either sacrament if the New Testament had never been written? If the Church had had to rely on nothing but oral tradition and a tradition of practice in order to administer these sacraments properly and appreciate rightly their significance for two hundred, for three hundred, for five hundred or for a thousand years, what would have happened to them? Would they today be recognizable as ordinances instituted by Jesus Christ? Would they even be in existence? Without the Scriptures, the sacraments are little more than trumpets that give an uncertain sound.

The appearance in the history of the Church of books purporting to give an authoritative account of correct Church practice, of custom and rite, is a phenomenon which demands explanation. From the end of the second to the end of the fourth century they appear in a fairly steady succession: the *Epistula Apostolorum*; Clement of Alexandria's *Ecclesiastical Canon or Against the Jews* (which is not extant but sounds as if it belonged to this company), Hippolytus' *Apostolic Tradition*, the *Didascalia Apostolorum*, the *Church Ordinances*, the *Apostolic Constitutions*. Indeed their appearance constitutes quite a strong argument for including the *Didache* (whose full title is 'The Teaching of the Twelve Apostles') in this group and regarding it as compiled about 200 in response to the need which apparently produced the other works. By the time the earliest of these works appeared the bulk of the New Testament had virtually been canonized; by the time the latest appeared the New Testament in its entirety had long been recognized as inspired and authoritative Scripture. The evidence for the Church's doctrine had been finally registered. But what about the evidence for its practice? Human nature is weak, and to expect the Church indefinitely to prolong the situation prevailing in the second century whereby each local church was allowed in happy toleration to maintain its own tradition of *praxis* was to expect too much. The period of ecclesiastical empire-building, and of the elimination of local authority and local usage and custom by the authority of the great sees, was beginning even in the third century. More centralized organization demanded more uniform practice. But where was the uniform practice to find its source and authority? These manuals of practice were perhaps written to supply this need. Even so, none of them received anything approximating to the canonization which the New Testament received. In the early Church the Christian showed his veneration for his Bible by copying it out; he showed his respect for his manual of traditional practice by putting interpolations into it. This is the difference between Scripture and tradition.

At the same time, it would be wrong to underestimate the importance of the tradition of custom. Behind it lies something of supreme importance and that is the very life of the Church itself. The ingenuous attribution to the personal institution of the apostles themselves of contemporary Church practice by almost all the writers of the early Church was an indirect compliment to the Church's life, just as their ingenuous doctrine of the inspiration of the Bible was an indirect compliment to the importance which they attached to the Bible. Without the Church's life, even the Bible would have been long ago forgotten, even the Gospel would have disappeared long ago from the face of the earth. This fact has been effectively stated by Pittenger:

> It is the living community alone which brings the fact of Jesus Christ before all succeeding generations of men. Without that community he would be an historical figure, but he would not be the figure that in Christian experience he has been seen to be.
>
> Let us suppose, for example, that in the days after the Resurrection, perhaps at the time of the Fall of Jerusalem, the entire Christian fellowship had been wiped out by Romans or by Jews. Let us suppose that the documents which had been written about Christ during the intervening half-century had been hidden in some secret place—like the Dead Sea Scrolls, perhaps, in a cave where they would be safe from marauders. Christianity would not have existed after the destruction of the community and the hiding of its documents. Then in our own time, let us suppose, archaeologists discover the documents. They translate them, make them available to the general public, and thus bring before the eyes of the modern reader the figure of Jesus— both as the Man of Nazareth and as the One believed to have risen from the dead and known as such in the literature which reflects the first days of the now non-existent fellowship.
>
> Can anyone imagine that by such a procedure the Christian faith in our Lord would be re-constituted? Would it not be next to a complete

impossibility to make Jesus Christ, thus 're-discovered', a living reality in the experience of men? And does not this suggest that it is precisely the continuing life of the Christian Church which has in fact played a major role not only in preserving the records about the origins of Christianity but also in making the Christian faith a vital and vitalizing factor through succeeding generations down to the present hour? . . . it is by such a 'tradition' or handing-on of Christ as the word 'Church' denotes . . . and by such a tradition only that we can be brought into a personal relationship, even today, with the historical origins of our faith.[1]

The Bible is only a dead letter written in dead languages until made living in the life of the Church; sacraments and liturgies are only empty gestures and barren formulae unless they are activated in the life of the Church; doctrine is only academic propositions until it is applied and made real in the prayer, the worship and the activity of the Christian community. This is not to say that the life of the Church controls the Christian Gospel, or the evidence for it in the Bible, or subordinates it to itself; on the contrary, the Gospel controls the Church, and the Church submits itself to the Bible. But both Gospel and Bible are designed for a living community, and are not the living force which the Holy Spirit means them to be until they are functioning in a living community. This was what the fathers ultimately intended when on the one hand they innocently ascribed to contemporary custom and practice an apostolic institution and on the other made it plain that they regarded this tradition as less important than the tradition of doctrine.

5. *Two Examples from the Fourth Century*

The main aim of this work is to examine the evidence for tradition in the period which must be regarded as critical and important above all others for this subject, the years between the emergence of Irenaeus as a writer and, to take an approximate closing point, the Synod of Antioch which condemned Paul of Samosata, roughly between the years 170 and 270. But it will be illuminating to investigate briefly the attitude of two fourth-century fathers to the subject of tradition, especially as one is very often quoted as an authority by those who write upon this subject.[2]

The first of these fathers is Athanasius. He uses the phrase 'ecclesiastical *canons*' to mean rules governing the administration of the Church, and

[1] N. Pittenger, *The Word Incarnate*, pp. 57–58.
[2] See also Congar, *La Tradition*, pp. 59–64; Turner, *The Pattern*, pp. 321–2.

regards them as traditional customs to be observed with reverence.[1]
'For the *canons* and formulae were not given to the churches recently',
he says, 'but were properly and authoritatively handed down from our
fathers; nor did the faith originate recently, but it has descended from
the Lord through the disciples to us.'[2] He is here protesting about the
irregular intrusion of Gregory the Cappadocian into his see in the year
340. Writing later of the same incident, he complains of Gregory, 'He
did not receive installation by any ecclesiastical rule, nor was he appointed
bishop according to the apostolic tradition; but he was despatched from
Imperial Headquarters with a company of soldiers and an escort.'[3] He
tells us that when after the defeat of Magnentius, Constantius, feeling
himself master of the whole Roman world, summoned the leaders of the
opposition to Arianism in the West, Paulinus of Treves, Lucifer of
Calaris, Eusebius of Vercelli and Dionysius of Milan, and commanded
them to sign a document condemning Athanasius and declaring their
willingness to communicate with the Arians, he was met with the reply,
'This is not the ecclesiastical *canon*.' To this Constantius gave the brutal
rejoinder, 'But what I want should be considered a *canon*!'[4] Further,
Athanasius evidently approves of the policy of the bishops of Rome
appealing for authority to the tradition of their own church. In his
Apologia contra Arianos 21–35 he quotes a letter written by Pope Julius
about 340 to Eusebius of Nicomedia and other leaders of the Arian party
in protest against their intrusion of Gregory of Cappadocia into the see
of Alexandria. Julius subscribes to the prevailing view that 'ecclesiastical
canon' and 'apostolic tradition' are pretty much the same thing.[5] He does
not directly contradict the assertion of the Eusebian bishops that the
bishop of Rome had no more and no less authority than any other bishop
of a great see, but uses an *argumentum ad hominem*, exposing the pro-
clivity of Eusebius and his friends to secure translation from lesser sees
to greater ones.[6] But he does maintain that if the Eusebians had wanted
to oust Athanasius from his see of Alexandria in proper form, they should
first have consulted Julius himself. The see of Alexandria was an important one; why had they not written to him? 'Or are you unaware that this

---

[1] Athanasius, *Encyclical Letter* 1, 2, 6.

[2] *Encyclical Letter* 1: οὐ γὰρ νῦν κανόνες καὶ τύποι ταῖς ἐκκλησίαις ἐδόθησαν, ἀλλ' ἐκ τῶν πατέρων
ἡμῶν καλῶς καὶ βεβαίως παρεδόθησαν· οὐδὲ νῦν ἡ πίστις ἤρξατο, ἀλλ' ἐκ τοῦ κυρίου διὰ τῶν μαθητῶν εἰς
ἡμᾶς διαβέβηκεν. The phrase ἐκκλησιαστικοὶ κανόνες is used in much the same way in
Apologia contra Arianos 11 and 59 and *Historia Arianorum* 74; in *Apol. contra Ar.* 60
it means a tax imposed by a bishop on his flock.

[3] *Hist. Arian.* 14: μήτε ἐκκλησιαστικῷ κανόνι τὴν κατάστασιν εἶχε, μήτε ἀποστολικῇ παραδόσει
κληθεὶς ἦν ἐπίσκοπος· ἀλλ' ἐκ παλατίου μετὰ στρατιωτικῆς ἐξουσίας καὶ φαντασίας ἀπέσταλτο. Cf. 51.

[4] *Ibid.* 33.   [5] *Apol. contra Ar.* 21, 29, 30, 34.   [6] *Ibid.* 25.

M

was formerly the custom, that we should first be written to, and so after that the proper decisions should be taken ?'[1] Later, Julius says that the neglect of rules and customs in appointing bishops evinced by the Eusebians is utterly untraditional:

> The regulations of Paul did not hand down this sort of procedure, neither did the fathers . . . for what we have received from the blessed Peter the apostle this I reveal to you also; and I would not have written, thinking that these facts were clear to everybody, if these incidents had not disturbed us.[2]

Julius is evidently maintaining the claim made by his predecessors Stephen and Victor that all custom then known in the Roman church must be regarded as deriving from Peter.[3] It is not perhaps surprising that the Eusebians were not convinced by this letter. But it is clear that Athanasius did accept this theory. He applies it in the case of Julius' successor, Liberius, also. In his *Historia Arianorum* he imagines Liberius speaking to the imperial agent, an eunuch, who was endeavouring to persuade him to condemn Athanasius: 'This is not an ecclesiastical *canon*, nor did we ever hold a tradition like this deriving from the fathers who themselves received from the blessed and great apostle Peter.'[4] And he adds, somewhat rhetorically, 'Eunuchs cannot tolerate the declaration of Peter,' as if Peter spoke through Liberius.[5]

But Athanasius also regards orthodox doctrinal development before his day, or even in his day, as tradition to be reverently observed. He defends the decisions of the bishops at the Council of Nicaea thus:

> They did not write about the faith, 'We have decided', but 'This is the way the catholic Church believes'; and directly afterwards they profess how they believe, so that they should demonstrate that their thought is not an innovation, but apostolic, and what they wrote was not invented by them but this is what the apostles taught.[6]

---

[1] *Ibid.* 35: ἢ ἀγνοεῖτε ὅτι τοῦτο ἔθος ἦν πρότερον γράφεσθαι ἡμῖν, καὶ οὕτως ἔνθεν ὁρίζεσθαι τὰ δίκαια;

[2] *Ibid.* 35: οὐχ οὕτως αἱ Παύλου διατάξεις, οὐχ οὕτως οἱ πατέρες παραδεδώκασιν . . . ἃ γὰρ παρειλή-φαμεν παρὰ τοῦ μακαρίου Πέτρου τοῦ ἀποστόλου ταῦτα καὶ ὑμῖν δηλῶ· καὶ οὐχ ἂν ἔγραψα, φανερὰ ἡγούμενος εἶναι ταῦτα παρὰ πᾶσιν, εἰ μὴ τὰ γενόμενα ἡμᾶς ἐτάραξεν.

[3] But Julius seems to have improved upon his predecessors' claims by maintaining that no bishop should be appointed to a great see without his consent. The exact reference of the words which appear to express this claim is however uncertain.

[4] *Hist. Arian.* 37: οὐκ ἔστιν οὗτος ἐκκλησιαστικὸς κανών, οὔτε τοιαύτην πώποτε παράδοσιν ἔσχομεν παρὰ τῶν πατέρων, τῶν καὶ αὐτῶν παραλαβόντων παρὰ τοῦ μακαρίου καὶ μεγάλου ἀποστόλου Πέτρου.

[5] *Ibid.* 38. Even after Liberius had betrayed him, Athanasius speaks generously of him (41): ὁ δὲ Λιβέριος, ἐξορισθείς, ὕστερον μετὰ διετῆ χρόνον [i.e. in 357] ὤκλασε καὶ φοβηθεὶς τὸν ἀπειλούμενον θάνατον ὑπέγραψεν.

[6] *De Synodis* 4: περὶ δὲ τῆς πίστεως ἔγραψαν οὐκ "Ἔδοξεν, ἀλλ' Οὕτως πιστεύει ἡ καθολικὴ ἐκκλησία· καὶ εὐθὺς ὡμολόγησαν πῶς πιστεύουσιν, ἵνα δείξωσιν ὅτι μὴ νεώτερον, ἀλλ' ἀποστολικόν ἐστιν αὐτῶν τὸ φρόνημα, καὶ ἔγραψαν οὐκ ἐξ αὐτῶν εὑρέθη, ἀλλὰ ταῦτ' ἐστιν ἅπερ ἐδίδαξαν οἱ ἀπόστολοι.

The followers of Aetius had apparently been circulating the opinion that councils were futile, in order to discredit the Nicene council, maintaining that Holy Scripture is sufficient, and saying, 'If a council is necessary on this subject, there are the decisions of the fathers' (ἔστι τὰ τῶν πατέρων). Athanasius replies that the Nicene fathers knew of these arguments: 'But they also recorded this fine statement, so that those who sincerely search the formula of these bishops could by them be reminded of the cult of Christ which is declared in the divine Scriptures.'[1] The Arians consistently contended that the Nicene party were involving the historic faith in unnecessary dogmatic subtleties, and Athanasius, instead of replying, 'A formidable dogmatic superstructure is necessary', consistently maintained that the Nicene formula did not complicate the faith but merely safeguarded its original meaning. It does not remotely occur to him that the Council of Nicaea was producing new revelation; it was in his view simply interpreting Scripture, reminding men of its true meaning. The Arians, he declares, were virtually saying, 'Contradicting those who came before us, and transgressing the traditions of the fathers (παραβαίνοντες τὰς παραδόσεις τῶν πατέρων), we have decided that a council must take place', that is the Council of Ariminum, which Athanasius regarded as superfluous and held under bad auspices.[2] He makes a very strong protest against the Arian desire to overthrow the conclusions of the Council of Nicaea on the grounds that they are attacking their own fathers in the faith and disregarding tradition.[3] Against the argument that the fathers who condemned Paul of Samosata also condemned the *homoousion*, he says that we must not criticize the fathers, alleging that some decided wisely and some otherwise; nor must we divide up the time, saying that the early authorities must override the later.[4] Unless we are to prove bastards (νόθοι), we must approve of what the fathers said: 'From them we have the traditions and from them the teaching of true religion.'[5] He urges those who receive his letter to pray, 'remaining on the foundation of the apostles and holding fast to the traditions of the fathers'.[6]

But we must not allow this evidence to lead us into the error of thinking that Athanasius regards tradition as a second source of doctrine parallel

---

[1] *Ibid.* 6: ἀλλὰ καὶ ἔγραψαν οὕτω καλῶς, ὥστε τοὺς γνησίως ἐντυγχάνοντας τοῖς ἐκείνων γράμμασιν δύνασθαι παρ' αὐτῶν ὑπομιμνήσκεσθαι τὴν ἐν ταῖς θείαις γραφαῖς καταγγελλομένην εἰς Χριστὸν εὐσέβειαν

[2] *Ibid.* 7; *De Synodis* was written towards the end of the year 359, but some additions were made later.

[3] *Ibid.* 13 and 14.

[4] *Ibid.* 43.

[5] *Ibid.* 47: ἐξ αὐτῶν ἔχομεν τὰς παραδόσεις καὶ παρ' αὐτῶν τὴν τῆς εὐσεβείας διδασκαλίαν.

[6] *Ibid.* 54: μένοντες ἐπὶ τὸν θεμέλιον τῶν ἀποστόλων καὶ τὰς παραδόσεις τῶν πατέρων κατέχοντες.

with Scripture. Pollard, in a useful article,[1] has emphasized that Athanasius on many occasions professes belief in the sufficiency of Scripture.[2] He refers us particularly to *Ad Adelphium*[3] and *Epistula ad Serapionem* I 28. 'Tradition', he says, 'is not a source of doctrine apart from or supplementary to Scripture; it is rather the πίστις, διδασκαλία and κήρυγμα[4] which have been handed down through the ages from the Lord himself and the apostles. For Athanasius, then, tradition, the *regula fidei*, is a summary of the teaching of Christ and of the preaching of the apostles, a summary used from very early times in the instruction of catechumens and based on the baptismal formula of Matt. 28.19.'[5] Later[6] he discusses Athanasius' appeal to the scope (σκοπός) of Scripture; this is a concept like Irenaeus' 'main body of truth', the 'purport' (*ratio*) of Scripture in Tertullian and the 'analogy of faith' among the sixteenth-century Reformers. Pollard quotes a passage from the *Orationes contra Arianos*:[7]

> What has been briefly said above may suffice to show their misunderstanding of the passages which they then alleged; and that they certainly give an unsound interpretation of what they now allege from the gospels we may easily see, if we consider the scope (σκοπός) of that faith which we Christians hold, and, using it as a rule (κανών), apply ourselves, as the apostle teaches, to the reading of inspired Scripture.

Pollard comments that this does not mean that Athanasius is laying down the principle that the *regula fidei* is to be used as a rule (κανών) for the interpretation of Scripture; 'scope' means general bearing or drift. He goes on to say that the 'ecclesiastical scope', the 'scope of faith' and the 'scope of Scripture' are identical for Athanasius: 'By appealing to this scope Athanasius is simply asserting the principle that Scripture must be interpreted by Scripture, the part in the light of the whole. . . . When he appeals to the scope of Scripture, Athanasius is appealing to the witness of Scripture as a whole over against what might be deduced from any single isolated passage or verse.'[8] It is clear, then, that Athanasius took the same attitude to the rule of faith in relation to Scripture as was normal with the fathers of the second half of the second century and of the third century; in no serious sense did he regard it as a second source of doctrine parallel with Scripture. On the other hand, within the

[1] T.E. Pollard, 'The Exegesis of Scripture and the Arian Controversy'.
[2] Op. cit., p. 419.
[3] *Ibid.* p. 421.   [4] Faith, teaching and preaching.
[5] Pollard, 'The Exegesis of Scripture', p. 421.   [6] *Ibid.* pp. 422–5.
[7] *Ibid.* p. 423: the passage comes from III. 28; the translation is Pollard's.
[8] *Ibid.* p. 424. See also C. R. B. Shapland, *The Letters of Saint Athanasius concerning the Holy Spirit*, pp. 133–4.

concept of tradition Athanasius includes the development or formation of doctrine up to his day. And he seems to have subscribed to the view, widely entertained but not universally accepted before his day, that customs and practices relating to the life and the institutions of the Church which were known as of long standing could confidently be regarded as instituted by the apostles themselves.

The other example of fourth-century thought upon the subject of tradition which we shall look at is provided by the well-known passages referring to unwritten tradition in the book by Basil of Caesarea *On the Holy Spirit*.[1] In the course of this work Basil has occasion very strongly to defend the form of the traditional doxology which he regards as orthodox. His opponents prefer to say 'Glory be to the Father through the Son in the Holy Spirit', and he champions vigorously the formula 'Glory be to the Father with (μετά) the Son and with (σύν) the Holy Spirit.' For the words respecting the Son his opponents plead the force of church custom in their favour.[2] Basil replies[3] that both customs are prevalent among the faithful but that ancient tradition supports the 'with'. But he hastens to add, 'But it is not enough for us that this is the tradition of the fathers, for even the fathers followed the intention of Scripture.'[4] But when he comes to defending the form of words in respect of the Spirit he explicitly states that he has three sources of material: 'universal notions' (κοιναὶ ἔννοιαι) about the Spirit (by which he means the pronouncements of contemporary philosophy and in particular Neoplatonic philosophy); the ideas about the Spirit which he has collected from the Scriptures; the ideas which he has received from the unwritten tradition (ἐκ τῆς ἀγράφου παραδόσεως) of the fathers.[5] His opponents disallow this appeal to unwritten tradition,[6] but Basil insists upon its importance, and not least on the importance of preserving intact the baptismal formula; to depart this life without baptism is no worse than receiving a mutilated baptismal formula.[7] Then in his twenty-seventh chapter he gives his famous account of the contents and value of unwritten tradition, from which we must quote at length:

> Secret doctrines (δογμάτων) and public teachings (κηρυγμάτων) have been preserved in the Church, and some of them we have from written teaching (ἐγγράφου διδασκαλίας) and others we have received handed

[1] See Congar, *La Tradition*, p. 61.
[2] Basil, *On the Holy Spirit*, VII. 16.93b: ἐν τῇ χρήσει τῆς ἀδελφότητος τετριμμένον.
[3] *Ibid*. 93c.
[4] *Ibid*. 93d: ἀλλ' οὐ τοῦτο ἡμῖν ἐξαρκεῖ, ὅτι τῶν πατέρων ἡ παράδοσις· κἀκεῖνοι γὰρ τῷ βουλήματι τῆς γραφῆς ἠκολούθησαν.
[5] *Ibid*. IX. 22.108a. [6] *Ibid*. X. 25.112c; XXVII. 68.196a. [7] *Ibid*. X. 26.113a.

down to us in a mystery from the tradition of the apostles (ἐκ τῆς τῶν ἀποστόλων παραδόσεως). Both traditions have the same value for piety. And nobody will gainsay these facts who has the least experience of ecclesiastical institutions. For if we were to try to disregard the unwritten ordinances of custom (τὰ ἄγραφα τῶν ἐθῶν) on the ground that they had no great force, we would be unawares damaging the gospel in the most important points themselves (εἰς αὐτὰ τὰ καίρια), or rather, reducing the public teaching to a mere name. For instance (to mention the first and commonest example), who has taught in writing that those who have hoped in the name of our Lord Jesus Christ should be signed with the sign of the cross? What document ever taught us to turn to the east for prayer? Which of the saints left us in writing the words of the invocation (ἐπικλήσεως) at the offering (ἀναδείξει) of the bread of the eucharist and the cup of blessing? For we are not content with the things which the apostle or the gospel recorded, but we add other words before and after, on the grounds that they have great force in connection with the mystery, having received them from the unwritten teaching (ἀγράφου διδασκαλίας). And we bless the water of baptism, the oil of anointing and the person baptized himself as well. From what documents? Is it not from the secret and mystical tradition (ἀπὸ τῆς σιωπωμένης καὶ μυστικῆς παραδόσεως)? Again, what written account enjoined the anointing of oil itself? Where did the custom of a man being baptized thrice come from? Surely from this unpublicized (ἀδημοσιεύτου) and secret teaching which our fathers preserved in a silence proof against meddlers and busybodies (ἀπολυπραγμονήτῳ καὶ ἀπεριεργάστῳ σιγῇ), having well learnt the lesson that the holy nature of the mysteries is preserved in silence. For how could it be likely that the teaching of what it is not permissible for the uninitiated to gaze upon should be advertised (ἐκθριαμβεύειν) in writings.[1]

Then follow passages from Scripture to show that secret teaching was envisaged in the Old Testament. Then:

In just the same way, the apostles and fathers who were ordering the institutions in connection with the churches in the beginning used to preserve that which was sacred in the mysteries by a secret and undivulged method. For that which is published for common and chance hearing is not properly a mystery. This is the reason for the tradition of unwritten things (τῆς τῶν ἀγράφων παραδόσεως), to prevent the knowledge of secret doctrines becoming neglected and through familiarity becoming contemptible in the eyes of the majority. Secret doctrine (δόγμα) is one thing; public teaching (κήρυγμα) another. The

[1] *Ibid.* XXVII. 66.188a–189a.

former is preserved in silence; the latter is published. The obscurity which Scripture employs is a form of secrecy; it renders the meaning of the secret doctrines difficult to understand, for the benefit of those who study it.[1]

Basil then gives what he regards as the real reasons for the custom of turning to the east for prayer, for praying in a standing posture on Sundays and of the observance of Whitsunday.[2] Then he continues:

> Daylight would fail me were I to go through the unwritten mysteries of the Church (τὰ ἄγραφα μυστήρια τῆς ἐκκλησίας). I pass by all the others. But from what documents do we possess the confession of faith (τὴν ὁμολογίαν τῆς πίστεως)? For if, as is logical (because as we are baptized, so we should believe), we make our confession similar[3] to our baptism, following the tradition of baptism (ἐκ τῆς τοῦ βαπτίσματος παραδόσεως), then let them also agree with us by the same logic to render our worship similar to our belief. But if they reject the manner of the doxology as unscriptural (ἀγράφου), let them produce for us the written evidences of the confession of faith and of the other things which we have enumerated. In spite, then, of the existence of so many unwritten things, and of their possessing so great a force in connection with the mystery of religion, will they not accept from us a single word, which comes to us from the fathers, which we find surviving as an unexamined custom (ἀνεπιτηδεύτου συνηθείας) among those of the Church who are not perverted, a custom whose rationale is not insignificant and which to no small extent contributes completeness to the power of the mystery?[4]

Later Basil says that 'most of the mystic rites (τῶν μυστικῶν) are given recognition without written authority (ἀγράφως ἐμπολιτεύεται)' and that he thinks it 'an apostolic ordinance' to abide by the unwritten traditions. Then he quotes I Cor. 11.2 and II Thess. 2.15 (both of which mention traditions), and continues:

> One of these traditions is the one under discussion which those who were there at the beginning instituted and handed down to their successors; the use spread continually with the lapse of time, and rooted itself deeply in the churches through long usage.[5]

And in his last paragraph Basil declares that he must 'administer the formula which has been preserved down to our day by the continuity of

[1] *Ibid.* 66.189b and c.   [2] *Ibid.* 66.192a–c.
[3] Reading ὁμοίαν as an emendation for MSS οὐσίαν.
[4] *Ibid.* XXXVII. 67.193a, b.   [5] *Ibid.* XXIX. 71.200b.

memory deriving from the tradition of the fathers (ἐκ τῆς τῶν πατέρων παραδόσεως πρὸς ἡμᾶς ἀκολουθίᾳ μνήμης διασωθέντα)'.[1]

At first sight this looks like an attempt to turn Christianity into a mystery-religion or an ecclesiastical freemasonry and to canonize a tradition of custom which earlier Christian ages had regarded as wholly secondary. It certainly is a disastrously uncritical excursus into history on Basil's part. Previous ages had been content to assume generally that all customs and rites existing in their day had always existed, since the time of the apostles, but that each Church should nevertheless retain its own customs. Basil appears almost to be giving to the unreflecting assumption that all existing custom has always been there a status as *de fide*; we do not seem to be very far from Cardinal Manning's statement that the appeal to history is treason.[2] But we should avoid the temptation of reading much later ideas into Basil's words. He is convinced that the traditional formula which he favours supports, as the other does not, the doctrine about the Holy Spirit which he knows to be the true, indeed the biblical one. He cannot find direct support for his formula, exclusive of the other one, in the Bible, and so he falls back upon declaring that his custom is the apostolic one. This is the only way that he can devise for producing authority for customs. It is noteworthy that what Basil produces as examples of unwritten tradition are customs and rites, not directly doctrines, many of them customs and rites which we have heard about before from Tertullian and Hippolytus and Dionysius of Alexandria and Origen. Basil is not really claiming that he possesses in unwritten tradition a second source of doctrine parallel to the Bible and independent of it. Behind this unfortunate and totally unjustifiable claim for a genuine apostolic origin for the liturgical and customary practice of the contemporary Church lies an uncertainty about how to use biblical material. Basil, with all his contemporaries, assumed that the Bible was an authoritative manual of doctrine, a divinely guaranteed series of doctrinal oracles. As he searched the Bible for oracles to justify contemporary ecclesiastical practice, he had the insight and honesty to see that there were not any there; the Bible was not a manual of liturgy nor a code of ecclesiastical law. Therefore a legend of apostolic origin for rite and custom must be invented, and tradition, instead of being left as the word to describe doctrinal development and exploration in continuity with the original Gospel, becomes an historical fiction.

---

[1] *Ibid.* XXX. 79.217b.
[2] See N. Sykes, *Man as Churchman*, pp. 67–68, who quotes H. E. Manning, *The Vatican Council and Its Definitions*, pp. 66 and 119.

It is significant that the further we have moved away from the original revelation in history, the stronger we have found the claim that unwritten tradition is apostolic. This is a reversal of the law that governs genuine tradition. 'Tradition', says Salmon, 'is a thing which must be the purer the further we trace it back. The Church may get a new revelation, but cannot get a new tradition. . . . Tradition, as it were, hangs by a chain from the apostolic church, and when one part of the chain snaps, down comes all that is below it.'[1] But then we must remember that the second half of the fourth century was a period standing on the threshold of what might be termed the golden age of ecclesiastical forgery. As Basil was writing his book the author of the *Apostolic Constitutions* may have been compiling his work, and many similar inventions were soon to follow. Grant has reminded us effectively of this.[2] He describes how anyone living between 400 and 1400 or between 500 and 1500 would have regarded the early fathers:

> The Apostolic Fathers had been bishops of the catholic Church, appointed by the apostles themselves or, in one instance, by their immediate successors. They had been prolific writers, and most of their writings had been preserved by the Church. Clement of Rome had written a good many letters, but his most significant works had been the *Apostolic Constitutions* and the story of Peter contained in the *Recognitions* and *Homilies*. Ignatius of Antioch had written twelve letters which revealed that his doctrine was almost Chalcedonian. Polycarp of Smyrna had not written so much, but one could read the Acts of his martyrdom, as well as the biography of his admirer Pionius. (There were also martyr-acts of Clement and Ignatius.)
>
> By 500 one might prefer to remember the achievements of these early Fathers in the field of philosophical theology. In this area the supply was quite equal to the demand. Not only were there many writings of Justin, philosopher and martyr, in circulation, but also the treatises of Dionysius the Areopagite, convert of Paul and first bishop of Athens, were available. Along with the treatises went ten letters, including one to Polycarp, one to Titus, and one to the apostle John. It was obvious that Dionysius had been closely related not only to the apostles but also to their successors.[3]

Grant then gives the periods in which these forgeries had appeared. He points out that in the pre-Nicene era forgeries were relatively few and often detected. But

[1] G. Salmon, *The Infallibility of the Church*, pp. 133, 134.
[2] R. M. Grant, 'The Appeal to the Early Fathers'.
[3] Grant, 'The Appeal to the Early Fathers', p. 11.

The century after Nicaea saw the production and acceptance of a good deal of forgery. The father to whom most was ascribed was Clement of Rome, now thought to have written 'encyclical letters' on virginity, the Clementine *Homilies* and *Recognitions*, and the *Apostolic Constitutions*. . . . After the Council of Ephesus the appeal to early fathers meant that some of their writings had to be re-written.[1]

Consequently, the fifth century saw the appearance of interpolation in the letters of Ignatius, the forged letters ascribed to him, the treatises and letters ascribed to Dionysius the Areopagite. In the sixth and seventh centuries forgeries were ascribed to Justin, Melito, Irenaeus, Pantaenus, Clement of Alexandria and Hippolytus. 'Indeed, in the seventh century the whole picture of the early fathers was corrupted when the favourite early authorities were Dionysius and Justin.'[2] Werner is going much too far when he says that it was 'a period of unrestrained and increasing mendacity' which produced the doctrines of the Trinity and of the two natures of the incarnate Christ.[3] But it is certainly true that after the middle of the fourth century any appeal to the uniformity and consistency of Christian tradition, doctrinal or otherwise, is increasingly liable to be rendered invalid by forgery or invention or self-delusion. In this is revealed the weakness of tradition and its incurable inferiority to Scripture. Tradition can be corrupted; Scripture, once it is canonized, is incorruptible.

[1] *Ibid.* p. 23.   [2] *Ibid.* p. 23.   [3] *The Formation of Christian Dogma*, p. 301.

5

The Canon of the New Testament

1. *The Beginnings of a Canon*

THE FORMATION of the Canon of the New Testament is clearly a subject which cannot be left unexamined if we are inquiring into the concept and the state of tradition in the early Church. There is no intention, however, of giving in these pages a formal or an exhaustive account of the formation of the Canon. All that this chapter is concerned with is to discover how early a canon, or something like a canon, was formed; to consider what were the principles upon which the choice of documents to compose a canon was apparently made, and to estimate whether any genuine tradition has survived, or could have survived, in uncanonical documents.

The Muratorian Canon is the earliest known list of books of the New Testament regarded as authoritative; it is generally reckoned to come from the church of Rome somewhere near the end of the second century.[1] But it is possible to trace the existence of a list of books concerned with the new revelation given in Christ earlier than this. Van Unnik has shown with laborious scholarship that the anonymous anti-Montanist writer who addressed his work to Abercius Marcellus in Asia Minor about 192, when he referred to 'the list of the New Testament of the Gospel' must have meant a written and determined testament, a collection of writings.[2] This is the first certain use of the phrase 'New Testament' in this sense. The Muratorian Canon contains no such phrase; a fragment from Miltiades written against the Montanists is a possible, but not a certain exception, for the language might refer to a period of revelation, now terminated, rather than to a list of books.[3] And the use of the phrase

---

[1] See *Some Early Lists of the Books of the New Testament*, ed. by F. W. Grosheide, pp. 5–11.
[2] τῷ τῆς τοῦ εὐαγγελίου καινῆς διαθήκης λόγῳ, Eusebius, *HE* 5.16.3; Van Unnik, 'De La Règle μήτε προσθεῖναι μήτε ἀφελεῖν dans l'Histoire du Canon'.
[3] Eusebius, *HE* 5.17.2; see Van Unnik, 'De la Règle', p. 5.

'the books of the Old Testament' in a fragment of Melito of Sardis[1] does not compel us to assume that the writer must also have used the phrase 'the New Testament'. Irenaeus, writing about 180, refers to 'the multitude of apocryphal and spurious writings' and contrasts them with 'the writings of truth'.[2] The first translation of the New Testament into Latin was probably made in Roman North Africa; the Latin translator of Irenaeus' *Adversus Haereses* and Tertullian are the earliest and the chief authorities for it. Westcott dated this *Vetus Latina* as no later than 170.[3]

But Souter concludes that the translation of the Greek New Testament into Latin began 'not later than 150', though we cannot trace in detail the development of what was certainly a piecemeal process. Tertullian must have possessed copies of translations of Luke, John, Galatians, I Corinthians, Romans and Ephesians.[4] The Scillitan martyrs, who were executed in 180, possessed copies (no doubt in Latin) of 'the books and letters of Paul, an upright man'.[5] It is well known that Marcion made his own canon of the New Testament, which comprised a mutilated version of Luke, Romans, both letters to the Corinthians, Galatians, Ephesians (probably known to him as Laodiceans), Philippians, Colossians, both letters to the Thessalonians and Philemon. The Prologues which either he or one of his disciples wrote to the selection of epistles in this collection have been identified in a Latin version.[6] They emphasize, to the exclusion of any mention of the really important contents of the epistles, the relation of Paul to the recipients of the letter, and whether he had to vindicate himself against false apostles in it, and use such phrases as 'the true evangelical faith', 'the word of truth'.[7] It has hitherto been almost universally assumed that Marcion's formation of his collection of reliable books for witnessing to the Gospel, probably between the years 150 and 160, in Rome, was the first attempt to form a canon, and that it stimulated the Church, in self-defence, to imitate him and form a counter-canon of the New Testament. But, as we shall see, this assumption has now become precarious, and it is more likely that Marcion picked and chose among an already existing collection, just as he picked and chose

---

[1] τὰ τῆς παλαιᾶς διαθήκης βιβλία, Fragment III in E. J. Goodspeed, *Die Ältesten Apologeten*, p. 309; see Van Unnik, 'De la Règle', p. 1.

[2] τὸ πλῆθος ἀποκρύφων καὶ νόθων γραφῶν contrasted with τὰ τῆς ἀληθείας γράμματα, *Adv. Haer.* 1.13.1.

[3] *Canon of the NT*, pp. 262–3.

[4] *Text and Canon*, p. 33.

[5] J. A. Robinson, *Acts of the Scillitan Martyrs*, p. 114, 1.20: *libri et epistulae Pauli viri iusti.*

[6] See above, p. 81.

[7] *veram evangelicam fidem*; *verbum veritatis.*

his text from an already existing one. The Second Epistle of Peter, which is usually dated some time between 120 and 150, says 'as our beloved brother Paul wrote to you according to the wisdom which was given to him, as indeed he does in all his letters whenever he speaks in them about this subject, in which there are some things hard to understand, which the unlearned and unstable distort for their own ruin as they do also the other writings' (τὰς λοιπὰς γραφάς, 3.16). This certainly suggests that the writer knows of a collection of Paul's letters, whatever we may think about the expression 'the other writings'.[1] One may indeed go on to ask, which of Paul's letters does the writer think was addressed to his own audience? In view of the dedication of the letter to 'those who have obtained a faith of equal standing with ours',[2] and the writer's description of himself as Symeon Peter (1.1), one might hazard the guess that the passage in 3.16 is a reference to the Epistle to the Hebrews, and that the writer is thinking of such passages as Heb. 5.11 to 6.10 and 12.4–13.[3] This list might have been in existence, as far as II Peter is concerned, any time between 120 and 150. Other evidence has recently appeared that a list of books of the New Testament was known and was regarded as in some sense authoritative as early as 140, and probably considerably earlier, in Rome. This evidence comes from the recently discovered *Gospel of Truth*, which the Nag-Hammadi find has yielded. Though all judgements upon this document must at the moment be tentative, it is widely held that this work was written by Valentinus, who came from Alexandria to Rome, and in Rome joined the Christian Church, but at the election of Pope Pius left the church to found his own heretical sect, and shortly afterwards wrote this work. It can tentatively be dated, then, 140–145.[4] Quispel tells us that this *Gospel of Truth* betrays the fact that its author 'was acquainted, not only with the Synoptic Gospels and the Gospel of St John, but also with the Epistles of St Paul

---

[1] So Souter, *Text and Canon*, p. 151. See below, pp. 206, 223–4.

[2] τοῖς ἰσότιμον ἡμῖν λαχοῦσιν πίστιν; RV: 'a like precious faith', NEB: 'who share our faith and enjoy equal privilege with ourselves'; the translation in the text is that of the RSV.

[3] The pseudonymous author of II Peter would, on this hypothesis, be purporting to write, as Peter, apostle of the circumcision, to the same audience as Paul had addressed in his letter to the Hebrews; Heb. 5.11 admits that the subject touched on is δυσερμήνευτος.

[4] Van Unnik in *The Jung Codex*, p. 91, gives the reasons for this dating: Clement of Alexandria (*Strom.* 7.17.106.4; PG 9.548–9) says that Valentinus began teaching under Hadrian (117–138) and was active in the reign of Antoninus Pius (138–160). Irenaeus (*Adv. Haer.* 3.4.3) says that Valentinus came to Rome in the time of Pope Hyginus, was at his zenith under Pope Pius (who acceded about 140) and survived as long as Pope Anicetus. Justin (*Dial.* 35.6) mentions Valentinians as active in Rome (i.e. 155–160); cf. *Newly Discovered Gnostic Writings*, pp. 39 and 64. Doresse (*Les Livres Sécrets*, p. 27) says that Valentinus flourished 136–165.

and even with the Epistle to the Hebrews and the Apocalypse of St John, already existing as a collection';[1] but this writer did not know the Pastoral Epistles.[2] This means that well before Marcion formed his *Apostolicon* or Marcionite Canon a list of authoritative books connected with the Christian dispensation had been formed and was known in Rome at least. It may well be that this was the collection to which the author of II Peter was referring when he mentioned the epistles of Paul. It was not Marcion's drastic higher criticism which set in motion the process of forming a canon of the New Testament, for such a canon was known before the middle of the second century. It has been suggested[3] that Ignatius is referring to a collection of evangelical and apostolic writings when he speaks of himself as 'having fled to the gospel as to the flesh of Jesus, and to the apostles as to the presbytery of the church.'[4] But this reverence is far from definite, and the suggestion is unlikely. It is, however, perhaps worth noting that the early fathers, when they refer to the subject of the Canon, which is not often, assume unquestioningly that it was formed very early indeed, before the deaths of the apostles. Origen says that Peter in his letter calls Mark his 'son' (I Peter 5.13) because Mark had written his gospel, based on Peter's reminiscences,[5] and Eusebius repeats the statement that Peter approved of Mark's composition.[6] Eusebius can also conjecture that when Philo says (*De Vita Contemplativa* 3) that the Egyptian Jewish monks, called the Therapeutae, study 'the writings of the men of old' (συγγράμματα παλαίων ἀνδρῶν) he probably means not only the Old Testament but also 'the writings of the apostles, and probably some writings interpreting the prophets of old, such as the letter to the Hebrews and many other letters of Paul contain'.[7] Eusebius also assumes that when the Second Epistle to Timothy (2.8) says 'according to my gospel', this was Paul referring to the Gospel according to St Luke.[8] Origen before him had taken the phrase 'the brother whose praise is in the gospel' (II Cor. 8.18) to mean Luke and his written gospel.[9] We cannot take seriously these suggestions, except in as far as they serve to remind us that the New Testament was thought by the fathers in some sense to take the place of the apostles,

---

[1] *The Jung Codex*, p. 49. Van Unnik confirms this, *ibid.* pp. 109–21, 124–5, *Newly-Discovered Gnostic Writings*, p. 64. For the evidence about the Epistle to the Hebrews, see below, p. 222.
[2] Van Unnik, *The Jung Codex*, pp. 109–21.
[3] Westcott, *Canon of the NT*, pp. 58–59.
[4] *Philad.* 5.
[5] Eusebius, *HE* 6.25.5.
[6] *HE* 2.15.2. They are no doubt both relying on Papias as an informant.
[7] *HE* 2.17.11, 12.   [8] *HE* 3.4.7.   [9] *HE* 6.25.6.

and that its Canon was theoretically supposed to close the era when apostolic witness was available.

It has generally been assumed that within this list of New Testament books the four gospels were the earliest to be recognized and collected. On the face of it this seems a likely theory, but it has to explain the undoubted fact that the fourth gospel had to overcome considerable suspicion and even opposition before it was given an unquestioned place in the Canon, whereas most of St Paul's letters seem to have won recognition early on and therefore may have circulated as a collection earlier than the four gospels circulated as a collection. Irenaeus expatiates in a famous passage upon why the gospels had to be four in number and four only, giving all sorts of fanciful reasons. He concludes that nobody has a right to add to or to subtract from their quadruple number, 'in the one case so that they should appear to have discovered more than the truth, and in the other so that they should reject the dispensations of God'.[1] Earlier than this, perhaps as early as the eighth decade of the second century, Tatian had formed his harmony of the gospels called the *Diatessaron*.[2] One would be inclined to hail this as a sign of the recognition of the four, were it not that there is some evidence that Tatian included a fifth gospel in his harmony.[3] Irenaeus mentions a Valentinian heretic who ascribed the fourth gospel to 'John the disciple of the Lord', and who expounded the prologue of this gospel,[4] and later he names him as Ptolemaeus. We know Ptolemaeus in his letter to Flora to have said 'further, the apostle said that the creation of the world was the Saviour's own work and that all things came into existence through him and that nothing came into existence without him.'[5] We have already seen that Valentinus, about 140, apparently recognized the four canonical gospels.[6] Earlier still Basilides, who probably taught at Alexandria from 125 to 130,[7] as we shall see presently, not only quoted the fourth gospel in his writings but referred to the 'gospels' in the plural, and therefore probably knew all four, though we cannot be sure that he did not recognize more

---

[1] *Adv. Haer.* 3.11.12.

[2] The Old Syriac version of the gospels, or the *Evangelion da-Mepharreshê* (the 'Gospel of the Separated', in contrast to the *Diatessaron*), represented by the Sinaitic and Curetonian Syriac MSS, may originate from a translation made about 200 by Palut, bishop of Edessa, assisted by Sarapion, bishop of Antioch. It of course contained the four canonical gospels. See Souter, *Text and Canon*, pp. 52–54.

[3] See below, pp. 229–30.

[4] *Adv. Haer.* 1.8.5. See Sanders, *Fourth Gospel*, pp. 56, 62–63.

[5] ἔτι γε τὴν τοῦ κόσμου δημιουργίαν ἰδίαν λέγει εἶναι, τά τε πάντα δι' αὐτοῦ γεγονέναι καὶ χωρὶς αὐτοῦ γεγονέναι οὐδὲν ὁ ἀπόστολος, PG 7.1281D; the quotation is from John 1.3. Tatian quotes the same passage for the same argument, *Oratio* 19 (4). Ptolemaeus also refers to 'Paul the apostle' (1288C and 1289A).

[6] See above, pp. 189–90. [7] So Van Unnik, *Newly Discovered Gnostic Writings*, p. 24.

than four. The earliest grouping together of the four gospels which we recognize today, therefore, seems to have taken place in Gnostic circles,[1] and Irenaeus is the first orthodox writer of whom we can be certain that he recognized the authority of four and of four only. Perhaps we may conjecture that somewhere between 170 and 180 the four gospels were widely recognized in the Church as exclusively authoritative. But it is highly likely that a collection of St Paul's epistles was regarded everywhere as authoritative before that period.

The reasons which lead us to place a recognition of the exclusive authority of the four gospels at so comparatively late a date will become obvious if we look a little more closely at the history of the reception of the fourth gospel as far as we can trace it. We can find no certain traces of the fourth gospel in *I Clement*, in Ignatius, in Polycarp, in Hermas, nor in *II Clement*.[2] The first known writer to quote this gospel is (if we can trust Hippolytus) Basilides. In his *Elenchos* Hippolytus quotes Basilides as citing John 1.9: the world, when created, was a seed containing the seeds of the whole universe; 'and this, he says, is that which is stated in the gospels: this was the true light which lighteneth every man coming into the world'; the ascent of the 'spiritual' to the supramundane regions will happen in due time, as is shown by John 2.4 ('my hour is not yet come'). And, according to Basilides and his followers, 'everything concerning the Saviour took place just as it is written in the gospels.'[3] Witnesses to the fourth gospel not much later than Basilides, even if they are not contemporary with him, are found in a number of fragments of early apocryphal gospels. There were published in 1935 four fragments of a Greek papyrus codex acquired by the British Museum in 1934, now called *Egerton Papyrus 2*. Experts in palaeography place the 'book-hand' (i.e. near-cursive) script with some confidence about 150, and perhaps a little before it; to set broad limits, after 130 and before 165. These fragments come from a 'gospel' (i.e. a record of the sayings and doings of Jesus, more like our synoptic gospels in form than the *Gospel of Thomas*) containing reminiscences, echoes and possible quotations from the fourth gospel, though the quotations cannot be regarded as certain.[4] Again there is the famous P52, a papyrus fragment from Egypt containing a

---

[1] So Sanders, *Fourth Gospel*, p. 47.

[2] Westcott, *Canon of the NT*, pp. 33, 52, 184 (in the last instance the parallels from *II Clement* for the fourth gospel are far from convincing); Sanders, *Fourth Gospel*, pp. 11–17.

[3] γέγονε πάντα ὁμοίως κατ' αὐτοὺς τὰ περὶ τοῦ Σωτῆρος ὡς ἐν τοῖς εὐαγγελίοις γέγραπται, *Elenchos* 7.27.8; also 7.22.4 (John 1.9); 7.27.4 (John 2.4); see Westcott, *Canon of the NT*, p. 301; Sanders, *Fourth Gospel*, pp. 52–53; Turner, *The Pattern*, p. 185.

[4] See *Fragments of an Unknown Gospel*, ed. H. I. Bell and T. C. Skeat.

copy of John 18.31–33 and 37–38, which experts declare must be placed in the first half of the second century, perhaps between 120 and 140. The *Apocryphon of James*, a document from the Nag Hammadi find, which may come from the first half of the second century, betrays knowledge of the fourth gospel, though exact quotations cannot be identified.[1] It is also wise to take into account the possibility of the influence of the fourth gospel on the *Gospel of Thomas*. Here again, however, we are in a region of uncertainty, for it is a highly debatable question whether we can detect such an influence on this 'gospel'. Van Unnik says categorically: 'No characteristic Johannine sayings appear at all.'[2] Grant and Freedman list no less than nineteen parallels to John's gospel in the *Gospel of Thomas*, though four of them are modified by marks of interrogation.[3] Wilson says of the logia in this 'gospel' which are not parables, 'Evidence for the use of John is comparatively slight, and indeed the similarities would seem to be more in the realm of ideas than of actual citation,'[4] and can say no more for the parabolic material than 'evidence for the use of John has been somewhat more prominent, but is still by no means strong.'[5] On the other hand, it is impossible to avoid the conclusion that Valentinus' *Gospel of Truth*, written probably between 140 and 150, betrays a knowledge of the fourth gospel and in several passages, without ever directly quoting it, is either writing a Targum or commentary on it or has passages from it in mind.[6] We have already noted the interest shown by the Valentinian Gnostic Ptolemaeus in the fourth gospel.[7] The terms Word (λόγος), Life (ζωή) and 'the Only-begotten' (ὁ μονογενής) figured in the systems of Valentinus and of his pupils, and they called Jesus 'the Paraclete',[8] and it is probable that an exposition of St John's Prologue to be found in Clement of Alexandria's *Excerpta ex Theodoto* is Valentinian.[9] Above all we can recover from Origen's *Commentary on St John* considerable fragments of the Valentinian Gnostic Heracleon's

---

[1] Van Unnik, *Newly Discovered Gnostic Writings*, pp. 83, 87.
[2] *Ibid.* p. 55.   [3] *The Secret Sayings of Jesus*, p. 104.
[4] R. McL. Wilson, *Studies*, p. 87.   [5] *Ibid.* p. 116.
[6] E.g. *Gospel of Truth* 16.31–17.1 (88–89) could be a commentary on John 1.1–13; 21.25–9 (93) could be based on John 10.3–4; 24.10 (96) mentions the Father's breast (κόλπος), cf. John 1.18; 1–20 (103), though clearly Gnostic in tone, could be inspired by several Johannine passages, and finally this passage has an unmistakably Johannine ring: 'and the Father is in them and they are in the Father, being perfect [and] inseparable from that truly good (ἀγαθός) Being' (42.26–30 (110)). The quotations are given from *Evangelium Veritatis*, ed. M. Malinine, H.-Ch. Puech and G. Quispel; I give first the page of the text, then, after a full stop, the lines of the text, and then, in brackets, the page of the ET. Van Unnik, *Newly Discovered Gnostic Writings*, p. 90, agrees that the *Gospel of Truth* knows the fourth gospel.
[7] See above, p. 191.
[8] Sanders, *Fourth Gospel*, pp. 58–59; the first two terms can be found in the *Gospel of Truth*.   [9] Sanders, *Fourth Gospel*, pp. 63–64.

N

commentary on St John's Gospel, written probably between 170 and 180, where it is quite clear that Heracleon regards the fourth gospel as fully authoritative. Apocryphal gospels, acts and epistles dating from the second half of the second century, most of them to a greater or lesser extent under Gnostic influence, show clear signs of acknowledging the fourth gospel. We can list the *Gospel of Peter*,[1] the *Epistula Apostolorum*,[2] the *Acts of Paul*,[3] and the *Acts of John*.[4]

On the other hand, orthodox writers before Irenaeus, or at any rate before Tatian (if we can call him orthodox), are apparently disinclined to acknowledge the fourth gospel as authoritative. The Second Epistle to Peter may refer (1.14) to John 21.18, 19, but the writer may be here relying on oral tradition. Much ink has been spilt on the subject of Justin's relation to the fourth gospel. We have seen that even Westcott was not quite certain that Justin's reference to the remark of Nicodemus proved that he quoted the fourth gospel;[5] the parallels which he produces in Justin's works (nine in all) are not sufficient to rank as quotations.[6] We cannot ignore the remarkable fact that when Justin uses the expression 'the reminiscences of the apostles', he never includes the fourth gospel in this description.[7] We must be content with the conclusion of Sanders:

> Certain passages are most naturally explained as reminiscences of the fourth gospel, while there are few, if any, which can certainly be said to be dependent upon it. It is therefore going farther than the evidence warrants to say that the theology of Justin is based upon the teaching of the fourth gospel. Justin's writings illustrate rather the first tentative use which was made of the fourth gospel by an orthodox writer, and this tentativeness makes it difficult to believe that Justin regarded the fourth gospel as Scripture or as the work of an apostle.[8]

There can be no doubt that Tatian knew of the fourth gospel when he wrote his *Oratio*, during the lifetime of Justin, i.e. between 160 and 165 or only shortly after that period.[9] He quotes the fourth gospel four times, thrice without any introduction.[10] But once he does give it a rubric: 'And

---

[1] See Grant and Freedman, *Secret Sayings*, pp. 37, 38, 40, 42.
[2] M. R. James, pp. 485–503; see *Epistula Apostolorum*, 3, 5, 15, 17, 18, 29, 31.
[3] M. R. James, pp. 270–99.   [4] M. R. James, pp. 228–70.
[5] See above, p. 170; the allusion to Nicodemus occurs in *Apol.* 1.61.5.
[6] *Canon of the NT*, p. 170.   [7] See below, pp. 203–4.   [8] *The Fourth Gospel*, p. 31.
[9] He refers (*Oratio* 18.2) to ὁ θαυμασιώτατος Ἰουστῖνος, which suggests (though not certainly) the eulogy of a living philosopher, not a dead martyr; and he mentions Crescens (19.1) as anxious to encompass Justin's death, though he had apparently not yet gained his object.
[10] In *Oratio* 4.1 he quotes John 4.24; in 5.1 he quotes John 1.1; in 19.4 he quotes John 1.3.

this is that which is said, The light does not comprehend the darkness . . . now the light of God is Word, and the uncomprehending soul is darkness.'[1] He also refers to 'the genuine reminiscences', apparently meaning the gospels, though he does not tell us which gospels he means.[2] This is not quite the language of one who believes in a canon of four gospels only, each of equal authority. On the other hand, Tatian later included John's gospel in his *Diatessaron*. We have seen how confidently Irenaeus speaks of a canon of four gospels and four only. And Irenaeus, as is well known, is greatly concerned to supply the fourth gospel with an apostolic authorship, and an historical pedigree to guarantee the genuineness of the tradition of apostolic authorship. Irenaeus certainly did not invent this tradition; Ptolemaeus, and probably Papias, knew it before him; but he may have considerably elaborated it. Theophilus of Antioch certainly recognized the fourth gospel as authoritative and associated it with the holy Scripture.[3] On the other hand, we can agree with Sanders when he concludes that neither Justin nor Tatian nor Theophilus nor Athenagoras were decisively influenced in their doctrine (not even in their doctrine of the Logos) by the fourth gospel.[4] It should also be noted that in some orthodox circles there was considerable opposition to the fourth gospel, both in Irenaeus' day and later. Irenaeus tells us that some reject this gospel, and he brands them as those 'who would like to be "would-be prophets" ';[5] apparently these people took exception to the account in the fourth gospel of the promise of the Paraclete. A party, whom Epiphanius[6] calls the Alogi, at Rome at the beginning of the third century rejected both the fourth gospel and Revelation and attributed them to the Gnostic heretic Cerinthus. There is evidence, too, that Gaius, an ecclesiastical writer in Rome contemporary with Hippolytus, praised by Eusebius, whom we know to have been a violent opponent of Cerinthus,[7] rejected as unauthentic both the fourth gospel and Revelation.[8]

We are not therefore justified in saying that the four gospels were the earliest part of the New Testament to receive recognition as canonical.

---

[1] *Oratio* 13.1, 2: καὶ τοῦτό ἐστιν τὸ εἰρημένον· ἡ σκοτία φῶς οὐ καταλαμβάνει . . . λόγος μέν ἐστι τὸ τοῦ θεοῦ φῶς, σκοτία δὲ ὁ ἀνεπιστήμων ψυχή (the quotation is of John 1.5).

[2] *Oratio* 21.2: τὰ οἰκεῖα ἀπομνημονεύματα, but the passage may be corrupt; Schwartz supposed a lacuna between οἰκεῖα and ἀπομνημονεύματα.

[3] *Ad Autolycum* 2.22. See below, pp. 211–12, for further treatment of this passage. Sanders (*Fourth Gospel*, p. 35) seems rather captious in refusing to allow a full recognition of John's gospel on the part of Theophilus.

[4] Sanders, *Fourth Gospel*, pp. 20–27, 35, 36.

[5] *qui pseudoprophetae quidem esse volunt*, *Adv. Haer*, 3.11.12. See Sanders, *Fourth Gospel*, pp. 37–38.   [6] *Panarion* 2.22.   [7] Eusebius, *HE* 3.28.1, 2.

[8] The evidence is summarized by Lawlor and Oulton, *Eusebius*, Vol. II, p. 208, on *HE* 6.20.3.

A better case could be made for assuming that a collection of St Paul's epistles was the first part of the canon of the New Testament to circulate as a collection of documents with special authority; perhaps it was in circulation as a collection before the year 120. The synoptic gospels were known very early, of course, and perhaps known as a collection of three, though testimony for Mark's inclusion in a collection is notoriously faint. The *Gospel of Thomas*, for instance, certainly knows Matthew and Luke, but its attestation to Mark is less certain, though on the whole probable.[1] The evidence concerning the recognition of John's gospel suggests two separate processes taking place. Among heterodox Christians, that is those whose Judeo-Christian or Gnostic proclivities led them outside even the flexible boundaries of second-century ecclesiastical doctrine, this gospel was known and valued early, at least as early as the year 130, though we cannot be sure that apostolic authorship is attributed to it as early as this. It is perhaps faintly discernible in the *Gospel of Thomas* and in other fragmentary 'gospels' from Egypt.[2] We can discern a strong, though unacknowledged, influence from the fourth gospel in the *Gospel of Truth*. Ptolemaeus attributed the work to the apostle John, and so probably did his contemporary Papias who derived much of his information from the twilight region between Judeo-Christian and Gnostic-Christian religion. Heracleon acknowledges the fourth gospel wholeheartedly and thereafter Valentinian Christians, and most other Gnostic Christians, have no difficulty in recognizing it. Among the orthodox, recognition of the fourth gospel follows a not dissimilar process, but it is later and more cautious. To an orthodox Christian living about the year 150, the fourth gospel must have appeared at first sight suspiciously unlike the three gospels he was used to and suspiciously like a number of other so-called 'gospels', the *Gospel according to the Hebrews*, the *Gospel of Peter*, the *Gospel of Truth*, some ancestor perhaps of our *Gospel of Thomas*, until he looked closely into it and discovered that it had stronger claims than those upon his attention. Therefore, though we can see that perhaps even Ignatius knows that 'Johannism is already in the air', and Polycarp too, they do not refer to the fourth gospel as an authority. Justin has read it but does not include it among 'the memoirs of the apostles'. Tatian quotes it, but only at the most with the introductory words, 'This is that which is said.' The Apologists as a whole do not rely on it for their doctrine. Irenaeus is the father who first clearly

[1] See Wilson, *Studies*, pp. 49, 56, 87.
[2] Wilson (*Studies*, p. 87) quotes the judgement of E. White on the earlier Oxyrhyncus fragments that they come from 'a period when Johannism was already in the air but still nascent and undeveloped', and suggests that it can apply to the *Gospel of Thomas*.

recognizes that this document, far from being a potentially heterodox reinterpretation of the older memorials of the works and words of the Saviour in the interests of a near-Gnostic version of Christianity, is in fact the best bulwark against Gnostic or Docetic versions of the Christian faith, and that it provides a basis for presenting Christianity to the philosophically minded intellectuals of the Roman Empire without in the process abandoning or distorting the original gospel.[1] He eagerly seizes upon the tradition, already circulating, that this work was by the apostle John, the brother of James and son of Zebedee, and does his best to support it with other evidence; he decides that the Canon of the gospels must now be closed, and confined to four, and these four only. Tatian has meanwhile included the fourth gospel with the other three (and perhaps with a fifth) in his harmony and translated it into Syriac. Latin-speaking Christians in North Africa have perhaps by this time translated all four gospels from Greek into Latin. Not long afterwards the Muratorian Canon tries to lend added weight both to the exclusive authority of the four and to the Gospel of John as the fourth by inventing or publishing an unlikely legend retailing the circumstances in which John began writing his gospel and making out that it contained the memoirs of all the apostles.[2] The Church as a whole accepts the judgement of Irenaeus, though even in the third century there are some who cannot see in this gospel anything except a heterodox document with a spurious pedigree. The fact, however, that the gospel followed much the same process in winning acceptance both among the Gnostics and among the churchmen should suggest, even if other indications were lacking, that it was not invented by the Gnostics, but only first recognized by them.

In fact there is plenty of evidence that the Gnostic heretics recognized and respected the books of the New Testament, as far as they were acknowledged in the second century.[3] Those who refused to acknowledge the New Testament, or who regarded only part of it as authoritative, were the exception rather than the rule. Basilides not only recognized the fourth gospel; he also knew and used some of St Paul's epistles. He thought that the phrase in Rom. 7.9, 'I lived without the law once' meant that Paul had experienced a previous incarnation.[4] He referred to the universe groaning and travailing together (Rom. 8.22)[2] and to the

---

[1] See Sanders, *Fourth Gospel*, pp. 68–84.

[2] Lines 9–16. Clement of Alexandria seems to know a version of this legend; Eusebius, *HE* 6.14.7; see below, p. 220–1.

[3] See Turner, *The Pattern*, pp. 167–87, and Note D, pp. 194–6, which is a mine of information on this subject.

[4] Origen, *Comm. on Romans* 5.2.   [5] Hippolytus, *Elenchos* 7.25.5.

expression in I Cor. 2.13, 'not in words which man's wisdom teacheth, but which the Spirit teacheth',[1] and his followers and those of Valentinus discussed the significance of the synoptic accounts of the dove at the baptism of Jesus.[2] Irenaeus declares that all the heretics use different gospels among the four, the Valentinians especially favouring St John's, and that this is in a way a testimony to the gospels' reliability.[3] The Naassenes used Rom. 1.20–23, 26–27 as one of their texts to establish their doctrine about the soul, and they also used some tags from the Epistle to the Ephesians.[4] They quoted Mark 10.18 and Matt. 19.17 and 5.45 as support for their doctrine of the origin of all things,[5] and they allegorized the parable of the Sower to fit their own theories.[6] They interpreted John 1.3, 4 to suit their doctrine also, joining it to a grotesque allegorization of the reference to Joseph's drinking cup in Gen. 44.2, 4, 5, and to a drinking-song of Anacreon![7] In the Gnostic document from Nag Hammadi, *The Hypostasis of the Archons*, there is not only a quotation from Eph. 6.12, but it is introduced by the phrase, 'The apostle says.'[8] The Carpocratians interwove texts from the canonical gospels in order to produce a narrative with a Gnostic meaning.[9] It may well be that Wilson is right in his suggestion[10] that when Papias wrote of Matthew's logia that every man interpreted them as he was able he was referring to 'interpretational' compilations such as these. The heretic Justinus said that Jesus on the cross left his body to Edom, the carnal evil power, and said to her 'Woman, thou hast thy son!'[11] Tertullian speaks of the heretic 'corrupting the very word of God . . . either by interpolation or by interpretation, introducing also secret sayings in apocryphal works, legends of blasphemy';[12] but this does not really suggest the rejection of books of the New Testament, only the use of others beside them. Elsewhere, as Westcott pointed out, Tertullian can say that the heretics argue from the Scriptures because otherwise they would not be able to convert anybody.[13]

---

[1] *Ibid.* 7.26.3.   [2] *Excerpta ex Theodoto* 5 and 16.   [3] *Adv Haer.* 3.11.10.
[4] Hippolytus, *Elenchos* 5.7.16.   [5] *Ibid.* 5.7.24.
[6] *Ibid.* 5.8.29, 30. Grant and Freedman give several examples from Epiphanius' *Panarion* of the Naassenes interweaving texts from the canonical gospels (*Secret Sayings*, pp. 92–95). Grant ('Notes on the Gospel of Thomas') gives more details to support the same point.
[7] *Ibid.* 5.8.4, 5, 6; cf. 5.8.10; they used the *Gospel according to the Egyptians* too, *ibid.* 5.7.8, 9.
[8] Doresse, *Les Livres Secrets*, p. 335. He notes, pp. 335–9, how largely Gnosticism borrowed from St Paul in vocabulary and subject-matter.
[9] Irenaeus, *Adv. Haer.* 1.25.4–5; see Grant and Freedman, *The Secret Sayings*, pp. 89–90.   [10] *Studies*, p. 144.
[11] γύναι, ἀπέχεις σου τὸν υἱόν (John 19.26); Hippolytus, *Elenchos* 5.26.32.
[12] *ipsum sermonem dei . . . vel stilo vel interpretatione corrumpens, arcana etiam apocryphorum superducens, blasphemiae fabulas, De Resur. Mort.* 63.6.
[13] *De Praescr. Haer.* 14; Westcott, *Canon of the NT*, p. 277.

Irenaeus had said 'they profess the Scriptures indeed, but they alter their interpretations',[1] and Tertullian allowed that Valentinus used the entire New Testament without mutilating it (in contrast to Marcion) and was content to adapt his system to the Scriptures rather than *vice versa*.[2] That Heracleon became the first writer in history to compose a commentary on a book of the New Testament is perhaps the most impressive testimony of all.[3]

Some have believed that the Gnostic heretics were anxious to displace or depreciate the books of the New Testament in favour of esoteric or apocryphal works.[4] In view of the evidence which we have just surveyed, it is hard to believe this. It is much more likely that Ptolemaeus in his *Epistle to Flora* gives us the usual attitude of the Gnostic heretic to this subject. He 'measures very carefully every word by the teaching of the Saviour,' but he is also anxious to impart to his devotees 'the apostolic teaching which we have received by succession'.[5] This spurious esoteric teaching might well be conveyed in apocryphal works, but it was regarded as supplementing, or as conveying the correct interpretation of, the already acknowledged books rather than as replacing them. When Valentinus' *Gospel of Truth* is mentioned by the fathers,[6] they do not suggest that Valentinus designed it to supersede the other gospels. The *Gospel of Philip*, which is predominantly Valentinian in character, quotes in various places Matt. 3.10, 15; 6.6, and Mark 7.24–30; 15.34, and Luke 10.34 ff., and John 6.53; 8.32, 34, 56, and I Cor. 8.1; 15.50, and II Cor. 6.7; it may indeed be said to regard the four gospels, and probably St Paul's epistles also, as authoritative and to have made them the basis of argument and exposition.[7] The *Gospel of Thomas* uses Matthew and Luke, and probably Mark, as well as perhaps other sources. Wilson has

---

[1] *Scripturas quidem confitentur, interpretationes vero convertunt, Adv. Haer.* 3.12.12.

[2] *De Praescr. Haer.* 38; Van Unnik (*Jung Codex*, pp. 122–3) calls attention to the last two passages.

[3] Westcott makes the most of this, *Canon of the NT*, pp. 310–11, 333. If Heracleon is (as has been conjectured) the author of the *Treatise on the three Natures* discovered among the Nag Hammadi documents, then its marked depreciation of the Greek philosophers (see Quispel in *The Jung Codex*, pp. 59–60), reminiscent of the *Epistle to Diognetus*, Tatian and Hermias, may be designed to stress in contrast the value of the Scriptures.

[4] Puech (*Jung Codex*, p. 24) says that all these Gnostic apocryphal writings, like all other apocryphal writings, 'were intended to complete, if not to displace, the canonical gospels'. Van Unnik, however, denies this (*ibid.* p. 106 n. 1). Westcott had written 'Most of the first heretics impugned the authority of apostles and for them their writings had no weight' (*Canon of the NT*, p. 6)—a wholly inaccurate statement.

[5] See above, p. 24.

[6] Irenaeus, *Adv. Haer.* 3.11.12; Pseudo-Tertullian, *Adversus Omnes Haereses* 4.6.

[7] See *Gospel of Philip* Logion 9(101), 23(104–5), 67(115), 72(116), 89(120), 110(125), 111(126), 122(130), 123(130–2).

suggested[1] that Logion 13 of this gospel, which describes a questioning by Jesus of his disciples about the popular estimate of his significance, reminiscent of the scene at Caesarea Philippi recorded by the synoptic evangelists, and his then imparting three secret words of power to Thomas, is 'a substitute for the canonical narrative of Peter's confession, designed to give to Thomas the pre-eminence'. But it could just as well be regarded as an esoteric supplement to that incident, designed to supply for the benefit of privileged Gnostics the secret teaching which Jesus gave to the select few in contrast to the open and public teaching which he gave to all his disciples. There is an ingenuous confession at the end of the apocryphal *Acts of Paul* which probably represents reliably enough the attitude of all forgers of apocryphal material at that period. It runs:

> Now it is not surprising that Luke has not narrated this fight with the beasts along with the other Acts; for it is not permitted to entertain doubt because [or seeing that] John alone of the evangelists has told of the raising of Lazarus; for we know that not everyone writes, believes, or knows everything, but according as the Lord has imparted to each, as the Spirit divides to each, so does he perceive and believe and write spiritually the things of the Spirit.[2]

This is in fact an appeal to oral tradition surviving independently of the written; no doubt all apocryphal books rested upon such an appeal, without thereby intending to depreciate the publicly acknowledged books. It is perhaps significant that in this case the writer apparently, in defect of reliable oral tradition, had to rely upon his own imagination.

There are, of course, some exceptions to the general respect shown by the heretics to the books of the New Testament. Marcion clearly is one; he certainly rejected the Gospels of Matthew and Mark and would not admit the Gospel of John, the Epistle to the Hebrews, nor (if he knew them) the Pastoral Epistles.[3] But then Marcion was regarded as exceptional in this respect; it was this cavalier attitude to the New Testament which marked him off from others, even from other heretics. It is most significant that Marcion made no attempt to substitute another, apocryphal, gospel for the gospels which he had rejected, but was content to

---

[1] *Studies*, pp. 111–12.

[2] M. R. James, p. 292, *Acts of Paul* VIII. This is a fragment recovered from Nicephorus Callistus (a fourteenth-century Byzantine ecclesiastical historian), and referred to by Hippolytus (*Comm. on Daniel* 3.29), who took it as authentic.

[3] Did Marcion know, and did he reject or accept Acts? It is difficult to read the Marcionite Prologues without gaining the impression that the writer has got some information from Acts, e.g. his statements that the various letters were written *ab Epheso* or *ab Athenis*, and his saying of the Thessalonians *perstiterunt in fide, etiam in persecutione civium suorum*.

re-edit Luke's Gospel. Anyway, later Marcionites after Marcion accepted Matthew and John and possibly Mark too.[1] The other obvious exception is the Ebionites who, as is quite clear from the *Clementine Homilies* and *Recognitions*, rejected both St Paul and his literature. But once again these Ebionites stand rather outside the main stream of Gnostic thought, being conditioned by their peculiar heritage of Jewish Christianity. Again the syncretistic Helcesaite sect rejected, according to Origen, St Paul's writings altogether, though they used some of the New Testament writings as well as some of those of the Old Testament.[2] On the whole we may say with some confidence that the heretics neither dared nor desired to displace or suppress those books of the New Testament which had become widely recognized as authoritative in the Christian Church by about the middle of the second century. They realized that to do so would be to undermine their own position and would militate against their winning of converts. These books had been deeply entrenched in the mind of the Church before the middle of the second century; the possibility of supplementing them was still open, but not the possibility of suppressing or disregarding them. This conclusion also tends to support the view that the fourth gospel was known to the Church independently of its recognition by the heretics, at quite an early date. Heretics would not have dared to palm off a document which had arisen in an entirely heretical milieu, a *Gospel of Truth* or an *Apocryphon of James*, as a document comparable to the synoptic gospels. The fourth gospel was therefore probably known early, but it was for some time regarded as not possessing authentication or authority from the apostles.

2. *The Development from Evidence to Oracle*

Van den Eynde, after a careful examination of the quotations of the New Testament by the Apostolic Fathers, including their citation of apocryphal sayings and their reproduction of synoptic logia in versions differing from those known to us, comes to the conclusion that they did not precisely regard these sayings and quotations as Scripture.[3] Grant similarly, discussing Ignatius' handling of the Matthaean account of the star accompanying the magi and of Luke's Resurrection Narrative, concludes that Ignatius is deliberately rearranging these incidents for his

---

[1] The evidence for this is given in Turner, *The Pattern*, p. 176.

[2] Eusebius, *HE* 6.38, quotes a fragment of Origen dealing with this sect. See Turner, *The Pattern*, p. 179.

[3] *Les Normes*, pp. 39–51.

own purposes.[1] These rearrangements are perhaps better explained by assuming that Ignatius is here allowing himself to be influenced by the *Gospel according to the Hebrews*.[2] But in either case Ignatius does not give the impression of treating the gospels as holy Scripture. Before Ignatius we can observe Matthew and Luke using Mark with great freedom in modification and omission. It is highly likely that the fourth evangelist knew and used Mark at least, and many scholars have suggested that one explanation of his striking difference from the synoptic tradition in such matters as the time of the Cleansing of the Temple and the arrangement of the events of the Passion over the days of the Passover festival is that he was anxious to correct the evangelists who had gone before him. The twenty-first chapter of St John's Gospel itself is apparently an attempt to supplement the gospel on the part of somebody other than the author of the gospel, ending with an apology for the gospel not being a complete narrative of everything that Jesus said and did (John 21.25). The longest of the endings supplied to St Mark's Gospel after the eighth verse of the sixteenth chapter (Mark 16.9–20) was known to Tatian and to Irenaeus, and therefore must have been produced before 165, and probably in the first half of the second century. It suggests that the gospel was not at that period regarded as sacrosanct. If the epithet which Hippolytus[3] says was applied to Mark—'stump-fingered' or 'dock-fingered' ($\kappa o \lambda o \beta o \delta \acute{a} \kappa \tau \upsilon \lambda o s$) —referred, as seems very likely, to the apparently incomplete state of his gospel,[4] then it tells the same story. The very free way in which the Codex Bezae, whose tradition probably goes back to the first half of the second century, handles the text of the Book of Acts points in the same direction. So does the use, without acknowledgement, of most of the Epistle of Jude in the second chapter of the Second Epistle of Peter. Indeed, II Peter gives us a little more information on this subject. 'This, brethren,' says the author, 'is now the second epistle which I am writing to you' (3.2); he knows the First Epistle of Peter and puts his on a level with it. He can hardly be imagining that he is writing holy Scripture, any more than the author of the *Acts of Paul* imagined that he was doing so. He goes on to urge his hearers to remember 'the words which have been spoken before

---

[1] R. M. Grant, *The Letter and the Spirit*, p. 60; the whole of this fourth chapter, 'The Second Century', is relevant to this subject. The passages in Ignatius referred to in the text are *Ephesians* 19.2, 3; *Smyrneans* 3.2, 3.

[2] See below, p. 224.   [3] *Elenchos* 7.30.1.

[4] *Apparently* incomplete, because reputable scholars have in recent years persuaded themselves, and others, that the gospel was intended to end at 16.8. They have shown with devastating clearness how impossible it is to believe that the gospel was mutilated early, but they have produced no solid evidence at all against the hypothesis that, like many another well-known work of antiquity, it was left unfinished.

by the holy prophets and the command of the Lord and Saviour through your apostles'.[1] We have already seen instances of this appeal to the prophets, the Lord and the apostles in Ignatius and in the author of the last two chapters of the *Epistle to Diognetus*.[2] The commands or the very words of the Lord must always have been treated with respect; we can recall Polycarp's condemnation of anyone who misinterprets the words of the Lord.[3] But none of these phrases suggest that the writers regard those books of the New Testament which they know as holy Scripture, or as inspired oracles, in the same way as they had been taught by Judaism to regard the Hebrew Scriptures. We can make the same estimate of Papias' attitude towards the books associated with the new covenant. Of Papias R. M. Grant writes:

> As a historian, Papias regarded the work of the evangelists as not unlike his own. He cannot have believed that they possessed some special gift of inspiration for their writing, since he describes Mark's efforts in purely historical terms. He may well have believed that John's gospel was more closely related to the Truth who was Jesus, but if this inference is correct he valued John's closeness to historical events more than any inspiration he may have been given as an evangelist.[4]

Justin's language about the gospels is particularly instructive. He describes them as 'the memoirs of the apostles' (τὰ ἀπομνημονεύματα τῶν ἀποστόλων). The word translated 'memoirs' could mean 'reminiscences' or 'memorials'. It is the word used by Xenophon for the title of his book, *Recollections of Socrates*.[5] Philostratus, writing not long after Justin's day, in his *Lives of the Sophists* describes by the same word a collection of materials for the lives of sophists, consisting of their wise, witty and terse sayings, which he used for his own work.[6] Grant's researches on this word, however, suggest that it would be more accurate to translate the phrase 'records of the apostles' than 'memorials of the apostles'.[7] In his *Apology* Justin says that the apostles in their 'memoirs, which are called gospels' handed down the words of Jesus at the Last Supper,[8] and that at the Christians' weekly eucharist the 'memoirs' of

---

[1] Literally, 'of your apostles', τῆς τῶν ἀποστόλων ὑμῶν ἐντολῆς τοῦ κυρίου καὶ σωτῆρος, 3.2.
[2] See above, p. 96.   [3] Polycarp, *Philipp.* 7.1.2 and see above, pp. 54–5.
[4] R. M. Grant, *The Earliest Lives of Jesus*, p. 19.
[5] Ἀπομνημονεύματα τοῦ Σωκράτους. Westcott, *Canon of the NT*, p. 111 n. 12, thought that Justin was deliberately recalling this title.
[6] See Dibelius, *From Tradition to Gospel*, p. 154.
[7] R. M. Grant, *The Earliest Lives of Jesus*, pp. 119–20. Grant has several interesting observations about the use of this word and its cognates by Justin and by Papias, *ibid.* pp. 15–18.
[8] *Apol.* 1.66.3: ἐν τοῖς γενομένοις ὑπ' αὐτῶν ἀπομνημονεύμασιν, ἃ καλεῖται εὐαγγέλια.

the apostles or the 'compilations' (συγγράμματα) of the prophets are read.[1] He uses this word 'memoirs' in his *Dialogue* also of the evangelists' accounts of our Lord's Temptation and of his Agony in the Garden,[2] and on the second occasion he glosses the word with the explanation, 'the accounts, I mean, put together by his apostles and by those who were their followers'.[3] He has several other references to these 'memoirs',[4] and once he writes 'it is written in the gospel'.[5] It used to be thought that Justin was the earliest writer to use the word 'gospel' meaning a written document.[6] But now that Valentinus' *Gospel of Truth* has been found, this claim becomes uncertain.[7] In his mentions of the 'memoirs' of the apostles Justin never quotes or refers to a passage which could be attributed to the fourth gospel. Justin's statement that the 'memoirs of the apostles' were read every week at the eucharist led Westcott to believe that this meant that 'they enjoyed the outward rank of Scripture'.[8] But Eusebius has preserved for us a letter written about the middle of the second century by Dionysius bishop of Corinth to Soter bishop of Rome saying that Soter's letter to the church of Corinth had been read that day at the Sunday service, and that it would be read again, just as they profited from time to time by reading the letter which Clement of Rome had written earlier to their church.[9] We cannot therefore assume that just because a document was read at the Christian service of worship it was thereby given a status equivalent to that of the Old Testament, though this practice may indicate one stage in a process which was eventually to lead some of these documents to canonization. It is better to conclude that Justin regarded the gospels, and indeed all those books of the New Testament which he knew to be widely acknowledged, as valuable memorials (which is just what he called them), but not as Scripture in the full sense of the word. Flesseman-van Leer concludes, after her survey of the evidence, that the documents of the New Testament have for Justin the authority of the apostles, and behind the apostles of Jesus Christ, but that he has no theory of the inspiration of the New Testament.[10] Tatian, the pupil of Justin, uses exactly the same term, 'memoirs', upon which the Christians base their faith, in contrast to

---

[1] *Ibid.* 1.67.3.   [2] *Dial.* 103.6, 8.

[3] ἃ φημι ὑπὸ τῶν ἀποστόλων αὐτοῦ καὶ τῶν ἐκείνοις παρηκολουθησάντων συντετάχθαι.

[4] *Dial.* 101.3; 105.1, 5, 6; 107.1.

[5] ἐν τῷ εὐαγγελίῳ γέγραπται, *Dial.* 100.1.

[6] Van den Eynde, *Les Normes*, p. 33 n. 3; Flesseman-van Leer, *Tradition and Scripture*, p. 75.

[7] There is also the use of this word by Basilides; see below, p. 205.

[8] *Canon of the NT*, p. 169.

[9] *HE* 4.23.   [10] *Tradition and Scripture*, p. 77.

pagan myths.[1] He has no doubt at all about the divine inspiration of the Old Testament, but he does not speak of these 'memoirs' in the same terms. He regards them simply as entirely reliable evidence. Grant's investigation of the treatment of the four gospels in Tatian's *Diatessaron* leads him to conclude that 'in Tatian's opinion all the evangelists were subject to error. Though he made an effort to preserve every scrap of information they provided, he cannot have held the theory that their memories were infallible.'[2]

It has sometimes been thought that the use of the word 'Scripture' (γραφή) in the singular or plural, or of the term 'it is written' (γέγραπται), was a reliable indication of the status which the writers of the second century assigned to the books of the New Testament; Westcott, for instance, relied much on this argument. But this indication is a very uncertain one. Van den Eynde maintained that up to the end of the second century the word 'Scriptures' (γραφαί) was used exclusively for the Old Testament.[3] Had he applied this remark to the expression 'the holy Scriptures' (αἱ ἅγιαι γραφαί), he would probably have been correct; the only occurrence of this phrase to be found in the second century appears in Aristides' *Apology*,[4] and, even though it is confirmed by the Syriac, we cannot trust the exact wording of our version of this work. But the word 'Scripture' (γραφή) is used of the New Testament in the second century, though rarely. Basilides described a passage from I Cor. as 'the Scripture' (ἡ γραφή);[5] he had also introduced a passage from Romans with the words, 'as it is written' (ὡς γέγραπται),[6] and had used the phrase 'as it is written in the gospels'.[7] The *Epistle of Barnabas*, probably earlier than the time of Basilides, had said, 'Let us be careful lest we should be found as it is written (ὡς γέγραπται) "many are called but few chosen"' (Matt. 22.14). Polycarp, writing to the Philippians, had used the words, 'Only, as it is said in these Scriptures, "Be ye angry and sin not" and "Let not the sun go down upon your wrath."'[8] The first quotation is from Ps. 4.5, and the second from Eph. 4.26. It is not, however, quite certain that Polycarp is here equating Ephesians precisely

---

[1] *Oratio.* 21.2: τὰ οἰκεῖα ἀπομνημονεύματα. See above, p. 195.

[2] *The Earliest Lives of Jesus*, p. 26. See also the interesting remarks of Gerhardsson, *Memory and Manuscript*, pp. 197–200.

[3] *Les Normes*, pp. 21–22; he said that the terms used for the Scriptures were (as well as γραφή/αί), τὰ βίβλια and τὰ συγγράμματα. Congar has a very similar statement, *La Tradition*, p. 29.

[4] *Apology* 16: τῆς παρ' αὐτοῖς καλουμένης εὐαγγελικῆς ἁγίας γραφῆς.

[5] Hippolytus, *Elenchos* 7.26.3; the passage is I Cor. 2.13.

[6] *Ibid.* 7.25.2.

[7] *Ibid.* 7.27.8: ὡς ἐν τοῖς εὐαγγελίοις γέγραπται. See above, pp. 191–2.

[8] *Philipp.* 12.1.

with the Book of Psalms, in the first place because we have here only a
Latin translation to rely on, and in the second because the word 'Scriptures' here might apply only to the first quotation. Dionysius of Corinth
refers to 'the dominical Scriptures', contrasting their high value with the
low value of his own writings, and complaining that evil-minded people
tamper with both.[1] This expression could certainly mean, for a second-
century Christian, the Scriptures of the Old Testament, but as in the
same passage Dionysius has invoked upon these tamperers the 'Woe'
mentioned in Rev. 22.18, 19, it is more likely that he means the New
Testament, and may be referring to the Marcionites. Again *II Clement*
expounds Isa. 54.1,[2] and then goes on, 'And another Scripture says,
"I came not to call righteous, but sinners." '[3] The Second Epistle of
Peter in a famous passage says 'Paul . . . wrote to you as he did in all his
epistles speaking in them about these subjects, in which there are some
things hard to understand which the unlearned and unstable distort as
they do the other Scriptures' ($\tau\grave{\alpha}\varsigma$ $\lambda o\iota\pi\grave{\alpha}\varsigma$ $\gamma\rho\alpha\phi\acute{\alpha}\varsigma$).[4] Justin frequently
uses 'it is written' of passages in the gospels, sometimes without further
explanation, but never applies the phrase 'the Scripture(s)' to the New
Testament. The apocryphal, though fairly orthodox, *Epistula Apostolorum*
invokes a malediction on those who 'have taught other doctrine, [pervert-
ing] the Scripture and adding thereto'.[5] This could, of course, mean the
Old Testament, but in view of the production of apocryphal works by
heretics in the second century, we would be better justified in taking it to
apply to the New, and to group it with other warnings, such as that of
Dionysius of Corinth just mentioned, a phrase of Irenaeus,[6] and an
expression in the anonymous anti-Montanist[7] writer. Irenaeus writes,
concerning some antinomian Gnostics, 'therefore those of them who are
fully perfected fearlessly do all the forbidden things concerning which the
Scriptures ($\alpha\grave{\iota}$ $\gamma\rho\alpha\phi\alpha\acute{\iota}$) affirm that those who do them shall not inherit
the Kingdom of God'.[8] But then elsewhere Irenaeus refers to Hermas
as 'the Scripture' ($\acute{\eta}$ $\gamma\rho\alpha\phi\acute{\eta}$)[9] and Clement of Alexandria can quote four
different quite uncanonical sayings, calling each one of them 'the Scrip-

---

[1] Eusebius, *HE* 4.23.12; the phrase in question is $\tau\hat{\omega}\nu$ $\kappa\nu\rho\iota\alpha\kappa\hat{\omega}\nu$ $\gamma\rho\alpha\phi\hat{\omega}\nu$.
[2] *II Clem.* 2.1–3.
[3] *II Clem.* 2.4: 'another Scripture' is $\acute{\epsilon}\tau\acute{\epsilon}\rho\alpha$ $\gamma\rho\alpha\phi\acute{\eta}$ and the NT passage referred to is
either Matt. 9.13 or Mark 2.17.
[4] II Peter 3.16.
[5] *Epistula Apostolorum* 29 (M. R. James, p. 495).
[6] See above, p. 191.
[7] See above, p. 187, and the article of Bakhuizen van den Brink, 'La règle', etc. He
might have added this example to his list.
[8] *Adv. Haer.* 1.1.12; the reference is to I Cor. 6.9, 10.
[9] *Ibid.* 4.34.2.

ture'.[1] Tertullian even applies the term *scriptura* to Hermas' *Shepherd*![2] An anonymous author writing against the school of the Theodoti probably early in the third century, to whom we have already had occasion to refer,[3] complains that the heretics 'have shamelessly played fast and loose with divine Scriptures (γραφὰς θείας), they have set aside the rule of primitive faith, they have not known Christ, nor investigated what the divine Scriptures (αἱ θεῖαι γραφαί) say . . . deserting the holy Scriptures of God (τὰς ἁγίας τοῦ θεοῦ γραφάς) they devote themselves to the study of geometry.'[4] If we could be sure that all these references to the Scriptures meant the New Testament, this would be a most important passage. But in fact we cannot be sure of this. It is quite possible that they mean the Old Testament. If we are to judge by Tertullian's *Adversus Praxean* and Hippolytus' *Contra Noetum*, heretics of the type attacked here derived their doctrine rather more from the Old Testament than from the New. Even the statement of the same writer, in another fragment, that the claim of the followers of Artemon that the true faith was preserved until the time of Victor might be plausible, if in the first place the divine Scriptures (αἱ θεῖαι γραφαί) did not tell against them,[5] may refer only to the Old Testament.

There can be little doubt therefore that some writers in the second century did refer to the books of the New Testament as 'the Scripture' or 'the Scriptures'. But it is difficult to discover, once we have established this, just what force this word had for them. English speakers are apt to be misled when they translate this word *graphe* as 'Scripture', for the word 'Scripture' has for them a special meaning, exclusively confined to the Bible, whereas the word *graphe* to all Greek-speaking Christians meant 'writing' or 'document' as well as Scripture. Those who wanted to refer to special, peculiar and sanctified Scripture could use the phrase 'holy Scripture', or 'inspired Scripture', as the author of II Timothy does, referring, no doubt, to the Old Testament.[6] But these are phrases which the writers of the second century rarely use of the New Testament.[7] No doubt most of the cases of the use of 'Scripture' for the New Testament which we have been reviewing mark an increasing respect for these documents and a movement towards their canonization, but we cannot regard the phrase as decisive. The same applies, with perhaps greater force,

[1] See below, p. 226.
[2] *De Oratione*, 16. Quasten calls attention to this in 'Tertullian and "Traditio" ', p. 483.
[3] See above, p. 76. [4] Eusebius, *HE* 5.28.13. [5] *Ibid.* 5.28.4.
[6] II Tim. 3.16: πᾶσα γραφὴ θεόπνευστος.
[7] It should perhaps be conceded that Theophilus of Antioch does virtually use some such phrase of the New Testament. See below, pp. 211–12.

to the even vaguer phrase 'it is written' (γέγραπται). This means that some authority is being quoted, but we cannot tell precisely what sort of authority it was from this word alone.

A more reliable means of ascertaining how early the writers of the second century began to regard the New Testament as holy Scripture on a level with the Old Testament is to inquire how soon they begin to allegorize the New Testament. St Paul and many other Christians had interpreted the Old Testament with very much the same allegorizing technique arising out of early Jewish typology that we can detect in the Rabbinic scholars of the first two Christian centuries, and sometimes also in Philo.[1] They felt justified in doing this because they were convinced that the Old Testament was a divinely inspired book of inerrant oracles, which demanded an esoteric system of interpretation to unlock its esoteric secrets, and because, as the Jewish scholars found this the most useful way of creating out of the very diverse and often contradictory materials of the Hebrew Scriptures a consistent, rational and practical system of law for a people to live by, so the Christians found it the most useful way of compelling the Old Testament to witness directly in every part of every book, without regard to background or context, to Christ and to the whole Christian dispensation. When, therefore, we find Christians of the second century applying the same allegorizing technique to the New Testament (where the need to compel refractory material to yield a Christian message was entirely absent), this is a strong testimony to their estimate of the books as equal in sacrosanctity and in oracular power to those of the Old Testament. Perhaps the earliest example we can find of this practice is in the *Epistula Apostolorum* 43-45, where there appears an allegorization of the parable of the Wise and Foolish Virgins (Matt. 25.1-12). The five wise virgins are Faith, Love, Grace, Peace and Hope, and the five foolish are Knowledge, Understanding, Obedience, Patience and Compassion (foolish, not in themselves, but because they slept). Irenaeus allegorizes the parable of the Good Samaritan (Luke 10.30-35): the injured man is Adam; Jerusalem is Paradise; Jericho is the world; the bandits are hostile powers; the Samaritan is Christ; the wounds are disobedience; the ass is Christ's body; the inn is the Church; the Samaritan's promise to return is the Parousia.[2] Hippolytus allegorizes the parable of the Unjust Judge (Luke 18.2-5): the judge is Antichrist; the widow represents the Jews.[3] In the fragmentary remains of his works on the

---

[1] See *Allegory and Event*, caps. 1-3.
[2] *Adv. Haer.* 3.18.2. Compare his treatment of the Lost Sheep and of the Sign of Jonah, *ibid.* 3.20.3.
[3] *De Antichristo* 56 and 57.

Song of Solomon we can find several examples of an allegorical use of the New Testament, though none appears in his early *Commentary on Daniel*.[1] Elsewhere he tells us that some people treat the words of the poet Aratus like the words of Scripture: 'They liken them to the things said by the Scriptures and allegorize them.'[2] It was normal to allegorize Scripture (but not Aratus), and we may tentatively conclude that Hippolytus included the New Testament in the Scriptures. Clement of Alexandria, who first introduced Philonic allegory into the tradition of Christian exegesis of the Bible, also allegorizes the New Testament, but not nearly as often as he allegorizes the Old. He treats the Parable of the Good Samaritan in this way, but with a different set of meanings from those which Irenaeus gave it: Christ is the Good Samaritan, the good physician who heals the evil passions which the demonic powers inflict upon us as wounds; he pours 'wine, the blood of the vine of David', into our wounded souls; he binds us with love, faith and hope; he orders angels to look after us and gives them a great reward.[3] It is probably significant that we do not find much allegorization of the New Testament among the writers of the late second and early third century. Tertullian is no exception to this rule;[4] it is with Origen that the allegorization of the New Testament is fully and methodically developed. It is significant too that it is only when the Canon of the New Testament is taking firm shape, when the fourth gospel has been decisively accepted, and when the conception of a 'New' Testament, in contrast to and in addition to the Old, is beginning to appear, that we find writers allegorizing the New Testament.[5]

More indicative still of the conferring of a pre-eminent authority upon the New Testament are statements in the fathers to the effect that the gospels, or the New Testament as a whole, contain all relevant or all surviving information about Jesus, in direct contrast to the attitude which we have found expressed at the end of the *Acts of Paul*.[6] Irenaeus first voices this sentiment when he insists that nothing should be added to and nothing taken from the four gospels.[7] The Muratorian Canon repeats this conviction when it says, of the gospels:

---

[1] See *Allegory and Event*, pp. 113–16.
[2] *Elenchos* 4.46.2: ὡς τινες εἰς τὰ ὑπὸ τῶν γραφῶν εἰρημένα ἀπεικονίζοντες αὐτὰ ἀλληγοροῦσιν.
[3] *Quis Dives* 29.
[4] See 'Notes on Tertullian's Interpretation of Scripture'.
[5] The date of the *Epistula Apostolorum* is very uncertain; various indications, such as its knowledge of the fourth gospel and its witnessing to a relatively developed type of creed, as well as this allegorization (though a very simple type) of the New Testament suggest a date late rather than early in the second half of the second century.
[6] See above, p. 200.　　　　　　　　　　[7] *Adv. Haer.* 3.11.12; see p. 191.

O

And therefore, though different doctrines are taught in each of the books of the gospels, yet there is no difference for the faith of the believers, since everything in all of them is declared by the one governing Spirit, about the birth, about the Passion, about the resurrection, about the life with his disciples, and about his double advent, the first when he was despised in humility, which has taken place, the second in splendid royal power, which is to come. What is remarkable, then, if John represents each of the events so consistently in his letters, saying concerning himself, 'What we have seen with our eyes and have heard with our ears and our hands have touched, this we write to you.' For thus he professes himself not only a spectator and hearer but also a writer of all the miracles of the Lord in order.[1]

Similarly the author of the Canon insists that Paul wrote to only seven churches, just as John addressed only seven churches in his Revelation,[2] as a sign (seven presumably mystically signifying fullness or perfection) that he was really writing to all churches,[3] because Paul knew that 'one Church was spread over the whole earth'.[4] Further, the letters to Titus and to Timothy, though written out of personal affection, 'were consecrated in honour of the catholic Church for the ordering of ecclesiastical discipline'.[5] Tertullian echoes this idea about the ultimate catholicity in Paul's intention in writing his letters. He says that the titles of Paul's letters do not matter 'since the apostle wrote as much to everybody as he did to particular persons'.[6] The idea recurs in the *Testimonies* of Cyprian, a work deriving largely from a period earlier than Cyprian's, perhaps from the church of Rome in the early third century; it says that as the Revelation addressed seven churches, so Paul wrote letters to seven churches.[7] We can find the conviction that the New Testament contained all information that a Christian could want and that nothing should be added to it nor subtracted from it in the utterance of the anti-Montanist writer addressing his work to Abercius Marcellus about 192,[8] and probably also in the statement of Sarapion, bishop of Antioch about the year 200, that some things have been added (perhaps better 'interpolated in addition', προσδιεσταλμένα) by the *Gospel of Peter*, which the bishop has set out in a list in order to warn those to whom his letter on the

---

[1] Lines 16–34.   [2] Lines 48–49.   [3] Lines 57–59.   [4] Lines 56–57.
[5] Lines 61–63; cf. the Catholic Prologue (probably third-century) to I Timothy in the *Vetus Latina*: *Timotheum instruit et docet de ordinatione episcopatus et diaconii et omnis ecclesiasticae disciplinae.*
[6] *cum ad omnes apostolus scripserat dum ad quosdam, Adv. Marc.* 5.17.1.
[7] Cyprian, *Testimonia* 1.20.
[8] Eusebius, *HE* 5.16.3. See above, p. 187. This writer calls the books of the New Testament not Scriptures, but 'the list of the new covenant of the Gospel', τῷ τῆς τοῦ εὐαγγελίου καινῆς διαθήκης λόγῳ.

subject is addressed.[1] Similarly the anonymous mid-third-century author of *De Rebaptismate* implies that the four gospels contain all reliable information about Jesus when he says of an incident described in the *Preaching of Paul* that 'it is written in none of the gospels'.[2]

As the writers of the second century appear on the whole disinclined to call the New Testament 'the holy Scriptures', so they appear to be chary of speaking about the inspiration of the New Testament. There are many evidences of their belief in the inspiration of the *Old* Testament. Justin had declared that the words of the (Old Testament) Scriptures were not 'said by the inspired people themselves' but by the divine Word who prompted them,[3] and he held that the prophet Zechariah saw Jesus in a trance.[4] Irenaeus believed that even the LXX translation of the Old Testament was produced 'by the inspiration of God'.[5] Theophilus of Antioch called the prophets 'inspired (πνευματόφοροι) by the Holy Spirit' and 'possessed' (ἐμπνευσθέντες), and described them as 'instruments of God' (ὄργανα τοῦ θεοῦ).[6] Athenagoras went even further and characterized the prophets as men 'who, while the thoughts of their minds were under trance (κατ᾽ ἔκστασιν), the divine Spirit activating them, uttered what they were possessed with, while the Spirit used them to blow upon as a flute-player uses his flute.'[7] Tertullian, relying upon II Tim. 3.16, extends this inspiration to all Scripture (i.e. Scripture of the old covenant) useful for edification, even if it was not in the Jewish canon.[8] Hippolytus echoes this when he says that the inspiration of the prophets was like the inspiration of instruments (ὀργάνων) so that the Word played upon them as a plectrum plays upon a lyre;[9] and he believed that there was no superfluous word in the Old Testament.[10]

With two exceptions, there is no language at all as exaggerated as this used of the New Testament. The first exception is Theophilus of Antioch. He introduces a quotation from the fourth gospel with the sentence, 'that is what the holy Scriptures (αἱ ἅγιαι γραφαί) and all the Spirit-filled men (πνευματόφοροι) teach us, and among them John says . . .',[11] which might suggest that he does not quite regard the gospels as holy Scriptures but that he thinks that the evangelists were inspired, but which on the whole should be taken as an attribution of the status of

---

[1] *Ibid.* 6.12.6. See below, pp. 219, 225.
[2] *De Rebaptismate* 17 (90): *quod in evangelio nullo est scriptum.*
[3] *Apol.* 1.36.1 f.   [4] ἐν ἐκστάσει, *Dial.* 115.1–4.
[5] κατ᾽ ἐπίνοιαν τοῦ θεοῦ, *Adv. Haer.* 3.24.1.
[6] *Ad Autolycum* 2.9.   [7] *Supplicatio* 9.1.
[8] *De Cultu Feminarum* 3.3; he is defending the Book of Enoch.
[9] *De Antichristo* 2 (p. 4, l. 23–p. 5, l. 1).
[10] *Comm. on Daniel* 1.7.2.   [11] *Ad Autolycum* 2.22.

'holy Scriptures' to the New Testament. Elsewhere he says that the utterances of the prophets and of the gospels all spoke as 'inspired' (πνευματόφοροι),[1] and he calls St Paul's Epistle to the Romans 'the divine word' (ὁ θεῖος λόγος).[2] But at the same time it should be noticed that even Theophilus quotes the gospels very little and never allegorizes the New Testament.[3] The other exception is Clement of Alexandria, who said that John last of all 'exhorted by his acquaintances, inspired by the Spirit, produced a spiritual gospel'.[4] But Clement's conception of the activity of the Word in teaching and inspiring men of all ages is so far-ranging that we should be cautious about taking this as a formal definition of the inspiration of the Scriptures of the New Testament. It is not until we reach Origen that we can find a considered and uninhibited doctrine of the inspiration of the New Testament. For him the New Testament is precisely on a level with the Old in authority, inspired in a mysterious and divine manner, inerrant in that though it has mistakes those mistakes are deliberately inserted for a sacred purpose, directly written by the Holy Spirit as its author, every part possessing (in accordance with the doctrine invented by Philo to apply to the Old Testament) its own special spiritual sense, with every word and every letter carefully placed in order by the Holy Spirit.[5] Origen's disciple, Dionysius of Alexandria, even among the very few fragments of his writings which have come down to us, has left us one in which he declares that the Book of Revelation, even though he does not believe in its apostolic authorship, derives from 'some holy and God-inspired man'.[6]

The history of the treatment of the Canon of the New Testament from the time of Ignatius to the time of Origen, then, is a history of increasing authority being conferred upon it, an authority which gradually pushes it onto a lonely peak of eminence shared only by the Old Testament. But this process is a gradual one, in some ways a surprisingly slow one. One reason for this is that as long as the Church moved in a mainly Jewish milieu, the Old Testament was bound to remain in an unapproachably numinous position. Any suggestion that the Christians of the first century imagined themselves or others to be writing Holy Scripture is

---

[1] *Ibid.* 3.12. [2] *Ibid.* 3.14.

[3] G. Bardy has observed this in his edition of the *Ad Autolycum*, p. 229 n. 4. Sanders (*Fourth Gospel*, p. 35) concludes that these phrases mean that Theophilus regards the fourth gospel as Scripture but not quite as Irenaeus regards it.

[4] Cited by Eusebius, *HE* 6.14.7: τὸν μέντοι Ἰωάννην ἔσχατον . . ., προτραπέντα ὑπὸ τῶν γνωρίμων, πνεύματι θεοφορηθέντα πνευματικὸν ποιῆσαι εὐαγγέλιον.

[5] For the evidence for this doctrine set out in full, see *Allegory and Event*, cap. 7.

[6] Feltoe, *op. cit.*, p. 117, *On the Gospels* 4: ἁγίου μὲν γὰρ εἶναί τινος καὶ θεοπνεύστου συναινῶ, οὐ μὴν ῥᾳδίως ἂν συνθοίμην τοῦτον εἶναι τὸν ἀπόστολον.

absurd. It is easy to use the word, or the concept, 'inspired' loosely, as when Clement says that Paul wrote by the Holy Spirit,[1] or when Philo remarks that he himself is sometimes inspired in ecstasy. Philo did not for a moment imagine that he was adding to the books of the Torah, the Prophets and the Writings, nor Clement that St Paul had produced a book of the New Testament. The author of a Paschal Cycle in the middle of the third century claims that he is 'inspired by God himself'[2] in drawing up his scheme for calculating Easter, but we have no right to assume that he imagined himself adding to holy Scripture. The other reason is no doubt because the New Testament started its career, not as inspired Scripture full of mysterious oracles, but as evidence, as the gospels which describe truly what happened to the Lord (in Basilides' description of them), as the sayings of the Lord which must be regarded with particular care (in Polycarp's view), as the epistles of Paul and the Lord's command mediated by the apostles (as the author of II Peter saw them), as the 'memorials', the records or original witness to the words and works of Christ (in the thought both of Justin and of Tatian). It is only gradually that what begins as evidence comes to be turned into oracle, that these books are called holy Scripture, divine Scripture, inspired Scripture. These are the compliments which the Church paid to the books about Jesus as it formed a definite Canon and began to think in terms of a New Testament corresponding to an Old Testament.

3. Norms of Canonicity

The really critical decision about the formation of the Canon of the New Testament seems to have been taken between about 100 and about 120. There is virtually no evidence available for us deriving from that period which could help us to determine what were the standards by which the Church at that time decided which books were to join its collection of documents relevant to the new covenant and which were not. To decide this question, we have to rely upon indications given at a later period. We can, however, gain some idea of what were the norms of canonicity by examining this later evidence. Clearly, one of the most important qualities which any book to be admitted into the Canon had to possess was antiquity or apostolicity. The two are not entirely the same; as the phrase which we have observed Justin using suggests—'the

---

[1] *I Clement* 47.3 and *De Cherubim* 9.27. K. Aland has some interesting observations upon the conception of inspiration reflected in remarks such as Clement's in his article 'The Problem of Anonymity'.

[2] *De Pascha Computus* 1 (248).

accounts put together by the apostles and by those who were their followers'[1]—it was recognized that a document could contain valuable and early information even though it had not been written by an apostle. The Marcionite Prologues, with their emphasis, not just upon the apostolicity, but upon the exclusively Pauline apostolicity of the epistles of the New Testament, are a sort of caricature of the early Church's conviction of the antiquity of the documents which were being canonized. If the evidence put forward in these pages that the Church as well as the heretics knew the fourth gospel quite early, and that both heretics and orthodox only gradually recognized it, be accepted, then no doubt we can conclude that what held back both verdicts, and the orthodox longer than the heterodox, was uncertainty about the apostolic authorship of this gospel. It was only when Papias and Irenaeus between them produced enough evidence of the antiquity of the gospel to satisfy the not very critical mind of the second-century Church that the gospel was wholeheartedly accepted. Melito knew that in order to gain reliable information about an old document it is necessary to go 'to the place where it was preached and was done'.[2] Irenaeus rejects the writings of the heretics because they were recently written, not long ago.[3] The Muratorian Canon refuses Hermas' *Shepherd* a place in its list because it was written 'very recently, in our own day, in the city of Rome, when bishop Pius, brother of the author, was seated in the chair of the church of the city of Rome'.[4] Tertullian, like Irenaeus, points to the recent origin of the writings of the heretics;[5] he rejects as spurious the *Acts of Paul and Thecla* because they are known to have been forged by a presbyter in the province of Asia within living memory.[6] One notes with interest that the presbyter was degraded for this offence. Tertullian's language on the Epistle to the Hebrews is instructive also. He describes the Epistle to the Hebrews as 'the evidence of a companion of the apostles . . . suitable for supporting the moral standards of the masters by the right of propinquity'.[7] And he continues:

For there is also extant a work, *To the Hebrews*, of Barnabas, a man sufficiently attested by God as one whom Paul placed next to himself in the exercise of self-restraint, 'Or have I alone and Barnabas not the right of working?' [I Cor. 9.6]. And needless to say the *Epistle of*

[1] See above, p. 204.
[2] Melito, *fragment* III (Goodspeed, *Die ältesten Apologeten*, p. 309, cited from Eusebius, *HE* 4.26.14).
[3] *Adv. Haer.* 3.11.9.   [4] Lines 74–76.
[5] *De Praescr. Haer.* 30.   [6] *De Baptismo* 17.5.
[7] *comitis apostolorum testimonium . . . idoneum confirmandi de proximo iure disciplinam magistrorum, De Pudicitia* 20.1.

Barnabas is more welcome among the churches than that apocryphal *Shepherd* of the adulterers.[1]

A little later he refers to the author of the Epistle to the Hebrews as 'one who learnt from the apostles and taught alongside the apostles'.[2] Clement of Alexandria, as anxious as Tertullian to see apostolic authority, even at second-hand, in this Epistle, is the first to produce the theory that the letter was written by St Paul 'in the Hebrew language', but that Luke carefully translated it for the benefit of the Greeks, and that this is why its style resembles that of Acts, and why it is not headed 'Paul, an apostle'.[3] This information Clement professed to have received from 'an old man' (or 'a presbyter'). Origen, as we shall see, is, when he speaks as a scholar, very doubtful about the apostolic authorship of this work, even at second-hand, though he found other reasons for accepting it.[4] Dionysius of Alexandria tells us that even in his day there were people who 'rejected and discredited' the Revelation, basing their action on the book's obscurity, and on its unorthodoxy in predicting (presumably in Rev. 20.1–6) a literal earthly reign of Christ lasting for a thousand years, but also because the book (they held) was not by an apostle, but was by the heretic Cerinthus.[5]

The attitude of Eusebius to canonicity is worth studying in some detail. He rejects the Epistle of James, although he knows that it is read in many churches, on the grounds that 'not many of the men of old mentioned it';[6] he denies the authority of the Second Epistle of Peter for the same reason: 'we have not received from tradition that it is canonical',[7] though again he is aware that in his day it was much used. The First Epistle of Peter, on the other hand, he accepts because 'the elders of old' (οἱ πάλαι πρεσβύτεροι) made frequent use of it.[8] The *Acts, Gospel, Preaching* and *Apocalypse of Peter* he refuses because 'we have no knowledge at all of their being handed down by tradition among the Catholics'.[9] Hermas'

---

[1] *Extat enim et Barnabae titulus ad Hebraeos, a deo satis auctorati viri, ut quem Paulus iuxta se constituerit in abstinentiae tenore, aut ego solus et Barnabas non habemus operandi potestatem? Et utique receptior apud ecclesias epistola Barnabae illo apocrypho Pastore moechorum, ibid.* 20.2. For Tertullian's intense dislike of Hermas' *Shepherd*, at any rate in his Montanist period, see below, pp. 218, 219.
[2] *qui ab apostolis didicit et cum apostolis docuit, ibid.* 20.5.
[3] A fragment from Clement's *Hypotyposeis* quoted by Eusebius, *HE* 6.14.2–4. The earliest prologue in the *Vetus Latina*, which Souter (*Text and Canon,* p. 190) dates between 350 and 380, follows Clement in its account of the authorship of the letter. Eusebius seems inclined to adopt it, *HE* 3.38.1–3.
[4] See below, pp. 218–19. [5] Feltoe, *Dionysius,* pp. 114–15, *On the Gospels* 3.
[6] Eusebius, *HE* 2.25; 'men of old' is οἱ παλαιοί.
[7] *Ibid.* 3.3.1: οὐκ ἐνδιάθηκον μὲν εἶναι παρειλήφαμεν. [8] *Ibid.* 3.3.1, 4.
[9] *Ibid.* 3.3.2: οὐδ' ὅλως ἐν καθολικοῖς ἴσμεν παραδεδομένα; the phrase could mean 'among the catholic books'.

Shepherd, he tells us, has been rejected by some and welcomed by others, as useful especially for elementary teaching; but it was used 'by some of the most ancient writers'.[1] The First Epistle of John, he says, 'has been acknowledged by the men of today and also by the ancients' (καὶ τοῖς ἐπ᾽ ἀρχαίοις).[2] The fact that Clement of Rome in his Epistle quotes the Epistle to the Hebrews establishes for Eusebius both its early date and its Pauline authorship; Luke, or more likely Clement himself, probably translated it from the Hebrew.[3] The pseudo-Clementine literature, on the other hand, he rejects, both because it is not mentioned by the men of old and because it does not preserve 'the quality of apostolic orthodoxy.'[4] It appears, in short, that what matters above all to Eusebius for establishing canonicity is early attestation or antiquity; recognition by the Church contemporary with Eusebius hardly counts at all; orthodoxy is a point which has to be considered, but it is doubtful if this alone would be enough to ensure a book's canonicity if its early attestation was uncertain. At one point in his discussion of the Canon of the New Testament Eusebius attempts to divide the books in question into three groups, a division which (as we shall see)[5] he derived from Origen, genuine, mixed and spurious.[6] The mixed are 'disputed' and of them he says, 'Nevertheless we have been compelled to make a catalogue of these also, distinguishing those writings which the tradition of the Church (κατὰ τὴν ἐκκλησιαστικὴν παράδοσιν) has deemed true and genuine and acknowledged from the others outside their number, which, though they are not canonical (ἐνδιαθήκους), but even disputed, yet are recognized by most churchmen.'[7] This list comprises the *Acts of Paul*, Hermas' *Shepherd*, the *Apocalypse of Peter*, the *Epistle of Barnabas*, the *Didache*, Revelation of St John, the *Gospel according to the Hebrews*, the First and Second Epistles of John, the Epistle of James, the Epistle of Jude and the Second Epistle of Peter. Of the books in the group marked 'spurious', Eusebius says: 'None of these has been deemed worthy of any kind of mention in a treatise by a single member of successive generations of churchmen; and the character of the style also is far removed from the apostolic manner, and the thought and purport of the contents are so absolutely out of harmony with true orthodoxy (πλεῖστον ὅσον τῆς ἀληθοῦς ὀρθοδοξίας ἀπᾴδουσα) as to establish the fact that they are certainly the forgeries of heretics.'[8] In this list are included the *Gospel of*

---

[1] *Ibid.* 3.3.6.   [2] *Ibid.* 3.24.17.   [3] *Ibid.* 3.38.1–3.
[4] τῆς ἀποστολικῆς ὀρθοδοξίας χαρακτῆρα, *ibid.* 3.38.5.
[5] See below, p. 218.   [6] *HE* 3.25.1–7.
[7] *HE* 3.25.6; this passage and the next quoted are given in the translation of Lawlor and Oulton.   [8] *HE* 3.25.6, 7.

Peter, the *Gospel of Thomas* and the *Gospel of Matthias*. In his summary of the discussion of the Canon Eusebius again reverts to a division into three groups.[1] But Lawlor and Oulton point out[2] that, if we are to judge by his remarks about the Johannine and Petrine Epistles and Jude elsewhere, and his general attitude to them, these works form a fourth group in his mind, separate from the other 'disputed' books, though he does not tell us what is his criterion in distinguishing them. It is easy to conclude glibly from the facts which have just been reviewed that Eusebius based his Canon of the New Testament on the authority of tradition, but we must define carefully what sort of tradition it was. If by tradition is meant the judgement of the contemporary Church, it must be said that this had very little weight with Eusebius. His tradition was wholly historical and not at all theological; for him, tradition meant the earliest information available about the books in question, attestation from a period as near to the apostles as possible. Orthodoxy was certainly important; a very old work with obviously heretical opinions in it he presumably would have rejected. But then, orthodoxy was only the test of antiquity put in another form. The earliest documents were orthodox, not because the Church guaranteed them as orthodox, but because the Church guaranteed them as early. Eusebius would have wholeheartedly endorsed the verdict of Westcott:

All the fathers at the close of the second century agree in appealing to the testimony of antiquity as proving the authenticity of the books which they used as Christian Scriptures. And the appeal was made at a time when it was easy to try its worth.[3]

At the same time it must be recorded that the test of soundness of doctrine was one widely applied to those books which were, so to speak, candidates for the New Testament. The Muratorian Canon says that 'One [letter] to the Laodiceans is in circulation, and another to the Alexandrians, forged in the name of Paul for the heresy of Marcion, and many others which cannot be received into the catholic Church, because it is not fitting to mix gall with honey.'[4] It was because of its doctrine, not primarily, one suspects, because of its apostolic attestation, that Irenaeus so resolutely championed the fourth gospel.[5] 'What does it matter', says Tertullian, 'even if the philosophers trespassed on those fields which in our sight are condemned by their being branded apocryphal books, for we are confident that nothing is to be accepted which is not

---

[1] *HE* 3.31.6.   [2] *Eusebius*, Vol. II, pp. 100–4.
[3] *Canon of the NT*, p. 352.   [4] Lines 63–68.
[5] So, very persuasively, Sanders, *Fourth Gospel*, pp. 66–84.

consistent with the prophets' enterprise, which is genuine and indeed has
an origin earlier than the period of the philosophers themselves?"[1] He
rejects Hermas' *Shepherd* with scorn on the grounds that the leniency
which it shows to the sin of adultery is wholly inconsistent with the rest
of Scripture.[2] In one remarkable passage he suggests in effect that
Scripture, unsupported by tradition, imposes itself as true by its compelling appeal to reason:

> Hitherto I have dealt with arguments designed to buttress the inten-
> tions of all the Scriptures which promise the restoration of the flesh.
> Since so great an authority of reasonable support favours this subject,
> I mean the honours paid to the flesh itself, the powers of God, the
> examples of their exercise, the reasons for judgement and the necessity
> of this process, then of course it will be proper that the Scriptures
> should be interpreted according to the principles of these impressive
> authorities and not according to the ingenious suggestions of heretics.[3]

We can recall the judgement of bishop Sarapion of Antioch whose letter
to the church at Rhossos, written about 200, warned its recipients that
their practice of reading the *Gospel of Peter* in their services, which he
had previously tolerated, was now leading them into danger because
though most of the letter was orthodox (τοῦ ὀρθοῦ λόγου τοῦ Σωτῆρος),
yet there was certain additional matter which was not. He makes no
mention of whether he regarded the work as primitive or not.[4] Origen
divided the books claiming to be inspired into three classes: genuine
(γνήσιον), spurious (νόθον) and mixed (μικτόν),[5] but he does not in
practice often keep to this division. Presumably the only way of determining (in the absence of the knowledge of historical criticism) where a
book in the 'mixed' class was genuine and where otherwise was by testing
the soundness of its doctrine. This was a test which Origen certainly did
employ. In the vast majority of his references to the Epistle to the
Hebrews Origen is content to attribute it to Paul, but in the one passage
from the *Homilies on Hebrews* preserved to us, where he is speaking as a
scholar, he admits freely, as is well known, that the tradition concerning

---

[1] *De Anima* 2.3: *quid autem si philosophi etiam illa incursaverunt quae penes nos apocryphorum confessione damnantur, certos nihil recipiendum quod non conspiret germanae
et ipso iam aevo pronatae propheticae paraturae?*
[2] *De Pudicitia* 10.12; see below, p. 219, and above, p. 215.
[3] *De Resur. Mort.* 18.1: *hucusque praestructionibus egerim ad muniendos sensus omnium
scripturarum, quae carnis recidivatum pollicentur. cui cum tot auctoritates iustorum
patrociniorum procurent, honores dico substantiae ipsius, tum vires dei, tum exempla
earum, tum rationes iudicii et necessitates ipsius, utique secundum praeiudicia tot auctori-
tatum scripturas intelligi oportebit, non secundum ingenia haereticorum.*
[4] Eusebius, *HE* 6.12.1–6; see above, pp. 210–11.   [5] *Comm. on John* 13.17.

its authorship is wholly uncertain; he records various contemporary conjectures, but allows that they are merely conjectures. But he says two more things about the work: the ideas in the letter are admirable (θαυμάσια) and not a whit inferior to the ideas of Paul expressed in his acknowledged writings, and, 'if therefore any church finds this letter attributed to Paul, let it treat it as authentic even because of this attribution, for the men of old did not hand it down as Paul's for nothing.'[1] Sound doctrine is of very great importance in enabling him to form his judgement here, and tradition, though it is by no means decisive, has its part to play; Origen seems to think that there is just enough tradition sufficient to allow the fine quality of the book's doctrine to tip the balance in its favour. Dionysius of Alexandria, in debating whether it is right to retain Revelation within the Canon, is very much influenced by considerations of the style and the subject of the book itself.[2] We have already seen[3] that the question of whether a book contained sound doctrine was an important one for Eusebius when he was discussing its claim for inclusion in the New Testament.

'The formation of the Canon', says Westcott, 'was an act of the intuition of the Church, derived from no reasoning, but realized in the course of its natural growth as one of the first results of its self-consciousness.'[4] There is a certain amount of evidence that at quite an early date the canonicity of books was sometimes decided by the official authority of the Church rather than by its intuition. Bishop Sarapion of Antioch seems to think himself empowered to decide whether the church of Rhossos shall or shall not read the *Gospel of Peter*.[5] Tertullian says that the *Shepherd* of Hermas, his *bête noire*, 'is stigmatized as belonging to the apocryphal and spurious writings by every council of the churches, even of *your* churches' (he is, as an avowed Montanist, addressing the Catholics).[6] But the impression expressed by Westcott certainly is supported by the greatest weight of evidence. The general verdict of tradition is what most of the fathers appeal to in referring to the Canon. 'Nowhere', writes Flesseman-van Leer, of Irenaeus, 'does he appeal to the tradition of the church for ascertaining the canon [but] . . . Irenaeus is

---

[1] Eusebius, *HE* 6.25.11–14. In two other places Origen seems to acknowledge slightly the uncertainty attaching to the supposed Pauline authorship, *Comm. on Matthew*, Comm. Ser. 28, and a fragment of a *Commentary on Ps. 40.6* (PG 12.1409).
[2] Feltoe, *Dionysius*, pp. 114–25.
[3] See above, pp. 215–17.
[4] *Canon of the NT*, p. 57; cf. pp. 274, 356.
[5] Eusebius, *HE* 6.12.1–6. See above, pp. 210–11, 218.
[6] *De Pudicitia* 10.12: *si non ab omni concilio ecclesiarum, etiam vestrarum, inter apocrypha et falsa iudicaretur.*

undoubtedly convinced that in the church the right canon is to be found.' Yet she adds that this simply expresses a factual situation; the Church does not self-consciously regard itself as responsible for fixing the Canon.[1] The Muratorian Canon has to take account, when discussing the *Apocalypse of Peter*, that 'some people among us are not willing to read it in church.'[2] Clement of Alexandria refers to 'the four gospels handed down to us', in contrast to the *Gospel according to the Egyptians*, which was not guaranteed by tradition in this way.[3] Souter comments on this statement: 'So far as we know, even the early Church possessed no knowledge of who it was handed these works over.'[4] Similarly Origen speaks of himself as 'learning as in a tradition about the four gospels, which alone are undisputed in the Church of God under heaven'.[5] We cannot be sure what exactly Origen meant by '*as* in a tradition', because we have only this fragment of the original passage preserved by Eusebius. But Origen usually uses some such phrase as 'the Scriptures circulating in the churches of God' or 'the undisputed examples among those which are recognized as inspired books',[6] and his test of canonicity is very often whether the book in question is widely acknowledged in the Church.[7] We can even see his favour towards one particular book, the *Shepherd* of Hermas, cooling during his lifetime, presumably as he became aware with greater experience of other churches how uncertain was its support in the Church at large.[8] Similarly Dionysius of Alexandria refuses to reject the Revelation of St John mainly because 'many of the brethren warmly favour it'.[9]

What was the value of this 'tradition' which supported the authority of this Canon? As far as individual pieces of information go, it can have had very little value. Eusebius gives us the 'tradition of the primitive elders' (παράδοσιν τῶν ἀνέκαθεν πρεσβυτέρων) as recorded by Clement of Alexandria in his *Hypotyposeis*: Mark wrote his gospel while Peter was in Rome in order to provide a written record of Peter's teaching, and Peter neither approved nor disapproved. John, exhorted by his friends 'observing that the bodily things (τὰ σωματικά) are displayed in the

---

[1] *Tradition and Scripture*, pp. 132–3.
[2] Lines 72–73.
[3] *Strom.* 3.13.93.1 (PG 8.1193): τὰ παραδεδομένα ἡμῖν τέτταρα εὐαγγέλια.
[4] *Text and Canon of the NT*, p. 146.
[5] ὡς ἐν παραδόσει μαθὼν περὶ τῶν τεσσάρων εὐαγγελίων ἃ καὶ μόνα ἀναντίρρητά ἐστιν ἐν τῇ ὑπὸ τὸν οὐρανὸν ἐκκλησίᾳ τοῦ θεοῦ, Eusebius, *HE* 6.25.4.
[6] For the translations of these phrases, and their references, see *Origen's Doctrine of Tradition*, p. 138.
[7] See *ibid*. pp. 138–9.
[8] See *ibid*. pp. 139–40.
[9] Feltoe, *Dionysius*, p. 116, On the Gospels 3: πολλῶν αὐτὸ διὰ σπουδῆς ἐχόντων ἀδελφῶν.

gospels' hitherto written, wrote a 'spiritual' gospel.[1] Every one of these statements is open to question and encounters grave difficulties. Origen similarly, as we have seen, gives us the tradition as he knew it in his day about the authorship of the Epistle to the Hebrews.[2] It was, as on this occasion he clearly recognized, quite untrustworthy. It looks very much as if the fathers accepted apostolic origin of the Canon of the New Testament much as they accepted the apostolic origin of the custom and rite of their day, or as they accepted the apostolic origin of the rule of faith of the Church as they knew it. They trusted confidently that the Church, at a time when the Church was near enough to the historical origin of Christianity to make a sound judgement, had judged soundly enough in the main to assemble a collection of documents which witnessed to the truth with sufficient clearness to enable men to be saved. They recognized that there might well be uncertainty, and even error, over details. They did not accept their canonical books uncritically; they tried to be sure, as well as they could according to their lights, that the books were written by apostles or by men who had lived with the apostles. They did their best to see that the canonized books were orthodox according to the standard of orthodoxy of their day. But their readiness to accept as useful and even informative non-canonical books and to quote non-canonical passages in their works[3] show that this judgement was in their view only an approximate judgement, or rather that they regarded the Canon as a division with ragged and uncertain edges. It was a luminary clear in the centre, where were the four gospels and the main epistles of St Paul, but towards the periphery its lineaments became dimmer and dimmer. As the fathers were sure that the Church perceived and taught the main body (σωμάτιον, Irenaeus) or purport (ratio, Tertullian) or scope (σκοπός, Athanasius) or drift of the teaching of Scripture, so they were sure that the Church had the central and important elements of a collection of inspired or authoritative books of the New Testament. They had been handed on by tradition from a period beyond living memory. But of course, as Eusebius clearly recognized in his treatment of the Canon, this appeal to tradition could not be maintained indefinitely. A point must arrive when the appeal to the contemporary usage of the Church will have been rendered ineffective by the lapse of time, and when it must be supported by an appeal to the earliest known references to the books under discussion. Eusebius believes that such a time has arrived by his day.

---

[1] Eusebius, HE 6.14.5–7.
[2] Cited by Eusebius, HE 6.25.11–14.

[3] See below, pp. 224–9.

That this tradition worked rather erratically and produced some inconsistent results is clear from even a brief consideration of the careers of some of the books which eventually reached inclusion in the Canon. The Epistle to the Hebrews, for instance, was known in the west very early, when *I Clement* was written; Hermas may have known it; Valentinus betrays signs of knowing it in his *Gospel of Truth*; the author of II Peter may have known it. Tatian knew it. Irenaeus knew it, though he probably did not attribute it to St Paul. As we have seen, Tertullian knew it, attributing it to Barnabas.[1] The writers of the eastern church welcome it from Theophilus of Antioch, through Clement of Alexandria and Origen to Dionysius of Alexandria, Gregory Thaumaturgus, Methodius and the authors of the Epistle of Hymenaeus, and to Eusebius himself.[2] And the third-century papyrus, P46, includes it. On the other hand, from about the year 200 for nearly two centuries writers in the western church refused to recognize or to quote the Epistle to the Hebrews. The Muratorian Canon makes no mention of it, or rather, if by its 'letter to the Alexandrians' it means this work, then it rejects the work as spurious. Hippolytus betrays no knowledge of it. Eusebius tells us that Gaius in Rome about the year 200 rejected the Epistle as not by Paul, and that even in his day there were some among the Romans who did not consider it to be Paul's. The Syrian *Didascalia*, surprisingly, shows no knowledge of it. Cyprian's *Testimonia* has no reference to it at all though there are several passages in this work where the words of the Epistle to the Hebrews would have been very relevant. Cyprian himself is silent about it. Novatian at least did not regard it as canonical. The work was regarded with uncertainty by several writers even in the fourth and the fifth centuries before it was finally accepted by the western church.[3]

---

[1] For *I Clement* see cap. 17.1; 36.1–6; 43.1. Westcott (*Canon of the NT*, p. 178) thought he could detect Heb. 2.12 in Hermas, *Visions* 2.3.2, and Heb. 11.13 f. and 13.14 in *Similitudes* 1.1 f. Heb. 2.17 and 9.16, 17 appear to be behind *Gospel of Truth*, p. 20, ll. 10–11 and 15–17 (92). For the reference in II Peter, see above, p. 189. Tatian, *Oratio* 6.1, quotes Heb. 9.26. For Irenaeus' reference to Hebrews see Eusebius, *HE* 5.26. For Tertullian's attitude to the letter, see above, pp. 214–15.

[2] Theophilus, *Ad Autolycum* 2.25, may be quoting Heb. 5.12. For Clement of Alexandria see above, p. 215, and for Origen pp. 218–19. For Dionysius of Alexandria see Feltoe, *Dionysius*, p. 8, *Letters* I and Westcott, *Canon of the NT*, p. 372; for Gregory and Methodius see *ibid.* pp. 392–3. For the *Epistle of Hymenaeus* see Routh, *op. cit.*, p. 299.

[3] Muratorian Canon, l. 64; Eusebius, *HE* 6.20.3 for Gaius; Connolly, *Didascalia Apostolorum*, introd. lxxii; Fausset, *op. cit.*, p. 123 (on *De Trinitate* 31). For the work's vicissitudes in the west in the fourth and fifth centuries, see Souter, *Text and Canon*, pp. 174–5. But pseudo-Tertullian, *Adv. Omnes Haereses* 8.3, quotes Heb. 5.6. If this work is (as some think) written in Rome, perhaps by Pope Zephyrinus in the early third century, we must modify our opinion about the entire rejection of Hebrews in Rome in the third century.

THE CANON OF THE NEW TESTAMENT

The Second Epistle of Peter, on the other hand, encountered quite a different history. It is extremely difficult to find any recognition of this work, favourable or the opposite, until the middle of the third century. The Muratorian Canon does not even mention it as apocryphal. Supposed allusions in Irenaeus and in the *Epistle of Barnabas*, in Theophilus of Antioch, in the *Acts of the Martyrs of Lyons and Vienne*, in Hippolytus and in Firmilian of Cappadocia are all either uncertain, very tenuous or readily explicable as coming from other sources.[1] It is not until the middle of the third century that Origen acknowledges the existence even of a second letter ascribed to Peter, with the words, 'Peter may have left a second letter, for it is disputed.'[2] The author of *De Singularitate Clericorum* quotes II Peter 2.13–14 under the rubric 'whom the holy Peter named when he said . . .'.[3] Eusebius, as we have seen, regarded it as at the best of very uncertain authority.[4] The Canon of the Codex Claremontanus (perhaps about 300, of uncertain provenance), a North African Canon of about 360, the Canon of the Council of Laodicea (about 360), and the Canon of Athanasius evidence the acceptance of this work as sacred Scripture by about the middle of the fourth century.[5] Ambrosiaster (second half of the fourth century) is apparently the first individual theologian in the west to receive it without hesitation. A late but gradually increasing acceptance of a rather similar sort can be traced for the Epistle of Jude, and a history not very dissimilar from that of the Epistle to the Hebrews, consisting of a very early recognition followed by considerable hesitations later before a final, late acceptance is achieved, could be recounted of the Revelation of St John. The uncertainty about who exactly wrote the Epistle to the Hebrews seems for long to have counterbalanced the undoubtedly early origin of the letter, and the same uncertainty, complicated by a fear of the encouragement it gave to millenniarism, seems to have held back Revelation. On the other hand a very late start

---

[1] II Peter 3.8 is reproduced in *Epistle of Barnabas* 15.4, Irenaeus, *Adv. Haer.* 5.23.2 and 5.28.3, and in Hippolytus, *Comm. on Daniel* 23.5 and 24.5, but this logion is more likely to be either derived from the *Epistle of Barnabas* by II Peter and all the others who quote it, or simply a popular saying evolved out of Ps. 90.4. The other two possible allusions in Hippolytus (*Comm. on Dan.* 22.4 (II Peter 2.19) and 10.4 (II Peter 3.9)) are too tenuous for argument to be founded on them, and the same applies to *Acts of Martyrs of Lyons and Vienne* (Eusebius, *HE* 5.1.45), where the phrase may be no more than an ordinary cliché (II Peter 1.8), and to Theophilus, *Ad Autolycum* 2.13 (II Peter 1.19) and Firmilian, *Ep.* 75.6.2 (where *Petrum et Paulum in epistolis suis* does not necessarily imply that more than one letter of Peter is known).
[2] Eusebius, *HE* 6.25.8. Origen never quotes II Peter in any of his works extant in Greek, but he does in works extant in Latin.
[3] *De Sing. Cler.* 28 (204): *quos sanctus Petrus designaverat, dicens . . .*
[4] See above, p. 215.
[5] Grosheide, *Some Early Lists of the Books of the New Testament*, pp. 16–19.

and a very late origin did not prevent the spurious claims of the Second Epistle of Peter to authorship from carrying it eventually into the Canon, and perhaps the same applies to the Epistle of Jude. It seems to follow that any tradition about the origin of a book which cannot be traced before the year 200 or thereabouts is worth very little, no matter how heavily the Church may later have endorsed it. The tradition of the Canon is, in short, an historically conditioned one, a tradition enshrining an historical judgement made at a certain period in history, and not capable of guaranteeing the tradition of the Church at later points of its development.

4. *Uncanonical Tradition*

The early fathers of the Church, however, in the period with which we are concerned, experienced no embarrassment in quoting from books which we would call apocryphal and which most of them must have known were not regarded as authoritative by the Church, and even from books part of whose contents they must have known to be heterodox. Ignatius, for instance, quotes from the *Gospel according to the Hebrews*, recounting from there a resurrection appearance of our Lord, and he reproduces a saying 'Near sword is near God' which may come from the same source and which reappears in another form in the *Gospel of Thomas* and is also quoted, but with some hesitation, by Origen.[1] The anonymous *II Clement* quotes five different sayings which probably come from apocryphal works, one of them paralleled in the *Gospel of Thomas*.[2] Justin gives several sayings and facts and other details not to be found in the canonical gospels which may have come from apocryphal books or may derive from floating tradition. He quotes the divine voice at Christ's baptism as saying 'Thou art my Son, this day have I begotten thee' (with D and the Old Latin).[3] He says that when Jesus descended to the

---

[1] Ignatius, *Smyrn.* 3.2 and 4.2; see *Gospel of Thomas*, logion 82; Origen, *Hom. on Jeremiah* 20.3 (PG 13.532; not in GCS). Origen vigorously rejects the *Gospel of Thomas*, *Hom. on Luke* 1 (on Luke 1.1–4). For comments on these passages in Ignatius, see Daniélou, *Théologie*, p. 34; Grant and Freedman, *Secret Sayings*, pp. 85–86, 170, and Jeremias, *Unknown Sayings*, pp. 54–56. Jeremias accepts as authentic the last-named saying.
[2] *II Clem.* 8.5, a saying like that of Luke 16.10, but not identical with it; 4.5 quite a long sentence (rather reminiscent of Matt. 7.23 and Luke 13.27); 5.3, a dialogue between Jesus and Peter about lambs and wolves (reminiscent of Matt. 10.16, 28 and Luke 10.3; 12.4, 5); 9.11, 'My brethren are those who do the will of my Father', quoted by Epiphanius as from the Ebionites; and 12.2, a very Gnostic-sounding saying paralleled in *Gospel of Thomas*, logion 22, and attributed by Clement of Alexandria to the *Gospel according to the Egyptians*. See Westcott, *Canon of the NT*, pp. 186–8, and Grant and Freedman, *Secret Sayings*, p. 75.   [3] *Dial.* 103.6.

water of Jordan, a fire was kindled; this is a detail supplied in several Jewish-Christian works, and probably to be found in a very fragmentary bit of *Egerton Papyrus 2*.[1] He says that those who saw Christ's works called him 'a magician and a deceiver of the people'.[2] He implies that Jesus was a carpenter, for he refers to 'the works of carpentry' (τὰ τεκτονικὰ ἔργα) which he made, and instances ploughs and yokes.[3] He quotes the saying, 'In whatsoever I find you, in this will I also judge you.'[4] He attributes to Jesus the prophecy, 'There shall be schisms and heresies.'[5] Finally he quotes a saying about the new law brought in by Christ instructing us to keep sabbath in a new sense every day.[6] As well as betraying knowledge of the last-mentioned saying, Irenaeus quotes another, 'Blessed is he who existed before he was made man,' and another 'Often have I desired to hear one of those words, and I did not have anybody to say it.'[7] Irenaeus also, as we have seen, quoted Hermas' *Shepherd*, as did the anonymous mid-third-century Latin work, *De Aleatoribus*.[8] We have already had occasion to notice the attitude which bishop Sarapion of Antioch took to the predilection of the Christians of Rhossos for the *Gospel of Peter*.[9] What is perhaps most remarkable of all about this incident is that though Sarapion had always rejected the *Gospel of Peter*, when he first learnt that the people of Rhossos were fond of reading it in church, he had permitted them to read it, saying, 'If this is the only thing that causes small-mindedness (μικροψυχίαν) among you, let it be read.'[10] Athenagoras produces a very odd and quite unidentifiable saying which he attributes to 'the Word', and which he may have derived from some apocryphal work, 'If anyone for this reason kiss for a second time, because it pleased him.'[11] Tertullian quotes three uncanonical sayings, 'Thou hast seen thy brother; thou hast seen thy Lord,' and

---

[1] *Dial.* 88.3; *Egerton Papyrus 2*, frag. 2 verso; here Jesus sprinkles something on the water, and as a result people are amazed. See also below, p. 230. Cf. too the statement of the anonymous author of *De Rebaptismate* 17 (90) that the *Preaching of Paul* described a fire upon the water at Jesus' baptism. See also p. 230.

[2] *Dial.* 69.7.

[3] *Dial.* 88.8.

[4] *Dial.* 47.5, also quoted by Clement of Alexandria, *Quis Dives* 40.

[5] *Dial.* 35.3, also quoted in *Clementine Homilies* 16.21 and Lactantius, *Inst. Div.* 4.30. See Jeremias, *Unknown Sayings*, pp. 59–61.

[6] *Dial.* 12.3, paralleled in *Gospel of Thomas*, logion 27, and Irenaeus, *Demonstration* 96.

[7] *Dem.* 43, paralleled in *Gospel of Thomas*, logion 19; *Adv. Haer.* 1.13.2, paralleled in *Gospel of Thomas*, logion 92.

[8] Eusebius, *HE* 5.8.7; Irenaeus, *Adv. Haer.* 4.34.2; *De Aleatoribus* 2 (94), quoting *Mand.* 4.1, 9. See above, p. 206.

[9] See above, pp. 210–11, 219.

[10] Eusebius, *HE* 6.12.1–4.

[11] *Supplicatio* 32.3; but this may be a jumbled quotation from some OT book or apocryphal work.

P

'Repent, and I will make thee whole,'[1] and 'nobody will attain the kingdom of heaven without enduring temptation'.[2] Perpetua, in her visions as recorded in her *Passion*, seems to have been influenced both by the *Shepherd* of Hermas and the *Apocalypse of Peter*.[3] Hippolytus certainly knew and believed some early variant of the legend about Simon Magus' opposition to Peter in Rome,[4] and he refers to a part of the *Acts of Paul*, regarding it as authentic,[5] and it is worth remarking that he regards as formally possible the survival of genuine tradition outside the Scriptures, for at one point he denies that the heretics 'constructed these systems by taking them from holy Scriptures or reached their heights of speculation by preserving tradition in continuity (διαδοχήν) from any holy man'.[6] Clement of Alexandria quotes apocryphal works and *agrapha* with the abundance of a cornucopia. He quotes the *Gospel according to the Hebrews*, the *Gospel according to the Egyptians*, the *Epistle of Barnabas*, the *Apocalypse of Peter*, the *Preaching of Peter*, the *Shepherd* of Hermas, the *Traditions of Matthew*, the *Didache*, and *I Clement*.[7] We can recover several uncanonical sayings from him: 'Ask for the great things and the small things shall be added to you';[8] 'Where I shall find you, there I shall judge you.'[9] Four other uncanonical sayings he describes as 'the Scripture' (ἡ γραφή): 'Thou art my lyre and flute and my temple,'[10] which may be a fragment from an early Christian hymn; 'those who draw ropes and weave nothing';[11] the expression applied to the Blessed Virgin Mary 'she has borne and not borne'[12] and a variant of logion 2 in the *Gospel of Thomas*.[13] He also in the *Excerpta ex Theodoto*[14] quotes as the words of our Lord 'Save thyself, thou and thy life'. He also quotes a long and delightful story of John the apostle in his old age, whose authenticity we have already discussed.[15] He is also among

---

[1] *De Oratione* 26.1 and *De Paenitentia* 4.1.

[2] *De Baptismo* 20. See Jeremias, *Unknown Sayings*, pp. 86–87.

[3] So J. A. Robinson, *The Passion of S. Perpetua*, introd., pp. 26–36 and 37–43. The Muratorian Canon, ll. 71–73, mentions the *Apocalypse of Peter*, apparently accepting it, but remarking that some do not do so.   [4] *Elenchos* 6.20.2.

[5] *Comm. on Daniel* 3.29; *Acts of Paul* VIII (James, p. 292).   [6] *Elenchos* 1, introd. 8.

[7] For references see *Origen's Doctrine of Tradition*, pp. 127–30.

[8] *Strom.* 1.24.158.2 (PG 8.905), also cited by Origen, *PE* 2.2, but with the addition, 'Ask for the heavenly things and the earthly things shall be given unto you.'

[9] See above, p. 225.   [10] *Protreptikos* 1.5.3 (PG 8.60).   [11] *Strom.* 1.8.41.2 (PG 8.737).

[12] *Ibid.* 7.16.94.2 (PG 9.532). Tertullian attributes this saying to the group of Gnostic heretics called *Academici* (*peperit et non peperit, virgo et non virgo*), but soon afterwards refers to *de vacca illa quae peperit et non peperit* which he believes to be a quotation from Ezekiel, *De Carne Christi* 23.2, 6.

[13] *Strom.* 5.14.96.3 (PG 9.141); he quotes it again, as from the *Gospel according to the Hebrews*, in *Strom.* 2.9.45.5 (PG 8.981).   [14] 2.2: σώζου συ καὶ ἡ ψυχή σου.

[15] See above, p. 48. He also quotes a variant of *Gospel of Thomas*, logion 22, as from the heretic Cassianus (*Strom.* 3.13.92.2; PG 8.1193), but does not accept it as authentic.

the very long list of fathers who quote the uncanonical saying of our Lord 'Be ye approved money-changers.'[1] Origen is markedly stricter than Clement in his attitude to apocryphal works. He rejects the *Gospel according to the Egyptians*, the *Gospel of the Twelve*, the *Gospel according to Thomas*, the *Gospel according to Basilides*, and the *Gospel according to Matthias*.[2] But he does in fact quote apocryphal works in his own writings. These include: the *Gospel of Peter*, the *Gospel according to the Hebrews* (four times), the *Preaching of Peter*, the *Acts of Pilate*, the *Clementine Recognitions*, *I Clement* and the *Epistle of Barnabas*.[3] He also refers to the *Shepherd* of Hermas and the *Acts of Paul*, though he appears to have grown uncertain about the authority of both these works in later life.[4] He quotes, in order to defend his belief in the perpetual virginity of the Blessed Virgin Mary, from an apocryphal book the statement that the 'brothers' of Jesus were sons of Joseph by a previous marriage.[5] He also quotes as if they were recognized sayings a number of *agrapha* not hitherto recorded here: 'How is it that many are round the well and no one goes into it?'[6] and 'Blessed is he who even fasts in order that he may feed a poor man',[7] as well as the well-known, 'Be ye approved money-changers';[8] he also quotes a version of *Gospel of Thomas*, logion 82, 'Whoever is near to me is near the fire.'[9] Dionysius of Alexandria, in the very passage in which he too uses this *agraphon*, 'Be ye approved money-changers,' tells us that he was encouraged by a dream, which he believed to be divinely sent, to read heretical literature[10]. As late as the end of the third century or beginning of the fourth the anonymous North African bishop who wrote the *De Aleatoribus* can quote both Hermas' *Shepherd* and the *Didache* as Scripture.[11]

---

[1] γίνεσθε τραπεζῖται δόκιμοι. For this list see Jeremias, *The Unknown Sayings of Jesus*, pp. 89-93.

[2] *Hom. on Luke* 1 (on Luke 1.1-4). Grant and Freedman, *Secret Sayings*, p. 86, note this stricter attitude of Origen.

[3] For references see *Origen's Doctrine of Tradition*, pp. 138-9.

[4] See *Origen's Doctrine of Tradition*, pp. 139-41; see also M. R. James, p. 297, on *Acts of Paul* XI.

[5] *Comm. on John*, frag. 31; the apocryphal book was the *Birth of Mary*; see Grant, *Earliest Lives of Jesus*, p. 82, and M. R. James, pp. 19-20.

[6] *Contra Celsum* 8.15, 16; paralleled in *Gospel of Thomas*, logion 74. This however is a saying supplied by Celsus, but not previously known to Origen.

[7] *Hom. on Leviticus* 10.2.

[8] *Hom. on Luke* 1.1 (on Luke 1.1-4).

[9] *Hom. on Jeremiah* 20.3 (PG 13.532; not in GCS).

[10] Feltoe, *Dionysius*, p. 53, *Letters* V 3 (1).

[11] *De Aleatoribus* 2 (94), quoting loosely *Mandates* 4.1, 9, and 4 (96) quoting *Didache* 14.2, again loosely. But it should be added that Audet believes that the *Doctrinae Apostolorum* here referred to is not the *Didache*; further, this bishop does not appear to have known the Bible very well, because he omits to mention those passages in the Old Testament which do refer to dicing, though he is very anxious to find Scriptural

This uncanonical material has of course attracted the attention of many scholars. Recently Jeremias has surveyed anew, in his *The Unknown Sayings of Jesus*, all such material known before the discovery of the Nag Hammadi documents, and has come to the conclusion that a surprising number of the uncanonical sayings are genuine utterances of Jesus, including 'Ask for the great things and the small things shall be added to you' and 'Be ye approved money-changers'.[1] Papyrus fragments from Egypt discovered at various times during the last eighty years have greatly enlarged our store of these *agrapha*. A portion of an apocryphal gospel, probably to be identified with *Gospel of St Peter*, was found at Akhmîm in 1886–7. At Behneseh, the ancient Oxyrhynchus, a leaf of a papyrus codex, dating from the first half of the third century, was found in 1897; it contained a collection of these logia (*Oxyrhynchus Papyrus 1*). In 1903 a very similar document (though not certainly the same work as *Oxyrhynchus Papyrus 1*), also of the third century, was discovered, written on the back of an official register (*Oxyrhynchus Papyrus 654*); it too contained logia, and was in form slightly more like a synoptic gospel. Since then there have been found *Oxyrhynchus Papyrus 655*, a fragment of an unknown gospel, probably the *Gospel according to the Egyptians*, *Oxyrhynchus Papyrus 840*, a fragmentary record of a conversation between Jesus and a chief priest in the temple, and *Egerton Papyrus 2*.[2] The *Gospel of Thomas* has brought to light a second appearance of several of the sayings found in these papyri, though we should be on our guard against lightly assuming that the logia appear in precisely the same form or from precisely the same tradition in the Oxyrhynchus papyri as in the *Gospel of Thomas* and the fathers.[3] The sayings in the *Gospel of Thomas* are obviously of a composite origin. Some are rankly Gnostic, but others are clearly not influenced by Gnosticism. For instance, logion 28, beginning, 'Jesus said: I stood in the midst of the world, and I appeared to them in flesh', is clearly not Gnostic in its ready admission of the Incarnation.[4] It has been strongly argued by Grant and Freedman in *The Secret Sayings of Jesus*, and by Grant alone in his article, 'Notes on the Gospel of Thomas', that the sources of the *Gospel of Thomas* consist solely of sayings taken from the four canonical gospels and adapted or

---

support for his attack on this vice. For two western mid-third-century possible quotations of apocryphal works see *De Montibus Sina et Sion* 13 (117) and *Ad Vigilium* 4 (124).

[1] Jeremias, *Unknown Sayings*, pp. 87–89, 89–93.

[2] Already described above, p. 192. Most of these finds of papyri are translated in Grant and Freedman's *The Secret Sayings of Jesus*.

[3] Wilson, *Studies*, pp. 28–29, sounds this warning.

[4] So Wilson, *Studies*, p. 41. Jeremias knew the first half of it from an Oxyrhynchus papyrus, and accepted this as authentic (*Unknown Sayings*, pp. 69 ff.).

rearranged to serve the purpose of Gnostic interpretation, and that there
are no other original or very early sources at all in this document. Some
of the sayings in the *Gospel of Thomas* certainly are mere reproductions
of synoptic material (whether we can trace the influence of the fourth
gospel here is another question), and some no doubt represent Gnostic
distortions and adaptations of synoptic material. But there remain several
sayings which cannot readily be explained on these lines. Logion 54, for
instance, runs, 'Jesus said: Blessed are the poor, for yours is the kingdom
of heaven.' Luke's version (Luke 6.20) runs 'Blessed are the poor, for
yours is the kingdom of *God*', and Matthew's (5.3) 'Blessed are the poor
in Spirit, for theirs is the kingdom of *heaven*.' The author of the *Gospel
of Thomas* seems to avoid using the name of God. Is he altering Luke,
in accordance with Matthew, or is Luke altering the more accurate
original preserved in the *Gospel of Thomas*, which has also been modified
by Matthew in his version? Or alternatively, has the originally Lucan
saying been transmitted to the author of the *Gospel of Thomas* through
a Jewish-Christian milieu? It is not easy to give a confident answer to
those questions.[1] It is not easy, generally speaking, to see a clearly
Gnostic pattern in the rearrangement of the apparently synoptic sayings
in the *Gospel of Thomas*. 'They are strung together,' says Wilson, 'without
any obvious indication of design, save that of association of key-words.
The closest analogy is not with a gospel, canonical or Gnostic, but with
an anthology, a testimony book, or such a collection as the Sentences
of Sextus.'[2]

   If we cannot easily account for the material in the *Gospel of Thomas*
which looks like synoptic material by saying that it is simply a reproduction of synoptic material, in an eccentrically rearranged pattern, then
we are faced with the possibility, which has lurked in the background
ever since we began to discuss the subject of uncanonical tradition, that
we have here some examples of genuine tradition preserved by the
sources of the *Gospel of Thomas*, independently of the synoptic gospels.
This possibility has been taken very seriously by Quispel, who in three
articles has investigated the affinities between some of the sayings in the
Gospel of Thomas and some other documents which show signs of knowing
a Jewish-Christian tradition of sayings not that of the synoptic gospels.[3]
He believes that the pseudo-Clementine literature, Tatian's *Diatessaron*
and the 'Western Text' of the synoptic gospels, witness to an independent

---

[1] Wilson poses them, *op. cit.*, pp. 55–56.
[2] *Ibid.* pp. 16–17.
[3] G. Quispel, 'L'Évangile selon Thomas et les Clémentines'; 'L'Évangile selon
Thomas et le Diatessaron'; 'Some Remarks on the Gospel of Thomas'.

but similar tradition of the words of Jesus. Tatian, in such of the remains of his *Diatessaron* as can be recovered, shows that he knew, Quispel thinks, some logia very like some in the *Gospel of Thomas*, which were not derived from the *Gospel of the Ebionites* nor the *Gospel of the Nazarenes*. These included, among other material, the account of a great light on Jordan at the baptism of Jesus, and a saying of Jesus during a post-resurrection appearance, a variant of Luke 24.39, to be found in the *Diatessaron*, as witnessed to in a Syriac translation of a work by Titus of Bostra, and in the *Gospel of the Nazarenes* (a fragment found in Jerome, *De Vir. Ill.* 16), where this gospel is probably reproducing the *Gospel according to the Hebrews*.[1] Quispel thinks that evidence of this sort points to the conclusion that Tatian used the *Gospel according to the Hebrews* as a fifth gospel in his *Diatessaron* (there is no reason to think that the name *Diatessaron* was Tatian's own title for his work), and that the *Gospel of Thomas* is ultimately indebted to the same work for all its early non-canonical material. This gospel he conjectures to have been of Jewish-Christian origin, written in Aramaic and containing a tradition of sayings independent of the tradition used by the synoptists. This document was not Q, but Q may have been a Greek translation of this document, used by Luke (and presumably Matthew), but not by the *Gospel of Thomas*; this Aramaic document may have been the Aramaic logia of Matthew mentioned by Papias.[2] Quispel thinks that the *Gospel of Thomas* probably used the *Gospel according to the Egyptians* for its Gnostic adaptations of original material.

The whole hypothesis of Quispel is of course in a tentative stage, but it clearly must be taken seriously. Neither Van Unnik[3] nor Wilson[4] are prepared to reject it. Wilson, who must impress his readers as a cautious scholar, inclines, though he has not the same credulity as Jeremias in accepting uncanonical material as authentic, to think that some sayings in the *Gospel of Thomas* have a good claim to be taken on their own merits as original however we may explain their history before they were included in this 'gospel'. Logion 55, about hating father and mother, brothers and sisters in order to be a disciple (parallels Luke 14.26–27,

---

[1] See 'L'Évangile . . . et le Diatessaron', pp. 106–17. For the relation between the *Gospel of Thomas* and the *Gospel according to the Hebrews* see also Grant, 'Notes on the Gospel of Thomas', p. 171. For the great light on Jordan, see above, p. 225.
[2] See above, p. 37.
[3] *Newly Discovered Gnostic Writings*, pp. 55–71.
[4] *Studies*, p. 140. H. W. Montefiore, after a careful consideration of the evidence, comes to conclusions very similar to those of Quispel and Wilson (against Grant), see 'A Comparison of the Parables of the Gospel according to Thomas and of the Synoptic Gospels'.

Matt. 10.37–38) he inclines to think may be such a saying.[1] Logion 31
is another:

> Jesus said: No prophet is acceptable in his village
> No physician heals those who know him.[2]

The same applies to logion 39, which is this gospel's version of the saying
about the Pharisees' possession of the keys of knowledge (Matt. 23.13;
Luke 11.52),[3] and also to logion 102, which, surprisingly, includes a
reference to the proverb of the dog in the manger.[4] Logion 79, which
looks like a combination of Luke 11.27–28 and 23.29), the reply of Jesus
to a woman who invoked blessings on his mother, Wilson thinks could
be readily explained as deriving from an independent tradition which
Luke has either broken up or received in a fragmented form.[5] And he is
impressed by the version in the *Gospel of Thomas* of the parable of the
Wicked Husbandmen (logion 65).[6] Its clarity, logical order and minimum
of addition and interpretation certainly cannot fail to strike the reader.

One observation must, however, be made. Even if the hypothesis of
Quispel were to be proved, or widely accepted, to be correct in its most
extreme form, it could not be said that what had been discovered were,
in the proper sense, any *new* sayings of our Lord. All that this hypothesis
might lead to was a new line of tradition testifying to ultimately the same
material as is in the synoptic gospels, or rather, a different presentation
or translation or edition of the material which is in fact reproduced in the
synoptic gospels in their particular translation or edition. If in one source
of the *Gospel of Thomas* we really have to do with a new tradition of the
sayings of Jesus, originally independent of the tradition which finally
found its way into the synoptic gospels, then this material constitutes an
impressive testimony to the accuracy and reliability of the synoptic
gospels. If we really can now check the synoptic gospels by another
tradition, then we can be sure both that they have preserved all that was
available for preservation of the sayings of Jesus within a few years of the
resurrection (for nothing significant is added by this independent tradition) and that they have preserved it in a reassuringly unmodified form
(for the differences to be found in this independent tradition, though
intensely interesting, are not great). If Quispel's hypothesis, or anything
like it, is widely accepted, then many assumptions made by scholars of
the Form Critical school in recent years about the wholesale alteration

---

[1] *Ibid.* pp. 56–57; Bartsch and Quispel regard this logion as original.
[2] *Ibid.* pp. 60–61.   [3] *Ibid.* pp. 75–76.
[4] *Ibid.* pp. 76–77.   [5] *Ibid.* p. 81.   [6] *Ibid.* pp. 101–2.

of the gospel material in the process of transmission will have to be abandoned.

It is worth while looking a little more closely at what we know about the presumed source of this uncanonical tradition in the *Gospel of Thomas*, that is, the *Gospel according to the Hebrews*. Wilson maintains that it must be distinguished from all other apocryphal gospels; the latter are generally worthless and legendary, but the former is, he says, quoting Lietzmann, always referred to by the fathers with respect.[1] Daniélou attributes the first evangelizing of Egypt to Jewish Christians (not necessarily Judaizing Christians, who are quite a different group). To this type of early Christianity he attributes the *Gospel according to the Hebrews*, the *Sibylline Oracles* and the *Epistula Apostolorum*. He thinks that to this group belonged 'the presbyters' referred to by Papias, by Irenaeus and by others, and he thinks that references to *gnosis* or to secret teaching by the author of the *Epistle of Barnabas* and by Clement of Alexandria derive from the same type of Christianity.[2] Hegesippus, we know, reproduced some material from the *Gospel according to the Hebrews*.[3] Jeremias takes the version given by this gospel of the story of the Rich Young Ruler as more authentic than the version of it in the synoptic gospels.[4] By far the most interesting point about the *Gospel according to the Hebrews*, however, is that it almost certainly has supplied one passage in the New Testament which has entered into the very heart of the Christian heritage, has formed a theme for painters and poets, and has given a proverb to the English language, the story of the Woman Taken in Adultery (John 7.53–8.11). It is well known that the passage containing this story has extremely poor manuscript support and quite certainly was not an original part of the fourth gospel. It is printed only in the margin of the latest edition of the Greek New Testament by Nestlé and Kilpatrick, and is placed by itself after the end of the fourth gospel in the New English translation of the Bible. The earliest known attestation of it is found in the *Didascalia Apostolorum* (third-century, emanating probably from Syria).[5] But Eusebius tells us that Papias 'produces also another story about a woman accused of many sins in the presence of the Lord, which the *Gospel according to the Hebrews* contains'.[6] It is wholly likely that this

---

[1] Wilson, *Studies*, pp. 2–3.
[2] Daniélou, *Théologie*, pp. 19, 27, 35.
[3] Eusebius, *HE* 4.22.8; for Hegesippus, see above, pp. 39–41.
[4] *Unknown Sayings*, p. 35; the story in this version appears in Origen, *Comm. on Matthew* 15.14; see above, p. 18.
[5] Connolly, *Didascalia*, introd. p. lxxi and text, cap. VII, p. 76; it appears in the Latin as well as the Syriac version.
[6] Eusebius, *HE* 3.39.17.

THE CANON OF THE NEW TESTAMENT

story is the *pericope de adultera*. This would mean that this story is not really a late piece of invention, but that it was contained in a document circulating perhaps as early as Ignatius' time, and one which included some material with good claims to authenticity. The impression of authenticity made by the story itself confirms the suggestion that this is part of the contents of the *Gospel according to the Hebrews*, perhaps the longest section of it to survive intact.

But it is certain that for centuries the Church refused to regard the story of the Woman Taken in Adultery as canonical. It is unlikely that this was because the *pericope* was regarded as late, because in fact in all probability it was not late. It is much more likely that the story was suspect because it came from the *Gospel according to the Hebrews*. We have seen that this gospel was well known in the early Church, indeed that it was respected. Yet it was never thought of as canonical by any orthodox writer, with the doubtful exception of Tatian. Origen expressly rejected it, as he expressly rejected the *Gospel of Thomas*.[1] It is probable that what excluded this gospel, for all its claims to authenticity, was the test of sound doctrine. If we look at the fragments of this gospel collected in M. R. James' *Apocryphal New Testament* (pp. 1–8) we can find, among a number of interesting stories and sayings which we know in the synoptic gospels, some suggestions of aberration towards Gnosticism. One of these is the preoccupation with 'rest' (in Greek versions probably ἀνάπαυσις), a concept which can be found appearing in the more obviously Gnostic parts of the *Gospel of Thomas* and in other Gnostic literature. Again, the mention no less than four times in the surviving fragments of 'my mother, the Holy Spirit' in this gospel, though it may reflect an Aramaic-speaking environment in which the word for 'spirit' is feminine, is also reminiscent of the introduction of a Mother-figure into many Gnostic systems.[2] Finally, the account given by Jerome, *De Viris Illustribus* 2, of the appearance of the Saviour to James the brother of the Lord after the Resurrection[3] may give us the *mise en scène* for this gospel. It may have been published in the form of a number of secret words imparted to James by Jesus after the Resurrection, just as the *Gospel of Thomas* and the *Apocryphon of John* and several other Gnostic gospels took this form. The fact that the heterodox, anti-Pauline, Jewish-Christian

---

[1] *Hom. on Luke* 1.1 (on Luke 1.1–4). Origen quotes this gospel in *Hom. on Jeremiah* 15.4 (εἰ δέ τις παραδέχεται); *Comm. on John* 2.12; *Contra Celsum* 5.61 and *Comm. on Matthew* 16.12.

[2] For a discussion of these heretical tendencies in the *Gospel according to the Hebrews*, see Appendix C.

[3] See James, pp. 3–4.

Ebionite sect seem to have adopted the *Gospel according to the Hebrews* as peculiarly their own no doubt rendered it doubly suspicious in the eyes of the fathers of the early Church.[1] Papias used it and Hegesippus used it, but the sources of neither of these writers are unimpeachable. When the fathers of the first three centuries gave their verdict upon the *Gospel according to the Hebrews* they had the full text of it in front of them. We have not, and we should not lightly assume that their judgement was mistaken. Far less are we justified in regarding this gospel as in any serious sense a rival of the canonical four.

4. *Conclusions*

After having made this survey of the way in which the Canon of the New Testament was achieved, it is worth while attempting to answer the question, Did the Canon impose itself? Some scholars think that this is the best way of describing the process of canonization.[2] But even a short consideration of the evidence which has been surveyed in this chapter should be enough to convince anybody that this is at worst an inaccurate and at best a romantic way of describing the process. The documents of the New Testament were chosen by the Church, at a period so early in Church history that it is difficult or impossible to determine how exactly the Church chose. But it was a conscious act of choice by the Church. The *Gospel according to the Hebrews* was rejected, the Gospels of Matthew, Mark, Luke, and finally John were chosen. The Epistles of St Paul were very early on collected into a group; the First Epistle of Clement and the *Epistle of Barnabas* remained in an uncertain position and were finally rejected. No doubt it was the intrinsic qualities of the material in these books, its convincing appearance and authentic ring, which caused them to be chosen rather than the others, but then it was necessary that a Church should exist to recognize these qualities, a Church capable of knowing authentic doctrine and evidence from unauthentic. Again, in what sense could the Epistle of Jude and the Second Epistle of Peter be said to have imposed themselves? A modern reader might well find them much less imposing than the Letters of Ignatius or even *I Clement*. It would be foolish to evade the obvious truth that it was the Church which determined the Canon of the New Testament.

It must, however, be recognized that the Church made this choice at

---

[1] Turner (*The Pattern*, p. 177) suggests that this gospel rewrote the account of our Lord's baptism 'in the heretical interest'.
[2] Notably Karl Barth (*Doctrine of the Word of God*, p. 120), as quoted, apparently with approval, by J. K. S. Reid, *The Authority of Scripture*, p. 200.

a period in history when it was open to the Church to do so, and that this period was by the nature of things a limited one.[1] Between the years 100 and 150 the Church was in a position to know what were authentic and original records of Christianity and what were not; but as the years went on the Church inevitably found itself no longer in this position. The long hesitations over the admission of the Epistle to the Hebrews and Revelation and the very late admission of II Peter suggest a Church gradually losing its grip on the necessary assessment of historical evidence as it recedes further and further away from the historical events to which the foundation documents of Christianity testify. If it is accepted that the primary function of the books of the New Testament is, and always was, to act as evidence, as the first four verses of St Luke's Gospel, and the first three of the First Epistle of John, suggest, then the conclusion is inescapable that in forming the Canon of the New Testament the Church put itself under the authority of the New Testament's witness and abdicated its right (if it ever possessed such a thing) of adding to or subtracting from this witness. A Canon of Scripture is meant to be exclusive and sufficient; otherwise there is no point at all in forming it. This is the real significance of the epithets such as 'holy' or 'divine' attached to the Scriptures of the New Testament by the fathers, and by their declaration that the New Testament was inspired. In many ways inspiration is a most unsatisfactory quality to ascribe to them, incapable of adequate proof or adequate definition. But it does serve to emphasize the uniqueness and the sufficiency of the New Testament. Where the ancient fathers said inerrancy and inspiration we today would prefer to say uniqueness and sufficiency.[2] But as far as the function of the Canon is concerned, they mean the same thing. The formation of a Canon meant that the Church placed its teaching under this Canon, regarding it henceforward as its doctrinal norm.

It was the advance of history and the lapse of time which made this move to form a Canon and treat it as paramount for doctrine a wholly unavoidable measure. Christianity is a deeply historical religion, not, of course, wholly conditioned by nor contained within history, but bound to the belief that God did authentically commit and reveal himself in the career of a really historical character. The fathers, for all their lack of modern critical insight, had a firm grasp of this truth. Even Origen, deeply dyed Platonist though he was, submitted to its demands. The time therefore had to come when Christianity would have to register once and

---

[1] See Cullmann, *The Early Church*, pp. 87–98; Flesseman-van Leer, *Tradition and Scripture*, p. 180.   [2] See my article 'The Inspiration of Holy Scripture'.

for all the historical evidence for the Event which constituted the religion itself, and abide by this registration ever afterwards. We have been during the course of this work studying the period when this registration took place. The reader must have been conscious all through of surveying a period which was as it were a watershed, a divide between two eras, the era of oral tradition and the era of written tradition, when gradually the oral tradition no longer suffices, the situation when oral and written tradition exist side by side passes, and the Church has to go forward into history, as far as sources of doctrine are concerned, connected with the apostles only by the New Testament, when the New Testament has become in this sense the successor of the apostles.[1]

And yet we must recognize that the fathers during the period that we have been studying were quite ready to admit that some uncanonical material could well be genuine, and honest scholarship must allow the strong possibility of some uncanonical sayings attributed to our Lord being perfectly authentic and original. The Canon of the New Testament may not be as an historical document exhaustively informative. Conversely, some small portion of the contents of the New Testament, such as the Second Epistle of Peter, and perhaps the Epistle of Jude, may have no serious claim to be regarded as in any real sense original and authentic evidence nor foundation documents of the Christian faith. They were canonized when the Church was no longer in a position to make a reliable decision about the originality and antiquity of the documents of the New Testament, and when the carefree fluidity and flexibility of the first two and a half centuries had been succeeded by a tendency towards fixity and precise definition. The significance of these facts must not be disregarded in the desire to emphasize the sufficiency of Scripture. The fathers found the New Testament sufficient for a norm of faith but did not pretend that it included every single actual piece of information about Jesus Christ. This is a fact which we must not forget when we make our final estimate of the significance of the Canon of the New Testament to the tradition of the Christian Church.

[1] See Cullmann, *The Early Church*, pp. 91–92; also Westcott, on Justin, *Canon of the NT*, p. 168, and *Origen's Doctrine of Tradition*, pp. 189–92.

6

Tradition as Interpretation

1. *Tradition as a Source of Evidence*

TOWARDS THE end of his classic work, Van den Eynde marshals all the arguments he can to prove that during the period with which we have been concerned in the first five chapters of this book the fathers of the Church consistently subordinated Scripture to tradition. He points to those passages where Irenaeus and Tertullian say that the rule of faith could survive without Scripture, and to the fact that the fathers often evince a conviction that 'tradition' (i.e. the men of old, or some such phrase) had decided the Canon of the New Testament.[1] He maintains that Irenaeus, Tertullian, Clement of Alexandria and Origen all teach that the Scriptures must be interpreted according to the rule of faith.[2] He points out that it is indisputable that the fixing of the New Testament Canon was an example of the acceptance of an unwritten tradition, and he adduces the fact that several authors, such as Tertullian, Origen, the author of the *Didascalia Apostolorum* and Hippolytus, assume that many customs, practices and rites existing in their day from time immemorial derive from original unwritten apostolic tradition, and he appears to think that they probably did derive thence.[3] Earlier he had shown that one of the main appeals of Irenaeus had been to the actual faith of the Church throughout the whole world guaranteed as genuine by apostolic succession, and had identified this as the definition of tradition proper,[4] the definition which Van den Eynde's own church regards as the best and clearest account of tradition. It may be that this definition is the one which would best suit the thought of the Eastern Orthodox church as well, for the definition of tradition given by P. L'Huillier, Professor at the Orthodox Theological Seminary in Paris, in a recent article,[5] appears to resemble this one closely. Tradition,

---

[1] *Les Normes*, pp. 260-7.   [2] *Ibid*. pp. 267-74.
[3] *Ibid*. pp. 275-80.   [4] *Ibid*. p. 164.
[5] 'The Ecclesiastical Hierarchy and the Magisterium.'

says L'Huillier, is not simply 'the Church's official exegesis of the Bible'.[1] He goes on:

> But on the other hand to understand tradition solely as the authorized exegesis of holy Scripture is inadequate, because in the organization of the Church and in its sacramental and liturgical life there is a whole series of fundamental rules not mentioned in the New Testament, but which have dogmatic implications and come to us from the apostolic age. St Basil remarks on this, in a weighty fashion, in the well-known passage of his *De Spiritu Sancto*, which was inserted into the body of the canon law of the Eastern church by the Quinsext Council in 692.[2]

Again, Sergei Bulgakov once wrote: 'This is always the way of Church tradition; it is not only conservative but creative.'[3]

Enough evidence has perhaps been produced in the first five chapters of this book to show on how tenuous a basis claims such as these must rest. The claims to autonomy for the rule of faith made by Irenaeus and Tertullian are not impressive and are not repeated by any later fathers. It is meaningless to regard them as 'subordinating' Scripture to the rule of faith because they, with all the other fathers of the period under review, consistently prove the rule of faith from Scripture. The choice of the Canon of the New Testament was made, in its essentials, very early in the history of the Church, at a period when oral tradition had not yet become uncertain and untrustworthy; this period passed, and with it the possibility of trusting oral tradition. In dealing with the Canon the fathers of later periods either recognize this fact or in canonizing books rely upon oral traditions which are manifestly untrustworthy. The appeal to unwritten tradition is always made by those writers of the period under review who make it as an appeal to something which is secondary, which can easily be allowed to vary from church to church and from place to place, and which cannot seriously be compared as an authority to Scripture. It is consistently thought of as a tradition which regulates praxis, not doctrine. If Van den Eynde and L'Huillier mean, as they appear to mean, that there is reliable evidence for the existence in the early Church of a tradition of doctrine or of important information about Jesus Christ, independent of the Bible and consciously recognized by all as authentic and original, and capable of being preserved in the Church intact for an indefinite period right up to our own day, then we must give an absolute negative to this theory. Careful, historical investigation of the relevant facts leaves no room for doubt here. By the year 250 such

---

[1] 'The Ecclesiastical Hierarchy', p. 21. [2] *Ibid.* p. 22. [3] 'Eucharistic Dogma', p. 67.

a tradition certainly was not known to exist in the Church, and therefore certainly did not exist. No words of Basil, a hundred years later, nor of the Quinsext Council four hundred and fifty years later, nor of any individual or authority a millennium or more later, could possibly conjure it into existence. Either we must believe that the laws of history have miraculously been suspended and that historical evidence is irrelevant for deciding matters of history, or we must accept this absolute No.

But there is a more recent variant of this theory which has been advanced by Congar in his book *La Tradition et les Traditions*. Congar does not believe that original doctrine or information about Jesus has survived independently of the Bible. He denies that there are 'truths of faith' which have been transmitted orally from the beginning; he will not allow an esoteric tradition nor a *disciplina arcani* which might authenticate such a theory as this; he believes that a sound doctrine of development can dispense with such unsatisfactory aids as these. Tradition is not a second source besides the Scriptures conveying part of the truths of faith, but is another way of communicating these truths, complementary to the Scriptures.[1] He defines tradition (which includes and carries Scripture) as 'the living continuity of the faith quickening the people of God',[2] and as 'an accumulation at compound interest (*thésaurisation*) of religious meditation made by generation after generation upon the biblical text.'[3] Interpretation, he insists, was there from the beginning, and he does not hesitate to call this Christian *midrash*. 'The Church has lived and will live to the end under a régime of *midrash*.' Fact and interpretation interact.[4] The deposit of faith, he says, is entrusted to a Church which lives the history of salvation in the middle of secular history. 'It leaves room for a sort of "midrashic" activity of actualization and even in this sense of accomplishment: to preserve it, "with the help of the Holy Spirit", is to live in it.'[5] One of his proofs for this theory is that for the writers of the second and third centuries 'there existed equally an unwritten part of the tradition of the apostles'[6] (as well as a written part). He thinks that Cullmann's statement that the very fixing of the Canon implies the rejection as norm of any other traditions not defined in writing by the apostles is contradicted by 'the numerous texts of the second and third centuries, and later of the fourth and fifth centuries, which demand that we should also take as norms unwritten traditions going back to the apostles as well as the others';[7] later he gives a list of unwritten customs

---

[1] *La Tradition*, pp. 75–76.   [2] *Ibid.* p. 16.   [3] *Ibid.* p. 18.
[4] *Ibid.* pp. 30–31; cf. pp. 56–57.   [5] *Ibid.* p. 33, quoting II Tim. 1.13–14.
[6] *Ibid.* p. 49.   [7] *Ibid.* p. 54.

culled from Irenaeus, Tertullian, Clement of Alexandria, Origen, Dionysius of Alexandria and Cyprian,[1] which does not differ in any important respect from that given by Van den Eynde. His summary of the fathers' conception of tradition includes a Christological exposition of the Old Testament and the understanding of the mystery of Christ and the Church as the Scriptures witness to them; liturgical and disciplinary practices which, though not witnessed to in Scripture, appeared to have come from the apostles; and the Scriptures read and interpreted in the Church and according to the Church's tradition of reading them.[2] G. H. Tavard, in an interesting and irenic book, has taken a not dissimilar position to Congar's.[3]

With this position all students of this subject should have some sympathy, because it is concerned to bring into prominence the existence of the Church as a living organism to be reckoned with by all who are exploring the subject of tradition. Further, the possibility is open that when we examine the very earliest period of the Church's history what we find is not Gospel separately and interpretation separately, but Gospel and interpretation fused inseparably together. It is the argument, as we have seen, of Nineham and of Evans[4] that this is in fact the case. Other scholars, such as A. Richardson,[5] maintain that the Church's interpretation in its earliest period can be shown to be based upon the teaching of Jesus himself. Though we certainly cannot rule out the possibility that the earliest version of the Gospel which we can recover is, so to speak, a Church-shaped Gospel, Congar's assumption that this situation could and should continue indefinitely, indeed permanently, is an unwarrantable one. He can only make it by ignoring the significance of the formation of the Canon. In an attempt to do justice to one factor in the situation he ends by putting the whole possibility of revelation in jeopardy.

The analogy with *midrash* is an unfortunate one. By the first century AD in Rabbinic Judaism all the *halakah* that was accepted as valid was attributed confidently to oral tradition stemming from Moses on Sinai. Every piece of traditional teaching which formed part of current practice was by ingenious reasoning somehow, by hook or by crook, supplied with

---

[1] *Ibid.* pp. 64–66.
[2] *Ibid.* p. 75.
[3] *Holy Writ or Holy Church*, especially cap. 1, The Patristic View. For a useful and concise account of modern Roman Catholic, and other, attitudes to tradition, see also K. E. Skydsgaard's essay, 'Tradition as an Issue in Contemporary Theology', in *The Old and New in the Church*.
[4] See above, p. 14.
[5] See his *Introduction to the Theology of the New Testament*.

justification from the Torah. Torah and *halakah* merged indistinguishably together.[1] In moden Judaism also there is recognizable a process of inter-action between the text of the Hebrew Scriptures and their interpretation, which has been called 'the dialectic of production by way of interpreta-tion', and included in the concept of tradition is 'the totality of life as shaped and conveyed from generation to generation', in other words, the whole life of the Jewish people as the *traditio passiva* as well as *activa*.[2] There can be no ultimate distinction between Torah and life flowing from Torah and consequently no finally objective standards of doctrine whereby the doctrine and the living out of doctrine can be distinguished. The once-for-all givenness of revelation witnessed to by Scripture has been abandoned. If the tradition of the Christian Church is a Christian form of *midrash*, then the declaration of the word of God becomes, in the words of J. K. S. Reid, a 'monologue which the Church carries on with itself'.[3] 'Every attempt', says A. L. Lilley, 'to exalt the authority of the Church at the expense of that of Holy Scripture is not only illogical but suicidal.'[4] Again, we cannot dismiss as insignificant the fact that Jesus himself criticized the *halakah* and did not regard it as sacrosanct. Surely his words should warn us against the danger of setting up a Christian *halakah* as a part, or even as an aspect, of revelation. It needs must be, perhaps, that *halakah* should occur. But our Lord himself warns us against the danger of identifying it with revelation.

These are strong *a priori* objections to Congar's theory of tradition. But if we return to the historical facts and ask whether the evidence from the first three centuries really bears out his case, we shall find even stronger objections. His theory reduces itself either to a truism or to a misapprehension. It is indeed true that ever since the Gospel first existed, ever since 'Jesus came into Galilee preaching the gospel of God' (Mark 1.14) there has in some form existed a Church. It is true that the Church's function is to preach the Gospel, that the very existence of a Gospel implies the existence of a Church. It is true that the Church, as it preaches the Gospel, is bound to interpret it, and especially when the Gospel is formally enshrined in and witnessed to by a body of documents like the New Testament a process of interpretation on the part of the Church is altogether unavoidable and necessary. But this does not in the

---

[1] Kümmel, 'Jesus und der jüdische Traditionsgedanke', pp. 105–17.
[2] See a thoughtful article by N. Rotenstreich, 'On the Notion of Tradition in Judaism'; the quotations are from p. 28.
[3] J. K. S. Reid, *The Authority of Scripture*, p. 121.
[4] A. L. Lilley, *Religion and Revelation*, p. 123. Turner, *The Pattern*, pp. 486–92, has some very impressive arguments against the view that Scripture and tradition form one indistinguishable whole.

least imply a permanent confusion or identification between the Gospel and the Church's interpretation of it. None of the fathers during the period that we have been reviewing in this book imagined that the Bible and the Church's interpretation together formed one indistinguishable whole. Most of them regarded the contents of the Church's teaching as for all important purposes identical, and all of them were anxious to prove the Church's teaching from the Bible. But this does not mean that by interpreting the Bible the Church has managed to squeeze a little more revelation out of the Bible than would be there without squeezing, nor that by interpreting from the very beginning the Church has always had a little bit of extra revelation. The statement $1 = 1$ cannot be made equivalent to the statement $1 = 1\frac{1}{2}$. Irenaeus could hold that the Church's teaching was equivalent to the contents of Scripture; he did not believe that revelation consisted of the Church's interpretation of Scripture *in addition to* the contents of Scripture. The very fact that the Church formed the Canon of the New Testament, the very fact that the Church from about 150 onwards always purported to interpret Scripture, shows that the Church believed that there was a given revelation witnessed to by Scripture which could not be subtly added to by interpretation. And if at the time of the Canon being formed the Church's oral teaching was held to be the same as the contents of the Bible, this only meant that the Church was then witnessing to an orally transmitted Gospel which could not be added to by interpretation.

Congar's case is made all the more untenable by the fact that at one period a situation did exist in which Gospel and interpretation of Gospel tended to mingle into one whole, and that this period passed away beyond recovery. In an interesting article K. Aland has suggested that up to some point between AD 100 and 150 several pseudonymous works by Christian writers were regarded by both the authors and their hearers as the written record of the utterances of the Spirit through the author and as perpetuating through the Spirit the teaching and the Gospel of the apostles. He thinks that this might apply to the *Didache*, the *Epistle of Barnabas*, the letters of Ignatius, the *Epistula Apostolorum*, Hermas' *Shepherd*, I and II Peter, Revelation, and perhaps the fourth gospel and the Johannine epistles, and conceivably to the Pastorals or to some of them.[1] One might add that the circulation up to this period of reliable oral tradition would contribute to this attitude to pseudonymous works. But Aland notes that in the middle of the second century a change takes place. 'The movement of the Spirit was losing impetus.' The expectation of the Parousia had

[1] K. Aland, 'The Problem of Anonymity and Pseudonymity', pp. 43–47.

failed. 'The Church, which had hitherto lived, as it were, a timeless existence, began carefully to distinguish between the apostolic past and the present. The considerations that determined the formation of the Canon show this very clearly. It was no longer possible to throw a bridge across the generations and to speak as the mouth of an apostle.'[1] This change to 'historicization' Aland places at about 125–130, the time of Quadratus, the first Apologist,[2] a period which corresponds strikingly with the suggestion made earlier in this book, as a result of independent investigation, that the crucial period for the formation of the Canon was between 100 and 120.[3]

Further, even the state of affairs that prevailed in Irenaeus' day could not last. Irenaeus and Tertullian could appeal to the orally transmitted rule of faith as an equivalent to Scripture, and those two fathers, with others, Hegesippus and Hippolytus, for instance, could appeal to apostolic succession to support their other appeal. But time moved on, and in time the appeal to an orally transmitted tradition becomes weaker and weaker. Readers of this book must have become aware of the fact that it has traced a period of Church history and of the development of Christian doctrine in which both these appeals fade out.[4] In 170 they were persuasive. By 250 it is no use employing them any longer. One could describe this extent of time as the period in which the New Testament became recognized by the whole Church as the only reliable and authoritative source of information about Jesus Christ. Even Van den Eynde and Congar in some sense recognize this. Van den Eynde allows that Irenaeus' respect for 'the presbyters' was based on the fact that they lived nearer to the time when Christianity originated than he did,[5] and this is a principle which, as it applies to this example of oral tradition, so presumably can apply to all examples of it. And Congar admits that as the time between the apostolic age and the age of the fathers increased, so the fathers were obliged in arguing with heretics to rely on an appeal to the Scriptures as documents which came from the apostles themselves and which were not to be gainsaid.[6] It cannot be stated too often that the appeal to an unwritten tradition of custom in the first two and a half centuries of the Church's existence is irrelevant to the discussion of the sources of Christian truth, because no father regarded this subject of custom as seriously affecting the question of doctrine. Later, when fathers such as Athanasius and Basil use language which could be held to support the theory of a reliable unwritten tradition of doctrine, it is too late to

---

[1] *Ibid.* p. 47.   [2] *Ibid.* p. 48.   [3] See above, pp. 187–213.
[4] See above, pp. 158–9.   [5] *Les Normes*, p. 164.   [6] *La Tradition*, p. 50.

make an appeal to this tradition. There is something almost ludicrous
in the fact that Congar can find more references to an unwritten tradition
among the fathers of the fourth and fifth centuries than he can among
those of the second and third.[1] Are we to argue that Athanasius and Basil
in the fourth century knew more about an unwritten tradition of doctrine
than Tertullian and Origen, and Cyprian and Dionysius of Alexandria
in the third who knew nothing of it? This would be to turn historical
probability upside down. It is only by ignoring (no doubt unwittingly)
the evidence of the third century that Congar can use the argument from
the fathers' references to the unwritten tradition of custom at all. But
historical evidence plainly obstructs this theory. The fragility of oral
tradition, even of an orally transmitted rule of faith, cannot be dismissed.[2]
Salmon's dictum about tradition cannot be gainsaid.[3] The untrustworthi-
ness of the historical sense of Athanasius and Basil is too palpable to
enable anyone to build an argument upon their estimate of historical
evidence unsupported by anything else.

The Church's interpretation of Scripture, then, if it is to be regarded
as an oral tradition either supplementing or conveying in a certain context,
or simply reproducing the contents of, Scripture, must be allowed to be
open to corruption, like all oral tradition. It has been pointed out more
than once already that tradition can be corrupted, whereas Scripture
cannot.[4] Perhaps we might modify this by saying that it is difficult to
corrupt Scripture just because it is a formally written tradition, recognized as public and as exclusive and as normative; and though Scripture
has on occasion been corrupted (the case of I John 5.7b and 8a springs to
mind) it is relatively easy to detect and reform corruption. But tradition,
a fluid, indefinite thing, not confined to registered written documents
and liable to vary with the vicissitudes of history and the development of
human thought, can very easily become corrupted, and has in fact on
many occasions suffered from forgery and from obfuscation. Though the
Church cannot do without tradition, it is a disastrous mistake to confuse or
identify tradition with Scripture. We cannot and should not return to the
charismatic atmosphere of the first century nor even to the situation in
which Irenaeus lived. History has moved on and we have no authority
for assuming that the manner in which the Holy Spirit guides the Church
is by guaranteeing the permanent and indefinite survival of either of
these two situations.

Finally, what *is* this Christian *midrash*? What are its contents? The

---

[1] See *La Tradition*, pp. 59–69.   [2] See above, pp. 50, 126–7.
[3] See above, pp. 35, 185.   [4] See above, pp. 175, 186.

Gnostic formulae of Ignatius? The angel-Christology of Hermas? The millenniarism of Justin or the economic Trinity of Irenaeus and of Tertullian? The modalistic monarchianism of Callistus and Zephyrinus? The graded Trinity of Origen? We have only to ask these questions to realize that no concrete contents can be given to this concept of Christian *midrash*. The Church has always interpreted the Gospel, and always will do so, sometimes with more success and sometimes with less. But the interpretation is not the Gospel, and never can be. It is not the interpretation which is creative, but the Gospel, the Word of God who reaches the minds of churchmen in the Gospel and who is dynamic, active and creative, and who judges and reforms his Church as he saves and cleanses it. The Lord of the Church himself has warned us against absolutizing the *halakah*. Christianity is not a baptized Judaism, and the tradition of the Christian Church is not a *midrash*.

2. *The Nature of the Canon of Scripture*

An inquiry into the concept of tradition in the early Church inevitably raises the question, what exactly is the Canon of Scripture? Is it a line dividing inspired books from uninspired books? This would be a very difficult case to maintain.[1] There are no satisfactory grounds for deciding that the Books of Esther or of Judges, for instance, are in themselves, apart from their use by the Jewish and Christian communities, inspired in a way in which the Thanksgiving Psalms of the Qumran Covenanters or the First Book of Maccabbees are not. How can anyone detect clear signs of inspiration in the style or the subject or the images of II Peter which are lacking in *I Clement* and in the letters of Ignatius, documents probably written earlier than II Peter? Unless we are to rely blindly upon the judgement of the Church and determine that because the Church chose these books they must all possess some quality of inspiration lacking in other books, no matter how complex and far-fetched our way of detecting this quality may be, we must abandon this account of the Canon. It is indeed much better not to connect the Canon with inspiration at all. It is much more satisfactory to define the Canon in terms of a body of documentary witness. To describe its function we may borrow some felicitous words of J. K. S. Reid:

> Neither in Scripture or anywhere else does the Christian faith possess a *system*, whether of doctrine or of conduct, to which it may point and

[1] For a further discussion of the meaning of inspiration, see below, pp. 249–52.

declare: Accept and obey this in order to be saved. The real ground of the sufficiency of the Scriptures is that they testify to him in whom in order to be saved men must believe; and the doctrine and the conduct, the faith and the life, have their origins there. In this sense, much less than what we have in the New Testament, always provided that it had the authentic character of witness or testimony, would suffice; and on the other hand there is no reason why we should not have had much more. The fact is, that, in the providence of God, through the careful guardianship of early believers, there has been handed down to us this actual quantity of authentic primary witness.[1]

It is important to add to this statement however the qualification that this witness takes the form of a body of documents. The form through which the Holy Spirit speaks or communicates in Scripture is historical evidence, and this form conditions and controls the whole normative function of Scripture. The Bible is indeed witness to the light. It reflects light and glows with light, and is illuminated by the light of which it is a medium. We might describe the Canon as a circle of light, with dazzling light at the centre and twilight at the edges. If some parts reflect this light only dimly and others scarcely at all or even not at all, this does not matter, because the whole effectively acts as a medium of light. To revert to our original point that the Bible is a body of evidence, it does not matter if some parts of the evidence are less relevant than others, and even a few not relevant at all, as long as the whole body conveys in its general drift a clear impression. Those who have read that first-rate piece of journalism, John Hershey's *Hiroshima*, may find an analogy here. This book includes a number of accounts of the explosion of the first atomic bomb written or given by different people and put together into a single account by Hershey. The different witnesses—a girl, a Methodist minister, a business man, a doctor, a Jesuit priest—describe the same event from different points of view arising from different experiences and backgrounds. Some of the accounts are inconsistent in detail with others; none of the contributors knew the whole story or the whole truth. Many of the details included are not particularly relevant and could have been omitted without spoiling the whole. Yet together these diverse pieces of evidence compose a magnificent picture of the whole dreadful occurrence. We can apply this analogy to the Bible, except that the occurrence here is supernatural, and joyful, not dreadful. All that the Church guarantees is that the documents of the Bible witness sufficiently to the truth to make us wise unto salva-

---

[1] *The Authority of Scripture*, p. 139. See also the useful remarks of W. D. Davies, *A Normative Pattern of Church Life in the New Testament*, pp. 15–22.

tion. The Church has no right to insist that all the documents are consistent with each other in every detail, nor that they contain only what is strictly relevant in order to witness to the truth and nothing more. The total impression which they convey is enough to disclose clearly the meaning and the demands of God's revelation of himself in Jesus Christ. Nothing more is needed; nothing more should be required. This does not necessarily imply that Scripture need be used only as a negative check against doctrine, so that what Scripture contradicts or condemns must be rejected, though what Scripture does not contain can be taught with impunity, as Congar appears to suggest.[1] The Bible is a body of documents witnessing to the revelation of God in Christ. Doctrines which have no basis in this witness or which cannot be drawn by implication from this witness must not be taught as a necessary part of the Christian Gospel. Doctrine which is not connected with this witness (whether consistent with it or inconsistent is irrelevant to this point) simply cannot be described as a part of Christianity. It might, for instance, be thought by some Englishmen that the British people are in some peculiar sense chosen specially by God to fulfil his purposes, and they might regard this as in itself very helpful and cheering doctrine. But this theory has no basis whatever in the biblical witness and therefore must be abandoned, no matter how fitting and consoling it might appear to Englishmen, even though the Bible does not explicitly condemn it. On the other hand, just because the Bible is a body or mass of witness we have no right to insist either that all its details are relevant or that no relevant detail has been omitted. All we have a right to ask is that no crucial or vitally important part shall have been omitted, and nothing either omitted or included which could affect the general impression made by the whole body of evidence. That is why we can view with equanimity the possibility that some words of our Lord may have been recorded in early gospels or other writings which were rejected by the Church, and not included in the four canonical gospels. Precious though any utterance of Jesus must be for every believing Christian, it is only the general drift and total impression of his words, taken in the context of his life and his works, that are indispensably important. An occasional utterance here and there which has escaped the net of the canonical gospels cannot seriously affect any fundamental doctrine. Even these few uncanonical sayings which may be authentic can only be recognized as authentic, or conjectured to be authentic, because we already possess a reliable standard of authenticity provided by the canonical sayings. In other words, the New Testament

[1] *La Tradition*, p. 54.

as we have it is indispensably and unalterably normative, though not necessarily an exhaustive glossary of all the sayings of Jesus. The very fact that the fathers themselves quote sayings from uncanonical sources in their writings shows that, whatever their doctrines about inspiration may have been, they did not in effect regard the Canon as drawing a hard and fast line.

It must of course be acknowledged that if we allow the possibility of the survival of authentic tradition, albeit of a very fragmentary character, outside the New Testament, we must also allow the formal possibility of the survival of authentic tradition outside the New Testament in the form of an oral tradition surviving indefinitely in the Church. But this possibility can be no more than formal, because of the difference of the two cases. Traditions of the words of Jesus preserved in such documents as the *Gospel of Thomas* may be regarded as valuable because there is reason to believe that they were written down at a comparatively early stage, that they have been, in the documents in which we encounter them, copied from earlier documents, such as the *Gospel according to the Hebrews*, and because we can check them by sayings in the synoptic gospels, in fact by early written evidence. But the theory of a survival in the Church indefinitely from the very beginning of an authentic unwritten tradition of doctrine has none of these advantages and has every consideration of historical probability against it. *A priori* arguments based on theological principles are useless here. One might perhaps believe that our Lord is likely to have bequeathed an unwritten tradition of this sort to the Church, that it is fitting that he should have done so, that it would be of great advantage to the Church, and so on. But these considerations are quite worthless if it cannot be shown that there is historical evidence pointing to the existence of such a tradition. At this point the honest historian must admit that he faces a hopeless deficiency of evidence.

The case of the fourth gospel raises an interesting question for those who are trying to determine the nature of the Canon of Scripture. Is it primary evidence coming from the earliest period of the works and words of Jesus? Few scholars would care to give a final negative to this question, but many would hesitate to answer it with a confident affirmative. The Church, as we have seen,[1] hesitated for some time before acknowledging it as authoritative. But once it was acknowledged as canonical it exercised a profound influence upon the development of Christian doctrine.[2] One might almost say that Christianity ever since has been Johannine Christianity. To regard the work as wrongly canonized, or as only

---

[1] See above, pp. 192–5.   [2] See M. Wiles, *The Spiritual Gospel*.

deutero-canonical, would be to demand a radical revision of Christianity. Versions of Christianity without the Johannine element in it, such as that presented by M. Werner in his *Formation of Christian Dogma*, do not encourage one to embark upon this enterprise. But if we recognize that the fourth gospel may be an example of canonized tradition, in the sense of interpretation rather than of original evidence, this perplexity may be resolved. That this gospel does contain a large element of interpretation, by any reckoning larger than the proportion of interpretation to be found in the synoptic gospels, very few would deny. What proportion of the Gospel represents the original teaching of Jesus and what the interpretation of the evangelist is a matter of considerable debate, by no means settled yet. But after all, St Paul's letters and the Revelation of St John and the First Epistle of Peter might well be described as examples of canonized tradition in this sense. These documents enshrine for us the comment and exposition and application of the teaching and the significance of Jesus by some of the earliest Christians, men who lived very near indeed to the historical source of light, men who had known the apostles or known others who had known them. The Church decided, with entire justice, that the comments of these writers constituted in itself witness so important that it must be regarded as normative. The same decision applies to the fourth gospel, with this difference that here we have an account of the earthly life of Jesus with an interpretation instead of letters concerned with the ordering of churches which incidentally interpret and witness to the significance of Jesus. The fourth gospel does constitute *early* interpretation; how early, it is very difficult to tell, but early enough to justify its canonization, early enough for us to be sure that it glows with the radiance of that light which came into the world to lighten every man nearly two thousand years ago, early enough to constitute one of the most valuable, though one of the most mysterious, components of the body of evidence which we call the New Testament.

It is only when we seek to link the Canon of the New Testament with theories of inspiration of the Bible that we find insuperable difficulties.[1] To say that the authors of the books were inspired rather than the books themselves or to attribute inspiration to the community which preserved the books, or to the persons who edited or revised the texts, only puts the difficulties one stage further back and leaves the anomalies unresolved.[2]

[1] For a fuller discussion of inspiration see *Allegory and Event*, cap. 7, my 'The Inspiration of Holy Scripture', and Grant, *The Earliest Lives of Jesus*, caps. 1 and 3. See also above, pp. 211–12, 234–5.

[2] In one comprehensive sentence, Congar (*La Tradition*, pp. 14–15) attributes inspiration to the biblical texts, the persons who have edited them, the historical life of the communities who transmitted them, and the holy words.

Theories of inspiration have so far in the history of the Church been paid to the Bible as compliments by those who loved the Bible, and, like other compliments, they have been high-sounding rather than accurate. It is of course true that the Bible was written from faith to faith. It has a power of evoking and of nourishing faith. It is not simply a body of ancient documents of high historical value (though it is this). Because of its subject, and because of its peculiar and exclusive closeness in time to its subject as a body of evidence, it is unique. It has been used by the Church as its foundation document for nearly two thousand years; by it Christians of all ages and of all ecclesiastical traditions have lived the life of faith since the beginning. If this is what is meant by calling it inspired, then inspiration in this sense can be accepted. But inspiration in this sense is a most misleading word; uniqueness would be a better one. Whenever anybody for the first eighteen centuries of the Church's existence called the Bible inspired, they meant something quite different from this. They meant that the words and statements of the Bible possessed in themselves some special 'sacred' quality (variously defined by various writers) which set them apart from all other words and statements in the world, and that the Canon was the line which separated these 'sacred' words or sentences or books from all others. But this function of the Canon is a purely imaginary one.

It should be obvious to those who have followed the argument of this book thus far that the function of the Bible as a norm is conditioned by the form which it takes as a norm, viz. as a body of historical evidence. It is not, for instance, a code of law nor a textbook of moral theology, though it contains within it law codes and discussions of moral problems. Tertullian made several determined attempts to turn the New Testament at least into a code of law, with how little success any reader of his works can determine. The Bible is not a series of disconnected inspired oracles which will yield the correct quantity of Christian doctrine to the mind which is capable of allegorizing them, as Origen apparently believed. It is not even a manual of doctrine, say of Christological or Trinitarian doctrine, waiting for the properly devout or properly educated mind to read off the right propositions from it, as several fathers from the third century onwards seem to have thought. It does not provide us with a ready-made blue-print for the ordering of the ministry and the administration of the sacraments; this was how Cyprian, who in some respects was immoderately biblical, constantly tried to use it. We marvel as we observe him finding texts in the obscurer parts of Leviticus and Numbers to determine the day-to-day problems of a diocesan bishop in North Africa in the middle of the third century. We are astonished to find Gregory Thaumaturgus in his *Canons* using texts from the Pentateuch as his guide in facing a few years after Cyprian's day the vexing problems presented by the aftermath of a severe Gothic invasion in the provinces lying to the south of the Black Sea. The Bible cannot even be regarded without qualification as a paradigm for conduct. *I Clement* may indeed with a charming confidence range freely all over the Old Testament to find examples of conduct both good and bad to hold up to its readers. But two can play at this game, as Marcion and Apelles were to show in the second half of the second century. The Gnostics could make a plausible case for the assertion that the Old Testament was full of evil examples apparently commended as good. Though the Bible is of course relevant for determining matters of doctrine, of morality, of the ordering of ministry and sacraments, it is relevant as a body of historical evidence, and not as law code nor as manual nor as blue-print nor as system of ethics. It is a body of historical evidence, against which all doctrine and all that implies doctrine must be matched. The New Testament is the record of what the Church believed, knew and taught at the very beginning of Christianity. Nothing incompatible with this, unconnected with this nor irrelevant to this should be imposed upon Christians. In this sense the New Testament is tradition *par excellence*, the earliest tradition both of historical information about Jesus and of doctrine about Jesus, recognized by the Church at a time when the Church was in a position to recognize it.

The casual nature of much of the material in the Bible is relevant to this point. In the Psalms we possess a miscellaneous collection of poems, some originally composed to express the personal reaction of some utterly unknown individual to some moment of joy or grief, some still incorporating rubrics or musical directions which have been incomprehensible for nearly three thousand years. In the law-books we have an assorted heap of legislation designed originally to deal with societies and situations which have long since lapsed into utter oblivion. When we read St Paul's letters we are eavesdropping upon the private correspondence of one who never remotely dreamed that his letters, sometimes hastily dashed off to deal with a temporary crisis, would eventually become sacred Scripture. This does not mean that the books we have been referring to are obsolete; because they truly witness to the activity of a living God they themselves live and become living to us. But it is impossible to regard them as oracles or manuals; it is only when we regard them as historical evidence that their true relevance appears. Our interpretation of them must be governed by the understanding of their nature and function. This does not mean that the Bible is a sheer chaos of inconsistent ideas which must be reduced to order and system by the ingenuity of scholastic theologians. The Bible has its own consistency, but it is the consistency of historical witness to an event, the consistency of John Hershey's *Hiroshima* rather than of Newton's *Principia*. We must not, for instance, imagine that the Bible will give us a complete and authoritative pattern for the Church's ministry nor a clear outline of eucharistic liturgy, any more than we must imagine that because these things are lacking the Bible can throw no light on ministry or liturgy. Interpretation is a subtler and more demanding discipline than either of these courses suggests. It is equally mistaken to imagine that because the Church must interpret the Bible therefore the Church can by some pleasing illusion supplement the Bible as an historical source. If, for instance, the Bible gives us no information whatever about the death of the Blessed Virgin Mary and the destiny of her body after death, it is quite illegitimate to invent, and wholly unjustifiable to persuade oneself of the existence, of such information. If it has not pleased God to give us this information, we must be content to be without it as long as this world stands. It is just as arbitrary to find patterns of ministry and forms of worship and lines of doctrine on other grounds and from other sources and then laboriously to find justification for them in the Bible. This was a weakness from which many fathers suffered, not least Origen and Cyprian. The task of interpreting the Bible is an arduous and exacting one, and it is never finished. It is exacting no less in its demand that we shall recognize our ignorance than in its insistence that we must be faithful to what we know.

3. *Tradition as the Scope of Scripture*

So far in this chapter our account of tradition as interpretation has been mainly negative. It has been necessary to make sure that tradition does not absorb or drown Scripture. But there is a very important positive aspect of tradition too. Flesseman-van Leer in one part of her book points out that in some of the usages of 'rule of truth' in Irenaeus the phrase 'cannot be anything but the real purport of Scripture . . . it is not a formal principle for exegesis, brought to the Bible from outside, but the real teaching of the Bible, that is, the revelation as embedded in Scripture.'[1] Elsewhere she repeats this dictum that the *regula* can mean the real purport of revelation and suggests that it is well expressed in Barth's definition of *the* Dogma, 'it is that which the dogmas try to express, the

---

[1] *Tradition and Scripture*, p. 127.

innermost meaning of all dogmatic sentences'.[1] We have already seen that
Bakhuizen van den Brink emphasized this aspect of the *regula*, that
Prestige wrote of the Gospel within the Gospel, and that Irenaeus
associated it with the σωμάτιον or main body, Tertullian with the *ratio*
or purport, and Athanasius with the 'scope' (σκοπός) of Scripture.[2]
Hägglund makes a great point of this meaning of the *regula*. It means, he
says, that 'the truth as such, that is the facts of creation and redemption
clearly evidenced in revelation, are the plumbline of the truth. The
concept does not lead us to a canon of ecclesiastical authority devised in a
conflict against the heretics, but to the revelation which lies behind the
Church's preaching and which is witnessed to continually in it.'[3] Later
he says that the *regula* cannot simply be identified with the Bible; it
means the contents or main teaching of the Bible.[4] Congar argues that
the fathers' whole interpretation of Scripture, and especially their typo-
logical treatment of it, constitutes an unwritten tradition, recognized
even in a sense by the Reformers.[5]

> It is evident that, in these conditions, there is in one sense *more* in
> the new application than in the fact of revelation or the scriptural
> attestation by which, however, it is justified. The scriptural reference
> is then less a literal or literary justification than an authentication, the
> deriving of an authorization from the intentions of God in so far as
> they are unfolded in the normative moment of the history of the people
> of God whose memorial is sacred Scripture.[6]

We cannot accept this as a serious account of unwritten tradition because
interpretation of this sort cannot perform the primary evidential function
of Scripture. But we may take it as another way, a particularly interesting
one, of stating the same conviction about the meaning of the rule of faith
which we have found variously described in Irenaeus, Tertullian and
Athanasius among the ancients, and in Prestige, Bakhuizen van den
Brink, Flesseman-van Leer, and Hägglund among the moderns. The rule
of faith interprets and detects the drift or burden or main body of
truth, the 'scope', of Scripture. This is as important a truth today as it
was in the second and third centuries.

It is perhaps only when we meet a point of view which denies this truth
that we realize its full significance. M. Werner, in his *Formation of
Christian Dogma*, is a spokesman for such a point of view. According to

---

[1] *Ibid.* p. 167. See above, pp. 128–9, where this quotation is given with references.
[2] See above, pp. 73 n. 5, 108–10, 116, 179–81.
[3] 'Die Bedeutung der "regula fidei" ', pp. 9–10.
[4] *Ibid.* pp. 13–14.   [5] *La Tradition*, pp. 76–91.   [6] *Ibid.* p. 84.

Werner, the Acts, the Pastoral Epistles and the fourth gospel were themselves a reinterpretation of the original tradition by the post-apostolic
Church, the original tradition being conveyed in the synoptic gospels
and genuine Pauline epistles. The process of de-eschatologizing and
Hellenization began in the 'Gnostic' fourth gospel, the Pastorals,
I Clement and Hermas, and the original Gospel was finally abandoned in
the fourth century, when the exponents of the true Christology, Arius,
Aetius, Eunomius and Eudoxius, were rejected. Werner takes eschatology
so literally that he regards Christianity as having seen its best days
already by about the year 60. He insists upon putting to this New Testament, soaked as its thought is in eschatology, the wholly uneschatological
question, 'Is Christ divine?' When he finds that the New Testament
gives no clear answer to this question, he incontinently assumes that from
the moment when the Church decided that Christ was divine it deviated
fatally from true Christianity. What Werner in effect repudiates is tradition, tradition precisely in the form of interpretation.[1] He does not
accept the idea that the Church has been from the beginning teaching
and preaching an interpretation of the Christian Gospel, attempting to
apply it to each contemporary situation and compare it with each contemporary philosophy, and that in these attempts nothing less than the
total impression or main truth or drift or 'scope' of the Scriptures is
variously conveyed. It is significant that if this idea (which indeed rests
upon an act of faith in Christ as found and encountered in the Church)
is abandoned, then the whole nexus of Christian doctrine falls to pieces,
as under Werner's analysis it does. One perceives that tradition (tradition
as interpretation) is necessary in order, to so speak, to hold the Bible
together. This does not really mean that the incongruous and contradictory ideas collected as in a patchwork within the leaves of the Bible
can only be regarded as a unity by a *tour de force* of intellectual ingenuity
which the Church in its wisdom (or should we say, in its cunning?) has
managed to provide. It means that there is a main body of truth, a 'scope'
to be found in the Bible, which the Holy Spirit intends us to find, and
that the chief intellectual task of the Church is to find it, and find it anew
every generation, and never to rest content with a final expression of it.
In the particular subject upon which Werner lays most stress, that of

---

[1] The same blindness to the necessity for allowing for tradition is found in E.
Schweizer's *Church Order in the New Testament* and in the work of Sohm on the origins
of the Church (see Linton, *Das Problem der Urkirche*, pp. 50–54, and J. L. Adams'
essay, 'Rudolf Sohm's Theology of Law and the Spirit', in *Religion and Culture*, pp.
219–35, and especially p. 233). W. D. Davies in his otherwise illuminating essay,
A Normative Pattern of Church Life in the New Testament, surprisingly does not mention
the subject of tradition. See also my essay, 'The Anglican Doctrine of Ministry'.

Christology, the fault of Werner (as of several other contemporary scholars) is to assume that we can discover the real Christology by concentrating upon one of the many Christological expressions in the New Testament—that which regards Jesus as an angel—and interpreting him by this one alone, rejecting all others as spurious. In fact the very variety of the categories applied to Jesus in the New Testament—Son of Man, Son of God, Messiah, Suffering Servant, Second Adam, High Priest, Shepherd, Logos, and so on—ought to suggest that there is some meaning behind all these which cannot be explained by any one of them, but only by taking the impression of the whole. This whole, this 'scope' is precisely what the tradition exists to express and attempts to express.

The Christian religion is translated into terms of creed, of doctrine, of practice, of life by a living community. Congar has reminded us of 'the living community of faith quickening the people of God'.[1] By feeding upon the Gospel the Church produces tradition. If we insist that this tradition mu/t be limited and controlled by the witness of the Bible, this is not because we are determined to shackle a living faith to a dead document. In the first place, it is ridiculous to call the Bible dead, seeing that it has had an extraordinary capacity for quickening the faith and kindling the religious imagination of countless people all over the world and in recent ages as well as ancient. No book has been translated into more languages; it is far and away the best-seller among books whether we reckon it by extent of demand or by sustained capacity to sell. If the Bible is a dead document, then many authors must wish that their books were as moribund! To read the writings of men whose minds have been nourished on the Bible, such as Hooker, or John Bunyan, or John and Charles Wesley, is to realize the ever-new life which flows from the Bible century after century. In the second place, the element of fixedness or permanence in the Bible is precisely the element of historicity which is an inseparable part of Christianity, because God did in fact choose to make his revelation in Christ through and in history. The fact that the Bible is an historical document, or rather a collection of historical documents, is the prime factor which prevents Christianity from becoming divorced from history, as, for instance, Hinduism and Buddhism have become divorced. Not even the sacraments of Baptism and Holy Communion, not even the ministry, which are all in some sense phenomena which stand in historical continuity with the origins of Christianity, can exercise so strong an influence as the Bible in mooring Christianity to the historical event upon which the whole religion is based. Christianity is

[1] See above, p. 239.

not historical merely in the sense that, like Buddhism and Mohammedan-
ism, it had its origins in historical events. It is a more thoroughly historical
religion than any other, because it teaches that God pledged and poured
himself into history, and that the historical particularity of the career of
Jesus Christ is the scandal which faith must accept. The Incarnation is
not over; Christ did not abandon his human body in the tomb; he is not
now remote from history and humanity. The very historical nature of the
Bible, the very fact that it can be described as a miscellaneous collection
of ancient documents of considerable interest for archaeologists and
historians of the ancient world, is the firmest guarantee of this truth.
That is why tradition must be bound and restricted by this collection of
historical evidence. To desire to emancipate tradition from this condition,
to envisage for it some fairy cornucopia of developing doctrine which need
owe no responsibility to historical evidence, is to evince an unconscious
desire to abandon the Incarnation. Christian doctrine consists of the
interaction of a living community and a body of historical evidence. This
precisely reveals the nature of Christianity, its unique paradox of once-
for-all event and transcendent Spirit.

Perhaps it is an overstatement to say that tradition *is* interpretation of
the Bible; it would be better to say (as we have already suggested) that
tradition is created and formed by interpretation. The two overlap and
interact. Bakhuizen van den Brink has some interesting words on this
subject:

> The Church's tradition and its interpretation of holy Scripture, at any
> moment of history, cannot be examined separately with any profit.
> The interpretation of Scripture is so much determined by tradition,
> and so much it creates tradition . . . The Church has read and inter-
> preted the Bible unintermittently and unweariedly in every period
> of its history. In interpreting the Scriptures it has alternately appro-
> priated them into its tradition and has corrected its tradition by the
> Bible. Its tradition has been by turns its vital principle and the stone
> of stumbling in its midst. This dialectic has continued into our own
> time.[1]

Interpretation has of course made serious mistakes in the course of Christian history, and still is open to a number of different distortions. There is
the temptation to take every word in Scripture equally as a direct command or word from God. Tertullian and Cyprian in their day fell to this,
and there are Literalists in our own day who imagine that this is the right

[1] 'La tradition dans l'Église', p. 272.

way to interpret the Bible and who forget that 'the flesh profiteth nothing'.[1] The result of this tendency, if it is pursued with rigour, is to turn the Bible into a mass of contradictions; it means treating the Bible, as someone has said, as if it were a railway guide. The opposite temptation is to turn the Bible into a manual of scholastic theology combined with a code of ecclesiastical law, and its results are just as unsatisfactory. Origen gave way in more than one respect to this tendency,[2] and those who today would, for instance, cite the story of Onan in order to find a ground for forbidding the use of contraceptives would seem to adopt the same method. But the Bible, as a body of historical evidence, is patient of neither type of interpretation.

The task of interpretation is not an easy one. But at the same time the Church must not and cannot avoid it. A characteristic sentence of Newman finely sets out this obligation:

> If the Church be the pillar and ground of the truth, and bound to contend for the preservation of the faith once delivered to it; if we are answerable as ministers of Christ for the formation of one, and one only, character in the heart of man; and if the Scriptures are given us, as a means indeed towards the end, but inadequate to the office of interpreting themselves, except to such as live under the Divine Influence which inspired them, and which is expressly sent down upon us that we may interpret them,—then it is evidently our duty piously and cautiously to collect the sense of Scripture, and solemnly to promulgate it in such form as is best suited, as far as it goes, to exclude the pride and unbelief of the world.[3]

And in fact the Church, however we define the Church and in whatever of its manifestations we like to observe it, is in innumerable ways interpreting the Bible all the time. It does so in worship, whether liturgical or free, in the private prayers of individual Christians, in preaching, in teaching, in the good works and in the moral decisions of its members. The Church may be said to live on the Bible as its spiritual and intellectual food. It is in fact either interpreting the Bible (which is its tradition *par excellence*) or it is living in illusion.

This work does not include within its scope the subject of the development of doctrine, though it will perhaps have supplied some material for those who wish to study this subject. It may perhaps be permissible to state the conviction that the subject of the development of doctrine and

---

[1] 'God says: Keep my Sabbaths. Are you keeping Sunday?' a poster observed in Sheffield Victoria Station in November 1960, is a brief and pithy example of this mistake.

[2] See *Allegory and Event*, cap. 11.   [3] *The Arians of the Fourth Century*, p. 86.

R

of the reformation of doctrine are equally alien to the thought of the early Church, because no writer had occasion to face seriously the question of what is to happen when the obligation to teach sound doctrine and the obligation to preserve the unity of the Church conflict with each other. This is the new problem with which the sixteenth century faced the Christian religion. The history of the early Church does not give an answer to it, any more than the Bible gives an answer to it. We are only justified in drawing the negative conclusion that the experience of the early Church gives no justification for assuming the existence of any source of sound doctrine outside the Bible. It may however be profitable to make one or two observations about the contents of tradition as we can observe them in the period which has been under review.

In the first place, it is valuable and interesting that it has been possible to make a rough estimate of the ingredients of the rule of faith.[1] It is clear that the subjects which were destined during the next two centuries to form the material for dogmatic and credal decisions were already well to the fore in the Church's consciousness, i.e. Christological and Trinitarian doctrine. The theological interpretation of the eucharist and the seat of authority in the Church were not considered to be part of the rule of faith and clearly did not occupy much attention, but it would be incorrect to say that they were totally beyond the Church's ken. More remote still was any thought about dogmatic statements concerning the status of the Blessed Virgin Mary, but even these cannot be said to be something irreconcilable with the interests of the churchmen of these early centuries. Whether these subjects should be made material for dogmas is a question whose answer will depend upon what theory of the development of doctrine we may hold. What does appear to be entirely ruled out by the doctrine of tradition held in the early Church is the possibility of the formation of any new doctrine or dogma dependent upon an historical event not recorded in Scripture. By no sort of theory could this be justified according to the lights of the early Church. If the dogma of the corporeal assumption of the Blessed Virgin Mary involves the belief in an historical fact (as well, of course, as the interpretation of fact), in some manner analogous to the dependence of the doctrine of the resurrection of Christ upon historical fact, then it can have no support whatever in the tradition of the Church of this period. If it is a fact, it is a fact wholly unknown to the writers of the second and third centuries. Tertullian can write a long treatise of sixty-three chapters *On the Resurrection of the Dead*, mentioning and discussing the Resurrection of Jesus Christ, the

[1] See above, pp. 86–91.

raising of Lazarus, the translation without death of Enoch and of Elijah, the returning from the dead of Moses for the Transfiguration, and even the preservation from what was humanly speaking certain death of the three young men in the fiery furnace and of Jonah in the whale's belly. He does not once even slightly mention, he does not once even remotely and uncertainly hint at, the resurrection or corporeal assumption of the Blessed Virgin Mary. Tertullian quite clearly, like all his contemporaries and predecessors, had never heard of this story.[1]

The second observation that can be made about the contents of the rule of faith is that clearly all the fathers of the period under review believed that there were primary and secondary doctrines as far as their importance was concerned. In his final summary Van den Eynde points out that all the authors of the second and third centuries distinguish between 'the essential doctrines in which all the churches agree and which are opposed to heresy, and the secondary points the negation of which constitutes error, adjudged less serious than heresy'.[2] We have seen that Origen even gives us a list, not only of what doctrines are included in the rule of faith, but also of what are not included,[3] not in order to list erroneous opinions but in order to leave himself room for speculation, unhampered by the rule of faith. Indeed, a rule of faith by its very nature implies a distinction between doctrines of primary and doctrines of secondary importance. Though the early fathers of course regarded the doctrines of their faith as connected by consistency and logic in an interior harmony belonging to revelation itself, they were very far from envisaging the construction of a *summa theologica* or imagining a doctrinal *totum* so well articulated that the removal or modification of minor or peripheral doctrines must affect the whole and involve its injury. Even Origen's *De Principiis*, far-ranging though it was, cannot be described as a rudimentary *summa theologica*. It can best be described as the first consistent and thorough attempt to give the Christian faith a philosophical basis. The fathers were too near to the historical origin of the Event which constituted Christianity to regard the task of doctrine

---

[1] The attempt of Daniélou (*La Théologie*, p. 261) to suggest that because one of the characteristic features of Judeo-Christianity was the belief that the bodies as well as the souls of some righteous men had been assumed into heaven before the general resurrection, therefore the dogma of the assumption of the Virgin 'appeared thus in the context of the primitive tradition', seems to rest on conjecture alone. In fact this idea first made its appearance in fifth-century Coptic Christianity under marked Gnostic influence. That these Jewish Christians did not include Mary in their list of spurious resurrections is all the more conclusive evidence that they had never heard of the doctrine of her assumption.

[2] *Les Normes*, p. 320.

[3] See above, p. 90.

as anything more than the filling out and application of the evidence to that Event provided by the Scriptures of the Old and New Testaments. This is one more indication that, whether they consciously realized it or not, their basic attitude about the Bible implied the recognition that the form which it took as revelation was the historic evidence for Christianity.

APPENDIX A

Cyprian's *Testimonia*

H. KOCH,[1] to support his argument that this work was by Cyprian, produced a long list of words and phrases from the *Testimonia* paralleled by similar or identical words or phrases from works which are universally acknowledged to be genuinely Cyprian's. This list, however, though it must preclude us placing this book in the list of pseudo-Cyprianic works, is not convincing enough to persuade us to regard it as wholly Cyprian's own, for the words and phrases adduced by Koch are either based directly on Scripture or are those which would be common to others and have no peculiarly Cyprianic tang about them. Koch admits that there are several reasons in the work to prevent our regarding it as typical of Cyprian's mature period. But quite apart from the question of whether we can trace a growth of maturity in the thought of one whose whole career in Christianity lasted only a little over ten years, there are things in this book so incongruous with the rest of Cyprian's work that it is not adequate to account for the incongruity by allocating the book to an early point in Cyprian's career. The main evidence for this incongruity is set out here:

1. This book shows readings in the text of the Latin New Testament unknown elsewhere in Cyprian:

    Test. 3.26: Matt. 7.23 is given as *recedite a me, operarii iniquitatis*; but in *De Unitate Ecc. Cath.* 15 Cyprian quotes this text as *recedite a me qui operamini iniquitatem*.

    Test. 3.32: Luke 20.35 is given as *non nubunt neque nubuntur*; but in *De Habitu Virginum* 22 Cyprian cites this text as *non nubunt neque matrimonium faciunt*.

    Test. 3.35: Rom. 2.4 is given as *quia bonitas Dei in paenitentiam te adducit*; but in *De Bono Paenitentiae* 4 Cyprian quotes this in the form *quoniam patientia et bonitas Dei ad paenitentiam te adducit*.

    Test. 3.119 cites Acts 15.29 thus: *abstinere vos ab idololatris et sanguine et fornicatione, et quaecunque vobis fieri non vultis, alii ne feceritis*; the omission of καὶ πνικτοῦ is indeed characteristic of Cyprian, as it is of Irenaeus and Tertullian, but the addition of the negative

[1] *Cyprianische Untersuchungen*, pp. 183–200.

version of the Golden Rule is not characteristic of Cyprian (it appears in D,614, sy^h, sa and Ir.).

2. The *Testimonia* uses some words and phrases which are markedly uncharacteristic of Cyprian: e.g.

Test. 1.18: *in evangelio cata Iohannem*, and according to Hartel's Apparatus several MSS read *cata* instead of *secundum* in most references to the gospels in this work. Elsewhere Cyprian always uses *secundum* in referring to the authorship of a gospel.

Test. 1.20; 2.16 (some MSS); 3.62 and in several other places this work refers to the books of Kings as *Basilon*. Elsewhere Cyprian refers to them as *Regum*.

Test. 2.2: *sacramento concarnationis*, meaning the Incarnation, a word not found elsewhere in Cyprian.

Test. 3.3: *Agapem et dilectionem fraternam religiose et firmiter exercendam*, where *agape* must mean Christian love, and not the agape-meal. Elsewhere Cyprian uses this word only of the meal.

Test. 3.98 uses the word *catachumenus*, which Cyprian employs only once elsewhere, preferring on all other occasions *audiens*. To H. von Soden, who pointed out these last two incongruities,[1] Koch replied that they are accounted for by the early date of this work and the influence of Tertullian. But a simpler explanation is that Cyprian was using or hastily revising somebody else's work.

Test. 3.36, 37, 39 refers to I Peter as *Petrus apostolus ad Ponticos*, an odd expression not used elsewhere by Cyprian.

3. The *Testimonia* betrays ideas which are not easily reconciled with Cyprian's characteristic teaching. E.g.

Test. 1.17 gives a series of quotations from the Old Testament designed to show that the old priesthood would cease and a new, eternal, priesthood be introduced. None of Cyprian's peculiar doctrines of sacrifice and priesthood appear here.

Test. 3.28: *Non posse in ecclesia remitti ei qui in Deum deliquerit*. This doctrine of certain sins—those 'against God'—being irremissible is Tertullian's and Hippolytus' and Origen's, but not Cyprian's. The parallels to this sentiment quoted by Koch[2] from *De Lapsis* 17 and *Ep.* 16.2 are not satisfactory, for all that these two passages declare is that the Church has no right to forgive sins against God *without proper delay and proper penance*. Against this we can set *Ep.* 55.26.2,

---

[1] *Quellen und Forsuchungen*, Bd. xii, 1909, 30, noted in Koch, *Untersuchungen*, (p. 200 n.).
[2] *Untersuchungen*, p. 193.

where Cyprian quite clearly allows forgiveness after penance to fornicators, in opposition to Novatian, who refuses it.

Test. 3.51: *Quod nemo in opere suo extolli debeat*; this sentiment is quite uncongenial to Cyprian's doctrine of merit. So is its emphasis upon faith (3.69, 87) and upon man's sinfulness (3.47, 54).

It is not satisfactory, in view of all this evidence, to be content with attributing this work to an early period in Cyprian's career as a Christian. We have no reason to assume that he used a different translation of the New Testament early in his career from the one which he used later, nor that he later changed his vocabulary, and little material for the theory that he considerably altered his theological ideas at any point in his career. Rendel Harris throughout the two parts of his *Testimonies* maintains that Cyprian was in the first two books of this work re-handling an older document which consisted of a series of proof-texts, with headings, against the Jews.[1] He suggested that 'the extent of the Testimonies from which Cyprian drew must have been larger than his first two books',[2] and that 'these two books showed traces of a derivation from a Greek original, however much they may have been remoulded by Cyprian himself'.[3] Harris' evidence strongly enforces the other evidence tending to the conclusion that *Testimonia* 1–2 at least represents an already existing document edited, but not originally written, by Cyprian. On the other hand, it must be pointed out that the evidence from readings in the Latin translation of the New Testament all comes from the *third* book of the *Testimonia*, and that some of the other evidence can be found in the third book as well as in the first two. The evidence for a Greek original seems to be confined to the first two books, and there is positive proof that the third book, even though it uses *catechumenus* instead of *audiens* and *agape* instead of *dilectio* or some Latin word, could not possibly have been a direct translation of the Greek. *Testimonia* 3.98 runs: *Catechumenum peccare iam non debere : Paulus apostolus ad Romanos : faciamus mala dum veniunt bona ; quorum damnatio iusta est.* Now, if this text from Rom. 3.8 is to apply to a catechumen, it must be translated 'Let us do evil while good things are on the way', and be directed against the catechumen's desire to have a last fling before baptism. But this is an impossible interpretation of the Greek[4] and could only have

---

[1] See *Testimonies*, Part 1, pp. 4, 5, 17, 33, 76, 94, 102, 104, 115, 121; Part 2, pp. 2, 3, 14, 18, 19, 21, 25, 33, 34, 36, 44, 63, 64, 65, 66, 73, 85, 87, 97, 100, 103, 106, 107, 126.
[2] *Ibid.* Part 1, p. 94.   [3] *Ibid.* Part 2, p. 2.
[4] ποιήσωμεν τὰ κακὰ ἵνα ἔλθῃ τὰ ἀγαθά. Vulgate (Wordsworth and White), *faciamus mala ut veniant bona*; Cyprian, in this passage, is apparently the only authority to read *dum veniunt*.

been imagined by somebody who knew his New Testament in Latin, and not in Greek.

It does not seem satisfactory to separate Book 3 from Books 1 and 2 so as to assume that Cyprian composed Book 3 himself whereas he used a source for the first two books. Book 3 is distinguished from the others both by its subject, which is concerned with ethics and church discipline and not with proof-texts against the Jews, and by Cyprian himself, who in his Preface to Book 1 mentions only two books but in his Preface to Book 3 explains that the man for whom he is writing, Quirinus, had asked him for a brief compendium of *disciplina* and that he is now supplying this. It is wholly likely that in Book 3 Cyprian was re-handling a source also, whether another part of the source used in Books 1 and 2 or a separate document it is difficult to say. These documents (or document) must have come from some church which used a Latin translation of the New Testament and was Latin-speaking, but had only recently changed from using the Bible in Greek. It must have had rigorist ideas, for (as we have seen) it regarded certain sins as irremissible and it took the line, adopted also by Tertullian, that marrying a pagan wife was equivalent in a Christian to fornication (*Test.* 3.62). The community which answers this description best is perhaps the church of Rome about the year 200, before the episcopate of Callistus.

APPENDIX B

Irenaeus, *Adversus Haereses* 3.3.1

THE Latin translation (the only version extant) of the sentence in this passage upon which discussion has concentrated most intensely runs thus:

> *ad hanc enim ecclesiam propter potentiorem* [v.l. *potiorem*] *principalitatem necesse est omnem convenire ecclesiam, hoc est, eos qui sunt undique fideles, in qua semper ab his qui sunt undique conservata est ea quae est ab apostolis traditio.*

For a brief account of the history of controversy about this text see N. Sykes, *Man as Churchman*.[1] The most important of the innumerable comments on this passage will be found summarized in Harvey, in his edition of the *Adversus Haereses* (*in loc.*), in Van den Eynde,[2] in Flesseman-van Leer,[3] and in Nautin.[4] The phrase *potentiorem principalitatem* has been here translated 'commanding position of leadership'[5] (assuming some such phrase as διὰ τὴν βεβαιοτέραν ἡγεμονίαν or διὰ τὴν ἰσχυροτέραν δύναμιν) as the result of a careful consideration of the translator's other uses of *principalitas* and its cognates.[6] Van den Eynde's conclusion, reached after a very similar survey, that behind this phrase must lie the word ἀρχήν or ἀρχαιότης, seems unacceptable, because the translator would have rendered ἀρχή by *origo*, a word which he uses elsewhere, and ἀρχαιότης will not bear the sense which Van den Eynde wishes to place upon it, i.e. 'qu'elle a l'origine plus fort', being founded by Peter and Paul.[7] *Convenire* has been translated here 'agree with' rather than 'travel to' because Irenaeus would hardly have said that the whole Church (or all churches) *must* travel to Rome. *In qua* has been taken to refer to *hanc ecclesiam*, and not to *omnem ecclesiam*, because the latter interpretation, though not impossible, would tend to make the last clause meaningless, and one would expect *ubique* rather than *undique* were this interpretation the right one. Nautin rejects Van den Eynde's reconstruction on rather similar grounds to these and proposes as the original διὰ δυνατωτέραν ἐξουσίαν.[8]

---

[1] pp. 39–48, 59–61.   [2] *Les Normes*, pp. 172–7.   [3] *Tradition and Scripture*, pp. 115–18.
[4] 'Irenée', pp. 64–76.   [5] See above, p. 145.
[6] See my article '*Potentiorem principalitatem* in Irenaeus, *Adversus Haereses* III.3.1'.
[7] *Les Normes*, p. 177.   [8] 'Irenée', pp. 46–49.

APPENDIX C

Heretical Tendencies in the *Gospel according to the Hebrews*

FOR the Gnostic affinities of a preoccupation with 'rest', see *Gospel of Thomas*, logion 90, which is only a variant of Matt. 11.28–30 (no doubt the saying which started all the speculation about 'rest', for it contains both ἀναπαύω and ἀνάπαυσις, the latter in a quotation from Jer. 6.16). But there is also further evidence:

Gospel according to Thomas, logion 50: 'If they ask you, what is the sign of your Father in you, say to them, It is a movement and a rest.'

Ibid. logion 51: 'When will the rest of the dead come about?'

Ibid. logion 60: 'You yourselves seek a place for yourselves in Repose, lest you become a corpse and be eaten.'

(All these words for rest translate ἀνάπαυσις).

Gospel of Truth, where the Coptic does not evidence the word ἀνάπαυσις, nevertheless contains the idea; see p. 37, ll. 15–21 (105), p. 40, ll. 30–34 (108), p. 41, ll. 12–14 and 28–29 (49); p. 42, ll. 21–22 and 30–33 (110); p. 42, l. 39–p. 43, l. 2 (110–111).

Compare with this the *agraphon* ascribed by Clement of Alexandria to the *Gospel according to the Hebrews*, 'He that wondereth shall reign and he that reigneth shall rest.'[1] Compare also the account of the baptism of Jesus from the *Gospel according to the Hebrews* quoted by Jerome on Isa. 11.2:[2] 'And it came to pass when the Lord was come up out of the water, the whole fount of the Holy Spirit descended and rested upon him and said unto him, My Son, in all the prophets was I waiting for thee that thou shouldest come and that I might rest in thee. For thou art my rest, thou art my first-begotten Son, that reignest for ever.' The *Gospel of Philip* also has several references to 'rest'; see logia 63 (114), 82 (119), 86 and 87 (120), 118 (128).

For the tendency of the Mother-figure to appear in Gnostic Christianity, see the quotations of the *Gospel according to the Hebrews* from Origen and from Jerome.[3] Compare with these the phrase found in the *Apocryphon of John*, 'the Father, the Mother, the Son';[4] the *Hypostasis of the*

[1] See James, p. 2, and above, p. 226.
[2] James, p. 5.
[3] James, pp. 2 and 5.
[4] Van Unnik, *Newly Discovered Gnostic Writings*, p. 70.

Archontes, in describing a creation made by Pistis-Sophia and Sabaoth, envisages a scene of celestial worship in which on the right of Sabaoth is enthroned Jesus Christ and on the left of him the Virgin and the Holy Spirit;[1] the *Treatise on the Triple Epiphany* brings on to the scene 'la Vièrge celeste appellée Mirothea';[2] Epiphanius[3] says that the Sethians introduced a Heavenly Mother into their system. The *Gospel of Philip* has several allusions to such a figure; Doresse remarks that 'we should note a development concerning Mary, the pure Virgin, whom no power has defiled',[4] and Schenke[5] makes a similar observation; cf. logia 17 (103) and 83 (119). The *Gospel of Truth* speaks of the All returning 'to the Father and the Mother'.[6] A Marcosian formula quoted by Irenaeus[7] runs, 'in the name of the unknown Father of all things into truth the Mother of all things.'

[1] Doresse, *Les Livres Secrets*, p. 199.
[2] *Ibid.* p. 199.
[3] *Panarion* 39.3.
[4] *Les Livres Secrets*, p. 241.
[5] *The Gospel of Philip*, p. 3.
[6] p. 24, ll. 6 and 7 (96).
[7] *Adv. Haer.* 1.14.2.

BIBLIOGRAPHY

Ancient Christian texts referred to in this book

ACTS OF MARTYRS
The Passion of St Perpetua   } ed. J. A. Robinson, Cambridge,
Acts of the Scillitan Martyrs   } 1891.
Acts of Justin and his Companions } ed. D. Knopf, rev. G. Krüger,
Martyrdom of Pionius   } Tübingen, 1929.
Martyrdom of Polycarp, ed. K. Lake, *Apostolic Fathers* II (LCL),
     London and New York, 1945.
APOCRYPHAL GOSPELS AND ACTS
The Acts of Paul
The Acts of John   ed. and tr. M. R. James, *The*
The Acts of Thomas   *Apocryphal New Testament*,
Gospel according to the Hebrews   Oxford, 1924.
Epistula Apostolorum
Gospel according to Thomas, Coptic text established and translated by
     A. Guillaumont, H.-Ch. Puech, G. Quispel, W. Till and Yassah 'Abd
     al Masih, Leiden and London, 1959.
Evangelium Veritatis, ed. M. Malinine, H.-Ch. Puech and G. Quispel,
     Zürich, 1956.
The Gnostic Apocryphon of John, summarized by W. Till, *Journal of*
     Ecclesiastical History 3, 1952, pp. 14–22.
The Gospel of Philip, tr. into German by H. M. Schenke, *Theologische*
     Literaturzeitung 84, 1959, pp. 1–26.
Egerton Papyrus 2 in *New Gospel Fragments*, British Museum, London,
     1955.
Fragments of an Unknown Gospel, ed. H. I. Bell and J. C. Skeat,
     London, 1953.
Apostolic Constitutions, ed. F. X. Funk, Paderborn, 1905.
ARISTIDES, *Apologia*, ed. E. J. Goodspeed, *Die ältesten Apologeten*,
     Göttingen, 1914.
ATHANASIUS
Encyclical Letter
Apologia contra Arianos
Encyclical Letter to Egyptian Bishops
Apology to Constantius   ed. W. Bright, *Athanasius'*
Apologia de Fuga   *Historical Writings*, Oxford,
Letter to Serapion   1881.
History of the Arians
De Synodis
ATHENAGORAS
Supplicatio, ed. E. J. Goodspeed, *Die ält. Apologeten*.

On the Resurrection of the Dead, ed. D. R. Bueno from the text of Schwartz and Geffcken (Padres Apologistas Griegos), Madrid, 1944.

Barnabas, Epistle of, ed. K. Lake, *Apostolic Fathers* I (LCL).

BASIL OF CAESAREA, *On the Holy Spirit*, ed. B. Pruche (SC), Paris, 1946.

CANONS OF COUNCILS

F. Lauchert, *Die Kanones der wichtigsten altkirchlichen Concilien*, Freiburg and Leipzig, 1896.

Mansi, *Sacrorum Conciliorum Nova et Amplissima Collectio*, Graz, 1960 (reprint of Welther's ed., Paris, 1902).

CLEMENT OF ALEXANDRIA

Stromateis
Protreptikos
Paedagogos }ed. O. Stählin (GCS), Leipzig, 1906 and 1936.
Eclogae Propheticae

Excerpta ex Theodoto, ed. R. P. Casey (Studies and Documents 1), London, 1934.

Quis Dives Salvetur, ed. P. M. Barnard, Cambridge, 1897.

CLEMENT OF ROME, *First Epistle* } ed. K. Lake, *Apostolic Fathers* I
PSEUDO-CLEMENT, *Second Epistle* } (LCL).

Epistola Clementis, ed. B. Rehm (GCS), Berlin, 1953.

CYPRIAN, *Epistles*, ed. and tr. into French by L. C. Bayard, Paris, Vol. I, 1945, Vol. II, 1925.

De Unitate Ecclesiae, ed. by E. H. Blakeney from Gersdorf's and Hartel's texts, London, 1928.

All other works, and also the *Vita Pontii* and the *Sententiae Episcoporum*, from *Cypriani Opera Omnia*, ed. G. Hartel (CSEL), Vienna, 1868.

PSEUDO-CYPRIAN

Ad Novatianum
De Aleatoribus
Ad Vigilium Episcopum de
  Iudaica Incredulitate   } ed. G. Hartel, *Cypriani Opera*
Adversus Iudaeos   } *Omnia*, Vienna, 1871.
De Singularitate Clericorum
De Pascha Computus
Auctor Anonymus, *De Rebaptismate*

Didache, ed. K. Lake, *Apostolic Fathers* I (LCL).

Didascalia Apostolorum, Syriac version tr. and Verona Latin fragments ed. by R. H. Connolly, Oxford, 1929.

DIONYSIUS OF ALEXANDRIA, *Letters and Other Remains*, ed. C. L. Feltoe, Cambridge, 1904.

Epistle to Diognetus, ed. K. Lake, *Apostolic Fathers* II (LCL).

EUSEBIUS, *Historia Ecclesiastica*, ed. E. Schwartz (GCS), Berlin, 1952.

GREGORY THEODORUS, *Profession of Faith*, ed. A. Hahn, *Bibliothek der Symbole und Glaubensregeln der alte Kirche*, rev. and supp. by L. Hahn and A. Harnack, Breslau, 1897, pp. 253–5.

PSEUDO-GREGORY. *Ecthesis tes kata meros pisteos*, PG 10.1103–24.

HERMAS, *Shepherd*, ed. Molly Whittaker (GCS), Berlin, 1956.

HERMIAS, *Irrisio Gentilium Philosophorum*, ed. H. Diels, *Doxographici Graeci*, Berlin and Leipzig, 2nd ed., 1929.

HIPPOLYTUS, *Elenchos*, ed. P. Wendland (GCS), Leipzig, 1916.
Apostolic Tradition, tr. and ed. by B. S. Easton, Cambridge, 1934, also by G. Dix, London, 1937.
Contra Noetum, ed. (as *Contre les Hérésies*) by P. Nautin, Paris, 1949.
De Antichristo, ed. H. Achelis (GCS), Leipzig, 1897.
Commentary on Daniel, ed. and tr. into French by M. Lefevre (SC), Paris, 1947.

HYMENAEUS, *Epistle of*, ed. M. J. Routh, *Reliquiae Sacrae* III, Oxford, 1846, pp. 289–99.

IGNATIUS, *Epistles*, ed. K. Lake, *Apostolic Fathers* I (LCL).

IRENAEUS, *Adversus Haereses*, ed. W. W. Harvey, Cambridge, 1857.
Demonstration of the Apostolic Preaching, ed. and tr. J. P. Smith (Ancient Christian Writers), Westminster, Maryland, and London, 1952.

JUSTIN, *Apology*
Dialogue with Trypho } ed. E. J. Goodspeed, *Die ält. Apologeten*.

MELITO, *Homily on the Passion*, ed. Campbell Bonner (Studies and Documents 12), London and Philadelphia, 1940.
Fragments, ed. E. J. Goodspeed, *Die ält. Apologeten*.

MINUCIUS FELIX, *Octavius*, ed. and tr. G. H. Rendall (LCL), London and New York, 1931.

Muratorian Canon, ed. F. W. Grosheide, *Some Early Lists of the Books of the New Testament*, Leiden, 1948.

NOVATIAN, *De Trinitate*, ed. W. Yorke Fausset, Cambridge, 1909.
De Cibis Iudaicis, PL 3.981–92.

Novum Testamentum Domini Nostri Iesu Christi (also referred to as the Vulgate), ed. J. Wordsworth, H. J. White, H. F. D. Sparks and A. W. Adams, Oxford, 1889, 1905, 1954.

ORIGEN, *Contra Celsum*, ed. P. Koetschau (GCS), Berlin, 1899.
Concerning First Principles (cited as *PA*), ed. P. Koetschau (GCS), Berlin, 1899.
Commentary on John, ed. A. E. Brooke, Cambridge, 1896.
Commentary on Matthew, ed. E. Klostermann (GCS), Berlin, 1933, 1935, 1941–5.
Homilies on Jeremiah, ed. E. Klostermann (GCS), Berlin, 1901.
Exhortation to Martyrdom, ed. P. Koetschau (GCS), Berlin, 1899.
Concerning Prayer (cited as *PE*), ed. P. Koetschau (GCS), Berlin, 1899.
Conversation with Heracleides, ed. J. Scherer, *Entretien d'Origène avec Heraclide*, Cairo, 1949.
Commentaires Inédits des Psaumes, ed. R. Cadiou, Paris, 1936.
Commentary on Romans, Greek fragments, ed. J. Ramsbotham, *JTS* 13, 1912, pp. 209–24, 357–68; *JTS* 14, 1913, pp. 10–20; also *Le Commentaire d'Origène sur Rom. iii. 5–v. 7*, ed. J. Scherer, Cairo, 1957.
Fragments on I Corinthians, ed. C. Jenkins, *JTS* 9, 1908, pp. 231–47, 353–72, 500–14; *JTS* 10, 1909, pp. 29–51.

Fragments on Ephesians, ed. J. A. F. Gregg, *JTS* 3, 1902, pp. 233–44, 398–420, 554–76.
All other works or fragments from PG 11–14 and 17.
POLYCARP, *Epistle to the Philippians*, ed. K. Lake, *Apostolic Fathers* I (LCL).
PTOLEMAEUS, *Epistle to Flora*, PG 7.1289–92.
TATIAN, *Oratio ad Graecos*, ed. E. J. Goodspeed, *Die ält. Apologeten*.
TERTULLIAN, *Adversus Praxean*, text and tr. by E. Evans, London, 1948.
De Praescriptione Haereticorum, ed. J. N. Bakhuizen van den Brink (Scriptores Christiani Primaevi), The Hague, 1946.
Apologeticus ⎱ ed. T. R. Glover (LCL), London and New York,
De Spectaculis ⎰ 1931.
All other texts of Tertullian, Corpus Christianorum, Turnhoult, 1954.
PSEUDO-TERTULLIAN, *Adversus Omnes Haereses*, Corpus Christianorum, Turnhoult, 1954.
THEOPHILUS OF ANTIOCH, *Three Books to Autolycus*, ed. G. Bardy, tr. into French by J. Sender (SC), Paris, 1948.

Books and Articles referred to in this Book

BOOKS

J. L. ADAMS, 'Rudolf Sohm's Theology of Law and the Spirit', essay 16 in *Religion and Culture*, ed. W. Leibrecht, London, 1958.
B. ALTANER, *Patrologie*, Freibourg, 1955.
L. P. AUDET, *La Didaché*, Paris, 1958.
F. J. BADCOCK, *History of the Creeds*, 2nd ed., London, 1938.
G. BARDY, *Paul de Samosate*, new ed., revised, Louvain, 1929.
E. W. BENSON, *Cyprian, his Life, his Times, his Work*, London, 1897.
F. BERTRAND, *Mystique de Jesus chez Origène*, Paris, 1951.
F. J. BETHUNE-BAKER, *Introduction to the Early History of Christian Doctrine*, 5th ed., London, 1933.
J. BONSIRVEN, *Le Judaisme Palestinien au Temps de Jésus-Christ*, Paris, 1934.
G. BORNKAMM, *Jesus of Nazareth*, ET London, 1960.
P. CARRINGTON, *The Primitive Christian Catechism*, Cambridge, 1940.
N. K. CHADWICK (ed.), *Studies in the Early British Church*, Cambridge, 1958.
Y. CONGAR, *La Tradition et les Traditions*, Paris, 1961.
F. L. CROSS (ed.), *The Jung Codex*, London, 1955.
O. CULLMANN, *The Early Church*, ET London, 1956.
The Earliest Christian Confessions, ET London, 1949.
Baptism in the New Testament, ET London, 1956.
A. D'ALÈS, *L'Édit de Calliste*, Paris, 1914.

J. Daniélou, *Théologie de Judéo-Christianisme*, Paris, 1958.
Menage Évangelique et Culture Hellénistique, Paris, 1961.
W. D. Davies, *A Normative Pattern of Church Life in the New Testament : Fact or Fancy?* London, [1950].
H. De Riedmatten, *Les Actes du Procès de Paul de Samosate*, Freibourg, 1952.
M. Dibelius, *From Tradition to Gospel*, ET of revised 2nd ed., London, 1934.
C. H. Dodd, *The Apostolic Preaching and Its Developments*, London, 1936.
J. Doresse, *Les Livres Secrets des Gnostiques d'Egypte*, Paris, 1957.
B. Drewery, *Origen and the Doctrine of Grace*, London, 1960.
A. Ehrhardt, *The Apostolic Succession*, London, 1953.
E. Flesseman-van Leer, *Tradition and Scripture in the Early Church*, Assen, 1954.
B. Gerhardsson, *Memory and Manuscript*, Uppsala, 1961.
R. M. Grant, *The Letter and the Spirit*, London, 1957.
The Earliest Lives of Jesus, London, 1961.
R. M. Grant and D. N. Freedman, *The Secret Sayings of Jesus*, London, 1960.
F. W. Grosheide, *Some Early Lists of the Books of the New Testament*, Leiden, 1948.
A. T. Hanson, *The Pioneer Ministry*, London, 1961.
R. P. C. Hanson, *Origen's Doctrine of Tradition*, London, 1954.
Allegory and Event, London, 1959.
A. Harnack, *Constitution and Law of the Church*, ET London, 1910.
J. Rendel Harris, *Testimonies*, Cambridge, Part I, 1916, Part II, 1920.
E. Hoskyns and N. Davey, *Commentary on St John's Gospel*, London, 1940.
J. Jeremias, *The Eucharistic Words of Jesus*, ET Oxford, 1955.
The Unknown Sayings of Jesus, ET London, 1957.
Infant Baptism in the First Four Centuries, ET London, 1960.
J. N. D. Kelly, *Early Christian Creeds*, London, 1950.
Early Christian Doctrines, London, 1958.
K. E. Kirk (ed.), *The Apostolic Ministry*, London, 1946.
H. Koch, *Cyprianische Untersuchungen*, Bonn, 1926.
Pronoia und Paideusis, Berlin and London, 1932.
H. J. Lawlor and J. E. L. Oulton, *Eusebius: Ecclesiastical History* (translated with introduction and notes), London, 1928.
A. L. Lilley, *Religion and Revelation*, London, 1932.
O. Linton, *Das Problem der Urkirche in der neueren Forschungen*, Uppsala, 1932.
E. Molland, *The Conception of the Gospel in Alexandrian Theology*, Oslo, 1938.
C. Montdesert, *Clement d'Alexandrie*, Paris, 1944.
J. H. Newman, *Arians of the Fourth Century*, reprint of 1st ed., London, 1854.
E. F. Osborn, *The Philosophy of Clement of Alexandria*, Cambridge, 1957.
N. Pittenger, *The Word Incarnate*, London, 1959.

G. L. PRESTIGE, *Fathers and Heretics*, London, 1940.
C. RAVEN, *Apollinarianism*, Cambridge, 1923.
B. REICKE, 'The Constitution of the Primitive Church', essay 10 in *The Scrolls of the New Testament*, ed. K. Stendahl, London, 1958.
J. K. S. REID, *The Authority of Scripture*, London, 1957.
A. RICHARDSON, *Creeds in the Making*, London, reprint, 1958, of 2nd ed. of 1941.
An Introduction to the Theology of the New Testament, London, 1958.
H. RIESENFELD, *The Gospel Tradition and Its Beginnings*, London, 1957.
J. M. ROBINSON, *The New Quest for the Historical Jesus*, London, 1960.
G. SALMON, *The Infallibility of the Church*, London, reprint, 1923, of 2nd ed. of 1890.
J. N. SANDERS, *The Fourth Gospel in the Early Church*, Cambridge, 1943.
E. SCHWEIZER, *Church Order in the New Testament*, ET London, 1961.
E. G. SELWYN, *The First Epistle of Peter*, London, 1947.
C. R. B. SHAPLAND, *The Letters of St. Athanasius concerning the Holy Spirit*, London, 1951.
K. E. SKYDSGAARD, 'Tradition as an Issue in Contemporary Theology', essay in *The Old and the New in the Church*, WCC Commission of Faith and Order Report, London, 1961.
A. SOUTER, *Text and Canon of the New Testament*, London, 1954 (ed. of 1913 revised by C. S. C. Williams).
E. STAUFFER, *New Testament Theology*, ET London, 1955.
N. SYKES, *Man as Churchman*, Cambridge, 1961.
G. B. TAVARD, *Holy Writ or Holy Church*, London, 1959.
V. TAYLOR, *The Formation of the Gospel Tradition*, London, 1933.
W. TELFER, *The Forgiveness of Sins*, London, 1960.
R. B. TOLLINGTON, *Clement of Alexandria*, London, 1914.
H. E. W. TURNER, *The Pattern of Christian Truth*, London, 1954.
D. VAN DEN EYNDE, *Les normes de l'enseignement chrétien dans la litterature patristique des trois premiers siècles*, Paris, 1933.
W. C. VAN UNNIK, *Newly-Discovered Gnostic Writings*, ET London, 1960.
F. E. VOKES, *The Riddle of the Didache*, London, 1938.
W. VÖLKER, *Das Vollkommenheitsideal des Origenes*, Tübingen, 1931.
H. F. VON CAMPENHAUSEN, *Kirchliches Amt und geistliches Vollmacht*, Tübingen, 1953.
M. WERNER, *The Formation of Christian Doctrine*, ET New York, 1957.
B. F. WESTCOTT, *The Canon of the New Testament*, 7th ed., London, 1896.
E. C. WHITAKER, *The Documents of the Baptismal Liturgy*, London, 1960.
M. WILES, *The Spiritual Gospel*, Cambridge, 1960.
R. McL. WILSON, *Studies in the Gospel of Thomas*, London, 1960.
Atlas of the Early Christian Church, F. Van der Meer and C. Mohrmann, ET London, 1958.
Dictionary of the Christian Church, ed. F. L. Cross, Oxford, 1957.
Dictionnaire Latin-Français des Auteurs Chrétiens, A. Blaise and H. Chirat, Strasbourg, 1954.

S

ARTICLES

K. ALAND, 'The Problem of Anonymity and Pseudonymity in Christian Literature of the First Two Centuries', *JTS* (NS), 12, 1961, pp. 39–49.

V. AMMUNDSEN, 'The Rule of Truth in Irenaeus', *JTS* 13, 1912, pp. 574–80.

E. W. BROOKS, 'The Ordination of the Early Bishops of Alexandria', *JTS* 2, 1901, pp. 612–13.

F. BÜCHSEL, Article παραδίδωμι and παράδοσις in *TWNT* II, pp. 171–5.

S. BULGAKOV, 'Eucharistic Dogma', tr. and abridged from an article originally published in Paris in 1930, *Sobornost*, Ser. 4, no. 2, Spring, 1960, pp. 66–76.

H. J. CARPENTER, 'Creeds and Baptismal Rites in the First Four Centuries', *JTS* 44, 1943, pp. 1–11.

C. P. CASPARI, 'Hat die alexandrinische Kirche zur Zeit des Clement ein Taufbekenntniss oder nicht?', *Zeitschrift für kirchlich Wissenschaft und kirchliches Leben* 7, 1886, pp. 352–75.

F. C. CONYBEARE, 'Newly-discovered Letters of Dionysius of Alexandria to Popes Stephen and Xystus', *English Historical Review* 25, 1910, pp. 111–14.

D. DE BRUYNE, 'Prologues bibliques d'origine Marcionite', *Revue Bénédictine* 24, 1907, pp. 1–16.

C. W. DUGMORE, 'A Note on the Quartodecimans', *Studia Patristica* IV, ed. F. L. Cross, Berlin, 1961, pp. 411–21.

C. F. EVANS, 'Bible and Tradition', *Theology* 60, 1957, pp. 487–94.

C. GORE, 'On the Ordination of the Early Bishops of Alexandria', *JTS* 3, 1902, pp. 278–82.

R. M. GRANT, 'Notes on the Gospel of Thomas', *Vigiliae Christianae* 13, 1959, pp. 170–80.

'The Appeal to the Early Fathers', *JTS* (NS) 11, 1960, pp. 13–24.

B. HÄGGLUND, 'Die Bedeutung der "regula fidei" als Grundlage theologische Aussagen', *Studia Theologica* 12, 1958, pp. 1–44.

R. P. C. HANSON, 'The Anglican Doctrine of Ministry', *Church Quarterly Review*, 1962, pp. 40–48.

'The Inspiration of Holy Scripture', *Anglican Theological Review*, April 1961, pp. 145–52.

'The Liberty of the Bishop to Improvise Prayer in the Eucharist', *Vigiliae Christianae* 15, 1961, pp. 173–6.

'Notes on Tertullian's Interpretation of Scripture', *JTS* (NS) 12, 1961, pp. 273–9.

'*Potentiorem principalitatem* in Irenaeus, *Adversus Haereses* III 3.1', *Studia Patristica* IV, ed. F. L. Cross, Berlin, 1961, pp. 362–5.

W. G. KÜMMEL, 'Jesus und der jüdische Traditionsgedanke', *Zeitschrift für die neutestamentliche Wissenschaft* 33, 1934, pp. 105–30.

J. LEBRETON, 'Les degrés de la connaissance religieuse d'après Origène', *Recherches de Science Religieuse* 12, 1922, pp. 265–96.

P. L'HUILLIER, 'The Ecclesiastical Hierarchy and the Magisterium', *Sobornost*, Ser. 4, no. 1, Autumn 1959, pp. 19–33.

E. MOLLAND, 'Irenaeus of Lugdunum and the Apostolic Succession', *Journal of Ecclesiastical History* 1, 1950, pp. 12–28.

H. W. MONTEFIORE, 'A Comparison of the Parables of the Gospel according to Thomas and the Synoptic Gospels', *New Testament Studies* 7, 1961, pp. 220–48, reprinted in *Thomas and the Evangelists* by H. E. W. Turner and H. W. Montefiore (Studies in Biblical Theology), London, 1962.

P. NAUTIN, 'Irenée "Adv. Haer." III 3.2, église de Rome ou église universelle?', *Revue de l'Histoire des Religions* 51, 1957, pp. 37–38.

D. E. NINEHAM, 'Eyewitness Testimony and the Gospel Tradition', *JTS* (NS) 11, 1958, pp. 13–25, 243–53; *ibid.* 13, 1960, pp. 253–64.

H. OPPEL, '*KANΩN* zur Bedeutungsgeschichte des Wortes und seiner lateinischer Entsprechungen (Regula-Norma), *Philologus*, Supp. Band 30.4, Leipzig, 1937.

T. E. POLLARD, 'The Exegesis of Scripture and the Arian Controversy', *Bulletin of the John Rylands Library* 41, 1959, pp. 414–29.

J. QUASTEN, 'Tertullian and "Tradition"', *Traditio* 2, 1944, pp. 481–4.

G. QUISPEL, 'L'Évangile selon Thomas et les Clémentines', *Vigiliae Christianae* 12, 1958, pp. 181–96.

'L'Évangile selon Thomas et le Diatessaron', *Vigiliae Christianae* 13, 1959, pp. 87–117.

'Some Remarks on the Gospel of Thomas', *New Testament Studies* 5, 1959, pp. 276–90.

N. ROTENSTREICH, 'On the Notion of Tradition in Judaism', *Journal of Religion* 28, 1948, pp. 28–36.

W. TELFER, 'Episcopal Succession in Egypt', *Journal of Ecclesiastical History* 3, 1952, pp. 1–13.

W. ULLMANN, 'The Significance of the *Epistola Clementis* in the Pseudo-Clementines', *JTS* (NS) 11, 1960, pp. 295–317.

J. BAKHUIZEN VAN DEN BRINK, 'Traditio in theologische Sinne', *Vigiliae Christianae* 13, 1959, pp. 65–86.

'La tradition dans l'église primitive et au xvie siècle', *Revue d'Histoire et de Philosophie Religieuses* 36, 1956, pp. 271–81.

W. C. VAN UNNIK, 'De la règle μήτε προσθεῖναι μήτε ἀφελεῖν dans l'histoire du Canon', *Vigiliae Christianae* 3, 1949, pp. 1–36.

INDEX OF NAMES

'Abd al Masih, Y., 18
Abercius, 31, 32, 187, 210
Abgar king of Edessa, 7, 49
Acts of Pilate, 224
Adams, J. L., 254
Aetius the Arian, 179, 254
Agrippinus of Carthage, 249
Aland, K., 13, 151, 213, 242–3
Alogi, 195
Altaner, B., 61, 84
Ambrosiaster, 223
Ammundsen, V., 65, 74, 75, 103, 109, 110, 124
Anacreon, 198
Ancyra, Council of, 84
Anicetus, Pope, 40, 157, 189
Annianus, 166
Antinous, 39
Antioch, Synods of, 82, 83, 175
Antoninus Pius, 57, 189
Apelles, 251
Aratus, 209
Ariminum, Council of, 179
Ariston, 36, 37, 38
Arius, 254
Arles, Council of, 71–72, 84
Artemon, 207
Asclepiades, 70
Audet, J. P., 172–4, 227
Augustine, 136
Augustus, 47

Badcock, F. J., 27
Bar-Cochbha, 165
Bardy, G., 82, 83, 117, 212
Barth, K., 128–9, 234
Basilides, 23, 119, 167, 191–2, 192, 197–8, 204, 205, 213
Basilides, Gospel of, 227
Bayard, L. C., 79, 141
Benevot, M., 153
Benson, E. W., 149
Bertrand, F., 83
Beryllus of Bostra, 84
Bethune-Baker, F. J., 27
Bonsirven, J., 15

Bornkamm, G., 14
Brooks, E. W., 166
Büchsel, F., 10, 21, 169
Bulgakov, S., 238
Bultmann, R., 14
Bunyan, John, 255
Butler, B. C., 173

Caecilius of Biltha, 68
Calixtus, catacomb of, 31
Callistus, Pope, 98, 121, 149–51, 245, 264
Carpenter, H. J., 62, 65, 68, 74
Carpocrates, 22, 198
Carrington, P., 130
Carthage, Councils of, 68, 79–80, 115, 141
Caspari, C., 62, 84
Cassianus the Gnostic, 226
Celsus, 35, 227
Cerinthus, 195, 215
Chadwick, Miss N. K., 20
Church Ordinances, 172, 174
Congar, Y., 11, 15, 27, 94, 163, 176, 181, 205, 239–245, 247, 249, 253, 255
Connolly, R. H., 34, 62, 78, 222, 232
Constantius, 177
Conybeare, F. C., 91, 100, 143
Cornelius, Pope, 81, 99, 125, 140, 143, 154
Cullmann, O., 11, 12, 13, 39, 54, 57, 65, 69, 71, 170, 235, 236, 239
Cyril of Jerusalem, 106

Daillé, J., 27
D'Alès, A., 149–50
Daniélou, J., 26, 27, 38–39, 43, 44, 45, 54, 56, 94, 110, 125, 224, 232, 259
Davey, N., 13
Davies, W. D., 246, 254
De Bruyne, D., 81
Decius, 34
Dedication, creed of, 83
De Riedmatten, H., 82, 83

Dibelius, M., 15, 20, 60, 203
Diodorus Siculus, 21
Dionysius the Areopagite (pseudo-Dionysius), 185, 186
Dionysius of Corinth, 204, 205
Dionysius of Milan, 177
Dionysius, Pope, 82
Dix, G., 61, 62, 94
Doctrina Apostolorum, 172, 227
Dodd, C. H., 10, 52
Domitian, 40, 41, 45, 47
Doresse, J., 17, 24, 25–26, 189, 198, 267
Drewery, B., 161
Dugmore, C. W., 50

Easton, B. S., 33
Ebionites, 201, 234
Ebionites, Gospel of, 230
Ehrhardt, A., 43, 61, 66, 161–2, 163, 165–6
Ephesus, Council of, 186
Ephraem Syrus, 170
Epiphanius, 57, 170, 195, 198, 224, 267
Essenes, 27
Eucratius of Thenae, 80
Eudoxius the Arian, 254
Eunomius the Arian, 254
Euodius, 167
Euphorbus, 47
Eusebius of Nicomedia, 177
Eusebius of Vercelli, 177
Evans, C. F., 14, 240
Evans, E., 67, 87, 93, 148

Fausset, W. Yorke, 63–64, 73–74, 116, 222
Felix of Buslacenae, 141
Firmilian, 80, 106, 141, 142, 152–7, 169
Flessemann-Van Leer, Mrs E., 25, 38, 55, 56, 59, 65, 75, 77, 96, 97, 103, 104, 109, 112, 116, 127, 128–9, 150, 158, 162, 168, 204, 219–20, 235, 252–3, 253, 265

Florinus, 41, 157
Funk, F. X., 84

Gaius, 46, 195, 222
Gebhardt, O., 60
Gerhardsson, B., 11, 15–16, 17, 19–20, 43, 56, 205
Glauceas, 23
Gore, C., 166
Grant, R. M., 18, 26, 50, 185–6, 198, 201–2, 203, 205, 227, 228–9, 230, 249
Grant, R. M. and Freedman, D. N., 18, 26, 193, 194, 198, 224, 227, 228–229
Greenslade, S. L., 81
Gregory the Cappadocian, 177
Gregory of Nyssa, 83, 84
Grosheide, F. W., 187, 223
Guillaumont, A., 18

Hadrian, 39, 57, 189
Hägglund, B., 65, 66, 67, 77, 86, 87, 101, 104, 109, 253
Hahn, A., 84
Hanson, A. T., 163
Harnack, A., 60, 84, 130, 150, 162, 163
Harris, J. Rendel, 263
Hegesippus, 39–41, 45, 84, 146, 157, 159, 164, 165, 167, 232, 234, 243
Helcesaites, 201
Heraclas, 143
Heracleides, 72
Heracleon, 193–4, 196, 199
Hershey, J., 246–7, 252
Hooker, Richard, 255
Hoskyns, E., 13
Hunter, A. M., 15
Hyginus, Pope, 157, 189
Hymenaeus, 82–3
Hypostasis of the Archons, 198, 266–7

Isidorus, 23
Iubaianus, 152

James, M. R., 61, 267
Jeremias, J., 19, 27–29, 32, 60, 139, 170, 224, 225, 226, 227, 228, 232
Jerome, 230, 233, 266
John the presbyter, 36, 37
Julius Africanus, 49, 164
Julius I, Pope, 59, 177, 178
Justin the Gnostic, 47, 198

Kelly, J. N. D., 29, 54, 55, 58, 60, 61, 62, 65, 66, 69, 71, 72, 74, 92, 94
Kirk, K. E., 163
Koch, H., 83, 150, 261–2
Kümmel, W. G., 16, 241

Lactantius, 225
Laodicea, Council of, 223
Lawlor, H. J. and Oulton, J. E. L., 41, 164, 165, 195, 216, 217
Lebreton, J., 123
Leo I, Pope, Tome of, 91
Leucius of Thebeste, 115
L'Huillier, P., 237–8
Liberius, Pope, 178
Libosus of Vaga, 134, 141
Lightfoot, R. H., 14
Lilley, A. L., 241
Linton, O., 163, 245
Linus, 164, 165
Lucifer of Calaris, 177
Lucius of Castra Galbae, 68

McLean, N., 91
Macrostich, the, 83
Magnentius, 177
Malinine, M., 23
Manning, H. E., Cardinal, 184
Manual of Discipline, 172
Marcellus of Ancyra, 59, 183
Marcion, 45, 65, 90, 110, 119, 162, 188, 190, 199, 200, 201, 217, 251
Marcus Aurelius, 57
Marcus the Gnostic, 44
Mariamne, 23
Methodius, 222
Miltiades, 43, 46, 187
Mohrmann, Miss Christine, 32
Molland, E., 22, 23, 95, 110, 122, 157, 162, 170
Montdesert, C., 27
Montefiore, H. W., 230

Naassenes, 23, 65, 198
Nag Hammadi, 15, 19, 24, 189, 193, 198, 199, 228
Narcissus of Jerusalem, 165
Nautin, P., 145, 146–7, 265
Nazarenes, Gospel of, 230
Neocaesarea, Council of, 78
Nepos, 117
Nero, 47
Nerva, 41, 48

Newman, J. H., 27, 65, 107, 257
Newton, Isaac, 252
Nicaea, Council of, 69
Nicephorus Callistus, 200
Nineham, D., 14, 15, 240
Noetus, 62, 71, 114, 121

Ophites, 63
Oppel, H., 84
Osborn, E. F., 122
Ostia, 106
Ostian Way, 46
Oxyrhynchus Papyrus 1, 228
  654, 228
  655, 228
  840, 228

Paion, 70
Palut of Edessa, 191
Pantaenus, 26, 167, 186
Papias, 35–39, 43, 45, 166, 190, 195, 196, 198, 203, 214, 230, 232, 234
Paul of Samosata, 82, 83, 176, 179
Paulinus of Treves, 177
Pectorius, 32
Peiratikoi, 23
Pella, 40, 41
Philo, 26, 49, 92, 107, 190, 208, 213
Philostratus, 20, 203
Pionius, 70, 185
Pittenger, N., 175–6
Pius I, Pope, 40, 189, 214
Plato, 21, 122
Pollard, T. E., 180–1
Polycarp, 36, 39, 41, 42, 43, 45, 64, 145, 147, 185, 192, 196, 203, 213
Polycrates of Ephesus, 50, 51, 75, 76, 125, 127
Pontianus, Pope, 164
Praxeas, 121
Prestige, G. L., 94, 109, 112, 116, 119, 149–50, 253
Priscilla, catacomb of, 31
Proculus, 46
Prologues, Marcionite and Catholic, 81, 188, 200, 210, 214
Puech, H.-C., 18, 199
Pythagoras, 47

Quadratus, 243
Quartodeciman controversy, 42, 50–51, 98, 136, 146

Quasten, J., 132, 207
Quinsext Council, 238, 239
Quispel, G., 15, 18, 189,
189–90, 229–30, 231–2
Qumran, 56, 172, 175, 245

Raven, C., 82
Reicke, B., 163
Reid, J. K. S., 234, 241,
245–6
Richardson, A., 54, 240
Riesenfeld, H., 12
Robinson, J. M., 14
Ropes, J. H., 60
Rotenstreich, N., 241
Rufinus, 59
Rusticus, 70

Sabina, 70
Salmon, G., 35, 185, 244
Sanders, J. N., 167, 191,
192, 193, 194, 195, 197,
212, 217
Sarapion of Antioch, 191,
210, 218, 219, 225
Saturninus the Gnostic,
119
Schenke, H. M., 267
Schweizer, E., 12, 162, 163,
254
Scott, Walter, 17
Selwyn, E. G., 130
Sentius Saturninus, 47
Sextus, Sentences of, 229
Shapland, C. R. B., 180
Sibylline Oracles, 232
Simon Magus, 49, 226
Skydsgaard, K. E., 240
Sohm, R., 245
Soter, Pope, 204
Souter, A., 81, 188, 189,
191, 215, 220, 222

Stephen I, Pope, 80, 91,
141–2, 143–4, 151–7, 178
Sykes, N., 151, 184, 265
Symeon, son of Clopas, 40,
41, 165

Tavard, G. H., 240
Taylor, V., 13
Telesphorus, Pope, 164
Telfer, W., 65, 149, 166,
167
Theodas, 22
Theodotus the Gnostic, 66
Therapeutae, 190
Thundering Legion, 46
Tiberius, 46
Till, W., 18, 24
Timothy Ailurus, 91
Titus of Bostra, 230
Tollinton, R. B., 122
Traditions of Matthew, 226
Trajan, 42, 84
Treatise on Three Natures,
199
Treatise on Triple Epiphany,
267
Turner, H. E. W., 22, 29,
50, 54, 65, 66, 75, 94,
130, 131, 137, 138, 144,
149–50, 154, 159, 162,
163, 164, 165, 166, 167,
176, 192, 197, 201, 234,
241
Twelve, Gospel of the, 227

Ullmann, W., 78, 164

Valentinus, 22, 77, 119,
148, 162, 167, 189, 191,
193, 198, 199, 204, 222
Van den Brink, J. N. B.,
29, 79, 101–2, 129, 131,
148, 206, 253, 256

Van den Eynde, D., 26, 27,
38, 43, 54, 55, 56, 59, 65,
66, 68, 75, 79, 94, 95, 96,
103, 104, 111, 119, 123,
124, 130, 140, 143, 147,
150, 153, 158, 161, 162,
163, 201, 204, 205, 237,
238, 240, 243, 259, 265
Van der Meer, F., 32
Van Unnik, W. C., 24, 167,
187, 188, 189, 190, 191,
193, 199, 230, 266
Vatican hill, 46
Vespasian, 40
Victor, Pope, 50, 51, 60,
147, 153, 156, 157, 178,
207
Vincentius of Thibari, 80
Vokes, F. E., 172
Völker, W., 83
Von Campenhausen, H. F.,
26, 43, 54, 149, 153, 162,
163, 168
Von Soden, H., 262

Werner, M., 15, 102, 186,
249, 253–5
Wesley, Charles, 255
Wesley, John, 255
Westcott, B. F., 36, 60, 167,
170, 188, 190, 192, 194,
198, 199, 203, 204, 205,
217, 219, 222, 224, 236
Whitaker, E. C., 169
Wiles, M., 248
Wilson, R. McL., 15, 19,
193, 198, 199–200, 228,
229, 230, 231, 232

Xenophon, 203
Xystus, Pope, 91, 100, 143

Zahn, T., 54, 60
Zephyrinus, Pope, 4–6, 76,
121, 222, 245

INDEX OF REFERENCES

I. BIBLICAL

A. OLD TESTAMENT AND APOCRYPHA

Genesis
44.2, 4, 5   198

Numbers
8.5–7   140
19.8, 9,
  12, 13   140

Psalms
2.12   115
4.5   205

90.4   223

Proverbs
1.8   139
23.9   34

Isaiah
7.10–17   110
11.2–3   160, 266
11.6–9   36

54.1   206
65.25   36

Jeremiah
3.15   115
6.16   266

Wisdom
3.11   115
14.15   21

B. NEW TESTAMENT

Matthew
3.10   199
3.14   170
3.15   199
5.3   229
5.45   198
6.6   199
7.6   34
7.23   224
8.2–4   18
9.13   206
10.16, 28   224
10.37–38   231
11.28–30   266
13.8   42
13.47–50   18
14.13–21   17
15.2   11
15.3, 6   10
16.18, 19   99, 100, 150,
             153
18.3   170
18.12–13   18
19.14   170
19.16–26   29
19.17   198
22.1–14   18, 42
22.14   205
23.13   231
24.26   107
25.1–12   208
25.14–30   18
26.29   42

27.62–66   29
28.4   29
28.19   80, 180

Mark
1.14, 15   52, 241
1.40–44   18
2.17   206
4.8   42
4.30–32   18
6.31–44   17
7.3   10, 11
7.5   10
7.8   10, 11
7.9, 13   10
7.24–30   199
10.14, 15   170
10.18   198
15.34   199
16.8, 9–
  20   202
16.17   80

Luke
1.1–4   224, 227, 233
1.2   10
2.22   139
6.20   229
9.10–17   17
10.3   224
10.30–35   199, 208
11.27–28   231
11.51   49

11.52   231
12.4, 5   224
13.27   224
14.26–27   230
15.12–14   18
16.10   224
18.2–5   208
18.16, 17   170
20.35   261
23.29   231
24.39   230

John
1.1–5   72, 110, 191,
             194–5, 198
1.1–13   193
1.9   192
1.10–11   110
1.18   193
2.4   192
3.3, 4   170
3.5   139, 170
4.21   114
4.24   194
6.53   199
7.53–8.
  11   232–3
8.32, 34   199
8.51–52   24
8.56   199
10.3–4   193
14.2   42
14.26   12

John–contd.
16.13   12
17.1–26 13
17.3   73
17.20   13
18.31–33,
  37–38 193
19.26   198
21.18, 19 194
21.25   8, 202

Acts
1.23   37
3.6   71
6.14   10
8.25   167
8.36   170
8.37   60, 69
10.47   70
11.17   170
15.29   261

Romans
1.3, 4   53
1.20–23,
  26–27 198
2.4   261
3.8   262
4.24, 25 53
6.17   10, 11
7.9   197
8.22   197
8.34   53
16.16   139
16.23   49

I Corinthians
2.13   198, 205
4.6   33
6.9, 10 214
7.10   11, 13
7.25   11
8.1   199
8.6   53
9.6   214
9.14   11
11.2   10, 11, 183
11.3   11
11.2–16 135

11.17–34 171
11.23   10, 11, 12, 13
12.8–10 160
14.1–40 171
15.1–7   8, 10, 11, 12, 54
15.11   12
15.25–28 42
15.50   199

II Corinthians
3.1–18   12
6.7   199
8.18   190

Galatians
1.1   13
1.9   11
1.12   11, 13
1.14   10
1.18   12

Ephesians
4.8   160
4.26   205
6.12   198

Philippians
2.5–11   54
4.3   165
4.9   11

Colossians
2.6   11, 12
2.8   10, 11, 12

I Thessalonians
2.13   11
4.15   11

II Thessalonians
2.15   8, 10, 11, 183
3.6   10, 11

I Timothy
2.5   53
3.16   10, 11, 53
6.13   54

II Timothy
1.13   81

2.8   53
3.16   207, 211
4.1   54
4.21   165

Hebrews
2.12, 17 222
5.6   222
5.11   28, 189
5.11–6.10 189
5.12   222
6.1, 2, 4,
  5, 8   28
9.10   28
9.16, 17,
  26   222
11.13–14 222
12.11–13 189
13.14   222

I Peter
1.21   54
3.18   53
4.6   125
5.13   190

II Peter
1.1   189
1.8   223
1.14   194
1.19   223
2.13–14 223
2.19   223
2.21   10
3.2   302–3
3.8   223
3.9   223
3.16   189, 190, 206

I John
5.7, 8   244

Jude
3   10

Revelation
13.14–18 28–29, 106
20.1–6   215
22.18, 19 206

II. PATRISTIC SOURCES

ACTS OF MARTYRS

Passion of S. Perpetua
See p. 226

Acts of Scillitan Martyrs
1.20   188
See also p. 70

*Acts of Justin and his
Companions*
II.4, 5   70
IV.6   70
VI.1   70

Martyrdom of Pionius
VIII.3   70
IX.6, 8   70

Martyrdom of Polycarp
14.1–3   171
See also p. 171

APOCRYPHAL GOSPELS,
ACTS, ETC.

Acts of Paul
VII.3.36 76
VIII   200, 226
XI   227
See also pp. 151, 194, 202,
214, 216, 226

Preaching of Paul
See pp. 211, 225, 227

Acts of John
85   171
95   96
109   171
See also p. 194

Acts of Thomas
49   171
158   171

Book of Thomas
See p. 24

*Gospel according to the
Hebrews*
See pp. 18, 196, 202, 215,
216, 224, 226, 227, 230,
232-4, 234, 248, 266-7

Epistula Apostolorum
5   61
29   206
43-45   208
See also pp. 174, 194,
232, 242

*Gnostic Apocryphon of
John*
See pp. 24, 201, 233, 266

Apocryphon of James
See pp. 24, 193

Gospel of Philip
(Schenke's logia)
9   199
17   267
23   199
63   266
67   66, 199
72   199
82   266
83, 86, 87 266
89   199
110, 111 199
118   266
122, 123 199

*Gospel according to the
Egyptians*
See pp. 198, 220, 226,
227, 228, 230

Egerton Papyrus 2
See pp. 18, 167, 192, 224,
228

Preaching of Peter
See pp. 215, 226

Gospel of Matthias
See pp. 217, 227

Gospel of Peter
See pp. 45, 194, 196,
210-11, 215, 216-17,
218, 225, 227, 228

Apocalypse of Peter
See pp. 215, 216, 220, 226

Birth of Mary
See p. 227

*Fragments of an Unknown
Gospel* (Bell and Skeat)
See pp. 167, 192

*Gospel according to
Thomas* (logia)
2   226
8   18, 224
16   18
19   225
20   18
22   224, 226
27   225
28   228
31, 39 231
50, 51 266
54   229
55   230-1
60   266
65   231
74   227
79   231
80   23, 23-24
82   227
90   266
92   225
107   18
See also pp. 193, 196, 199,
217, 227, 228, 229-31,
233, 248

Evangelium Veritatis
(pages and lines)
1-20   193

16.31-17.1
    193
18.11-15 23
20.10-11,
    15-17 222
21.25-29 193
24.6, 7 267
24.10   193
37.15-21 266
40.30-34 266
41.12-14,
28-29   266
42.21-22 266
42.26-30 193
42.30-33 266
42.39-
43.3   266
See also pp. 196, 199, 201,
204
(For other apocryphal
works, see Index of
Names)

APOSTOLIC
CONSTITUTIONS

VI.11   84
VI.15   170
See also pp. 171, 172, 174,
185, 186

ARISTIDES

Apology
15.1-3,
4-5   57
16   29-30, 205

ATHANASIUS

De Decretis
26   82

Encyclical Letter
1, 2, 6 177

Historia Arianorum
33   177
37   178
38   178
41   178
51   177
74   177

Apologia Contra Arianos
11   177
21   177
25   177
29   177
30   177
34   177
35   178
59   177
60   177

De Synodis
4   178
6   179
7   179
13, 14 179
43   179
47   179
54   179

Epistula ad Serapionem
I.28   180

Orationes contra Arianos
III.28 180

ATHENAGORAS

Supplicatio
9.1   211
32.3   225

On the Resurrection from the Dead
1   59
24   111
See also p. 118

EPISTLE OF BARNABAS

15.4   223
See also pp. 118, 167, 172,
    173, 216, 226, 227, 232,
    234, 242

BASIL

De Spiritu Sancto
VII   181
IX   181
X   181
XXVII   168, 181–3
XXIX   82, 183
XXX   183–4

CANONS OF COUNCILS

Council of Arles
VIII   71–72
XIII   84

Council of Ancyra
14   84
19   84
21   84
24   84

CLEMENTINE
LITERATURE

I Clement
5   46
7.2   56
17.1   222
36.1–6 222
42   44, 163
43.1   222
44.1–4 44, 163
47.3   213
59.3–61.3 171
See also pp. 130, 226, 227,
    234, 245, 251, 253

II Clement
2.1–3, 4 206
4.5   224
5.3   224
8.5   224
9.11   224
12.2   224
17.3–5 55
See p. 192

Pseudo-Clementines
(*Homilies* and *Recogni-
tions*)
See pp. 17, 49, 170, 185,
    186, 201, 216, 225, 227,
    229, 230

Epistola Clementis
2.4   77, 151
See also pp. 143, 164

CLEMENT OF
ALEXANDRIA

Stromateis
1.1.5   137
1.1.10   122
1.1.11–12 26, 97
1.2.20   122
1.5.28   122
1.8.41   226

1.12.56 26, 97
1.19.96 77, 137
1.24.158 226
2.9.45   226
2.20.117 48
3.4.25   48
3.6.52 f. 48
3.10.70 26, 106
3.13.92 226
3.13.93 220
4.15.98 77
5.10.63 26
5.14.96 226
6.5.4   122
6.7.61   26, 158
6.8.67   122
6.8.68   26
6.11.88 26, 106
6.15.124 106–7
6.15.125 77, 107
6.15.131 26, 97
6.16.124 77
6.16.146 26
6.17.159 122
6.18.164 26
6.18.165 77
7.7.41   77
7.7.43   137
7.7.108 98
7.15.90 67
7.15.92 26
7.16.94 77, 97, 107, 226
7.16.95 111
7.16.97 107
7.16.105 26, 77, 107
7.16.106 22, 23
7.17.106 189

Protreptikos
1.5   226
2.25   122
9.82   170

Paedagogos
2.1.4–5 137
2.1.16   48
3.11.54 122
3.11.81 137

Eclogae Propheticae
27   26, 43, 97, 114

Excerpta ex Theodoto
2   226
5   198
16   198
80   66

Quis Dives
29   209

Quis Dives–contd.
40   225
42   48, 162

Fragments, see p. 48

CYPRIAN

Epistles
4.1.2   99, 115
4.4.3   106
10.2, 3   68
16.2   262
33.1.1   159
43.5.1   140
43.6.1   99
45.1.2   99, 159
46.1.2   99
48.3.1   154
55.26.2   262–3
55.27.3   79
59.8.1   79
59.14.1   153
59.14.2   154
59.15.2–4   161
63.1.1   99
63.1.19   99
65.2.1   161
65.4.1   161
66.4.1   159
67.3.1   161
69.3.2   99
69.7.1   63
69.12.3   140
69.14.12   140
70.1.2   80
70.2.1   63, 169
71.3.1   141
71.13.1   141, 152
72.3.2   156
73.4   66, 152
73.5.2   90
73.10.1   106
73.13.3   152
73.15.2   99, 141
73.16.1, 2   152
73.21.2   106
73.26.1   152, 156
74.1.2   152, 154
74.2.2, 3   152, 154
74.4.1   68, 155
74.7.3   152
74.8   66
74.9.1, 2   79, 141
74.10.2   99
75.2.3   153
75.3.1   80, 153
75.5   66, 152
75.6.1, 2   152, 156, 223
75.10.5   80, 169

75.15.1   106
75.16.2   159
75.17.1, 2   153, 155
75.19.1, 3   152, 155
75.24.1, 2   153, 155
75.24.3   80
75, 25.1,
2, 4   152, 155
76.1.3   79

De Habitu Virginum
22   261

De Dominica Oratione
2   99

De Bono Patientiae
4   26

Ad Demetrianum
26   68

De Lapsis
2   99
7.13   68
17   262

De Unitate Ecclesiae
3   115
4   153–4
15   261
19   99

Testimonia
1.17   262
1.18   262
1.20   210, 262
2.2, 16   262
3.3   262
3.26   261
3.28   262
3.32, 35   261
3.36, 37,
39   262
3.47   263
3.50   34
3.51   263
3.53   121–2
3.54   263
3.62   262, 264
3.69   263
3.87   263
3.98   262, 263
3.119   261

Sententiae Episcoporum
1, 7   68
28   141
29   80
30   141

31   115
37   80
63, 70   141

PSEUDO-CYPRIANIC
LITERATURE

De Aleatoribus
2   225, 227

Ad Vigilium
4   227–8

Adversus Iudaeos
10   117

*De Singularitate
Clericorum*
1   81
22   161
28   223

De Pascha Computus
1   213

De Rebaptismate
1   142
6   142
10   169–70
15   142
16   170
17   211, 225
19   142

De Laude Martyrii
8   70
9   81
10   68

De Montibus Sina et Sion
1   115
11   115
13   227–8

DIDACHE

1.1–11.2   173
1–6   172
8.2   173
9.5   173
10.7   171
11.2–16.8   173
11.3   7
14.2   227
15.3   9
16   10
See also pp. 216, 226, 242

DIDASCALIA APOSTOLORUM

VII	232
XV	34, 89
XXVI	78, 89

See also pp. 172, 174, 222, 232

EPISTLE TO DIOGNETUS

4.6	30
6.4	30
7.1	30
8.2, 4	119
11.1–2, 6	96
11–12	88
12.1–13	106, 118

DIONYSIUS OF ALEXANDRIA
(pages in Feltoe)

8	222
47	91
53	143, 227
56	68
95–96	100
111–14	117
114–15	215, 219
116	220
117	212
177, 182, 198	82
257	117

EUSEBIUS OF CAESAREA

Historia Ecclesiastica

1.7.2–15	49
1.12.1–3	49
1.13.1–22	49
2.1.4, 5	47
2.9.2	48
2.14.1–6	49
2.15.1, 2	37, 48, 190
2.16.1	48, 166
2.17.1	49
2.17.11, 12	190
2.23.4–18	40
2.24	166
2.25	215
2.25.5, 6	46
3.1.1–3	49, 50
3.3.1, 2, 4	215
3.3.6	216

3.4.7	190
3.5.2, 3	40
3.11.12	40
3.17	41
3.18.1	41
3.19	41
3.20.1–6, 9	41
3.22	167
3.26.6–19	48
3.24.17	216
3.25.1–7	216
3.28.1, 2	195
3.29, 30	48
3.31.3	50
3.31.6	217
3.32.1–8	40
3.32.7	40, 84
3.38.1–3	215, 216
3.38.5	49, 215
3.39	36, 37
3.39.1	36
3.39.3	39
3.39.13	38
3.39.17	232
4.8.1	40
4.8.2	39
4.11.1	157
4.11.7	40
4.22.3, 4, 5–7, 8	110, 232
4.23	204
4.23.4	84
4.23.12	206
4.26.14	214
5.1.45	223
5.8.7	225
5.16.3	187, 201
5.16.7	136–7
5.17.2	187
5.20.4, 6	41, 157
5.20.7	42
5.23.1	51
5.24.2–7	51, 76
5.24.9–18	51, 147
5.24.14	42, 147
5.25	51
5.26	222
5.28.4	207
5.28.13	76, 207
6.12.1–16	218, 219, 225
6.12.6	211
6.13.8, 9	26, 42–43
6.14.24	215
6.14.7	197, 212
6.14.5–7	221–2
6.20.3	46, 195, 222
6.25.3	84
6.25.4	220
6.25.5, 6	190

6.25.8	223
6.25.11–14	219, 221
6.33.1	84
6.38	201
6.43.15	81
7.30.7	82

GREGORY THEODORUS

Profession of Faith, see pp. 83–84

Canons, see p. 251

Pseudo-Gregory, Ecthesis, see p. 84

HERMAS

Shepherd, see pp. 149–150, 192, 206, 207, 214, 215, 215–16, 216, 218, 219, 220, 222, 225, 226, 227, 242, 245, 253

HERMIAS

Irrisio, see p. 118

HIPPOLYTUS

Elenchos

1, introd. 1.2	22
1, introd. 1.6	160
1, introd. 1.8	47, 226
4.46.2	209
5.7.1	23
5.7.8, 9, 16	198
5.7.20	21, 22, 23
5.8.4, 5, 6, 10	198
5.8.29	198
5.9.4	55, 56
5.10.2	23
5.17.13	23
5.23.1	47
5.26.32	198
6.20.6	47, 226
7.20.1, 5	23
7.25.2	205
7.25.5	197
7.26.3	198, 205
7.27.4	192
7.27.8	192, 205

Elenchos–contd.
7.30.1   202
7.32.6   76
8.18.2   98
8.19.2   161
9.10–21   149
9.10.1   76
9.12.21   76
9.12.26   98
9.31.2   76–77
10.5.1, 2   76
10.9.3   23
10.25   161
10.32–34   121
10.34.1   76–77

Apostolic Tradition
(Dix's enumeration)
1.2, 3   137, 168
1.5   138, 168
6–9   171
15   161
21–22   169
21   98
23.13–14   32, 138, 160
36.12   43, 138
38   98
38.2, 3   138
40–43   171
See also pp. 62, 69, 98

Contra Noetum
1   62 63
2, 3, 9   114
16   121
17   63, 88
18   88
See also p. 207

De Antichristo
2   211
50   106
56, 57   208

Commentary on Daniel
1.7   211
3.29   200, 226
10.4   223
22.4   223
23.5   223
24.5   223

Epistle of Hymenaeus
(pages of Routh, Vol. VIII)
289, 290,
    291   83
299   83, 222
See also p. 82

IGNATIUS

Ephesians
12   164
18.2   154
19.2, 3   203

Magnesians
6   163
14   163

Philadelphians
5   163, 190
8.2   54

Romans
4   45

Smyrneans
1.1, 2   54
3.2, 3   202, 224
4.2   224

Trallians
9   54
13   163

IRENAEUS

Adversus Haereses
1.1.5, 8   22, 24
1.1.12   206
1.1.15   45, 205
1.1.20   65, 75, 105
1.2   86
1.3   45, 75, 95, 167
1.4   118–19
1.8.5   191
1.8.7   44
1.9.4   65, 109
1.13.1   188
1.13.2   225
1.14.2   267
1.15   86
1.20.2   23
1.21.3   61
1.25.1, 2   45
1.25.4, 5   198
1.27   157
1.28.7   23
1.29   24
2.33.3   25
2.40.3   25
2.41.1–3   29, 106
2.41.4   119
2.42.4   119
3.1.1   38, 45
3.2.1   22, 24
3.2.2   95, 157

3.1, 2   144–5, 157, 265
3.3.3   94, 145, 157
3.3.4   145
3.4.1   86, 95, 102
3.4.3   157, 189
3.5.1   25, 109
3.6.3   171
3.11.4   110
3.11.9   214
3.11.10   198
3.11.11,
    12   46, 191, 195, 199, 209
3.12.5   144
3.12.12   199
3.18.2   208
3.18.3   44
3.20.2   208
3.24.1   208, 211
3.25.1   110
3.38.1   106
4.4.6   44
4.7.4   110
4.11.2   45
4.27.1–2   45
4.34.2   206, 225
4.38.2   103
4.40.1   157
4.40.2   106, 159
4.42.1   160
4.42.2   42
4.53.1   86
4.53.2   95, 110, 160
5.5.1   42
5.17.4   44
5.20.1   96, 157
5.20.2   105
5.23.2   223
5.28.2, 3   29, 45, 106, 223
5.30.1–3   45, 106
5.33.3   36, 42
5.35.2   42
5.36   42

Demonstration
3   61, 65, 75, 113
6   61, 66, 113
7   61, 113
43   225
61   36
86   113
96   225
98   113
99, 100   66, 113

JUSTIN MARTYR

Apology
1.6.2   57–58

Apology–contd.
1.21.1	58
1.31.7	58
1.36.1 f.	211
1.42.4	58
1.46.5	58
1.61.4	170
1.61.5	194
1.61.9	169
1.65.3	58
1.66.3	203
1.66, 67	171
1.67.2	58
1.67.3	203–4

Dialogue
12.3	225
30.3	71
35.3	225
35.6	189
46.1	58
47.5	225
63.1	58
69.7	225
76.6	71
80.2, 5	59
85.1, 2	58, 71
88.3, 8	225
100.1	204
101.3	204
103.6, 8	204, 224
105.1, 5, 6	204
115.1–4	211
126.1	58
132.1	58

MELITO

Homily on the Passion,
see p. 88

Fragments
III. 214

MINUCIUS FELIX

Octavius
X.1, 4	30
XIX.15	30

MURATORIAN CANON
(lines)
9–16	46, 197
16–20	46
16–34	210
48–49	210
56–59	210

61–63	210
64	222
63–68	217
66–68	44
71–73	220, 226

See also p. 222

NOVATIAN

De Trinitate
1	73–74
9	73, 74, 90–91
11	73, 116
12	116
14	143
16	73, 74, 116
17	73, 74, 116
21	73, 74, 115
23	116
26	73, 74, 116
29	73, 74, 161
30	100, 116
31	222

See also pp. 63–64, 72–73

De Cibis Iudaicis
1	100
7	74

ORIGEN

Contra Celsum
1.56	48
2.62, 68	49
2.71	111
3.9	161
3.15, 16	112
3.30	161
3.60	33
4.8, 9	112
5.18–24	115
5.22	79
5.61	233
6.6	139
8.15, 16	227

Peri Archon
Origen's pref.
4–10	90
10	79, 93, 98, 112, 122
1 pref. 2	63
2.5.3	112
2.10.1	79
3.1.1	79
3.6.6	111
4.2.2	78–79, 98, 107

See also p. 259

Commentary on John
2.12	233
10.4	14
13.17	218
13.16	78, 115
13.44	115
32.3	63
frag. 31	227

Commentary on Matthew
11.17	79
13.1, 2	79
15.14	232
16.12	233
17.35	79
20.14	161

Comm. Ser.
12	161
25	49
28	78, 219
29	115
33	63
46	78, 107
47	107

Commentary on Romans
2.7	139
5.2	197
5.8, 9	139
10.33	139
10.41	49

Homilies on Jeremiah
4.3	63
5.4	78
5.14	79
15.4	233
20.3	224, 227
20.8	49

Homilies on Isaiah
6.3	139

Homilies on Ezekiel
12.3	161

Homilies on Genesis
14.3	49

Homilies on Exodus
8.4	67

Homilies on Numbers
5.1	139
13.12	69

Homilies on Leviticus
8.3	139
10.2	227
12.3	161

Homilies on Psalms
Hom. IV on Ps. 37.1 98

Commentaries on Psalms
(Migne)
On Ps. 27.5   79
On Ps. 89.12   49

Commentaries on Psalms
(Cadiou)
118, 119,
  142   161
Homilies on Luke
1   224, 227, 233
14   139
34   43

Fragments on I Corin-thians (Jenkins)
XIX   33
XXXVII 79
LXXXIV 78

Fragments on Ephesians
(Gregg)
XX   49

Exhortation to Martyrdom
17   67

Peri Euches
2.2   226
15.1   140
16.1   140
28.10 161

Conversation with Hera-cleides
  (pages of Scherer's text)
118–20   72
129–30   139, 140
144   79

Fragments
See pp. 49, 79 (thrice),
  115, 139, 219

POLYCARP

Epistle to Philippians
2.1   54–55
7.1, 2   55, 203
12.1   205–6

PTOLEMAEUS

Letter to Flora
See pp. 24, 26, 191

TATIAN

Oratio ad Graecos
1–3   117
4.1   194
5.1   194
6.1   222
13.1–2 194–5
18.2   194
19   191, 194
21.2   195, 204–5
40.1   117–18

Diatessaron
See pp. 24, 191, 195, 197,
  229–30

TERTULLIAN

Adversus Praxean
1   160
2   87, 113, 120
3, 5, 9,
  11, 13 113
20   109, 113
30   67
See also p. 207

De Praescriptione Haereticorum
2.1, 3   38
6.4   77
7.9   19–20
12   106, 109, 120
13.1–6   87
14   103, 108
15–18   103
19.2, 3 104
20   67, 104, 158
22–27   25
22.2   25
22.4, 5 147, 150
23.5   25
25.2   25
26.2, 9–10
         25
29.3   160
30   214
31.1, 3 104
32.1   158
32.3   147
36.2, 3, 5 148
38   110, 198
See also pp. 96–99, 103–105

Scorpiace
4.5   67
10   147, 150

14.3   46

Apologeticus
1.26, 56   49
4.1–3   46, 47
7.6   31
46.10   103
46.17   77

De Spectaculis
3   131
4   67
18   131
24   67

Adversus Valentinianos
1.1   22
4   148
4.1   77
4.4   160
5.1   46

Ad Nationes
1.7.8   46
1.7.13, 14,
  19   31
1.10.1   77

Ad Uxorem
2.5.4   31

De Paenitentia
4.1   226

Ad Scapulam
4.6   46

Adversus Marcionem
1.1.6   103
1.21.4   77
1.22   104
1.28.2   67
2.4.4   106
3.1.2   103
4.2.1, 2 110
4.2.5   103
4.5.1, 2 111, 147
4.13.6   147
4.19.10 47
4.36.12 77
5.1.2   68
5.3.1   77, 103
5.8.5, 8, 9 160
5.17.1   210
5.19.1   103

De Anima
1.4   67
2.3   217–18
28.5   47

De Anima—contd.
35.3   67
55.4   147
58.8   113, 160
58.9   120

De Carne Christi
2.3   103
7.3   147
23.2, 6   226

De Baptismo
1.1   97, 169
6–8   169
15.1   61
17   214
20   226

De Testimonio Animae
2.2   77

Ad Martyras
3.1   67

De Corona
2.1–3   132
2.4   131
3.1–2   132
3.2, 3, 4   61, 67, 134, 168
4.1, 4, 5, 6   133
9.1–4   133
11.1, 7   67
13.7   67

De Idololatria
6.1   67
19.2   67

De Monogamia
1.2   160
2.2   97
2.3   77
4.2, 4   131
8.3   147
11.1   67

*De Resurrectione
Mortuorum*
3.1, 6   121
18.1   218
63.6   198
63.9   113
21.3   77, 113
See also pp. 258–9

*De Ieiunio adversus
Psychicos*
2.1–3   136
5   160
8.4   136, 160
10.5, 6   97, 131, 136
10.7   67
13.1, 2   97, 136
14.1, 2, 3   136
16.1–4   136
16.8   160

De Pudicitia
1.5   114
1.6   150
8   109
8.12   106
9.16   67
10.12   149, 218, 219
13.7   149
16.22   149
20.1   214
20.2   214–15
20.5   215
21.1–4, 6   150
21.5   149
21.7   151
21.9–15   161
21.9   150
22.1, 2, 3   149

De Virginibus Velandis
1.1   134
1.3   87
1.3–5, 7   134
2.1, 2, 3   134, 136
3.1   134, 136

*   *   *

3.2–4   134
3.5   135
8.4   135
16.1, 2   114, 135
17.3   135

De Oratione
15.2   97, 131
16   97, 149, 207
22.1   131
25   131
26.1   226

Adversus Hermogenem
1.1   103

De Exhortatione Castitatis
4.2   131

De Cultu Feminarum
3.3   211

De Fuga in Persecutione
10.3   160

Adversus Iudaeos
8.11   47
8.14   160

*Pseudo-Tertullian,
Adversus Omnes Haereses*
4.6   199
8.3   222

THEOPHILUS OF
ANTIOCH

Ad Autolycum
2.9   211
2.13   223
2.22   195, 211
2.25   222
3.12   211–12
3.14   212
See also pp. 195 and 207